Sportbike
Performance Handbook
2nd Edition

Kevin Cameron

motorbooks

I dedicate this book to my mother, Sheila,
who explained to a very small boy how things work.

First published in 2008 by Motorbooks, an imprint of MBI Publishing Company, 400 First Avenue North, Suite 300, Minneapolis, MN 55401 USA

Motorbooks titles are also available at discounts in bulk quantity for industrial or sales-promotional use. For details write to Special Sales Manager at MBI Publishing Company, 400 First Avenue North, Suite 300, Minneapolis, MN 55401 USA.

To find out more about our books, join us online at www. motorbooks.com.

Library of Congress Cataloging-in-Publication Data

Cameron, Kevin, 1941–
  Sportbike performance handbook / Kevin Cameron. — 2nd ed.
     p. cm.
  Includes index.
  ISBN 978-0-7603-3183-5 (sb : alk. paper)
  1. Motorcycles—Customizing. 2. Motorcycles—Performance. 3. Superbikes. I. Title.
  TL440.C29 2008
  629.28'775—dc22
                                      2008029319

On the cover: When it comes to performance, sportbikes give the biggest bang for your buck. And even though a bone-stock sportbike is plenty of fun, a modified one can be even better—if you use the right combination of parts, machine work, and tuning procedures. *Kevin Wing*

On the title page: State-of-the-art sportbike performance: The Superbike World Championship. *Suzuki*

On the back cover: Suzuki's GSX-R1000

Editor: Lee Klancher
Designer: Mandy Iverson

Printed in Singapore

CONTENTS

	Acknowledgments	4
	Introduction	5
CHAPTER 1	Planning Power	6
CHAPTER 2	Fitting the Bike	9
CHAPTER 3	How Engines Work	12
CHAPTER 4	Choosing a Type of Engine	36
CHAPTER 5	Dyno Tuning	42
CHAPTER 6	Carburetion	50
CHAPTER 7	Exhaust Pipes	64
CHAPTER 8	Cylinder Head and Valvetrain	69
CHAPTER 9	Transmission, Clutch, and Final Drive	81
CHAPTER 10	Ignition	90
CHAPTER 11	The Electronic Motorcycle	95
CHAPTER 12	Turbocharging, Supercharging, and Nitrous Oxide	103
CHAPTER 13	How Suspension Works	108
CHAPTER 14	Suspension Tuning	125
CHAPTER 15	Chassis	135
CHAPTER 16	Tires	142
CHAPTER 17	Wheels	150
CHAPTER 18	Brakes	154
CHAPTER 19	Oils	164
CHAPTER 20	Fuels	171
CHAPTER 21	Weight Reduction	175
CHAPTER 22	Upgrading Yourself	180
APPENDIX A	Horsepower Junkie's Glossary	184
APPENDIX B	Performance Math	187
APPENDIX C	Suggested Reading	189
	Index	192

ACKNOWLEDGMENTS

Doing acknowledgments reminds me of the racer, up on the podium with the microphone in his face, taking a deep breath and hoping to remember everyone. "I wanna thank Kel Carruthers, I wanna thank Goodyear. . . . "

I do have a lot of people to thank, in particular my editor, Lee Klancher, whose idea this book was. I can assure you that my family did not relish the competition that this book gave them ("He's in his office again. . . ."), but they got on with it somehow and so did I. The first race bikes I ever laid hands on came from the dealerships of John Jacobson, whose years of supporting racing gave me the opportunity to get serious about this business. A long friendship with Erv Kanemoto has made top-level racing—its people and technology—seem less far away. When behind schedule and in quiet desperation, I called on people in and out of industry for photographs and line art, and was overwhelmed by the rapid and enthusiastic response. My long-time friend John Owens kindly opened his racing photo archive to me and photographed the piles of parts I brought him.

So I'm taking a deep breath now and getting ready to do the list, in strictly alphabetical order. Bear in mind that shortness of breath and/or memory may leave out irate contributors. I regret any omissions.

Jim Allen of Dunlop Tires, Ammar Bazzaz of Bazzaz Performance, Harold Bettes of SuperFlow Corporation, Don Burnett of Conoco Phillips, Jonathan Cornwell of the Ohlins trackside group, Bob Coy, Jim Czekala of C&H Dyno, Bob Franski of NOS, Miles Frederick of Street & Competition, Garry Gallagher of EBC Brakes, Robert Iannucci of Team Obsolete, Peter Kates of G.M.D. Computrack Network Boston, Dave Koshollek of Dynojet, Claude Le Roux of Michelin Tire, Jim Lindemann of Lindemann Engineering, Reynolds Mansson of Mansson Technologies, Jeff March, Doug Meyer of Muzzys Performance, Tony Mills, K. Nishi of Mikuni American, Jamie O'Hare of Performance Connection, David Peters of Snap-On, Mark Reese of American Suzuki Motor Corporation, Roger Slater of Slater Bros Motorcycles Ltd., Bob Starr of Yamaha Motor Corporation, Michael Tursky of Keihin Seiki U.S.A., Dirk Vandenberg of American Honda Motor Co., Steve Whitelock of AFAM Sprockets, John Wittner, Jerry Wood of the Penguin Roadracing School, and Andrew Wright of Superbike Parts.

Likewise, and in no lesser degree, I must thank all the people at the races who have shared their insights with me over many years.

—Kevin Cameron, January 2008

INTRODUCTION

What is a sportbike? Borrowing from Mr. Soichiro Honda's introduction to the 1959 Benly owner's manual, I quote, "Primarily, essentials of the motorcycle consist in the speed and thrill." A sportbike is a motorcycle whose enjoyment comes mainly from its ability to perform on all types of paved highway—its cornering agility, its handling, its thrilling acceleration and braking power, even (dare I say it?) its speed.

In a narrower sense, a sportbike is any one of the machines built since the early 1980s that could be production-raced in stock condition, beginning with Kawasaki's 550. These were the bikes whose off-the-showroom-floor performance started a new kind of roadracing in the United States—Supersports. But that would leave out their important ancestors, the still-popular Kawasaki, Honda, and Suzuki air-cooled giants of the 1970s, for which so much speed equipment is still available. These bulletproof monsters were to motorcycling what the DC3 was to aviation—the first of a new breed, over-built extra-rugged because no one knew yet how strong was strong enough! I can't say these bikes were agile, with their weight and flexing water-pipe chassis, but I include them because they were the first of the big four-stroke motorcycles, classics that still turn heads and tires.

Although there are suggestions in this book, it is not a cookbook that lists ingredients and their outcomes. It is my ambition that you the reader, in modifying, tuning, and perfecting your bike, should actively become your own expert, not passively relying on others for your choices. To that end, several of these chapters are written as in-depth practical explanations of how engines, chassis, and their components work. I have tried to write them in such a way so that you will not put the book down in disgust, finding that it's just another tiresome school text.

This book will provide an understandable framework of ideas as to how engines and chassis work. It will show what the various modifications do, and how to choose among them. Upon this framework, you can tack up the data points of your own experience as you set forth to become your own expert.

You're not an engineer? Neither were many of the motivated, hard-working people who created our material civilization. The basic ingredients of engineering are, first of all, a strong desire to achieve something or to solve some problem. Second comes a willingness to propose and test possible answers one after another until a direction is found, followed by pursuing that direction to a result. Third comes a willingness to dip into formal engineering when necessary. The heads of major bike racing teams are not engineers, either, but they do read the Society of Automotive Engineers (SAE) tech papers and know where to look for answers when they are stumped.

John Britten was not an engineer, but he created and developed the Britten V-1000 twin with all its innovations. He keenly wanted practical results, worked hard to test and prove his ideas, and was willing to study when necessary. Of the Wright Brothers, the same is true. They weren't engineers, but their work was definitely engineering—their airfoil testing, their crude but effective wind tunnel, their learning to fly on gliders, their final success. Rex McCandless, designer of the most-copied, most successful motorcycle chassis of all time, the Norton Featherbed, quit school at 13 and learned by working and thinking.

This way of thinking, of working, is not something reserved to graduates of engineering colleges. It's just part of human nature, part of our own "bundled software"—accessible to anyone with a problem to solve and energy to spend on solving it.

You want a better bike? Get to work.

At the center of sportbike territory—Suzuki's GSX-R1000. As delivered, modern sportbikes have amazingly seamless powerbands, good brakes, and capable handling. A good modification is one that preserves rather than destroys the balance of these qualities, while increasing overall capability.

CHAPTER 1
PLANNING POWER

To appoint yourself project leader on your own bike is exciting, but then you need a plan that you can actually carry through. And, assuming that you carry out the plan, you'll have to live with the result, good or bad. That plan had better be good.

What is the plan? First, some basic questions: If you aren't satisfied with your present bike, why not replace it with one you like better? Don't just dismiss the idea; think about it, because modifications take time, may involve learning new skills, and may not, in the end, satisfy you. Staying with a manufactured product is reasonable if you don't want to get involved with mechanical work, getting help from specialists, getting parts by mail order, and spending your downtime working on your bike. The strong point of the manufactured product is that it's already fully engineered. Streetbikes today have marvelously strong, wide powerbands, their handling is better than that of race bikes of 5 to 10 years ago, and you can get parts at any dealer.

"Well, I have this bike, and I don't have a lot of money. I can't afford an MV or a Ducati D16RR, but I do want something special. So I'm going to modify what I have."

Stop right there and ask yourself how much you can actually spend, just as a common sense protection against "catalog madness." The aftermarket has so much to offer that it's easy to be swept away by one's own enthusiasm. Have fun with the catalogs, but at the same time, figure out what you can actually use. Do you want primarily appearance changes? A suspension upgrade? Improved tires? Or can you handle (and do you need) engine work?

The big lesson of the past five years comes straight from MotoGP. I saw it up close in Valencia, Spain, in 2004. Rossi, leading the race, was not sliding, spinning, or wobbling. The farther I looked downfield, the harder the riders were working to hold their positions. Bringing up the rear were probably the most powerful bikes in the race, their engines full of F1 technology. They were spinning, sliding, and leaving big black lines off every corner. And they were last.

Rossi was leading, not because he was taking the biggest risks, but because his machine was so easy to use that he could safely use more of everything—power, maneuverability, brakes—than the others could. The others had to go slower because spiky powerbands provoked wheelspin at the touch of the throttle or because over-ambitious electronic controls were trying to assassinate them in every other corner.

The lesson therefore is this: By focusing on making your machine more easily usable, you will have the confidence to use more of whatever abilities it has. Keep this lesson in mind as you make your plan.

Here are some considerations. For a given horsepower, a smaller engine has to be tuned more aggressively than a larger one does. To make big power, the smaller engine needs longer-duration cams that narrow its power, requiring you to stir the gearbox more. That takes your attention from other tasks—like riding the bike. A bigger engine at the same power level has moderate cams that allow it to make good torque across a wider range of rpm. With it, you spend less time on "powerplant management" and more time on the riding task. As a result, you go faster. On the other hand, the bigger the engine, the heavier the bike—and the slower its rate of maneuver may be.

A mundane consideration is that by modifying a bike, you make it less road-worthy (will the dealer in Bozeman, Montana, have a spare piston for your big-bore kit?) and you may also lose the protection of any warranty from the manufacturer.

The basis of the Supersport roadracing class is suspension upgrades plus a pipe and engine re-mapping. Everything else stays stock. Supersport lap times eclipse those of decade-old pure racers—on DOT tires. This is Jason DiSalvo on the factory Yamaha. Akrapovic

Superbike racers are beautiful but expensive. A Superbike begins with a production machine, of which a specified number must actually be built (loosely based on factory size), and is now limited to use of many stock or stock-weight components such as pistons, crankshaft, and so on. Other parts—such as the swingarm and front fork—may be replaced with upgraded items. U.S. AMA Superbike pits 1,000cc twins against 1,000cc fours, but in World Superbike the twins now get 1,200cc. These bikes make just over 200 horsepower.

It's tempting to dream of super power but will you be able to ride it to work? Can you tolerate a blowup and the time it will take to fix?

Do you sometimes carry a passenger, or are you solo only? To carry two-up, especially pulling away from an uphill stoplight, you'll need a wide, muscular powerband, and it would be a drag to have to "ease" away from lights at 10,000 rpm. But if you build a solo-only ride with killer horsepower, do you realistically have the skill to handle it? Or only the enthusiasm? Always remember that you can learn riding skills faster on easy-to-ride bikes. Be realistic about yourself; it's silly to ride more bike than you can use.

Or maybe you've decided to take in a few production road races and want a mild, Supersport-type mod that remains streetable? There's a lot to consider, but if your determination to modify your bike remains, read on.

Let me offer you some rough categories.

First of all, split the plan into two basic aspects: performance and appearance. You may want all of one, all of the other, or a mixture, but the division is a real one. It's perfectly possible to build a stock-appearing "sleeper" or "Q-ship" that packs a surprising punch from a modified engine. The other extreme is a "titanium stocker," completely restyled with special wheels, glass, and paint, but retaining the drivability and easy maintenance of a stock engine.

Either of these extremes—or any mixture between—is perfectly valid, because you are the owner and project leader. It's up to you.

On the other hand, it must be pointed out that given a contest between a good rider on a junk bike and an indifferent rider on a good bike, the good rider wins every time. The all-titanium-and-carbon trick Ducati owner may be embarrassed at track days by well-ridden but scruffy stockers. No matter what kind of machine you build, it can't make you fast if you're not. Becoming fast is another game altogether. A good way to play it is to pick up a used middleweight and go production racing. Simple machines, run in stock condition, make learning to ride much easier—just as easy-to-ride MotoGP bikes have enabled ex-250 riders to succeed in the big class. It's therefore a good idea to soup up your own software before souping up the hardware.

Assuming that your software is up to the job and you're ready to plunge into hardware upgrades, you'll have to decide what you want from your modified machine. Within the engine performance area, I suggest three basic divisions:

(1) Engines whose character has not been compromised.

Such engines are easy to ride because they behave like stock, but are significantly stronger in performance. Their powerbands contain no spin-provoking spikes, no acceleration-stopping holes. This is what I strongly recommend for any bike to be ridden on the street—because it is **practical**, and does everything well.

(2) The second type accepts certain compromises in some areas to get much stronger performance in other areas. No one should build such an engine without knowing the trade-off. Drivability will be lower, reliability may suffer, and higher skills are required to get any value from such engines. A substantial amount of tuning work will be necessary to make this type of engine give its best.

(3) The third type is the racing-only engine, built with the most reliable (expensive) components. This kind of engine makes an all-out struggle to attain *one* kind of performance, and is consequently lousy at all other kinds. Reliability is still important (they only count the winners at the finish line), but is now measured in hundreds of miles, not thousands. Maintenance is continuous—changing valve springs, freshening the top end, inspecting the bike inside and out on a regular basis.

Appearance can also be divided, but along the lines of personal comfort. The more nearly upright you are on the bike, with hands and feet in natural positions, the more comfortable you'll be and the longer you'll be able to ride (do you lie down to operate a typewriter?). But that's not what some of you want, because I see plenty of riders tooting down the boulevard all leaned over on racy-looking low bars, peering over a low windscreen and hunching over a bulbous, race-style gas tank, their feet on high footpegs that drive their (bare) knees up into their lunch. Is this fun? It must be, because lots of people do it. If interrogated with modern police methods, I would confess to having done the same. At the time, I would never have admitted I was uncomfortable, so I don't expect today's low-bar riders to admit to their discomfort, either.

Instead, I will just offer the suggestion that you quietly, maturely consider comfort as you consider appearance.

Younger riders, as yet unaware that they have bones or joints, ride in the "GSX-R position" without ache or pain. Older ones, no longer able to get their feet behind their heads, may prefer a more "VFR-like" position. OK, fashion is passion, but you have to ride the thing after you've built it. Pick your poison. And remember that race teams work very hard to make their riders comfortable on the bikes. Passion is not penance.

Here are some sample styles.

1. Extreme Road Race: This one looks terrific but puts your weight on your arms and wrists, unless you are topped out doing 190 at Hockenheim. There is no room for a passenger. Footpegs are up high, suitable—as one of my former riders once said—for "six-foot people with eighteen-inch legs." Handlebars are genuine clip-ons. Color me red (or green, etc., according to brand madness), with plenty of attention-getting carbon fiber and titanium. As Peter Ustinov says in his racing send-up, *Grand Prix of Gibraltar*: "Man must be a slave to his machine."

2. Moderate Road Race: This is the style of the modern sportbike. It still suggests speed, but the required body contortions are less demanding. A passenger is possible, especially with one of those hide-away seats. Bars are higher, usually attached above the top fork crown, putting less strain on arms and wrists, but you can still tuck in if you like. Mainstream compromise.

3. The 1970s Superbike: This is the classic Reg Pridmore/ Steve McLaughlin sit-up-and-beg position adopted on the high-bar 1025cc Superbikes of the 1970s, based as they were on the unfaired "standards" or universal Japanese motorcycles (UJMs) of the period. Ride all day in comfort as long as the speed isn't high enough to make your cheeks inflate like Colonel Stapp's on his rocket sled. Carry a passenger with ease any time. Have a blast (of wind, for example) in an honored bygone style. Plenty of wannabe low-bar hot dogs have been humbled by experienced riders on these basic period bikes (supposedly obsolete, but skilled riding is never obsolete). Clothes (viewing motorcycles as haberdashery for the moment) do not make the man. Or woman.

4. Sport/Tourer (ratio of relative importance is up to you): This is the sportbike of (2) above, morphed into something more useful for high-speed highway travel by the odometer-minded rider. Wind protection is much better than in either (1) or (2) above, thanks to a fairly huge fairing. Rider position/ comfort as in (3) is the goal. Technology in service to mankind, with appearances sliding toward the "ship under sail" look. Such a machine can even carry (dare I mention it?) luggage.

I could go on, but that's up to you.

As to actual handling, I suggest you look at those chapters, and I'll restrict my remarks here to saying this: Hard suspension used to be considered racy, back in the days before competent chassis and suspension components existed. That's no longer true, so don't get sucked into building a bike that rides like a "lumberwagon" (Yvon DuHamel's words) because

Freddie Spencer's 1,025cc factory Honda. The muscular, basic appeal of vintage sit-up liter bikes makes them frequent choices of custom builders today. Looks aren't the only draw—there is new interest in this type of vintage racing as well. The Krober ignition boxes (seen just ahead of the top of the rear shock) identify this as a 1981 machine. In Superbike, Freddie won the races, but Lawson took the titles. John Owens Studio

Suzuki's 1,300cc Hayabusa. To build or to buy—that is the question. When you want more motorcycle than you have, seriously consider moving up to a stock machine of higher performance. A production bike is a fully engineered package, with a smooth powerband and a warranty. But a successful modified bike is your own achievement, representing your understanding of how all its systems work. Your choice.

of that outdated idea. Even if you choose to put race-quality components on your bike (those red springs and massive gold-colored fork legs are so sweet), don't spring and damp it so hard that you have to pee every 20 minutes. Riding is supposed to be a pleasure. Modern suspension components are plush.

Therefore my question in this section is: who are you? And, being who you are, what do you require from your motorcycle? Ask yourself.

CHAPTER 2
FITTING THE BIKE

Man ought not to be a slave to his machine, but too often is. We hop on a new bike and are so dazzled by its qualities that we don't even notice that the bars are at the wrong angle for our wrists, the brake pedal is set high enough to cause cramp, and the seat dips in the wrong place. This bike is great! Off we go.

In the days that follow, our minds and bodies make a million small adjustments—but they are all wrong. We are adjusting to our new machines, when in fact it ought to be the other way around. Indeed, because of the reasonable complaints of others like us, the makers of the bike have made it adjustable in many ways, and the aftermarket offers us an even wider range of options in fitting the machine to ourselves. Different bars, seats, windscreens, hand and foot controls—all these and more exist to help us adjust motorcycles so we can comfortably "wear" them.

Why bother? We should bother because many of the small adjustments that our backs, wrists, ankles, and hinder parts make to the machine put our muscles and ligaments in unnatural positions, imposing strain and generating fatigue that need not, and should not, exist. We have other uses for our concentration.

Similar conditions can exist—or come into existence—on machines we have owned for years. During every day of use, wear occurs. Cables dry out and begin to stick-slip instead of pull smoothly. Slack develops in throttle cables too long under stretch from an eager wrist. Rear brake shoes are worn and the pedal is a long way down—we haven't gotten around to pulling it back up with a few turns of the cable adjuster. Because these problems develop by small degrees, we may not even be aware of them.

Therefore, I suggest that any rider may benefit from this fitting process, this business of making the machine into the proper servant of man. This is, in fact, the very first step that factory teams take before they start testing with a new rider or machine.

Begin by sitting on the machine and thinking about your hands and feet. As you reach for the bars, are they at the angle that your hands naturally assume? If your bars are of the serrated, multi-position type, get out your Allen wrenches, loosen the adjusters, and swing the bars to new positions that suit you better. If your bars aren't adjustable, consider the aftermarket options. A fatigue-free rider rides better, safer,

A brake pedal set too high for comfort. This seems OK at first, but as the miles roll by, the tension required to keep that back brake from dragging gets to you. Take the time to adjust the pedal height to suit your riding position. John Owens Studio

and longer, and any annoyance that takes your attention away from riding is a potential danger to you.

The longer the handlebar, the lower the control forces. But the racer style insists that little shorty clip-ons are cool. That may have been useful back in the days of 18-horsepower 125s, when a rearview mirror caused a measurable loss of top speed, but we're talking 150-horsepower sportbikes here, and control is far more important than silly notions like drag caused by pinky fingers out in the wind. So if you'd like lighter steering, try longer bars. Eddie Lawson used longer clip-ons on courses that required a lot of muscle. Nothing is sacred here; if you don't like the clip-on style bars that came with your sportbike, find ones that you do like and use them.

Next, reach for the levers. Are they a natural pull for your hands, or must you twist your wrists uncomfortably up or down for them? It's a simple matter to slack off the pinch-bolts that hold master cylinder and clutch lever to the bar, and rotate them to a more comfortable angle. Is the brake lever too far out for your hand size, making combined throttle and brake control into a stretching exercise? Some master cylinders feature adjustable levers, and there are aftermarket levers made especially for smaller hands.

Now turn the throttle. Is there slack in the throttle cable(s), making initial throttle control uncertain? Don't put up with it. Whip out the wrenches and find the adjustment (on the carb or throttle body rack, under the tank, at the throttle assembly itself, or in the cable), and zero out the slack without making the cables so tight that they hold the throttles up fractionally. Swing the bars from side to side. This check is important because bending a cable housing makes it slightly longer, which can lift the throttles a tiny bit.

Maybe you've been irritated by the endless twist it takes to go from idle to full throttle. That's what aftermarket quick-throttles are for—to suit your taste. And how about the grips? Do they have ridges that make your hands look like charbroiled burger patties after an hour? Are they too squishy and vague? Don't put up with their tyranny; get the knife, slash them lengthwise, pull them off, and replace them with something you like better.

Pull the clutch. The bane of older bikes is a cable-operated clutch that isn't smooth because cable and housing have too long gone without lubrication. How can you get off the line smoothly, feathering the clutch, when there is nothing feathery about a clutch cable that moves only in a series of little jerks? Too tight a turn in the cable can have the same effect. Route the cable in gentle curves. Late-model bikes often have hydraulically actuated clutches that some competition riders find vague and uncertain in operation. Kits exist to convert them back to cable operation. Consider the options and please yourself.

What about seat height? Do your feet reach the ground well to either side of the machine at stoplights, bracing it with assurance? Or do you have to point your toes, hoping the wind doesn't blow you over? Seats can be lowered by removing padding, and machines these days can be raised and lowered on their suspensions. Make yourself at home.

Are your feet where you'd like them to be, or are the peg locations actually props from *Planet of the Apes*? Late-model bikes often have movable peg assemblies, and the aftermarket is ready to help those that don't. Put the pegs where you like them. Most people like to put their feet under their center of gravity, so that if they take their weight on the pegs, they are neither thrown forward nor backward. Think you'd like a set of racy-looking knurled metal pegs, like those on road race machines? Find them in the catalogs. If it's not in the catalog, do what the racers do: bolt an aluminum plate to the stock locations, and drill the plate to mount your pegs wherever you please. Those of you with machine-shop skills have special advantages here.

Now the foot controls. Can you shift with a quick toe dab, without having to lift or reposition your foot? That's the

ideal, but a surprising number of riders put up with having to go looking for the shifter every time they shift because it isn't where their toes are. The height of the shifter is almost always easily adjustable, either by relocating the pedal on its splined shaft, or by turning the length adjuster on a linkage-type shifter. If the pedal is too long or too short (not everyone is average), take it to a fabricating shop and have it changed to suit you, or look over other bikes from the same maker. Chances are that many of the shift pedals are interchangeable, and maybe one from another model will suit you better. A close look at any race bike will show similar mods—pedals shortened or bent, pegs shortened, and so on. Some people fear to make such mods because they are too impressed with their machines ("I could never do that to my 1098 . . ."), but the machine is nothing if it doesn't fit you.

On the other side, the rear brake pedal gets the same treatment. Set it high enough that it doesn't kiss Mother Earth in corners, low enough to prevent spasm as you struggle to keep from dabbing the pedal accidentally.

What about the seat? Do you have the feeling that you're always sliding down to where the seat wants to put you, then having to scoot back up to where you need to be? Then you have the wrong seat. Horsemen don't use generic saddles, why should you? Some people like a suede-like

This brake hand lever is set too high and will become unpleasant the farther you ride. A few seconds of work will make it fit you perfectly.
John Owens Studio

When the stock controls won't do, the aftermarket offers solutions. Rear sets, raised or lowered handlebars, and other ergonomic goodies tailor the bike to your needs. Street & Competition

surface on which they don't slide around, while others like the freedom to move that a slicker surface gives. Sometimes the adjustment is as simple as unfastening one edge of the seat cover and altering the foam padding underneath—something that's been commonly done in "production" racing for years. Replacing hard padding with softer stuff will lower your position, but keep the seat looking unchanged when you're not on it.

There are other potential sources of irritation on a motorcycle. Giacomo Agostini didn't like the pivot pin of a linkage-type shifter digging into the side of his ankle, so the bikes he rode all have a rounded, perforated disc there to act as a shield. Older bikes may have longer footpegs that hit the ground in turns, disturbing your feet. Do what racers do: cut them off, making sure to round the ends so they can't cut or gouge you in a get-off. Do you have to remember to scrunch your neck down to keep your helmet from hitting the windscreen? Cut the offending screen to suit you (as you can't get a smaller head) and round off the resulting sawn edge by sanding.

Be ruthless. Do what it takes to make your bike fit you like a custom suit of clothes. A comfortable rider is a better, more alert rider.

If you have to consider resale value, set aside the stock parts for later re-installation, and modify aftermarket parts to suit you.

CHAPTER 3
HOW ENGINES WORK

Internal combustion (IC) engines are based on a simple sequence of events.

1. A rising piston compresses a cylinder full of air.

2. That compressed air is heated by burning fuel in it.

3. Heating the air raises its pressure.

4. This pressure drives the piston forcibly back downward.

5. A crank mechanism links this piston motion to a rotating shaft.

6. During all this, the inertia of a flywheel keeps everything turning, even when the piston is not producing power.

All the rest of the IC engine's complexity is just housekeeping, concerned with emptying out the burned gases, refilling the cylinder with fresh air/fuel mixture, and with protecting the parts from breaking, seizing, or melting. The basic idea is simple. The housekeeping is complicated.

In the currently dominant four-stroke engine, it takes four end-to-end strokes of a piston to complete the engine cycle (hence the name, four-stroke). We call the maximum-volume piston position "bottom dead center" (BDC) and the minimum-volume position "top dead center" (TDC). **They are the four strokes referred to in the designation "four-stroke engine."**

INTAKE

The first stroke is intake. Intake valves open as the piston moves from TDC to BDC, drawing in a fresh charge of air and fuel.

COMPRESSION (2)

As the intake valves close, the piston begins the compression stroke, moving from BDC to TDC. This compression raises cylinder pressure from atmospheric (about 15 psi) to something like 175–200 psi. Just before TDC, the compressed air/fuel charge is ignited and quickly burns in 30–70 crank degrees, raising gas temperature thousands of degrees. With this comes a 5:1 or 6:1 rise in cylinder pressure. Peak pressure in a well-designed engine at full throttle is, as a rule of thumb, 100 times the compression ratio and can easily be 1,000 psi or more. It is typically reached at 14 degrees after TDC (ATDC).

POWER (3)

The crank rotates farther and the piston begins the power stroke, going from just after TDC and maybe 1,000 psi, down toward BDC and an end-of-stroke cylinder pressure of 100 psi or less. Near the end of the power stroke, the exhaust valves begin to open, giving the exhaust process a useful head start.

EXHAUST (4)

The crank turns further (driven by energy stored in its flywheel mass), driving the piston up again from BDC toward TDC on the exhaust stroke and chasing out remaining burned gases. The exhaust valves close as the intakes open again, and the cycle repeats with another intake stroke.

Four-Stroke Fundamentals: *the four strokes as we all learned them in high school.* **Intake Stroke:** *With the intake valve opening, the piston falls, creating suction in the cylinder which draws in fresh charge.* **Compression Stroke:** *Both valves close and the piston rises, compressing the air/fuel charge.* **Power Stroke:** *Once the spark has ignited the compressed charge and flame has burned it, gas pressure in the cylinder rises to about 100 times the compression ratio. This pressure now drives the piston downward, delivering power to the crankshaft.* **Exhaust Stroke:** *With the power stroke completed and the exhaust valve opening, the piston rises again, pushing the burned gases out of the cylinder through the exhaust port.*

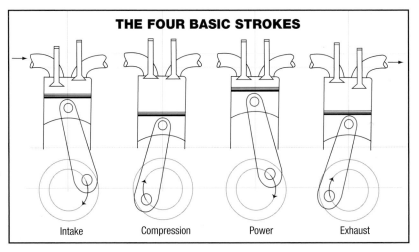

THE FOUR BASIC STROKES

Intake Compression Power Exhaust

WHY FOUR-STROKE?

The reason the four-stroke system is now dominant is that it gives a good combination of power and economy, and can be made to meet emissions standards relatively easily. The separation of its strokes is the basis of these qualities. The intake stroke draws in pure fresh charge (good for power), yet there is little chance of any fresh charge going to waste out an open exhaust port (good for emissions and efficiency) because the exhaust port is open only during the exhaust stroke.

EFFICIENCY—WHERE THE ENERGY GOES

A well-designed spark-ignition engine converts 25 percent of its fuel energy into useful work at the crankshaft. The rest is wasted as heat. This is like lighting four stove burners to make tea on just one. The largest part of the waste heat is left in the exhaust gas, whose pressure is too low for the piston to extract any further energy from it. Further energy can, however, be extracted from exhaust gas by fancy devices such as turbochargers, steam bottoming cycles, etc.

The next big slice of waste heat appears in the coolant—the fluid (water, antifreeze, oil) used to carry away heat from hot parts to prevent lubricant failure, melting, or seizing. This includes waste heat generated as friction. Well-designed engines typically have mechanical efficiencies of about 85 percent. This means that, of the total power delivered by expanding combustion gas against piston domes, only 85 percent makes it to the output shaft as net power.

The rest does the job of overcoming the various sources of friction. Piston and piston-ring friction, together with pumping loss, are the largest losses, followed by crank and rod bearings, valve mechanism, and all the internal thrashing of oil and air by the moving parts. The higher an engine revs, the greater its internal loads and the greater the friction loss. This is why recent, higher-revving sportbike engines have such light pistons and con rods.

FUEL MIXING

At 10,000 rpm, it takes about a hundredth of a second for the fuel to leave the injector or carburetor, travel down the intake

---

BEYOND THE BASICS

Unfortunately, they didn't tell us the whole story in high school. The fabled four strokes are not as separate as we were taught, and there is a lot of important action that goes on in-between them.

Post-BDC Intake Flow: The piston, accelerating downward, pulls a strong partial vacuum in the cylinder, and it takes measurable time for the airflow to catch up and begin to fill the cylinder. If the filling process isn't finished by bottom dead center (BDC), air will continue to rush in during the time when the piston is moving slowly near BDC. Even if the cylinder is full at BDC, the intake air is moving so fast that it keeps right on coming, converting its own velocity into pressure in the cylinder. In fact, flow can continue even against the rising piston. Therefore, we leave the intake valve open for a time after BDC (ABDC). In a racy two-valve, the intake may close as late at 80 degrees ABDC. In a four-valve, it is more likely to be 60 degrees or less ABDC.

Overlap: Overlap is the period near TDC, following the exhaust stroke, when the exhaust valve has not yet completely closed but the intake valve has already begun to lift. A well-designed exhaust pipe sends back a negative (suction) wave that arrives during overlap at peak-torque rpm. This wave pulls out the exhaust product remaining in the combustion chamber. This suction wave continues on through the intake valve, causing early intake flow to begin, even before the piston has begun to drop on its intake stroke. Using overlap this way is tricky, because the more overlap there is, the bigger the torque-boosting

effect—but at lower rpm, it is a positive wave that hits during overlap, stuffing exhaust back into the cylinder from the pipe and causing blowback from the throttle body. This positive wave is the cause of the dreaded flat spot in the torque curve.

Early Exhaust Opening: In the classic explanation, the exhaust valve is supposed to open right at BDC, but in practical engines that is much too late. It's hard work for the piston to pump the exhaust gas out of the cylinder. The engine can make more power if the exhaust valve opens some time before BDC, so the energy remaining in the exhaust gas does most of the work of pumping it out. This leaves a much lower pressure in the cylinder that the piston must overcome on the exhaust stroke, so power rises. A bit of the power stroke is wasted in this process, but it is at the low-pressure end of the stroke, so the waste is small compared to what is gained in lower exhaust-stroke pumping loss.

A SUPPLEMENT TO THE FOUR BASIC STROKES

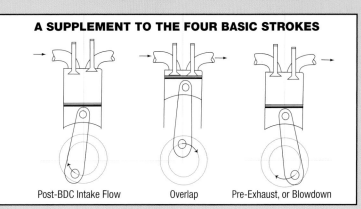

Post-BDC Intake Flow   Overlap   Pre-Exhaust, or Blowdown

port into the cylinder, and then be compressed. During this time, enough of the fuel must evaporate to form an ignitable mixture. Not all air/gasoline mixtures are spark-ignitable; mixtures richer than about 10:1 (1 part fuel to 10 parts air), or leaner than about 18:1 (1 part fuel to 18 parts air), cannot be ignited by a normal spark. Even with a correct mixture of about 14.8:1, if a significant part of the gasoline supplied fails to vaporize, the resulting droplet/vapor mixture can still be *effectively* too lean to be ignited. A spark can't ignite big, cold fuel droplets.

Rapid evaporation requires a highly volatile fuel—in this case, gasoline. Any serious loss of fuel volatility has prompt effects on engine performance, causing poor throttle response and worse. Engines run poorly when they are cold because the engine's metal parts are too cold to evaporate much of the fuel. The vapor part of the mixture is therefore lean, and the result is non-starting or the dreaded start-and-stall. To make a cold engine start, therefore, the mixture must be enriched in some way. Recent electronic fuel injection does this automatically, but older engines have chokes for cold-starting.

IGNITION

The ignition system quickly builds up a voltage difference across the spark plug electrodes. Any stray electrons in the gap are violently accelerated by this voltage difference, and they slam into atoms in their way, liberating more electrons. This is gap ionization, which provides enough conduction electrons in the gap to make it conductive. Almost instantly, a shower of electrons develops and becomes a considerable electric current across the gap. Bombarded by these conduction electrons, whatever is in the gap is highly heated. This breaks up chemical compounds, allowing atoms from fuel and air to recombine in the energy-releasing process called combustion. The spark is small and doesn't last long, so the "sample" of air/fuel mixture that it zaps is critical. If the mixture in the plug gap is correct, ignition will be prompt with a maximum chance that the tiny

flame kernel will swell into rapid combustion. If the sample is rich or lean, the flame kernel may take longer to get going, or may fizzle out, causing a misfire.

This model also explains why plug gaps for automobiles have grown so large. Many years ago they were at 0.024 inch, then 0.032, then 0.040, and now they are at 0.060 inch or more. This was done to counteract the misfire-producing effects of leaner mixtures adopted for emissions reasons. The bigger the gap, the bigger the sample of charge through which the spark jumps, and the greater the chance of hitting some correct mixture instead of a rich or lean zone.

One engineer friend of mine says, "One can tell approximately how much combustion pressure an engine makes by the kind of plug caps the owner has had to put on it." What this means is that the denser the charge, the more powerful the ignition must be to ionize and fire the gap, and the more elaborate the insulation has to be as a result. As the ignition system fires, it must build up voltage across the plug gap faster than it can leak away across any accidental high-resistance pathways, such as along carbon on the plug's insulator nose, or up a salty fingerprint on the external insulator surface. Such fast rise-time ignitions can create the opposite problem—that of popping right through the plug cap, or along the insulator surface beneath its grip. This has been a problem with some racing ignitions, and one fix is to carefully degrease both the plug insulator and the plug cap (checking for a close fit between) during assembly. Even a fingerprint is sometimes a culprit here. Degrease with alcohol, contact cleaner, or lacquer thinner.

COMBUSTION AND TURBULENCE

From the instant of the spark, until measurable pressure rise occurs in the cylinder, takes 10 or more crank degrees. This is called the ignition delay period, and it exists because the flame kernel, being small, has a small initial growth rate. Fifty or sixty more degrees are required for the flame to burn all of the mixture.

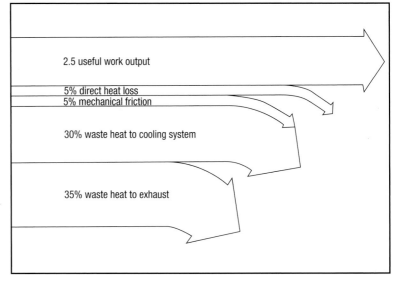

Efficiency Diagram. *Modern four-stroke motorcycle engines can convert only 20–25 percent of their fuel's energy into useful work at the crankshaft. Of the rest, some is direct heat loss, carried away by air in contact with the hot engine. Another bite is taken by mechanical friction—the shearing of oil films throughout the engine, mainly piston and ring friction, followed by the crank and rods, and the valve mechanism. Of the power actually delivered onto the piston tops by combustion gas pressure, maybe 85 percent reaches the output shaft, with 15 percent consumed by internal friction. The two major losses, of course, are waste heat in the exhaust stream, and heat loss to the cooling system. Unfortunately none of this energy is in a form easily convertible into useful work—it just makes our slipstream a little warmer.*

2.5 useful work output
5% direct heat loss
5% mechanical friction
30% waste heat to cooling system
35% waste heat to exhaust

It's important to understand that normal combustion is not in any sense an explosion. In an explosion, combustion spreads at or above the local speed of sound. This would produce a violent rate of pressure rise that would destroy an engine (see detonation section in Chapter 19). Even in a gun, propellant combustion is not an explosion for the same reason. Normal flame velocity in piston engines is a few tens of feet per second, giving a survivable rate of pressure rise, and is seldom as much as 40 psi per crank degree.

Combustion is largely symmetrical around top center. If the best-torque ignition point is, say, 36 degrees before TDC (BTDC), then combustion will end roughly 36 degrees ATDC. Thus, ignition and combustion will take one-sixth to one-fifth of a turn of the crank, or in round numbers, again at our example of 10,000 rpm, a thousandth of a second. This is quick and is only made possible by the nature of turbulent flames. If you mix gasoline and air in chemically correct proportions, let the mix become still, and then ignite it, it burns quite slowly—only a few inches per second. This is too slow to make a high-rpm engine possible. But if you stir up the mixture so it is swirling, tumbling, and eddying, the flame moves much faster. How? A turbulent flame front becomes so wrinkled and shredded that it gains huge surface area. This big area, multiplied times the modest local flame speed, quickly consumes the mixture. How quickly? Measure the distance from spark plug to the farthest part of the chamber; this is the maximum flame travel distance. Divide that distance by the combustion time in our example—a thousandth of a second. For a 70mm-bore engine with a central spark plug, the flame travel distance is 70/2 = 35mm, or 1.38 inches, so flame speed in our example is 1.38/0.001 = 1,380 inches per second, or 1,380/12 = 115 feet per second. That's brisk, yet this speed is completely dependent upon turbulence.

Ionization of the Spark Plug Gap. *This is a chain reaction process that ignites the air/fuel mixture in your engine's cylinders. As the ignition is triggered, a high voltage difference rapidly appears across the plug gap, with the centerwire preferably negative and the ground wire positive. Electrons in the plug gap are accelerated toward the ground wire, colliding with atoms of fuel and air in their paths, knocking loose further electrons from them. This rising population of electrons is in turn accelerated, creating yet more in an avalanche effect. Soon the whole gap is filled with rushing electrons and atoms with one or more missing electrons. This is called ionization. The necessary condition for electrical conduction is the presence of free electrons, so once the gap is ionized, it becomes a conductor. Therefore, a flood of electrons rushes across the gap, colliding with, and thereby greatly heating, everything in its path. Fuel and oxygen molecules are broken up and recombine with each other, releasing heat. This is a tiny flame kernel. If this kernel releases heat through combustion faster than it loses heat to the nearby plug electrodes and passing gas atoms, it will grow and may (we can but hope) lead to general ignition in the cylinder. If heat loss wins over heat release, we get only a misfire.*

And where does the turbulence come from? Most of it comes from the fast inrush of intake flow into the cylinder. At peak revs, intake velocity may play footsie with the speed of sound; all it takes to reach the speed of sound is a 0.53:1 pressure ratio across the orifice. Some turbulence is also generated by the piston near TDC, as it comes locally close to the cylinder head, squeezing mixture out from between in high-speed jets. Such turbulence-generating areas of close approach are termed "squish areas."

THE NEED FOR TURBULENCE

Lack of adequate combustion chamber turbulence is a major reason for soggy midrange in high-rpm engines. In the big ports these engines often have, midrange intake air velocity is low, so the engine lacks the turbulence to burn quickly and efficiently. In engines with very large bores, short strokes, and high compression ratios, the space above the piston near TDC may be too tight for air motion to continue. In such engines, turbulence dies away as the piston nears the head, leading to slow combustion and poor performance. This is a major problem for race engine designers. Some modern four-valve auto engines operate on only one intake valve up to a certain rpm, and then switch to both. This generates useful turbulence at lower revs by effectively doubling intake velocity.

This need for turbulence drives the current, progressive trend toward smaller ports for sports and racing engines.

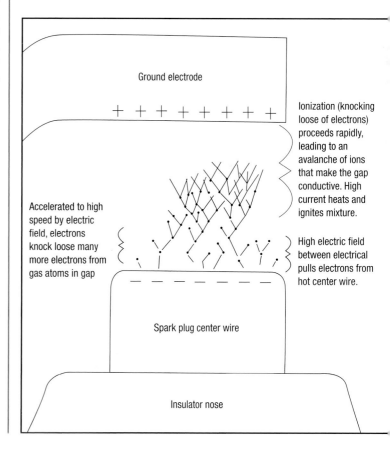

Ground electrode

$+ \ + \ + \ + \ + \ + \ + \ +$

Ionization (knocking loose of electrons) proceeds rapidly, leading to an avalanche of ions that make the gap conductive. High current heats and ignites mixture.

Accelerated to high speed by electric field, electrons knock loose many more electrons from gas atoms in gap

High electric field between electrical pulls electrons from hot center wire.

Spark plug center wire

Insulator nose

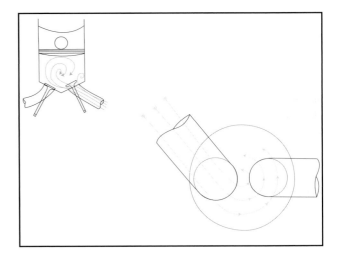

Sources of Turbulence. *On the right is a two-valve cylinder with an offset intake port to promote axial swirl (that is, rotation around the cylinder axis). Swirl is valuable because it provides a means to store the high-speed motion of the intake process until it can be converted, as the piston nears TDC, into the random small-scale turbulence that fast combustion requires. On the left is a section of a four-valve cylinder showing "tumble" motion—that is, motion in the same sense as the rotation of the crankshaft. This motion is controlled by intake port downdraft angle. The higher the port, the more flow is favored over tumble. The lower the port downdraft angle, the more tumble is favored at some loss to flow. The designer chooses the angle according to the needs of the application; for low- and midrange combustion enhancement, more tumble will be desirable. For peak power, lower tumble with higher flow is the choice.*

Big ports look impressive, but they drop dead in the midrange for the reason given. Better to have smaller, carefully streamlined ports that keep velocity and turbulence up—and still deliver enough air for top-end. The higher the intake velocity, the greater the in-cylinder turbulence it generates.

TYPES OF CHARGE MOTION

Turbulence is necessary for rapid combustion, but in-cylinder air motion can take different forms. In the 1930s, it was found that *axial swirl* was a good way to store intake motion until the piston neared TDC and the ignition point. Axial swirl is air motion around the cylinder axis and is typically generated by offsetting a single intake port, so its flow enters the cylinder more on a tangent than on a diameter. Near TDC, this systematic swirl motion can break up into the small-scale turbulence that leads to high flame speed. Swirl design can be seen in Kawasaki's venerable two-valve Z1. It can also be generated by oriented squish areas in the cylinder head.

Tumble is air motion in the same sense as crank rotation; air enters the cylinder, flows across the head, down the far cylinder wall, and loops across the piston crown and up again. This type of motion is favored in four-valve engines and was conceived by the late Keith Duckworth. The degree of tumble produced is controlled by the downdraft angle of the intake ports; high ports flow well but produce less tumble, while lower ports sacrifice some flow to boost tumble. Race engines, which run at higher rpm all the time, need less tumble than street engines, which must deliver usable low and midrange

power. As with swirl, tumble is just a way to momentarily store the energy of the intake process while the piston rises on compression, to ensure that there will still be vigorous motion during combustion. Near TDC, the tumble motion breaks up into smaller scale motions.

Turbulence is destroyed by two mechanisms. One is the rise in gas viscosity as the cylinder pressure rises during the compression stroke. The other is friction and disturbance caused by features in the combustion chamber, valves and their matching piston cut-outs, sharp edges, etc. A smooth combustion chamber performs better than one full of machined edges and angles.

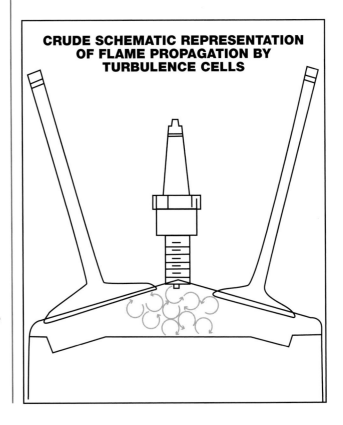

CRUDE SCHEMATIC REPRESENTATION OF FLAME PROPAGATION BY TURBULENCE CELLS

Flame Propagation by Turbulence Cells. *As the piston comes near TDC on the compression stroke, the orderly air motion of tumble disintegrates into random, variable-scale turbulence. To imagine flame propagation, think of these turbulence cells as little trains of gears. The spark ignites one, which must then rotate enough to present its inflamed region to the next, which must in turn rotate, and so on, across the chamber. The more rapid the rotation of these "gears," the sooner the flame will consume the entire charge.*

Squish as a Turbulence Generator.
In the left figure, the combustion chamber is divided into the squish zone (hatched) and the combustion space inside it. As shown in the right-hand figure, in squish the piston at TDC comes very close (0.025 inch, or 0.6mm, in a 70mm-bore engine) to the head, rapidly squeezing out air/fuel mixture trapped between, and forming fast-moving jets that enter and stir the mixture in the combustion space.

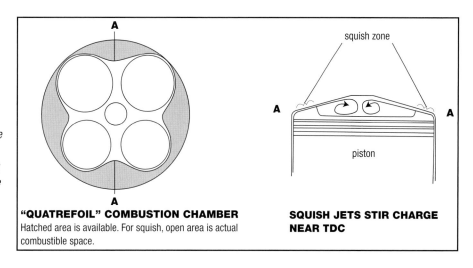

"QUATREFOIL" COMBUSTION CHAMBER
Hatched area is available. For squish, open area is actual combustible space.

SQUISH JETS STIR CHARGE NEAR TDC

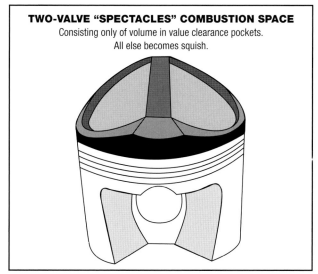

TWO-VALVE "SPECTACLES" COMBUSTION SPACE
Consisting only of volume in value clearance pockets.
All else becomes squish.

The Two-Valve "Spectacles" Chamber. *In this case, the combustion space is reduced to only the volume in the two valve clearance reliefs, plus access for the spark plug(s). All else becomes tight squish, barely thicker than the mechanical limit. This achieves maximum concentration of charge near the ignition source. Chambers like this can burn very quickly. Those of the Don Tilley/Dick O'Brien Battle of the Twins Harley* Lucifer's Hammer *of the mid- to late-1980s needed only 23 degrees of ignition lead. Quick combustion is free horsepower and often brings a reduced operating temperature, too. Machining such chambers and piston crowns is demanding, but worth it.*

FLAME PROPAGATION

As the piston nears TDC, axial swirl or tumble breaks up into smaller turbulence cells, and textbooks picture this process as if these cells were a train of gears. The spark plug lights the charge in one turbulence cell, let's say, and the flame reaches the next cell when the first cell rotates far enough to bring flame to it. Then the second cell must also rotate to bring flame to the third, and so on. From this simple model, it is easy to see why a wide, thin combustion chamber burns more slowly than a more compact, thicker one of equal volume. The thin chamber is filled by a train of many small gears (bigger ones won't fit the space), so many rotations are required to carry the flame to the cylinder wall. The compact chamber can be filled with fewer, bigger gears, so the flame is not delayed by as many rotations having to take place.

The combustion space is not, therefore, of equal thickness over the whole bore area. Instead, it is made into squish—as thin as mechanical considerations allow—everywhere but over the area occupied by the valves. This four-leaf clover area is the real combustion space, and it may be located in the head or, as Kawasaki has done it, in the piston itself. This helps combustion speed too, because a chamber smaller than the bore shortens the flame path.

The mixture forced into squish areas probably does not burn very well, so the volume of charge in squish is made as small as possible by making the piston come as close as possible to these areas. How do you know how close to set it? By getting it too close and seeing the bright areas that indicate piston-to-head contact! The great tuners stand head and shoulders above the others because of the size of the piles of broken parts upon which they are standing.

In highly developed racing two-valve engines, the chamber is reduced to a sort of "spectacles" area that includes the two valves and their reliefs cut into the piston crown, and the single or twin spark plug(s). The rest is squish. Regardless of the number of valves, the game is to put as much of the charge as possible, as close as possible to the ignition sources.

Recently motorcycle engine design has been forced to move on from its long hold at a bore/stroke ratio of 1.5. Engines with even higher ratios are becoming dependent upon squish to generate turbulence in their very tight combustion chambers.

PEAK PRESSURE

With the best power ignition timing, regardless of whether that be early or late, peak combustion pressure is reached at about 14 degrees ATDC. Why this relationship? Put a dial

A Deep Combustion Chamber. *This is the deep, wide valve-angle chamber of the classic Honda RC166 250cc six-cylinder road racer of 1964–1967. Because of slow flame propagation in its severely folded combustion space, this engine (and others like it, such as the Benelli fours) needed over 50 degrees BTDC spark timing! This engine's wide valve angle was made necessary by the need to get cooling air to the head, between the cams. In modern Formula One auto racing engines, compression ratio is sacrificed to obtain faster, more efficient combustion (too high a compression ratio makes the combustion chamber tighter, leaving little room for flame-speeding charge turbulence). Among motorcycles, the equivalent would be the late 1980s Yamaha FZ750 five-valve, which as a race engine could be built either to accelerate (using a high compression ratio) or give high top speed (using a faster-burning, lower-compression chamber), but not both.* John Owens Studio

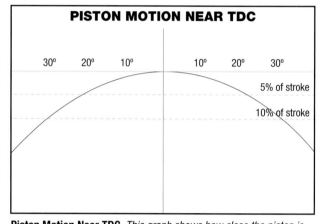

Piston Motion Near TDC. *This graph shows how close the piston is to TDC at various timings. A typical four-stroke production engine fires at about 35 degrees BTDC. No pressure rise is observed for about 10 degrees but after that, combustion speeds up quickly and pressure rise is rapid, peaking in the vicinity of 13–15 degrees after TDC (ATDC) if timing is set for best torque. In racing four strokes with bore/stroke ratios in the 1.0–1.3 range, combustion may require as little as 22–30 degrees BTDC ignition timing. But as the stroke is made shorter, combustion slows because the resulting combustion chamber becomes wider and thinner, a poor shape for sustained turbulence. Such short-strokers (bore/stroke = 1.5 or greater) may need 40 or more degrees BTDC ignition timing.*

gauge on a piston near TDC, and watch it read off piston travel as you swing the crank past TDC. The piston is pretty much motionless for the 30 degrees centered on TDC, but begins significant downward motion around 14 degrees ATDC. If peak pressure comes earlier, there will be heat losses as the hot combustion gas waits for piston motion. If it comes later, expansion by the piston will dramatically reduce peak pressure. Either way, power will drop.

The piston and con rod have zero leverage on the crankshaft at or near TDC, increasing to maximum at about 78 degrees ATDC (when the con rod and crank arm are at right angles to each other). It would be nice to have peak pressure later in the cycle, when leverage is greater, but combustion pressure falls very fast as piston motion expands the combustion gas. Thus, 80 percent of the recoverable energy in the combustion gas is delivered on the piston in the first half of the expansion stroke. This is fortunate because it allows us to use the last part of the expansion stroke for early opening of the exhaust valves, giving a valuable head start on the exhaust process—without wasting significant power.

EXHAUST

Reading through the four separate strokes, it appears that the piston must push the exhaust out of the cylinder. This is sometimes true, but it is more desirable to let the exhaust's own energy do most of the work, rather than take energy from the crank to *force* it out. For this reason, the exhaust valve(s) begin to open some time before BDC on the power stroke, allowing exhaust expansion to push itself out.

About half the heat rejected to coolant is transferred to the head through the walls of the exhaust ports. This is because velocity and turbulence are highest here. To avoid as much of this heat load as possible, exhaust ports are made as short and straight as practical, with the head pipes often extending deep into the cylinder head. In some cases, cylinder heads have been designed to fit in existing chassis, forcing an ugly exhaust port with a sharp turn in it to be used. An example of this is the rear head on Honda's V-twin Ascot.

It has been discovered recently that well-designed but smaller-than-stock exhaust ports and valves can flow more exhaust gas than many stock-sized items. In extensive modifications, this can sometimes make room for larger intake valves. Small is beautiful; small valves suffer less heat distress (shortened heat path), and small exhaust ports introduce less heat and distortion into cylinder heads.

COOLING

The compressed charge in the cylinder of an engine on full throttle jumps up 2,600 degrees Centigrade in temperature

Growth of Leverage as the Crank Turns. *At TDC there is no torque on the crankshaft because the effective lever arm is zero (crank arm pointing straight up). As the crank turns, however, the effective lever arm increases, as shown in the graph on the left, peaking at just before 80 degrees ATDC. In this peak leverage position, the crank arm and the con rod make a right angle. When this curve of increasing leverage is combined with the curve of falling cylinder pressure, the result is peak torque on the crank at somewhere close to 35 degrees ATDC; cylinder pressure is falling through one-half of its peak value, while the effective lever arm has grown to about half of its maximum value.*

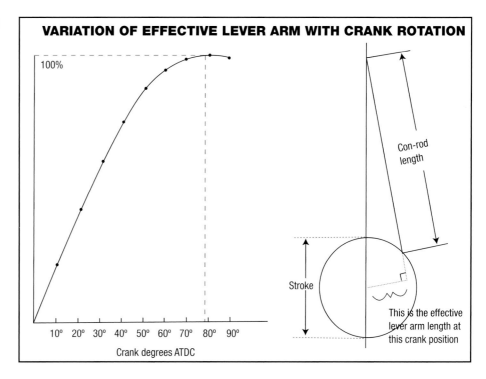

VARIATION OF EFFECTIVE LEVER ARM WITH CRANK ROTATION

100%

Con-rod length

Stroke

This is the effective lever arm length at this crank position

10° 20° 30° 40° 50° 60° 70° 80° 90°

Crank degrees ATDC

during combustion. That's higher than the melting point of any metal in the engine. How do the parts survive? There are three basic answers to this.

Cooling Is Provided (1)

Air traveling between cooling fins, or water/antifreeze circulating through cooling passages cast into the engine, carries away heat from the hot parts fast enough to hold their temperatures at survivable levels.

Combustion Is Intermittent (2)

Combustion takes about one-sixth of a crank revolution and doesn't occur in that cylinder again for another 1 5/6 revolutions. This means the heat is on less than 10 percent of the time, with the other 90-plus percent available for the hottest parts to cool by giving up their heat to cooler parts. Thus, glowing hot exhaust valves transfer heat to their valve seat rings, heat flows from the hot centers of piston crowns and outward toward the cooled cylinder walls, and so on. Heating and cooling are cyclical; combustion blasts temperatures up, but there is time for it to leak away to oil and coolant before the next heat shot.

Natural Insulation (3)

In a storm window, two layers of glass sandwich a layer of stagnant air between. That still air is an excellent insulator because of its low density and its stagnant state. Inside an engine, despite the turbulent entry of intake gas, the mad swirl of combustion, and the scouring exit of exhaust, there is a layer of essentially stagnant gas that clings to all the parts. This so-called boundary layer is stagnant because it is more

under the influence of the nearby surface than of the moving gas a few molecules away. A good thing, too! This "natural storm window" does a great job of limiting the amount of heat transferred from hot gas to engine parts. Without it, engines would (and regularly do, when conditions destroy the boundary layer) fail within seconds.

This is not to say that it's been easy. It took decades for adequate valve materials that did not melt, erode, crack, or stretch to be developed. It took a long time to develop the engine designer's body of useful knowledge about how cool is cool enough for each part.

LUBRICATION

Metal rubbing on metal is bad news because, unless something prevents it, the surfaces will micro-weld at their myriad tiny points of real contact, tear, generate wear particles that make it all worse, heat up, and eventually seize. Lubrication prevents this nastiness and makes machines possible.

Three forms of lubrication exist: hydrodynamic, boundary, and mixed.

Hydrodynamic (1)

This fancy word just means "fluid in action," and it describes the case in which a wedge of fluid—oil in our case—is encouraged to develop between the moving parts. The motion of the parts drags the oil into the wedge, where very high pressures may be generated toward the thin end to separate the parts. Think of it as a kind of mechanical surfing, or as flight in extremely low-altitude ground-effect. Machines lubricated entirely in this mode (thrust bearings of large

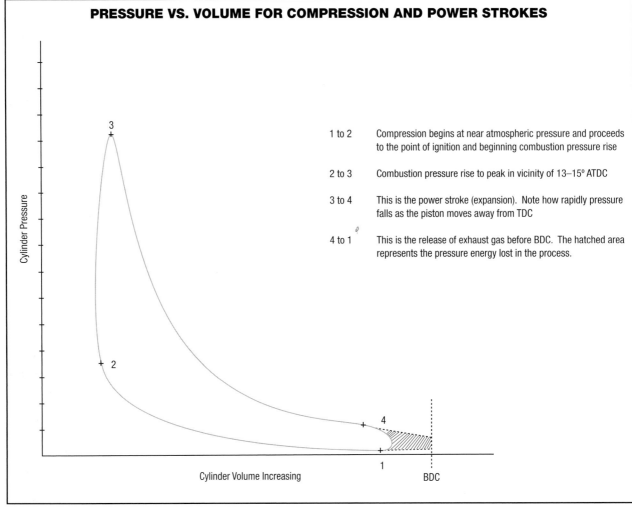

PRESSURE VS. VOLUME FOR COMPRESSION AND POWER STROKES

Cylinder Pressure

Cylinder Volume Increasing

BDC

1 to 2   Compression begins at near atmospheric pressure and proceeds to the point of ignition and beginning combustion pressure rise

2 to 3   Combustion pressure rise to peak in vicinity of 13–15° ATDC

3 to 4   This is the power stroke (expansion). Note how rapidly pressure falls as the piston moves away from TDC

4 to 1   This is the release of exhaust gas before BDC. The hatched area represents the pressure energy lost in the process.

Pressure versus Volume during Compression and Power Strokes. *This curve illustrates several things. First, the power delivered to the piston is represented by the area under the curve 3–4 (combustion gas pressure expanding against the piston), minus the area under the curve 1–2 (compression pressure opposing the piston's rise). It is obvious from this that the power lost by opening the exhaust early (the hatched area) is very small compared to the large area under the 3–4 curve. Note also how quickly pressure falls after its peak at point 3. The actual torque exerted on the crankshaft is this pressure, multiplied by the effective lever arm of the crankpin. This lever arm is zero at TDC, increasing to maximum at about 78 degrees ATDC. The result is that about 80 percent of the available energy in the combustion gas has been extracted before the piston has moved through half its stroke. This is why we can open the exhaust valves early without significant power loss.*

vertical hydroelectric turbines, for example) have run without shutdown for decades, showing zero wear and original tool marks when finally scrapped. This type of lubrication exists in running crank bearings and between pistons, rings, and cylinder walls over much of their travel. If we could keep all parts operating in hydrodynamic lube mode, they'd never wear out because they'd never touch each other.

Boundary (2)

This is what happens between cam and tappet as you start your engine. Most of the oil has drained away, so hydrodynamic lubrication can't occur until the oil pump summons the healing fluid from the sump or tank. What is left to carry the load

is some combination of *(a)* oil molecules adhering to metal surfaces via short-range forces and *(b)* oil additives that have formed protective layers on the metal surfaces, which are able to withstand a few cycles of scrubbing contact while the oil is on its way. Cold-starting and warmup are responsible for most engine wear. This is why expensive racing engines may have their oil systems externally pressurized before startup.

Mixed (3)

This is a combination of (1) and (2) and occurs wherever sliding speed is low. An example is piston-ring-to-cylinder wall friction near TDC or BDC, where piston velocity is very low, or between cam lobes and tappets at idle speed. In mixed lubrication, the

TWO KINDS OF OIL PUMPS

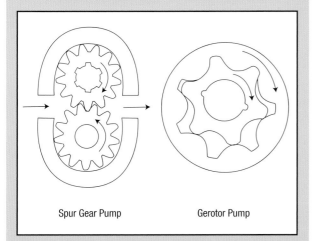

Spur Gear Pump   Gerotor Pump

Spur Gear Pump: On the left is a gear pump. Oil trapped in the tooth spaces is swept around from left to right, but is prevented from leaking back at the center where the teeth mesh. The scavenge pump in an oil system would be a thicker, higher-capacity pump, while the pressure pump would be smaller to ensure that scavenge keeps up with pressure despite air entrainment.

Gerotor Pump: The inner rotor is driven, carrying the outer rotor around with it. This type of pump has a smaller leakage path than a gear pump and is notably more compact, although both types are commonly used in engine oil systems. The suction and delivery ports are in the end plates, not in the outer housing as with the gear pump.

---

moving part is moving too slowly to "fly" on a full oil film, carrying the load that it does. Think of it as "incipient oil film stall." Some support comes from hydro, some from boundary. This is why additives are important, making false the old-timers' claim that "oil is oil."

Crank and con rods in modern engines run on so-called plain bearings. These are split shells, lined with layers of soft bearing metal that face the rotating journal itself. Various types of bearing materials are made for different duty levels. The housing of each main and rod bearing is itself split, with a cap retained by bolts or studs and nuts. Each pair of bearing shells is slightly too big for its bearing housing. This provides "crush," or installation preload, that will hold the bearing in place and prevent its spinning. Each bearing shell has an installation tab or other line-up device to ensure it is installed properly.

The oil pressure that supports the rotating parts results from the viscous sweeping action of the moving surfaces, carrying oil into the loaded zone of the bearing. Pressure here can peak as high as several thousand psi. Naturally, as the bearing rotates, oil is being continually squeezed out at the edges, but more is being swept into

the loaded zone to make good this loss and support the load. The oil swept in is provided by the pump continually pushing oil into the bearing's unloaded zone. The high-pressure flow of oil within the loaded zone generates heat that would soon destroy the oil's viscosity and load-carrying ability. This is prevented by flowing excess oil through the bearing simply as coolant.

Oil is picked up from the sump or tank and delivered to a main oil gallery, parallel with the crankshaft. From this gallery, drillings carry oil to the upper (less loaded) shell of each main bearing. The lower main bearing shells are normally ungrooved to maximize their load-carrying ability, but each upper shell has a groove that receives oil from the main gallery. Corresponding with this groove is a hole, or holes, in the crank journal, whose purpose is to collect oil from the groove and carry it to the adjacent con-rod bearing through drillings in the crank itself.

Sometimes this oil-delivery scheme is not enough. Note that oil must follow a tortuous path into the grooved upper main shell, around the groove, into the oil hole(s) in the crank journal, and inward against centrifugal force. Then it flows through the drilled passages to the nearby crankpin and, finally, out through its oil hole into the rod bearing. As the crank is whirling, this oil supply can become intermittent, and the oil delivered to the rod bearings can become marginal. Higher oil pressure sometimes helps, sometimes not. Engine designers sometimes resort to a different scheme—end feed—in which oil is fed into the center of the crank from one or both ends. This way, it no longer has to be pumped inward against centrifugal force, and every crankpin receives oil continuously—not just when a drilled passage happens to line up with a groove in an upper main bearing shell. The current Ducati D16RR, derived from that company's 990cc MotoGP engine, has an end-feed oiling system.

Not so long ago, engines and gearboxes were separate, and separately lubricated. Engines used engine oil, gearboxes carried gear oil. Today, save for two-strokes, the same oil is shared between engine and gearbox. This is unfortunate in a sense, because gears do best with aggressive, extreme pressure (EP) additives, so gears must be designed a bit oversized to last in non-EP engine oils. On the other hand, being lubed with engine oil has a power advantage. The old scheme was to fill the gearbox up to the shaft midline and let the splash of the rotating gears provide the lubrication. All this paddling around in gear oil generated heat and power loss. In new, shared-oil designs, both shafts are supplied with oil pressure, from which drillings lubricate the free-spinning gears on the shafts. There may also be an overhead oilway, from which downward-directed jets spray onto each of the five or six gear pairs. At high speed, this probably saves a horsepower or two.

As a negative example, Kawasaki's KR250 two-stroke road racer had a very tight gear case, and when it was given its "correct" fill of 1,100cc of gear oil in 1975–1976, it got so hot it burned the black paint right off the gearbox. Cutting the fill to 600cc made the situation tolerable if not desirable.

The Three Regimes of Lubrication. *At the top is full hydrodynamic lubrication, in which the relative motion of the surfaces, plus the viscosity of oil, drags oil into the loaded zone and maintains a lubricant film. This kind of lubrication is present in crank and con-rod bearings at normal operating speeds, and between piston rings and cylinder wall except at the ends of ring travel. In the middle is mixed hydrodynamic/boundary lubrication, in which some support is supplied by a partial oil film, and some is supplied by adsorbed or chemically bonded surface films. Mixed lubrication is normal between the piston rings and cylinder wall, when the piston moves slowly near top and bottom center. Cam-to-tappet lubrication is also likely to be mixed at or near idle speed, when the surfaces move too slowly to establish full-film lubrication. The bottom figure shows boundary lubrication, which occurs during startup, when oil has drained from working parts and before the pump can supply fresh oil. Surface layers, supplied by additives in the oil, protect moving parts in the absence of an oil film. If the protective layer is ruptured, it re-forms from additives in the oil.*

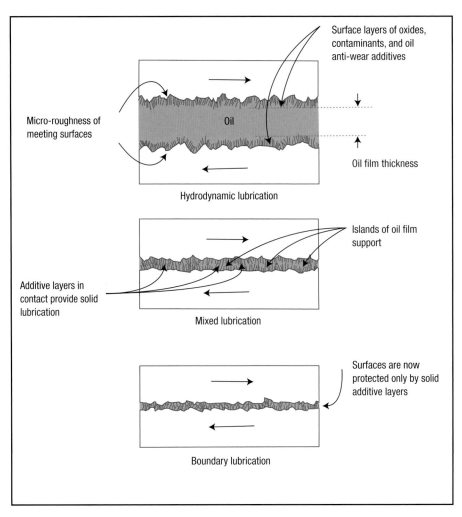

Primary gears are the fastest-moving gears in the engine, and so have the largest potential for wasting power through excessive oil churning. Oil from the pressurized shaft center emerges into the clutch, from which it is flung to create what is really the best condition for the lubrication of high-speed gears: air-oil mist.

Oil pumps are of two general types. In one, two meshing gears sweep oil around inside a tight-fitting case from intake to delivery. In the other, often called a gerotor pump, there is a gear-within-a-gear, which draws in oil at one point and delivers it at another. There is always a relief valve in any oil system, intended to prevent pump damage when cold startup would otherwise force the pump to do the impossible: pump stiff, cold oil at warmed-up rates of flow. To ensure adequate lubrication at idle and low speed, oil systems may produce excess flow at high speed, which is why some F1 engines now have two-speed oil pumps.

Oil makers like their products to run no hotter than a bulk temperature (meaning the oil temp in the sump or tank) of 180 degrees Fahrenheit. Bulk temps of up to 300 degrees are said to be routine in family cars towing trailers across Kansas in August, but this causes excessive viscosity loss and accelerates deterioration of some additives. Run an oil cooler if you find excessive temperatures. Otherwise, a cooler is just another fashion accessory!

Another source of friction in engines is so-called windage, which I would prefer to call "oilage" because oil is 600 times denser than air and is the primary source of this kind of loss. As the crank spins, oil is constantly thrown from its main and rod bearings. This constitutes a power loss if the crank is flinging this oil off at high speed. In GP car engines, there are slingers at each main bearing to deflect emerging oil away from the crank, so it can just drop to the sump without being accelerated along a crank cheek, robbing valuable momentum from crank motion.

A worse problem existed in early sportbike engines, whose oil sump levels were not sufficiently far below the bottom of the cranks. During braking or other maneuvering, oil could slosh up to the crank where it could be gathered up in large volume and whirled and flung everywhere, causing a several-horsepower loss and great oil heating. (Think of each horsepower as 746 watts, which is about what a red-hot toaster draws. Therefore, a 5-horsepower oil-churning loss can be thought of as five toasters, heating your oil.) Crank windage trays and oil deflectors and scrapers were conceived to prevent this loss.

CARBURETION

Previously I mentioned that gasoline vapor and air can be spark-ignited only within a certain range of mixture strength. Even within that range, the energy released varies with mixture strength. This is why engine tuners put so much effort into getting carburetion right; the right mixture gives maximum power, all others give less. You'll occasionally hear people reason as follows: "Fuel is power, so the more fuel I can make my engine burn, the more power it'll make." This sounds good, but it ignores the real nature of burning.

Air is roughly 80 percent inert nitrogen, 20 percent oxygen. To convert the chemical energy of fuel into heat, we have to rearrange which molecules are attached to which partners. To begin, we have to take apart the fuel and oxygen molecules. Gasoline is called a hydrocarbon because it is made up of chains or rings of carbon atoms, each one joined to one or more hydrogen atoms. Oxygen in the air is in the form of two-atom molecules. It takes some energy to knock all these structures apart so they can go back together in new arrangements that release heat in the process. This is why we have to add heat (a match, a spark) to start a fire. But when two molecules of hydrogen and a single molecule of oxygen rush violently together to form a water molecule, a definite, known amount of energy is released. If there is no oxygen, there is no energy release. When two molecules of oxygen rush to bond with a single molecule of carbon to form carbon dioxide, another definite quantity of energy is released. The reason air/fuel mixture is important is that maximum heat release occurs when the proportions cause every hydrogen, carbon, and oxygen atom in the original mixture to find a reaction partner and release energy. All this violent rushing together sets the collection of molecules into vigorous motion—and the average intensity of this motion is defined as temperature.

If there is too much fuel (rich condition), some carbon and hydrogen molecules will not find oxygen molecules and so will not react to release heat. The extra, unburned fuel cools combustion like throwing cold stones into a campfire—

These two bearing types support the same shaft diameters and widths, but the ball bearing on the right is much bulkier and heavier. Split plain-bearing shells allow a crankshaft to be forged in one rugged piece, not assembled from pressed together sections as with a roller crank. John Owens Studio

it absorbs heat from combustion and contributes nothing. If there is too little fuel (lean condition), there is oxygen left over after combustion that could have generated more energy if there had been enough fuel to combine with it.

In the latest emissions-controlled motorcycle engines, electronic fuel injection operates with an exhaust oxygen sensor (or lambda probe), enabling a correct mixture to be delivered at all times. This is closed-loop operation. Somewhat less sophisticated and effective is the earlier open-loop system, which uses data from atmospheric temperature and pressure sensors to enable the electronic control unit (ECU) to deliver an estimated correct mixture.

Because fuel evaporation and mixing are never perfect, because combustion near the cool chamber walls is partly quenched, and because some late combustion is terminated while incomplete by piston expansion, combustion is never quite perfect. Even at best maximum-power mixture, exhaust gas contains about 4 percent carbon *mon*oxide and the telltale stink of other products of partial combustion—aldehydes and ketones. Engines making peak power also generate sharp-smelling peroxides. This complex exhaust smell is what Soichiro Honda found so exotic about the first automobile he ever saw, causing him to run after it, filled with dreams of a new world.

The ideal is an engine whose combustion is fast enough that all of it can be completed with the piston very close to the cylinder head, at or near maximum compression. This gives the highest possible peak pressure. The slower combustion is, the earlier you have to light the flame, and the longer it burns after TDC. Both of these processes are wasteful: the first because it is negative work, the second because late burn occurs at a lower effective compression ratio, making a reduced contribution to peak pressure.

Modern roadracing engines waste some energy because their extreme bore/stroke ratios slow combustion, but what they gain as a result of being able to operate at higher rpm more than offsets this. Compromise is always with us.

ENGINE MIXTURE REQUIREMENTS

The ideal mixture that allows every fuel molecule to be completely burned—all hydrogen and carbon atoms finding just enough oxygen for complete combustion—is called a *chemically correct mixture*. You may also see this referred to as a *stoichiometric mixture*.

It would be dandy if all we had to do was give an engine this mixture all the time to get perfect performance. But problems with fuel evaporation change things in particular conditions. Gasoline is not a pure substance but a mixture of a hundred or so different varieties of hydrocarbon, some heavier, some lighter, each with its own volatility. At low temperature, only the most volatile hydrocarbons can form a vapor, while the rest remain liquid. Benzene, an excellent though carcinogenic fuel, actually freezes into a solid at Minnesota winter temperatures!

To cold-start, engines require an extremely rich mixture of 4:1 or so. In a cold engine, only the most volatile parts of the

Journal Rotating Off-Center in Bearing. *In this drawing, the load acts vertically downward from above. Oil is pumped into the unloaded zone at the top of the bearing, but it is the oil's viscosity that causes it to be swept around the clearance space by the rotating journal. Because this viscous "pumping action" drags oil into the bearing faster than it can leak out at the bearing's edges, the journal is "floated" off of the bearing shells by the oil. The heavier the load, the farther off-center the journal operates in the bearing—until at some critical load, the journal touches the bearing shell.*

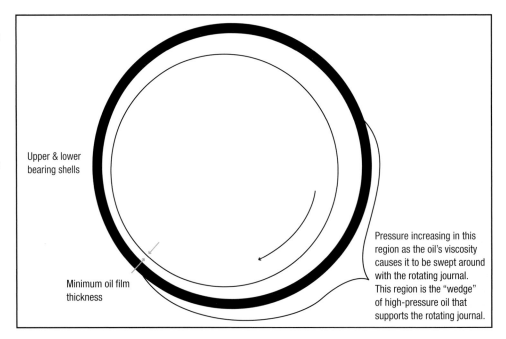

Upper & lower bearing shells

Minimum oil film thickness

Pressure increasing in this region as the oil's viscosity causes it to be swept around with the rotating journal. This region is the "wedge" of high-pressure oil that supports the rotating journal.

fuel will form vapor, and to make this vapor rich enough to ignite, huge amounts of fuel must be dumped in. The large part of the fuel that doesn't vaporize just dribbles through the cold engine, unburned or partially burned (stinky black smoke). A choke or other enrichment system supplies this special rich mixture. As the engine warms up, its rising temperature begins to evaporate more of the fuel supplied, making the vapor a fraction richer. Therefore, the rider of a carbureted machine gradually leans the mixture as the engine warms by moving the choke lever toward "off." The latest electronic fuel injection systems perform this function automatically.

Engines idle on a very rich mixture of about 10–11:1. This is necessary because vaporization conditions are poor at idle, when intake air velocity is low and mixing is poor. Consequently, low-volatility parts of the fuel remain liquid, creeping along the intake pipe walls, and do not burn. More fuel must be added to deliver a combustible vapor fraction.

Engines cruise on a chemically correct mixture (14.8:1) or even a bit leaner. This produces maximum economy and minimum emissions (with plenty of oxygen available, unburned hydrocarbons are minimized—every dancer has a partner).

Maximum power is achieved with a somewhat richer-than-correct mixture in the 12–13:1 range. The extra fuel gives the combustion gas a slightly larger specific volume, based upon a larger number of reaction product molecules. Adding more extra fuel than this reduces power.

The carburetors or fuel injection system must accurately deliver the right mixture for conditions. Maladjusted carburetors or injectors cause power loss, poor throttle response, stumbling, and so on. Mixture control—carburetion or the mapping of fuel injection—is therefore an art worth learning.

Because of the need to reduce engine exhaust emissions, carbureted stock machines were often so close to the lean misfire limit that the slightest inaccuracy in manufacturing led to unacceptable carburetion. Given a choice between official frowns from the Environmental Protection Agency (EPA) or private frowns from the vehicle owners, which do you think the manufacturers chose? To correct this problem, jet kits were widely sold in the 1980s and 1990s as a way to push carburetion back onto the good side of the misfire limit. More about that later.

A current promising development is four-stroke gasoline direct injection (GDI). It uses fine-particle-size injectors originally developed for direct-injection two-strokes. When fuel particle size is 10 microns or less (0.0004 inch), the resulting mist burns just as it would with full evaporation. Also called "dry injection", GDI needs less enrichment during cold starting, acceleration, and so on. This is good for both emissions and performance. Fuel particle size for conventional "wet" fuel injection is somewhat larger than for carburetors, being in the 50–150 micron range. As of April 2008, GDI had not yet arrived in motorcycle engines.

FLAME SPEED AND TURBULENCE

For best torque, any engine must burn to peak pressure at about 14 degrees ATDC. There is some combustion after this, but peak pressure at this position gives maximum torque. This is because the piston is essentially stopped for 11–15 degrees after TDC, but after that, it accelerates downward rapidly. This puts peak pressure just at the beginning of significant downward movement.

Flame speed varies with conditions: the denser and more turbulent the mixture, the higher the flame speed. As the mixture becomes either rich or lean, combustion slows. Thus on full throttle, flame speed is brisk, but slows as the throttle

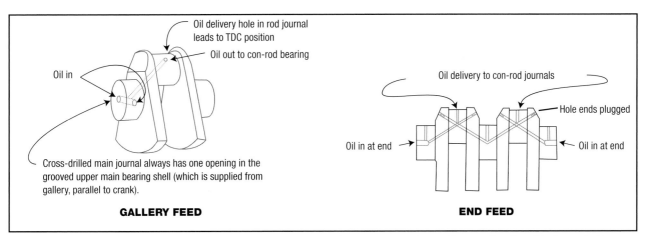

Oil Routes to Main and Con-Rod Bearings. *In the commonly used gallery feed, oil is pumped to a gallery running alongside the crank. From this gallery, oil enters each main bearing's grooved upper shell. This feeds the main bearing itself, while some oil also flows into the crank journal through one or more drillings, against centrifugal force, to supply the con-rod journals. Depending on the number of drillings provided, con-rod bearing lubrication may be intermittent. If the rod bearings show streaking or polishing, and there is no oil pressure problem, end feed may be the answer. Oil is pumped into the end(s) of the crank, making lubrication always available at all bearings. F1 auto engines and current MotoGP engines are end feeders.*

is closed. Where the exhaust pipe is helping the engine, the charge is denser so less advance is needed. Where the pipe produces a flat spot, cylinder filling sags and so does flame speed, thus requiring more advance. In effect, the ignition advance curve is the inverse of the torque curve. Research done by Honda in the early 1960s shows that in-cylinder turbulence and flame speed grow pretty much in step with rpm—even out to 27,000 rpm. This is why an engine does not require more and more ignition advance as it revs up.

A prime misconception is that more advance is better. Even the words we use conspire to make us feel this way. Would you rather be thought of as, *advanced* or *retarded*? The truth here is otherwise. The most highly developed engines require the least timing, because their combustion has been worked over to make it fast and efficient. Engineers refer to the optimum ignition setting as Minimum for Best Torque (MBT). If your modified engine makes best power with *less* timing than stock, you should be happy because this shows that you have achieved faster combustion. Slow combustion requires you to light the fire long before TDC (a disgraceful 45 degrees in the case of the old Yamaha FZ750), so that the piston must compress burning gases that have already generated some pressure. This is *negative work* that cuts your output. The longer combustion takes, the more time there is for heat loss. And not least, the longer combustion takes, the more likely detonation becomes. Therefore, designers and tuners try to speed combustion in any way they can by:

1. raising intake velocity to create turbulence;

2. providing tight squish areas between piston and cylinder head;

3. shaping the piston crown to push every possible bit of charge in close to the spark plug, to occupy a combustion chamber that is vertically roomy enough to allow turbulence to continue even when the piston nears TDC on compression. For equal volume, a hockey puck is a better combustion chamber shape than is a pancake or a CD.

Cosworth, builders of Formula One car racing engines, was able to get best power from its 85.7mm-bore double four-valve (DFV) engine with ignition at only 27 degrees BTDC. This was achieved by narrowing the valve angle to create a more compact combustion chamber and filling it with tumble charge motion. The builders of National Association for Stock Car Racing (NASCAR) stock car engines regularly get their 100mm-bore V-8s down to less than 30 degrees BTDC ignition timing. These chambers are also small, filled with vigorous charge motion. These concepts remain the basis of efficient combustion—a compact chamber that does not suppress charge motion near TDC.

The reverse side of this coin is exemplified by the terrible combustion chambers of the classic air-cooled racers of the 1960s, such as the Honda fours and sixes, and the Benelli fours, which need 55 or more degrees of ignition lead for peak power. Why such slow combustion? The traditional excuse is their high rpm (17,000 for Honda's 250 six), but current 600 sportbike engines rev nearly as high, yet make their power with much less ignition lead. The classic machines of the 1960s had large valve included angles and tall piston domes, so their combustion spaces resembled the peel of half an orange—thin and very spread-out. Being so thin yet of large area, they had no room for flame-speeding turbulence to persist near TDC.

A useful concept is *combustion efficiency*, which is the ratio of the heat value of the fuel supplied, divided into the actual heat generated. As you'd expect, it's easier to think about this than to measure it, but here's where the losses occur. Some of the mixture is quenched—extinguished—by being too close to cooler metal surfaces. There is a layer of incomplete combustion next to the metal walls of the combustion chamber, and there is some volume of gas trapped in squish zones and in piston-ring crevice spaces that doesn't burn at all, or burns so late in the cycle that it doesn't contribute to peak pressure. Then, too, the mixture is never perfectly accurate, or completely evaporated or mixed. This means that part of the fuel doesn't burn even if it isn't quenched—it's like the eligible bachelor who somehow never finds his mate.

Evidence of incomplete combustion is the strong smell of exhaust, containing sharp aldehydes and ketones, which are products of incomplete oxidation. Modern tuners may use an onboard exhaust gas analyzer.

SEALING

A major element in a successful engine is sealing. You can flow lots of air, compress the daylights out of it, and burn it in a "fast" chamber, but it's all for nothing if you have leaking valves or piston rings. They make performance "soggy." Good builders keep track of the condition of their engines with a leakdown tester. With it, you pressurize a cylinder to a given air pressure with its piston held at TDC, then measure the percentage of loss in a given time period. When the leakdown percentage exceeds some amount (20 percent is a number you'll often hear in this connection), the engine needs to be "freshened up." This means giving it a valve job and new piston rings, with honing of the cylinders to give a fresh surface for break-in. Drag racers cudgel their brains to push their new-engine leakdowns to tiny figures like 2–3 percent, but such numbers are irrelevant for engines that go for miles and miles.

A leakdown tester is not trivially cheap, but its results are interesting. If the state of your engine's sealing is very important to you, this is the way to know.

For any engine, there is a characteristic curve of power versus hours of operation. When a fresh engine is started, its power is somewhat low at first because break-in has not yet taken place. Sealing is imperfect and there is extra friction. Power rises through break-in, reaches a peak that may last a while, and then begins to drop as the valves accumulate under-head deposits, warp, and begin to leak, piston-rings become soggy, and bores wear. In production racing classes, the winning teams are often those which keep their engines up nearest this peak through constant maintenance. Much of the work involved in racing is "dirty dishes" labor of this kind—just keeping things in their best possible condition.

Now consider how piston rings work. Their springiness pushes them out against the cylinder wall, but the real sealing force is compression or combustion pressure. It enters the space above and behind the piston ring in its groove, pushing the ring outward to seal against the cylinder wall and downward to seal against the bottom of the groove (you can always tell

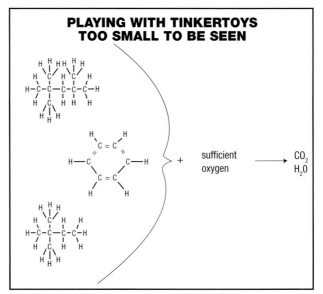

Fuel plus Oxygen Equals Power. *These chemical Tinkertoys represent fuel molecules. At the top is the branched-chain of isooctane, a major component in good fuels. At the center is the classic ring structure, benzene, with some single and some double bonds. At the bottom is isopentane, a volatile branched-chain species often used in gasoline to provide cold-starting ability. Pump gasoline contains more than a hundred different hydrocarbon species. The overall properties of the mixture must meet a variety of engineering standards. Racing gasolines may contain as few as three to six components in the interest of achieving high octane, high energy content, or whatever other quality may be desired.*

which face of a used ring goes downward, because it is the shiny one). But as the piston rises on its compression stroke, two forces are acting on the ring. Compression and then combustion pressure is pushing it down, but as the piston decelerates sharply near TDC, the ring's inertia is tending to lift it off the bottom of the groove. If it does lift off, the gas pressure behind it vents below the ring, and without pressure behind it, the ring stops sealing.

Well, you may reasonably propose, why not just make the groove tighter? A tight groove prevents gas pressure from getting behind the ring, leading to non-sealing at speed. A typical up-and-down clearance for piston rings is over 0.001 inch. Therefore, rings in high-speed engines have been made thinner and thinner over time to reduce the near-TDC inertia force tending to jerk them upward, off the bottoms of their grooves. In some types of drag racing, rings are run in tight grooves to prevent their being broken by ultra-high accelerations, as engines run to very high revs. These rings are inflated by combustion pressure fed behind them through small holes, drilled down from the piston dome. This is not a universal remedy, as it is also possible to have <u>too much</u> gas pressure behind the rings—enough to cause extra friction and premature wear in the near-TDC region.

Another interesting piston ring technique used in racing is crankcase evacuation. Racers have found that if crankcase pressure is kept negative by various means, lighter pressure oil rings can be used. Their lower friction sets free useful power. Case evacuation is handled by some combination of intake vacuum, vacuum piped from the header-pipe junction, timed breathers, or, in the case of F1 engines, actual pumps.

COMPRESSION RATIO

IC engines work by allowing hot, high-pressure gas to expand against a piston. Igniting a mixture at atmospheric pressure generates a moderate pressure rise of maybe 7 atmospheres (7 x 15 psi = 95 psi), but compressing the mixture first increases the pressure rise a lot (peak pressure in a non-supercharged race engine can be 1,000–1,200 psi). This is why the mixture is compressed before it is ignited. The ratio of the volume above the piston at BDC (full expansion), to the volume above the piston at TDC (full compression), is arbitrarily called the compression ratio, but we could just as accurately call it the expansion ratio. It is both.

MAKING THINGS HARD TO UNDERSTAND— THERMODYNAMICS

In heat engines, efficiency is governed by the difference between the maximum and minimum cycle temperatures: the bigger the difference, the higher the efficiency. This means that the higher the compression ratio (CR), the higher the efficiency and the more the air/fuel charge is heated by compression, and to this temperature is added the 2,600 or so degrees Centigrade that comes from combustion of a healthy charge. This is the maximum cycle temperature, and raising the CR does, indeed, raise it. The minimum cycle temperature is that of the exhaust gas when the exhaust valve opens. Viewed from the power stroke, the higher the CR, the more the gas will be expanded, and the cooler it will be at the moment of exhaust. Thus, again, a higher CR also lowers the minimum cycle temperature (one non-intuitive result of this is: the higher the CR, the cooler the exhaust valves run).

A major reason diesel engines deliver higher efficiency than do spark-ignition engines is their higher CRs of between 17 and 23:1, If you run an engine on an instrumented dyno, you will see the effects of changing to a higher compression ratio. Brake-specific fuel consumption will fall as the CR is pushed higher.

BRAKE MEAN EFFECTIVE PRESSURE (BMEP)

BMEP is that constant net pressure which, if it acted on the piston throughout the power stroke, would produce the same power as the actual varying pressure during combustion and expansion. BMEP is the *effect* of many things acting together: cylinder filling, combustion efficiency, heat loss, friction, and compression ratio. BMEP is the profit left after all the engine's internal bills have been paid. To raise BMEP, go after those losses in detail.

A higher compression ratio, better cylinder filling, lower heat loss or friction, or higher combustion efficiency, all tend to raise BMEP. Unsupercharged engines with exceptional breathing and combustion may reach a BMEP of 230 psi at peak torque. Well-developed sportbike engines are currently around the 190 psi mark.

DETONATION SETS THE LIMIT OF POWER

When higher CRs were tried in the early years, the result was delightful: more power *and* greater economy. But theory often collides with practice. When engine CRs were raised sufficiently, strange knocking noises were heard as engines overheated and parts broke. This was the phenomenon of *engine knock* or *detonation*. High-speed photographs, made through transparent

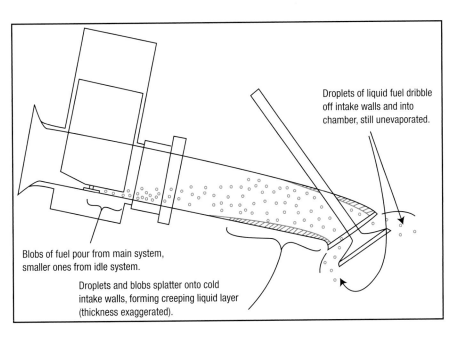

Droplets of liquid fuel dribble off intake walls and into chamber, still unevaporated.

Blobs of fuel pour from main system, smaller ones from idle system.

Droplets and blobs splatter onto cold intake walls, forming creeping liquid layer (thickness exaggerated).

The Intake System during Cold Starting.
Ideally, all the fuel should evaporate by the moment of ignition, but when the engine is cold, there isn't enough heat to accomplish this. The evaporated part of the fuel is too lean to fire, so the starting mixture is enriched to provide enough evaporated fraction to be ignitable. The liquid portion of the fuel passes through the engine unburned. As the engine warms up, more of this liquid fuel is evaporated, enriching the mixture. To counter this, the ECU responds to rising engine temperature by leaning out the mixture. The engine then is hot enough to accept normal throttle without choke, and the rider rides away.

cylinder heads, showed what was happening. The spark ignited the mixture and the flame front expanded, compressing and heating the unburned charge ahead of the flame. When the flame nearly reached the farthest bits of unburned mixture out near the cylinder wall, bright flashes appeared in that unburned mixture. This was auto-ignition of the so-called end-gas, or last charge to burn, and it truly exploded, burning at sonic speed. The resulting shockwave caused the knocking sound and the destructive effects.

This process—detonation—is caused by heat acting on the unburned charge. Heat effects begin during compression and speed up greatly once the charge is ignited. The expanding ball of burned gas compresses and heats the remaining unburned charge ahead of it. Heat breaks down some of the fuel molecules into active fragments that are really an explosive, and if this process goes far enough, this chemically changed charge goes off by itself. To avoid this, early engines had to run inefficient low CRs, like the *3:1* of the Model T Ford. The discovery of the effective anti-detonant *tetraethyl lead* in 1923 allowed CR to rise to 5:1 or 6:1.

Intensive development of fuels for supercharged aircraft engines during World War II pushed fuel octane number up over 100, allowing a sharp rise in postwar automotive CRs.

SENSE AND NONSENSE ABOUT COMPRESSION

Raising the CR increases the compression heating of the charge, and thereby raises peak flame temperature. This dumps more heat into your engine's cooling system. You can tolerate a lot of compression for a short time without knock, but as the parts heat up, the hot engine begins to knock and soon destroys itself. This is how drag racers can get away with 16:1 compression ratios. This extra compression gives extra torque to get those big slicks turning in the crucial first 50 feet, but the engine is run as cold as possible, which is what lets it survive. A World Superbike road race engine may have 13–14:1 compression, but you'll notice the huge radiators they carry to deal with all the heat this compression pushes into their coolant. When the goal is all-out power, builders get the best fuel they can find and push compression up until they find the edge of detonation—and they operate there, barely on the safe side. A street-ridden engine needs more margin of safety than this; pump fuel quality varies and lower rpm operation allows more time for detonation to develop, so lower compression ratios are safer. Honda engineers have a term they use for this margin of safety that separates normal operation from detonation: they call it "combustion toughness." Others call it simply "detonation margin."

The bigger the cylinder, the less compression tolerant an engine is. This is partly because the bigger chamber takes longer to burn, and partly because heat must flow farther from the hot centers of the pistons, outward to the cooled cylinder walls. Higher piston temperature pushes the end-gas closer to detonation. Where a small-bore (70mm) street sports engine may have a 13:1 compression ratio, it's normal for a big-bore engine (90–100mm) to be 1 or 1 1/2 numbers lower.

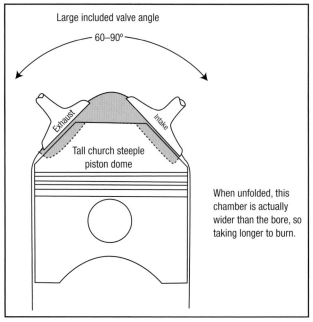

Combustion Chamber Evolution. *Two-valve engines in former times needed a large valve-included angle just to fit in adequate valves. Honda's classic racing four-valves of the 1960s also had large included angles, but only to make room for adequate fin area between the cam boxes. To get high compression with such deep chambers, high piston domes were necessary, resulting in thin, folded combustion spaces—and slow combustion. Early two-valves had extravagant 100-degree valve angles, but later engines such as the classic Z1 Kawasaki had more-compact chambers with narrowed valve angles nearer 60 degrees. Keith Duckworth brought compact, narrow-valve-angle chambers to the four-valve engine, and sensible designers have been using it ever since.*

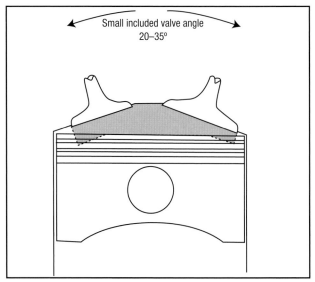

A compact, quick-burning combustion chamber results from adoption of today's 20–30-degree valve included angle, with a flat piston crown. The central spark plug provides the minimum flame path length.

ADVANTAGES OF WATER COOLING

Water-cooled engines have "heat toughness" in the form of three strong defenses:

1. If the engine generates more heat, the thermostat opens a bit more, sending more of the coolant stream through the radiator and less directly back into the engine.

2. Even after the thermostat is fully open, water has a very high specific heat (it takes a lot of heat energy to raise its temperature—1 calorie per gram, per degree Centigrade, which is 3 times higher than that of aluminum, and 9–10 times that of steel). This puts the brakes on further temperature rise.

3. If *that* fails, there is the fact that it takes a *fortune* in energy to actually *boil* water—a whopping 540 calories per gram to convert water at 100 degrees Centigrade, into steam at the same temperature. This protects the engine from local hot spotting, for example near hot valve seats.

By contrast, an air-cooled engine has no such reserves—the only way it can dissipate more heat is to get hotter. Because of this, air coolers must be run a bit on the conservative side in the compression department. Many, many races have been won by air-cooled engines with no more than 10.5:1 compression.

The limit on compression is indicated in either of two ways:

1. The engine begins to detonate; or

2. The power gained from more compression can't keep up with the extra heat lost into the cooling system. More compression, even with a non-detonating fuel, is then pointless. The curve of *theoretical* benefit from increased compression ratio goes up steeply at first—that's why Model T Ford–based racers got such a boost from going to 5:1 from the stock 3:1. Then the curve gets pretty flat after 12:1.

Always remember that the higher the compression, the smaller and tighter the combustion chamber becomes. To retain mixture turbulence all the way to TDC, the chamber must contain some fairly open volume in which the charge can move. Otherwise, combustion speed is reduced. Because of this, the best compression ratio is often determined by the needs of combustion (lower CR gives more room for turbulence) rather than pure thermodynamics (higher CR is better). Lots of builders go nuts on compression because it has done wonders for their drag engines. Then they wonder why it won't do the same for their road-race or street engines. Fact is, very high compression works off the line when the engine is revving lower, maybe even below its torque peak, but such an engine is too "tight" in the combustion chamber to burn fast enough to top-end well. In drag racing, winning in the first 50 feet is super-important. Speed out in the lights is secondary. For a sports/road-race engine, the compromise has to be different because there is no first 50 feet.

AIRFLOW IN AND OUT

Airflow in engines is not as simple as it seems. In a simple view, the intake valve would open at TDC and the piston would draw in a cylinder full of mixture as it moves to BDC.

Then the intake valve would close so compression could begin. But in real life, no valve can open or close instantly. That would require infinite acceleration/deceleration forces, which would destroy the valve and its mechanism (as well as being impossible anyway). Therefore, real valves take significant time to open and close. That being so, and since we need to have the valve substantially open when the piston is moving fastest near 78 degrees ATDC (this is where con rod and crank arm are at right angles to each other), we have to start the intake valve opening process early—*before* TDC.

Even though we give intake this early start, at higher rpm the cylinder-filling process is not complete by the time the piston reaches BDC. This is because air has inertia, and when the intake begins opening and the piston pulls down on its intake stroke, it takes some time for the air to accelerate and follow the moving piston. The higher the engine revs, the more the intake process lags behind piston motion.

When we look at a graph of cylinder pressure versus piston position taken from an engine running at high revs, we first see a steep pressure drop as the piston pulls a vacuum in the cylinder. Then we see the pressure rise smoothly back up as the mixture in the intake port accelerates toward the cylinder and begins delivering high-speed airflow. If we closed the intake valve at BDC, we would be wasting the ability of this high speed flow to keep charging into the cylinder—*even after the piston has started back on its compression upstroke.* It is to take advantage of this inrush of air that we leave the intake valve

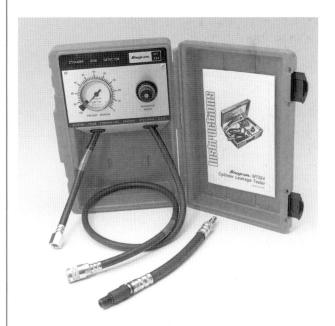

This leakdown tester allows you to pressurize any cylinder, seal it off, and see how long it takes for the pressure to fall. This quickly determines if your engine needs freshening up, and it even tells you (by listening for where the hiss is coming from) where the problem is. This is a Snap-On unit. John Owens Studio; Tester courtesy of Snap-On Tools

open *after* BDC. In a racy two-valve engine, intake closing might be as much as 80 degrees ABDC. Four-valve engines don't need as much timing because they have more flow area, but they may close their intakes 50–60 degrees ABDC.

This is a stinky compromise, because by leaving the intake open past BDC to improve cylinder filling at high rpm, we are *degrading* cylinder filling at lower revs. This is because at lower revs, intake velocity is too low to continue its inrush after BDC. When the piston starts back up on compression, it will stop this slower moving intake flow, then reverse it, pumping charge *back out of the cylinder*. The result will be less charge trapped in the cylinder, so less torque will be produced. Such backflow may also blow fuel mixture back into the air box, where it then makes the next cylinder's intake stroke too rich.

In other words, cam timing that works best at peak revs works poorly at lower revs. As a result, cam timing is *always* a compromise: not enough timing for best power on top, but too much timing for good power off the bottom.

EXHAUST

Now consider the exhaust. It takes power to push exhaust out of the engine, but we have other uses for that power (fun! total victory!). Therefore, instead of opening the exhaust valve close to BDC, we open it early, allowing exhaust pressure to begin the work of emptying the cylinder. At first this seems wrong because early exhaust valve opening appears to shorten the power stroke. But as noted before, 80 percent of the available energy in the combustion gas has done its work in the first half of the power stroke. This is because combustion pressure peaks at about 14 degrees ATDC and falls quickly as the piston moves away from TDC on its power stroke. Therefore, early exhaust opening is wasting very little *useful* power stroke. As the exhaust valve begins to open 50–70 degrees BBDC, hot gas rushes out from its own pressure at or above the speed of sound. If this process is right, very little exhaust will then have to be *forced* out of the cylinder by the piston, during the formal exhaust upstroke. And that means little power will be wasted.

OVERLAP AND EXHAUST PIPE ACTION

Now we come to the period called *overlap*, which is the time around TDC at the end of the exhaust stroke, when the intake valve is beginning to open, yet the exhaust valve has not yet completely closed. This is a crucial period in the valve cycle because it can potentially allow direct energy exchange between the pressure waves in the exhaust pipe and the intake process that is about to begin.

As the exhaust valve opens, a positive pressure pulse is discharged into the exhaust pipe. It travels to the end of the pipe (or its junction with a collector, megaphone, etc.) and expands there, reflecting back toward the engine with its sign reversed; that is, the positive wave has now become a negative one, or a suction pulse. If the pipe length and engine rpm are about right, this suction pulse will reach the engine

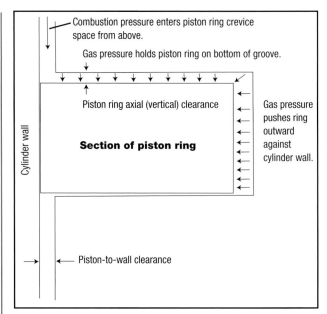

How a Piston Ring Seals. *High-pressure combustion gas enters the ring crevice spaces by traveling down between the piston's top land and the cylinder wall. This gas pressure "inflates" the ring by (a) pressing it outward against the cylinder wall, and (b) downward against the bottom of its groove (which is why the lower face of a used piston ring is always shiny). If the engine revs so high that the ring's inertia during deceleration, nearing TDC, overcomes the pressure holding it down against the bottom of the groove, gas pressure behind the ring will be lost and it may collapse inward. This cycle, repeated, is called "ring flutter," and shortly leads to ring breakage. If ring axial (vertical) clearance is too small, gas pressure cannot reach the space above and behind the ring. An engine with tight grooves of this kind will not break in and will not seal.*

during overlap, and it will travel into the cylinder through the still-open exhausts to help pump out the exhaust residuals still present in the combustion space. Because the intake valve is just beginning to open, this suction wave also travels out to the intake system, causing flow toward the cylinder to begin. These two actions—extra cylinder scavenging, and giving an early start to the intake process—result in *improved* cylinder filling and increased torque.

Now as you can see, if we increase the overlap period, we create a wider window through which exhaust pipe action can assist cylinder filling, and torque at this speed range increases. That's the good news.

But at some lower engine rpm, the negative exhaust pipe wave reaches the cylinder too soon, and it is the next wave in the pipe—a positive one (they alternate, positive-negative-positive, and so on, indefinitely)—that hits during overlap. The positive wave stuffs exhaust gas from the pipe back into the cylinder, and may even blow some back through the intake valve and port. By contaminating the cylinder with extra exhaust and delaying the intake stroke, this positive wave *reduces* torque. And—you guessed it—when we widen the overlap period to get more torque up at design rpm, we also get less torque at lower rpm. It's as though the act of pulling the torque curve *up* at higher revs simultaneously pulls it *down* into a big hole at lower revs. Compromise.

COMPROMISE BREAKING

The four-valve engine breaks out of this by providing what the engine needs (prompt airflow) without imposing its own needs on the process (the two-valve engine's need for longer timings in which to complete the valve cycle).

The squared-cubed law says that as parts are made smaller, they lose weight faster than they lose area, Thus, two smaller intake valves can be made lighter in relation to their flow area than can a single larger valve. With less valve mass in relation to stem cross-section, they can be accelerated harder. This is the mechanical basis for the switch to four valves per cylinder.

ABOUT FIVE VALVES

When Yamaha introduced its Genesis engine family in 1985, there was much interest in the possible advantages of five, six, or even seven valves per cylinder. The low-lift flow advantage of a four-valve is present in even greater degree in engines with five or more valves, and this should make them able to run even shorter cam timing and deliver even wider powerbands.

But the road to success proved rocky. The resulting combustion chamber was tight and compromised. If you wanted acceleration, you had to do without top-end because the high compression chamber was too "tight" to burn quickly at higher revs (it had too little "headroom" for turbulent charge motion). The early Genesis engines ran as much as 45 degrees of spark lead—a clear indication of combustion problems. To run on top, compression had to be

dropped, resulting in soggier acceleration. The later engines were improved by Jim Leonard and others, and have won their share of Daytona 200s. In MotoGP, Yamaha switched from five valves to four just before the 2004 season.

Ferrari's experience with five valves ran straight into the classic problem of valve seat distortion. As early as World War I, engineers understood that the more holes you put into the head, the more it tends to distort from heat (especially if the engine is air cooled), leading to valve leakage. Ferrari's five-valve endurance-racing engines were sometimes unable to re-start after pit stops. The advantages that beckon so invitingly from a sheet of calculations cannot always be realized.

LOSING OUR MINDS—AIRFLOW

Besides the dyno, the most frequently used tool of the engine developer is the flow bench. This is a glorified vacuum cleaner/blower to push or pull air through the port under study, equipped with some type of orifice meter for measuring airflow. It costs a moderate $1,500 to $2,000 to get into this game and begin testing at a pressure of 10–15 inches of water. An inch of water is the pressure it takes to lift a column of water one inch. Atmospheric pressure is about 32 *feet* of water, so 1 inch is 1/(32 x 12) = 0.002604 atmosphere, or 0.0383 psi.

If you listen, you will hear rumors that NASCAR teams are testing flow at much higher pressures, which may foster the belief that since this must be better, testing at lower pressures must be useless. Not true at all! Lots of good work goes on at 10–15 inches—work that produces solid power gains. The reason for testing at higher pressures, I believe, is that big engines with small valves and ports reach intake velocities near the speed of sound. This can produce local shocks and other effects that would be invisible in low-pressure flow testing.

In flow testing, your cylinder head is attached to a dummy cylinder of the same bore as your engine. This is done to accurately model any valve masking or other effects caused by the presence of the cylinder wall. This dummy cylinder is then attached to the flow bench. A device is used to hold open the valve(s) of the port under test by any desired amount. It's usual to test at 0.050 inch, 0.100 inch, 0.150 inch, and so on to the maximum lift of

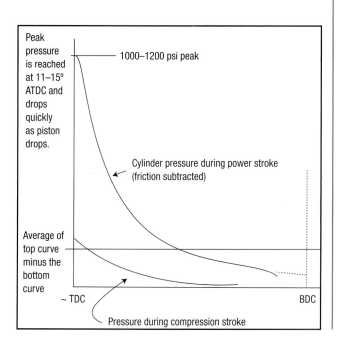

Peak pressure is reached at 11–15° ATDC and drops quickly as piston drops.

1000–1200 psi peak

Cylinder pressure during power stroke (friction subtracted)

Average of top curve minus the bottom curve

~ TDC

BDC

Pressure during compression stroke

The Average versus the Real. *Here we see averaged combustion pressure versus the real pressures acting in the engine. The "kangaroo tail" is the pressure-volume curve we saw earlier, with one change: friction has been subtracted from it. The upper curve of the tail is the pressure doing work on the power stroke, while the lower curve is the work taken from the crank to compress the charge on the compression stroke. The flat line is the average of the area under the top curve, minus the area under the bottom curve. Imagine that the kangaroo tail is a piece of ice sandwiched between glass; when it melts, the resulting water level is the flat line you see—which we call the Brake Mean Effective Pressure (BMEP). The simple meaning is that this is the stroke-averaged combustion pressure, with compression work and friction subtracted from it.*

the cam to be used. Then a curve is drawn, connecting the test points to produce a graph of flow versus lift.

Airflow changes with temperature, and on the popular Superflow flow benches, the blower motor is cooled by the airflow, which therefore heats up as the bench runs. This must be compensated for with arithmetic, as must the changes in barometer. It is all very tedious to end up with apples to compare with apples to be sure you really know what you are doing. Naturally, there are computer programs to make this easier. No end of procedural errors is possible in flow testing. Many are the red faces that have been caused by air leaks between parts, or by the simple error of leaving out the spark plug from the cylinder head under test. Wow! That last tweak really did the job! Oops, guess I'd better redo that run . . . .

Hearing protectors will keep you in a better mood as the hours of testing flow by. The flow bench is a serious research tool, and research rewards only the careful and methodical. The airflow researcher who gets the decimals right and tests without prejudice is the one who smokes 'em.

The trend in port development is to get more air through stock-sized (or even smaller) ports and valves. The advantage is that as intake velocity rises, there is more and more energy in the inflowing stream of charge at BDC. This energy is (as old Newton taught us) velocity squared, times the mass of what is in motion. Ports are designed to have only part of the intake charge at really high velocity, to avoid unnecessary flow losses. Typically, a part of the port just behind the valve, equal to 20 to 25 percent of the cylinder volume, is made small to generate this velocity. As the piston sits still at BDC, this intake energy spends itself in supercharging the cylinder, continuing to rush in until it is used up in compressing the charge in the cylinder. Then, ideally, the intake valve is just closing, trapping this extra pressure.

Thinking from this model: it's easy to see why we should push intake velocity higher with smaller ports, not lower it by "hogging out" the ports. Velocity squared is a powerful relationship. If we raise intake velocity by 10 percent, we are raising the BDC intake energy by 1.1 x 1.1=1.21, or 21 percent. But if we *drop* intake velocity by that same 10 percent, we have 0.9 x 0.9 = 0.81, or a 19 percent *loss* in BDC intake energy.

Getting power out of higher BDC intake energy is not always as simple as just making everything smaller (in some cases it's just that simple), because at a sufficiently high velocity, flow friction eats up the gains. Always remember that above an orifice pressure ratio of about 0.53, a shock will form somewhere in the duct. After that, the piston can suck as hard as it likes, but there will be no further increase in flow because no pressure signal can flow upstream through a shock. This is sonic choking. The velocity game is to raise velocity and airflow at the same time, and that calls for subtle streamlining. Some distinctly non-intuitive things are learned along the way.

Be prepared, if you venture into airflow work or begin a collaboration with an airflow specialist, to see some ugly ports

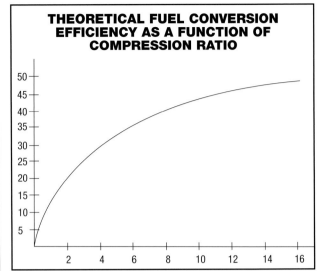

THEORETICAL FUEL CONVERSION EFFICIENCY AS A FUNCTION OF COMPRESSION RATIO

Rise of Power with Compression Ratio. *Power rises with compression ratio, but the gains flatten out at the higher numbers. Detonation sets an upper limit on compression ratio in any case. As compression ratio is increased, heat loss from hotter combustion gas to the piston and combustion chamber also increases. At some point the efficiency gain from higher compression is canceled by increased heat loss. Compression ratio must sometimes be compromised with the need for a combustion chamber roomy enough to burn efficiently. If the chamber is too tight, it cannot sustain the turbulent air motion necessary for rapid flame propagation.*

that flow massive air and some beautiful-looking ports that mysteriously act like they're full of rocks.

A great deal of the magic in porting occurs at or very near the "choke point," which is the valve seat. Its shape and dimensions are therefore critical. This is why a five-angle or blend valve job is basic to Supersport-level performance.

Intake testing should be performed either with the engine's complete intake tract in place (rubber manifold, carb, and bell mouth, if any) or with some standard, smooth bell mouth attached to the head. Otherwise the air will not enter the port in a realistic way.

Likewise, blowing air out through an exhaust port will produce wacky results unless you use either the engine's proper exhaust system or a piece of pipe or a cone that is the same in all tests. This is because there is a large expansion loss as the air exits the head into the atmosphere. Just holding a crude paper cone up to the port can magically increase flow by an apparent 30 percent.

A DANGEROUS AIRFLOW MYTH TO AVOID

The concept of energy exchange is basic to all flow work. The piston drops on the intake stroke, pulling a sudden vacuum in the cylinder. This vacuum creates a pressure difference across the intake duct, accelerating the air in it and converting that pressure difference into the rising kinetic energy of motion in the accelerating intake gas. After BDC, that kinetic energy is transformed back into pressure, supercharging the cylinder to some degree. Each time an energy exchange like this is performed, there is some loss involved, because no process is 100 percent efficient.

The process of converting velocity into pressure is called diffusion, and the device that does the job is called a diffuser. A diffuser is a duct that *expands* along the flow direction. Most people believe that if they place a funnel facing large-end first in an airflow, the pressure will increase as the air crams down into the smaller end of the funnel. *This is not true!* To make efficient conversion of velocity into pressure, the airflow must be slowed down gradually. To do this, we must turn the funnel around the other way. Air at high velocity enters the *small end* of the funnel and decelerates gradually as the funnel enlarges. This process is most efficient if the included angle of the funnel is small—10 degrees or less. At larger diffuser angles, the flow tends to separate from the diffuser walls, wasting energy in the creation of eddies.

As an example, before he got his factory ride, Tom Kipp Jr. and his father did a lot of private small-scale research. One of their projects was to create a ram air box for their 750 five-valve Yam, with a forward-facing intake and diffuser. If the intake

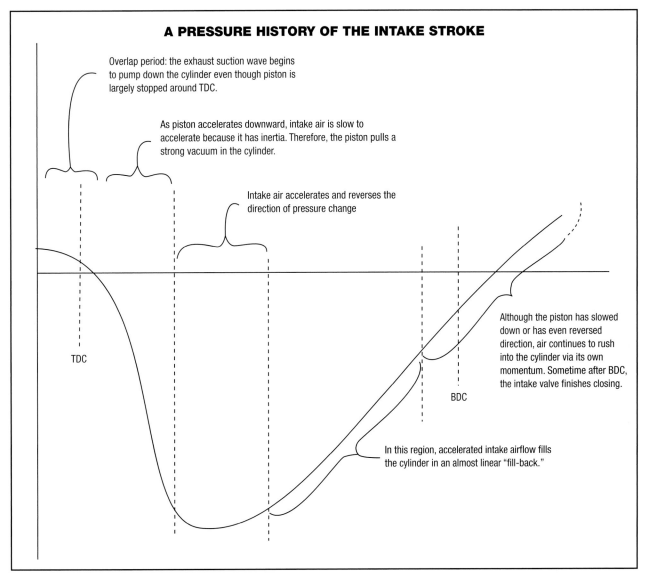

A PRESSURE HISTORY OF THE INTAKE STROKE

Overlap period: the exhaust suction wave begins to pump down the cylinder even though piston is largely stopped around TDC.

As piston accelerates downward, intake air is slow to accelerate because it has inertia. Therefore, the piston pulls a strong vacuum in the cylinder.

Intake air accelerates and reverses the direction of pressure change

TDC

BDC

Although the piston has slowed down or has even reversed direction, air continues to rush into the cylinder via its own momentum. Sometime after BDC, the intake valve finishes closing.

In this region, accelerated intake airflow fills the cylinder in an almost linear "fill-back."

Pressure History of the Intake Stroke. *The industry uses tiny rugged microphones to record cylinder pressure as engines run. This is a typical trace made during an intake stroke. Note that the piston moves before the air can follow it, pulling a deep partial vacuum in the cylinder. Atmospheric pressure then pushes the intake air toward the low pressure in the cylinder, accelerating it rapidly to a velocity of some hundreds of feet per second. This flow then fills the cylinder back up—and may keep right on filling it after BDC, if its velocity is high enough.*

Good and Bad Results of Overlap Flow.
During overlap, both intake and exhaust valves are slightly open at the end of the exhaust stroke. The exhausts are just closing while the intakes have just begun to open. If the engine is "on the pipe," it is a negative wave that arrives back at the cylinder during overlap, sucking out exhaust and giving a head start to the intake process by pulling mixture from the intake system, even before the piston has moved from TDC. If the engine revs are below pipe rpm, a positive wave will arrive during overlap, cramming more exhaust back into the cylinder, and possibly blowing exhaust back through the carburetor. In carbureted engines, this inert blowback picks up fuel from the carb and is carried back into the cylinder when the intake stroke begins, carbureted a second time, making the engine over-rich as well as weak from intake delay.

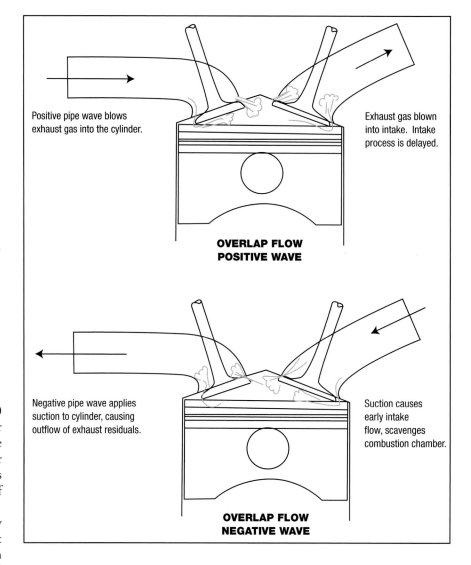

Positive pipe wave blows exhaust gas into the cylinder.

Exhaust gas blown into intake. Intake process is delayed.

**OVERLAP FLOW
POSITIVE WAVE**

Negative pipe wave applies suction to cylinder, causing outflow of exhaust residuals.

Suction causes early intake flow, scavenges combustion chamber.

**OVERLAP FLOW
NEGATIVE WAVE**

diffuser and box had worked at 100 percent efficiency at 160 miles per hour, the box pressure would have been about 12 inches of water, but for various reasons, only about 8 inches were obtained. This is an efficiency of 8/12, equal to 0.67, or 67 percent.

The classic airflow energy converter is the venturi—a duct that first decreases in diameter, then increases again. It is sometimes called a convergent-divergent nozzle. As air enters the duct, it must accelerate as the duct tapers down. In doing so, it *loses pressure* as Bernoulli noted so many years ago. The accelerating air is gaining velocity energy as it loses pressure energy. At the throat of the venturi (the minimum cross-section), the velocity is maximum and the pressure is minimum. As the flow expands from there, velocity smoothly decreases while pressure increases. There is practically no end-to-end pressure loss through a well-designed venturi, operating at a considerably subsonic throat velocity.

A carburetor is a venturi, and so is the intake port. In the carb, a venturi is used to create a pressure difference signal that will flow fuel (see Chapter 6 on carburetion.). In the intake port, the airflow must accelerate to pass through the restriction between valve and seat, which is why seat and valve shapes are so important. As airflow exits from beneath the seat, there are ways to make the inside surface of the cylinder head act at least somewhat like a diffuser, reducing the sharp expansion losses that otherwise occur.

When a diffuser works well, it can be really dramatic. Back in 1978, the American Motorcycle Association (AMA) decided that the two-stroke TZ750 racers had to be slowed down, and it imposed its infamous orifice rule, Tech Bulletin 78-1, requiring all airflow to each cylinder to pass through a 23mm round hole. The early attempts to make power with this little hole failed because they used a diffuser angle too steep to recover pressure efficiently after the orifice. Yamaha engineers knew their business, however, and provided a gentle 10-degree diffuser of maximum length on the engine side of the orifice, with only a short, rounded entry upstream. This recovered pressure from the high throat velocity so effectively that factory rider Kenny Roberts not only won the Daytona 200, but also set a new record in doing so. This was despite having the engine's intake area cut in half by the orifice rule.

In a sense, the rider's back and the sides of the machine are diffusers turned inside-out. Their job is to keep airflow attached, slowing it down from its maximum speed as it

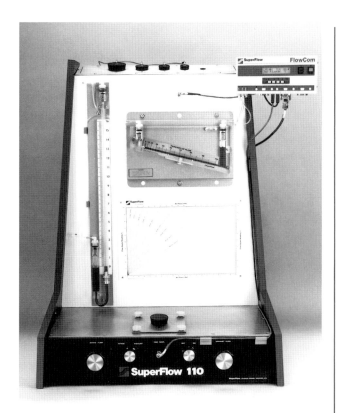

The Flow Bench. *This is a Superflow 110 Flowbench, the low-priced machine that put thousands of engine builders into the serious airflow measurement business. The steady flow of the flow bench replicates the pulsed flow in a real engine well enough for an improvement on the bench usually to translate to a real-world power gain. Warning: Flow testing can be habit-forming. In this photo, a rubber cork plugs the test orifice, on which you place a dummy cylinder with your cylinder head bolted to it. The flow bench can optionally interface to a computer to speed data formatting. Superflow Corp.*

flows around the machine's thickest part. You can clearly see "diffuser stall," or flow separation, on a tucked-in rider's back as fluttering of his jacket. If you go to the races, you'll sometimes see riders raise their butts on long,

fast straightaways, making the "diffuser angle" of their backs less steep to prevent flow separation. Riders report they can gain 150–200 revs in top gear by doing this. Why do they go faster? The airflow, instead of separating into turbulent eddies, remains attached to the rider's back, its smooth pressure exerting a slight but measurable forward shove on this sloping human "diffuser."

And on and on. Engines are full of simple physical phenomena, exploited in clever, often unobvious ways. The people who make progress in these areas are of two basic kinds: energetic triers who test everything, and thinkers who employ physical intuition. Experience makes everything better, because it gives you a feel for what you are working with. Engineering knowledge is useful, but it can be misused to build a box you can't get out of, so you end up not testing things you "know" can't work. Keep an open mind.

SQUARED-CUBED

Some idea of how size affects the ratio of a valve's mass to its area can be had by comparing two cubes, one measuring 2 x 2 x 2 inches, the other 1 x 1 x 1 inch. Each side of the 2-inch cube measures 2 x 2 = 4 square inches, while its volume is 2 x 2 x 2 = 8 cubic inches. Each side of the 1-inch cube is 1 x 1 = 1 square inch, while its volume is 1 x 1 x 1 = 1 cubic inch. Halving the dimension of the cube has cut its area in four, but has cut its weight in eight. A valve is not a cube, but the same dimensional logic applies.

The flow basis for four valves is that two smaller intakes expose flow area faster per increment of lift than can one larger valve of equal total head area. Low-lift flow area is valve total perimeter, multiplied by lift. The four-valve wins here because *(a)* valve perimeter is about 40 percent larger and *(b)* the smaller valves, as already noted, can be lifted faster as well. These two effects multiply, greatly shortening the time it takes to expose a given flow area. This means a four-valve needs less

overall valve timing for a given performance level. It therefore inherently delivers a wider powerband.

On the other hand, two-valve engines are capable of excellent flow and cylinder filling. This is partly because the flow from a single valve is unobstructed by flow from any other valves. The specific flow, in cubic feet per minute, per square inch of valve area, of a single intake valve is higher than that from the paired intakes of a four-valve—given careful design in both cases. The four-valve wins the rpm contest because enough extra total valve area can be crowded into a cylinder to offset its lower specific flow. And, of course, the four-valve has the higher safe rpm tolerance.

Back in the 1950s, the British Racing Motors (BRM) team built the P25, a very short-stroke, large-bore 2.5-liter two-valve four for GP car racing—but the problem of moving very large valves at high accelerations without breakage could not be solved. Four valves are not better than two in every way, but they are the best current compromise for high-rpm engines.

CHAPTER 4
CHOOSING A TYPE OF ENGINE

You can make a highly tuned small engine give as much power as a mildly tuned big one, and this can seem mighty attractive because of the giant-killer aspect. But something unpleasant happens to the little engine's power curve when it's pushed so hard. It's going to need big carbs or throttle bodies, ports, and valves, with long cam timings and big overlap. It's going to have to turn high revs to get the power to slay giants. In the process, we're going to trade away the pleasant driveability of a stock engine, leaving it gutless or, at best, indifferent below 10,000 or 12,000. If that's OK with you, and you're willing to learn to ride its "billspike powerband" and tolerate the constant revving, fine. But if you were expecting your modified engine to be just like stock, only more powerful, you're going to be disappointed. The bike you need is one with a bigger engine!

Keep in mind the lesson of MotoGP, which is that riders go faster on bikes that are easy to ride fast. Making riding difficult with narrow powerbands and steep torque curves usually just slows you down.

Torque curves are not perfectly smooth, but have large and small peaks and dips in them. Usually, these peaks and dips are caused by wave action in the engine's intake and exhaust pipes, affecting cylinder filling. In certain rev ranges, the waves help to stuff more mixture into the engine, so you get a peak. In between those peaks, there will be dips or flat spots, caused by the reverse part of those same intake or exhaust waves *sucking out* some of the mixture the engine just sucked in. There are ways to play games with these peaks and dips, mixing and matching effects, but the simple truth is that they are never going to go away completely. Wave action is too useful in making power for us to ignore it, but for every positive effect, there's a negative at some other rpm.

There are two basic approaches to this problem:
1. Find a combination of cam timing and other variables that results in a smooth, driveable torque curve, and forget about going for absolute maximum torque at high revs; this is what the manufacturers do to produce both rideable stockers and fast racing machines.

The Perils of Power. *Superbikes are tuned for a few hundred miles of top-end power and little else. The result may put the racer on the podium, but the cost is often long hours working to get the bike ready to race.* Brian J. Nelson

A PRIVATEER IN SUPERSPORTS RACING

Supersport is just one more in the endless series of attempts to create a cheaper, more democratic racing class, and it fails, as they all do, on this point (which is the First Law of Racing, by the way): in racing, everyone spends all that he or she can afford, no matter what the rules are. If the rules allow carbon-fiber-core fork tubes that cost $40,000 apiece (no joke—they exist), someone will have them. If the rules say all parts must be stock, some other way will be found to use that money to an advantage. If we are considering 600 Supersports, we have something else to consider, too. The 600-class is a top-selling class. To a manufacturer, it's worth spending a few dollars to defend a good position in that market.

Let's consider the possibilities. You or I—ordinary mortals—can go to the dealer and buy the brand of our choice, then roll it into the shop and go through the rule book. It allows us to change the suspension springs and the rear shock, eliminate the lights and horn, simplify the wiring, and toss any stands and turn signals. There is no weight limit. Fuel delivery may be changed. Air box and filter must remain stock and functional. The pipe can be replaced.

You get busy. While you wait for the suspension parts and Power Commander III to arrive, you break in the engine. This is critical, because it determines the engine's sealing ability. Motul, for one, makes a special break-in oil, so you will fill up on this or something similar and set off, alternating hard acceleration with deceleration to allow local heat to dissipate and wear particles to be carried away. Or you go to the dyno for the break-in and make the prescribed baseline run, followed by 20 hard pulls. You look over the sheets to see if power is still climbing. If it is, you follow the trend. When you're done, you drain the oil and refill with your choice of racing synthetic. You check engine sealing with a leakdown test; it's good to know where you're starting from.

Now the head goes to a good shop to get a slick blend valve job. Supersport rules allow any mods to the iron valve seat rings, and this is a critical area; a good valve-to-seat prep is worth power. You build up again, replacing stock cam sprockets with slotted, adjustable ones that have arrived. You put the cams in to set clearances.

You decide to start with figures like 99/101 intake/exhaust lobe centers, and you set about degreeing your cams. You install the pipe, Power Commander, and the suspension parts. You pull off all remaining heavy street junk that the rule book allows you to take off.

Now it's back to the dyno for fuel injection calibration with a Power Commander or similar, and to zero-in the cam degreeing.

Off to the track for a test day, with a bike at some baseline suspension setup: ride heights, preloads, compression, and rebound damping. There are good tires on the wheels, good brake pads in the calipers, and good hoses making the connections. You do the work of finding a good setup. It all goes into your permanent notebook for ready reference. It hurts to have to create the same information twice.

Before you go off to the first race, you run another leakdown to see how the seal is holding up.

At the races, you find yourself wheezing out long before the checkered flag, and you resolve to fix that quickly with a program of physical training. No more late nights, no more crazy eating. You have to build yourself as carefully as you built (are building, and will continue to build) your bike. It is all an ongoing process. It is a unique kind of life—intense, special. You feel yourself to be different from others now, on a different track.

When the leakdown begins to sag, after some mileage, you decide it's time to "freshen up" the top end. Before pulling the head, you check lobe centers to see how far they've moved. It's good to know how long the "good time" lasts and what's bringing it to an end. The head gets a good look-over to see that all four cylinders are burning equally, but you knew that because you've been looking at the plugs, too. Then it goes to the shop for another careful valve job. You notice that there is a lot of repetitive work of a rather unglamorous nature. Half of success, says ex-F1 driver Niki Lauda, is having the machine on the start line. That means being willing to do all the dirty-dishes, smelly-laundry work that absolutely has to be done to put you there, reliably, weekend after weekend, on a machine that has competitive power and handling.

As your sophistication increases, you will add more activities to this already full schedule. You will, for example, make an arrangement with the biggest dealer in your area (who should certainly be one of your sponsors, if there is any justice in this world) to let you flow-bench-test any replacement or warranty heads the dealer happens to have. You trade in your own carefully prepared head every time you find one that flows promising numbers. You play with highly touted oils on the dyno. You check differences in racing gasolines—including ones that smell so bad you worry about your health.

Then you get into the nitty-gritty—tearing down the engine to check all internal clearances. Will it make more power with more piston clearance, or with relaxed main and rod clearances? You begin to notice yourself unconsciously going to cheaper restaurants, because all this is costing a lot of money. Your girlfriend or wife, who once bravely announced, "He was like this when I met him, and I know he's not going to change to please me," has now begun to look a little less happy. But you have to test the theory that a loose-clearance oil pump sets free 1 whole horsepower. You scrape up cash to buy a wreck, which gives you lots of spares and new test opportunities. You're happy, because you feel yourself expanding into something you genuinely like to do, and you're becoming good at it. It's all tremendously exciting.

The list of possible modifications is endless, and no doubt there are people who put so much energy into bending the rules that they have little left with which to ride their bikes. In any case, it does no good to get hung up on what the other riders might have in their bikes—you can't do anything about that. One thing is sure. Good preparation, hard riding, and constant maintenance are essential. If you can ride, and your bike is as good as you can make it, it will show. That—and luck—are what move you ahead.

continued on page 38

continued from page 37

When in the course of your hard work, you become overtired, under motivated, and on the point of giving up and going to bed, you are confronting racing's Big Question, the one that confronts every single rider and crew member many times a year: Are you in, or are you out? There's no halfway in this game. So do it. Yes, it's 4 a.m., and the engine isn't in the chassis yet. Just keep on doing everything the best way you know how, carefully and one step at a time, because that machine has to roll out on time for practice.

Fine-tuning the motorcycle is part of the program for racers, and that process takes place as much on laptop computers as it does with wrenches these days. This is Anthony Gobert's bike being tuned up at a tire test. Brian J. Nelson

2. Go for broke on top-end, setting cam timing and other variables for that condition only, and to hell with bottom performance. Don't feel badly if you've done this—several major companies with strong engineering departments chose this approach in trying to break into MotoGP—and they all failed. Motorcycles can make the most of their limited tire grip only when everything happens very smoothly.

Clearly, these are two very different kinds of engines. Engine (1) can be ridden and enjoyed by anyone because it requires no special skills, no special gearbox, and no constant revving. Engine (2) makes impressive but narrow power and not much else. Valentino Rossi described one such engine (the 500 Honda built for Alex Criville for 2000) by saying that while you might make one fast lap on it, "twenty-four laps are another story."

There are different ways to make the same power, and some of those ways are more pleasant than others. Look at the horsepower equation:

$$HP = \frac{RPM \times BMEP \times Displacement}{793,000}$$

where RPM is revolutions per minute, BMEP is stroke-averaged net combustion pressure in pounds per square inch (normal range for modem engines is 125–230 psi),

The middle ground between factory and privateer is the "satellite team," like Jordan, which has some factory connections. We hope it can provide more good rides for up-and-comers. Brian J. Nelson

and displacement is in cubic inches. 793,000 is simply a constant that makes the answer come out in the desired units.

Many soup-up tricks increase BMEP on top-end by reducing it on bottom-end. This is what gives us a harder-to-ride type (2) engine. But if we leave BMEP pretty much alone, and instead increase displacement with a big-bore kit (or wisely trade up to something with a bigger engine), we will retain a type (1) engine, but with more power.

The bigger the engine, the less hard we have to push it to get the power we want. The harder we try to get the last possible scraps of power, the bumpier the power curve becomes. This is what happens to make a highly-developed race engine obsolete; —to keep it competitive, driveability has been steadily traded away for power. To return to a

workable combination, a redesign becomes necessary. The prime example is Honda's RC30 in its Superbike form, which started life with a wide, useful powerband. Later, as other designs with more performance appeared, it had to be tuned more sharply to stay with them. This involved sacrifices in the midrange. At first there was no power below 10,000, then nothing below 10,500, and so on until the engine had become virtually unrideable and the design had to be replaced.

Take another perspective. If you're not satisfied with the power of your small engine, but do like its smooth, usable type (1) power, trade up to a bike with a bigger type (1) engine and forget about all those fascinating but potentially powerband-destroying mods. Never forget that performance is more than engines; you can make your bike faster by making it lighter, by making it handle better, or most of all by gaining skills yourself. Streetbikes are *heavy*. Duck soup to lighten older streetbikes a bunch and increase the capability of their suspension.

As I will say in other places in this book, my real objective here is not so much to guide you to a better bike, as it is to push you into learning how to build or otherwise get what you want. I want you to become the expert, to make the experiments with cam-timing, compression, and pipes that will allow you to confidently go from simpler to more complex projects, with *pleasure in the results*.

MODERATION

Now that I've suggested that over modified bikes are a waste of time, let me say what I really mean. A big-bore kit is *not* the only useful modification. You *can* benefit from a cam, bigger carbs or throttle bodies, porting, compression—properly chosen and integrated. But the temptation is to over order rather than combine compatible elements into a useful, rideable package.

The temptation is like that faced by the gourmet chef who always wants to put in more rich cream, tasty herbs, and other overpowering ingredients. We ignore the cam whose ad blurb says "moderate boost for street" and go straight to the "super-power for all-out competition," or "Bonneville double-throwdown killer eliminator." When too many superlatives have been put together, the result is off-scale and not much use.

Your bike is just a tool for getting down the road. If you build a tool that you can't use confidently and well, you won't get down the road as well as with one that suits the job.

The itch in the back of the mind keeps saying, "Yeah, this guy says 'everything in moderation,' but I know I can handle it. I'll be OK with the killer motor. It'll be fun." I have to tell you that even professional racers prefer type (1) engines in almost all cases. They hate what happens when engines are squeezed the way the RC30 had to be squeezed. The big example here is Honda's experience in developing its 900RR. Concerned lest inexperienced street riders might have trouble with such a capable machine, engineers worked hard to smooth its power and eliminate all surprises. The real surprise came when they put professional test riders on the prototype—and they went faster than they had previously gone on more sharply tuned versions.

Top-end gets you down the straight, but the dead midrange leaves you between gears in critical corners, getting blown off on early acceleration by everyone with a fatter powerband. In pre-1993 season GP testing, Kevin Schwantz was offered numerous engine and chassis choices. One of the engines had *smaller* carburetors and *smaller* reed valves. It was unusually tractable, and it accelerated. Schwantz said, "This is something I can ride." What professional racers want is a smooth, controllable streetbike engine, but with killer top-end. That's what we all want. Fortunately, there are ways to get it.

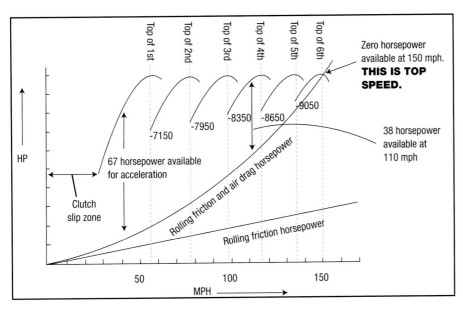

Acceleration and Available Power.
This presents horsepower versus road speed, with curves showing the rise of horsepower consumed by drag. I have repeated the horsepower curve of a typical sportbike engine for each gear, showing how the power left over after drag is subtracted gets smaller as road speed rises. Gearbox ratio splits narrow as you upshift, to keep average horsepower always high enough to keep accelerating in the next gear—until you get to top speed.

PICKING A SHOP

What you are looking for is competence, value for money, and the ability to deliver on time. You will have to look for them by reputation. Sometimes a dealership will maintain a real service shop that includes someone who knows the speed business and is equipped to practice it. More often, though, these people will have their own, non-franchised shops. Personal styles vary; some shop operators are neat-freaks with gleaming bench tops, lots of lighting, and late-model equipment with no chips in its paint. Others work out of hole-in-the-wall shops, dingy and messy, but the troll inside somehow knows where everything is, who it belongs to, and when it has to be done. Both are OK, provided the practitioner gets the job done.

Your relationship with the builder will be the basis of the work to be done. I cannot sufficiently emphasize this point.

You will discover this place by asking questions—at your dealer, at the drags, at the road races. Seek a builder who does the kind of work you are seeking; don't ask a drag engine builder to build your road race engine, and vice versa. Likewise, if possible, find someone who specializes in your brand.

Don't be put off by a brusque manner. People in this business are as talkative as anyone, but talk is the enemy of work. Therefore they discipline themselves to say the minimum. The most hated time-waster is the telephone; no professional likes to have his time wasted in answering vague questions over the phone. Form a clear idea of what you want so you can be as businesslike as possible. Ask for an appointment to discuss your needs. Have your aims and your facts straight. Be prepared to spend some money. There was an old saying in NASA years ago: "If you can't afford to do it, don't do it."

IS TOO MUCH JUST ENOUGH?

Another temptation is the big, highly modified engine—type (2) characteristics in a great big engine. Some people want such an engine in the same way that others want to climb Everest without oxygen and in tennis shoes. What they typically end up with is a really scary machine, so hard to ride that they are slower on it than they would be on a stocker—except in a straight line.

A good example of this is what has sometimes happened in unlimited roadracing. Big 1,000 and 1,100 motors were built to the limit, generating dyno rumors of 185 horsepower. Impressive! But when they went up against "little" 750 factory Superbikes whose powerbands had been "professionally ironed" into a smooth and usable shape, they were easily beaten. Why? Their power, while large, was lumpy and full of terrifying surprises.

Like to have your horsepower suddenly double during a corner exit? Privateer builders, lusting after killer horsepower, unwittingly create powerbands that jump up out of a deep flat spot, right onto a tall torque peak only a thousand rpm higher up the scale. Since this sudden power onset is too steep for any human rider, you compensate by using less of it—and

go slower. As that great rider of the 1960s and 1970s, Gary Nixon, once said of the peaky 750 Suzuki two-stroke, "That'd be a nice little motor if it weren't so damned hard to ride." And that's just what big, type (2) engines are.

THE MIDDLE GROUND

What everyone needs is power that is strictly proportional to the throttle opening and smoothly increases with rpm in a predictable, no-surprises way. With this kind of power, the rider knows that the rear wheel isn't going to suddenly snap loose as the throttle is rolled on out of a corner. Smooth power isn't full of holes that the engine can't climb out of either. Every racer and many builders of modified sportbikes have had the experience of trying to accelerate, only to hear a sickly moan from the engine as the tach needle sits still.

Here are the principles:

1. The bigger the engine, the softer the tune should be. A big, tame bear doesn't need a bodybuilding course. Big engines, because they have more knockdown power to begin with, should have the smoothest power of all. Therefore, concentrate on the mods that are not rpm-dependent for their operation: mixture correction, big-bore kit, possibly higher compression, more valve lift without a lot more duration, minimum increase in valve overlap (overlap deepens the powerband flat spot). Use four-into-two-into-one pipe (smoother power, shallower flat spot), rather than simple four-into-one. Keep carbs or throttle-bodies at stock size, or get small size increase with big-bore kit. Air box must *not* be removed, because its resonant action contributes significant

MUZZY'S TEN COMMANDMENTS

Back in 1983, I went to interview Rob Muzzy about his success in creating the useful tool with which Eddie Lawson won the Superbike title. At the time, I saw in Muzzy's remarks a kind of informal "ten commandments" of successful preparation, which were later printed in the former *Cycle* magazine. Here they are:

1. Analyze the work to be done—reliability first, performance second.
2. Work on jobs that pay off quickly. Don't pin down talented people on low-yield projects.
3. Keep away from the dyno and the flow bench unless you know what you want and why you need it.
4. Run combinations that work together. An engine is a system, not a parts list.
5. In a system of parts that must work together, choose the cheap parts to complement the expensive ones.
6. If there are two good ways to do a job, one simple, the other complicated, use the simple way.
7. Use everything you know in your work, even if it seems irrelevant. Do everything you can in your own shop.
9. Have enough of the things you know you'll need.
10. Big numbers on the dyno are no substitute for races won.

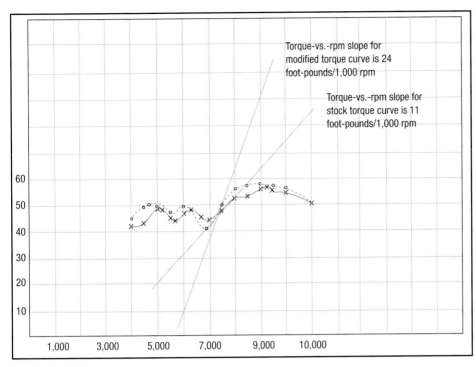

Torque-vs.-rpm slope for modified torque curve is 24 foot-pounds/1,000 rpm

Torque-vs.-rpm slope for stock torque curve is 11 foot-pounds/1,000 rpm

Torque Curve Showing Sudden Rise out of Flat Spot. *These curves are taken with two different cam timings on the same engine. What has happened here is that the high-power curve has longer valve overlap, while the lower-power stock curve has less. Just as the "window" of overlap lets the pipe help more in the 7,500–10,500 range, it also lets the pipe's positive wave hurt torque more in the 6,500–7,500-rpm range—the dreaded flat spot. The large-overlap engine gives a much more sudden rate of torque increase in the 7,000–8,000 range. Drag racers might not care, but while accelerating out of a turn, the steep curve may break traction before you know what's hit you. A big, smooth powerband beats a big, lumpy one every time.*

power. If you absolutely **must** go further, consider ported head, but stock port and valve sizes (keeps power coming on low down, rather than pushing power up the rpm scale).

2. With a smaller engine, go as far as you can with the above principles, because that will preserve the original easy-to-ride powerband. Reduce weight wherever you safely can. If you **must** have more power, a bigger motorbike is the first choice. If class rules or other constraints eliminate this choice, you must go on to those mods that tend to boost the top but do somewhat weaken the bottom. These include longer duration cams with greater-than-stock overlap, a more sharply tuned pipe with larger-than-stock header diameter and carb/throttle body and valve sizes to match, and a flowed head. See how you like the result after the fuel mixture is worked out, and if there are unacceptable problems, tackle them. Some engines are critical on cam timing, so it will be worthwhile to try varying cam timing on the dyno. This sounds time-consuming, but a day spent this way can find a lot of extra power, and you will learn a lot in the process. Remember to check valve drops if you have a higher lift cam or get far from stock cam timing settings (a valve drop test measures the minimum piston-to-valve clearance in the overlap area, and is performed with light "checking springs" in place of the normal valve springs). It's good to have 1mm as minimum valve-to-piston clearance, especially on the exhaust. While at the dyno, vary ignition timing either way from stock, as some modified engines will need a new setting. If you find a trend, follow it as far as the gains continue.

Dick O'Brien, head of Harley's race department for years, was working with Don Tilley on his famous Battle of the Twins bike *Lucifer's Hammer*. After a fresh build, the new engine failed to give normal power on the dyno, and after checking everything, O'Brien said, "We'll have to dyno time the SOB." With the engine running at peak power, they first advanced the timing but the torque dropped. So they began to retard it. The torque came up, so they pulled it back some more and got even more torque. Finally they had the magneto pulled around so far it was ridiculous—almost hitting the cylinder—and they found MBT, the peak torque setting. When the engine was shut down, they went back to check the timing, and this big two-valve air-cooled was firing at 23 degrees BTDC! A "normal" ignition timing for this engine would be somewhere in the range of 32–36 degrees, but by ignoring what's "supposed to happen" and following the trend of increase as far as it went, they got 116 horsepower and a remarkably cool-running engine (this was a 1000cc air-cooled H-D twin).

Thereafter, the late Bobby Strahlman (for many years "the Champion Man" at the races) said of this engine, "Every once in a while you'll get one like that, that burns real quick and makes a lot of power. Consider yourself lucky when it happens."

The moral of this story is that the final, detailed truth about engines is in the engines themselves, not in books or expert advice, and not in our expectations. You have to go in and get it.

CHAPTER 5
DYNO TUNING

Even through double glass, the sound of your engine is strong and insistent as the dyno operator smoothly brings the throttle up to full and then hits "run." The computer takes over, and the engine accelerates up the rev range, stopping just short of the limiter, then dropping to idle. A moment later, the printer behind you begins to graph out the run. You all gather around to see the results of the latest change or adjustment. Dyno tuning is like Christmas every day.

The recent greater availability of dynamometers—now found in many shops or even on the backs of pickup trucks at the races—has changed everything. Formerly the dyno was shrouded in mystery. Users were magicians who debated the merits of $100,000 German dynos versus $100,000 English or Japanese dynos. Now, because Superflow and Dynojet

This is the unit that created an industry—the Dynojet inertia-wheel acceleration dyno, pictured here with a Yamaha YI F750 in the test position. The roller under the rear wheel simulates the inertia of acceleration on the highway, and a computer converts the roller's rate of energy increase into horsepower and torque information. A dyno run takes only seconds to complete. These units are in use all over the world. Dynojet

acceleration dynos are everywhere and anyone can make as many runs as desired for less than the price of dinner each, the discussion is ended. A new standard is established, infinitely more available. Anyone who wants it can have real horsepower data.

The old-timers will continue to debate test methodology. The time-honored research system is called step-and-hold, in which the engine is held at a particular rpm, the readings are taken, the revs are advanced to 50 or 100, held at that point, and so on. The dynos you are likely to find in a performance shop use an acceleration test method instead, in which the engine accelerates steadily and the torque and rpm readings are taken by computer. Old-timers and university researchers swear that step-and-hold is the only correct test method—and in some cases they even step back down the rpm scale as well, to be sure the results agree. Whatever the truth about accuracy, the step-and-hold method holds your engine shrieking at high rpm for minutes at a time, while the operator waits for temperatures to stabilize to take data. This is the technique that puts teeth into the old remark that nothing wrecks engines faster than the dyno. Step-and-hold is an infinitely long straightaway.

Do real engines sit at constant rpm, or is it really their acceleration that interests us? Maybe if you are going air racing, you need to know constant-speed horsepower, but otherwise, acceleration testing gets my vote.

The most widely used dyno in the bike business is the Dynojet, which employs an inertia wheel to load your engine. Another you will often find is the Superflow, which can operate in step-and-hold or in acceleration mode. A third general type is the older dyno that has been updated with modern, computerized controls, such as the Depac. Finally, there are a few, super-expensive, industrial-type Schenck, Meidensha, Froude, or GE dynos.

Another choice that sometimes faces you is whether to test with the engine in its own chassis, or set into a cradle that is part of the dyno setup. A lot of people are still impressed by the "factory" feeling of cradle testing, and some will vote for the ease of servicing the engine when tested in this way. But to test in a cradle, you will have to provide everything that the engine has in its own chassis (air box, fuel tank and pump, cooling, etc.) and your engine will still not vibrate or operate as it does in its own chassis. Therefore, I urge you not to scoff at whole-machine dyno testing as I once did. I got over it, but it took me

Dyno tuning is a crucial part of the tuning process. This is a Dynojet unit. Some units are also built on trailers so they can be brought out to racetracks and other events. Dynojet

some time and a bit of thinking to do it. Whole-bike testing is convenient and it is realistic.

Traditional dynos absorb power by making the test engine either pump water or generate electricity, and in this way they can provide engine load at constant speed for as long as desired—as is useful, for example, in life-testing. Superflow, Froude, and Stuska machines are "controlled water pumps," while the famous Schenck is an electric eddy-current device. Still other older machines (GE, Meidensha) are DC generators. Such machines do excellent work, but they are complex and expensive. All of these machines measure horsepower by taking two pieces of information: torque and rpm. All of these dynos load the engine and measure the torque reaction against the absorption unit. There is a tachometer to measure the dyno's shaft speed. The exception to this rule is the Dynojet, which uses inertia to load your engine.

There are some simplified semi dynos that attempt to measure power by pumping hydraulic fluid through a restricted loop and measuring the pressure, or by measuring the output of an electric generator across resistors. Such units may work for crude comparisons, or for engine break-in, but they are not accurate enough for engine development. Hydraulic fluid loses viscosity as it heats up, and the efficiency

of generators varies with the temperature of their windings. Both of these factors will change during extended running. Therefore seek either an inertia dyno or one that takes data in the form of torque and rpm.

The Dynojet makes your bike's rear tire accelerate a heavy roller weighing about 900 pounds (Superflow has a similar machine). Your engine accelerates just as it does on road or track. A digital sensor reports roller position to a computer (just like the toothed wheel used in anti-lock brakes, or ABS), which then computes roller speed. Knowing the mass of the roller, this yields roller energy at any given rpm, so the computer can then calculate horsepower at any instant from the rate at which energy is being added to the roller. Horsepower is figured continually as your engine accelerates across its powerband, and a printer prints the results in whatever form is desired.

Your bike is rolled onto the unit and strapped down. A tachometer sensor is attached to an ignition wire. The engine is started and warmed up. An electric fan supplies cooling air. The bike is put in gear and, with the clutch, the roller is brought up to a speed that corresponds to the lowest test rpm. The throttle is opened and the engine accelerates across its rev range—a matter of a few seconds. When the run is over, the spinning roller is stopped either by a separate brake (not all Dynojets have these), or by your bike's rear brake (it will get plenty hot, so spare rear pads aren't a bad idea).

The beauty of this test methodology is that it closely reproduces the real conditions your engine will see in use. It is in its own proper chassis, vibrating just as it will in the real world, breathing from its own air box. It is accelerating, as bikes do on street or track, and not being held at constant revs as if it were an airplane engine on a transoceanic flight. This is how you will actually use the power as you ride. You can upshift on this dyno, permitting you to see just how your fuel system responds. Once the data are in the computer, you can process them to give other useful measures of performance. Want a torque curve instead of horsepower? A few keystrokes and the printer starts again. Think you'd like averaged horsepower across a particular rev range? No problem.

Other dyno operators have whole-bike test setups using other dyno types. Some connect to your drive chain, some to your output sprocket via shaft and universal joints. Such machines have research advantages, such as the ability to measure other variables such as air and fuel flow, temperatures at various points, air box pressure, or pretty much whatever you are interested in. These are more development-oriented dynos, while the extreme convenience and simplicity of the Dynojet and Superflow inertia-wheel machines are well-suited to tuning in modified engines and solving fuel mixture problems.

I strongly recommend that you use the dyno to find out what you have achieved with your stock or modified bike and to fine-tune it. This can provide some of the cheapest horsepower you can find. After all, what use is new hardware that is not adjusted to give its best? On the dyno, you will learn what cam timing your engine "likes," and, with the aid of equipment like Dynojet's Power Commander, you can reprogram fuel injection to work with non-stock parts. After a day on the dyno, there is nothing as pleasant as a meal with the dyno crew, when the day's activities are reviewed, stories are told, and the next day's testing is planned.

READING ENGINE PERFORMANCE CURVES

Your printout will display both horsepower and torque, with horsepower numbers up on the left side of the graph and those for torque on the right side. The horsepower curve is a more or less gradual up-slope that rises to a peak, then falls sharply. The torque curve rises steeply from low values at low revs, stays high with some ups and downs across much of the rev range, and then slopes down gradually.

Torque

Torque is the twisting force your engine generates, and it is the direct result of combustion pressure. A torque curve and a BMEP curve (Brake Mean Effective Pressure is averaged combustion pressure), drawn on the same rpm scale, have identical shapes. As a rule of thumb, each ft-lb of torque per cubic inch of displacement is equal to 151 psi of BMEP. Thus, a 750cc engine (45.8 cubic inches), making a peak torque of 60 ft-lb (or 1.3 ft-lb per cubic inch), is making a BMEP of 1.3 x 151 = 196.3 psi, which is very good indeed.

The more fully the cylinders are filled, the higher the resulting combustion pressure, and the higher the torque. The ideal torque curve—the one every tuner works hard to approximate—is not a curve at all. It's a straight, flat line, representing high, constant torque across the widest possible range, from low down to the highest mechanically safe rpm. This is the kind of torque characteristic that makes a machine easiest to ride well, because it is consistent and free from surprises.

Real engines can't quite achieve these curves. Torque is not flat because:

1. Cam timing is a compromise. Intake valves close too late for best cylinder filling at low revs, too early for best filling at high revs. Because of this, the low-rpm part of the torque curve will sag. At the rpm at which cam timing is ideal, cylinder filling will be maximum, and the torque curve will reach its peak. Above that, there will no longer be time to completely fill the cylinder, so again the curve will sag. The result is a rise from low torque to a peak or plateau, followed by a drop-off after peak.

Even if you had automatic, variable cam timing, your torque would still peak, then fall. This is because air friction in the ports increases with speed, eventually choking the engine off as revs rise.

2. Other effects raise or lower the torque in specific rev ranges. For example, the exhaust pipe will add torque at, say,

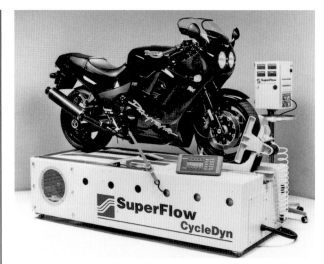

Superflow Corp., whose 901 computer-controlled absorption dynos put a lot of people in the dyno business, has an inertia-wheel unit of its own, the CycleDyn. This machine is available with a continuous absorption capability, allowing steady-state testing for variables like fuel and air consumption. Superflow Corp.

9,500 rpm and 5,500 rpm, but will create a low (flat) spot midway between those rpm. The intake system, because of its length and the waves that bounce back and forth within it, also has an rpm range in which it works best. This will add a sub-peak of its own. On bikes with a sealed air box, there will be an air box resonance effect that puts a useful bump somewhere in the torque curve.

Each engine system—valve timing, port sizes, intake and exhaust lengths, and air box resonance—has a torque contribution of its own, and the resulting, actual engine torque curve is the sum of all these. This is exactly how engineers create the flat, very rideable torque curves that modern sportbikes have, by moving the peaks of the several torque-contributing systems around until the sum of their effects is the best approximation to the ideal flat torque curve. Conversely, bikes with practically unrideable torque curves, full of holes and sudden wheelspin-provoking peaks, are those whose systems have been put together without thought for what their total result would be. Sometimes, of course, there is little choice. When a design is near the end of its useful lifetime, tuners may need top speed so much that they are forced to sacrifice acceleration to get it. Then they tune all subsystems to chime in together, high in the rev range. This can make a lot of power, but it also plays havoc with the midrange. Suzuki was forced to do something like this late in the two-stroke 500GP era.

Horsepower

Horsepower is torque, multiplied by rpm, divided by 5,252, so power is force (torque) times speed (rpm). Fifty ft-lb of torque at 5,000 rpm is 47.6 horsepower, but 50 ft-lb at 10,000 revs is twice as much, or 95.2 horsepower. That is because the same

STOCK VERSUS MODIFIED

These four illustrations are sample real-world dyno curves, stock and modified. These curves are shown not to suggest specific mods, but to give you an idea of how you'll be spending your time, puzzling over your own curves and what they may mean, while planning your next move. Performance Connection

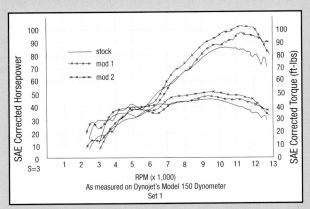

1993 GSX-R750 Suzuki *(both horsepower and torque shown). Mod 1—Vance & Hines four-into-one pipe and Powerpack jet kit, 117 main jets, needles third clip, new chain and sprockets. Mod 2—As Mod 1, but now degreed cams. Note that both modified power curves hold on much better after 10,500, while only the run with degreed cams shows a boost in the 7,000–8,500 area. Note both mod runs show a flat spot in the 6,000 rev area.*

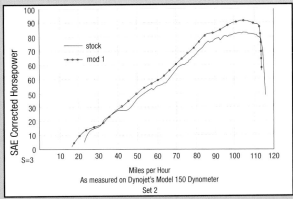

1996 CBR900RR Honda *(horsepower only). Mod 1—Ported and milled head (milled means compression raised), stock pistons, open air Factory Pro jet kit, Erion ER2 and ER3 cams, 142/140 mains, needles third clip. This one really holds on nicely after 10,000 and is almost as smooth and lump-free as stock. Serious parts, serious work.*

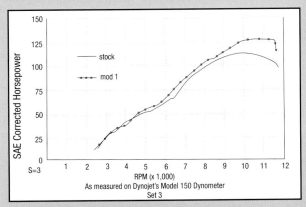

1997 GSX-R600 Suzuki *(horsepower curves only). Mod 1—Yoshimura stainless race 4-2-1 duplex pipe, Dynojet jet kit, K&N air filter; 104/106, needles third clip. It's all gravy in this picture, probably because the 4-2-1 pipe gives nothing away down low. This is a classic Supersport-type engine mod.*

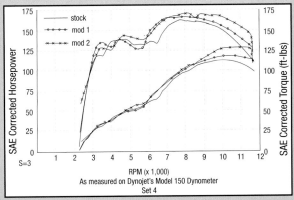

1996 CBR900RR Honda *(horsepower and torque shown). Mod 1—Two Brothers 4-2-1 race pipe, Factory Pro AirBox Plus. Mod 2—As above but milled and ported head, Erion drop-in ER2 and ER3 cams, open air jet kit, 142/140 mains, needles third clip. Note that the pipe and jet kit lifted the curve somewhat, especially above 10,000, but pulled a big flat spot in the mid-5s. Adding compression has helped fill it in. Cams and porting have added a lot above 9,000. Engines want air!*

force is moving twice as fast. When we take the ideal flat torque curve and convert it to horsepower, therefore, the result is a straight, upward-sloping line.

There's a lot of argument as to which is "better," power or torque. The truth is, neither is any use without the other. Torque by itself can't move your bike. If you put a torque wrench on a tight head bolt and apply 65 ft-lb of torque and the bolt doesn't turn, you are accomplishing nothing; nothing moves, so horsepower is zero. Likewise, a tiny electric motor with essentially zero torque turning 25,000 rpm isn't accomplishing much either. Grab the madly spinning shaft between thumb and forefinger and it stops. There are lots of revs, but they are empty.

These are extremes, but there are real-world approximations. The engines of large cruiser bikes have impressive torque at bottom revs, but it fades with hardly any rpm capability because these bikes have short valve timing and poor-flowing ports. Their strong initial acceleration fades out and stockers struggle even to reach 100 miles per hour. Conversely, Yamaha's old TA125 racer could reach 14,000 revs, but was lucky to make 20 horsepower. Millions of revs, no power.

A Trick of Language

When an engineer or physicist says torque, he means twisting force in the strict sense. Our measure of torque is the ft-lb, which means the twisting force created by a 1-pound force, acting on a 1-foot-long lever. In metric countries, this translates to kilogram-meters; one kg-m is a force of 2.2 pounds, acting on a lever that is 3.281 feet long, or 2.2 x 3.281 = 7.218 ft-lb.

When riders talk about engine characteristics, they use the term torque differently, loosely. When they say an engine is torquey, they mean it gives strong acceleration across a wide rpm range. This is the opposite of peaky—giving strong acceleration only across a very narrow range. The peaky engine may actually have more ft-lb of peak torque than the torquey-feeling engine, but that's not the idea the speakers are trying to get across. Don't let these two different usages confuse you in your work with engines.

There's another small complication. People with formal education will sometimes insist that torque be stated, not in ft-lb, but in the technically correct pounds-feet. This is to distinguish torque from another physical quantity, work. A ft-lb of work is what it takes to lift 1 pound 1 foot. A ft-lb of torque is a twisting force. A ft-lb of work is a measure of energy. Confusion is possible if they both go by the same name. Therefore we now refer to torque in pounds-feet (lb-ft) and to energy in foot-pounds (ft-lb).

The horsepower curve is just the curve of torque times rpm. This factoring in of rpm is what gives it its rising trend. The sag in the torque curve at both ends causes the horsepower curve to have a similar shape, and the dynamic effects of pipe, intake length, and so on, superimpose their peaks and dips on that.

It's typical for the horsepower peak to occur higher on the rpm scale than the torque peak. This happens because although torque falls after its peak, it often falls slowly. If torque falls slowly, horsepower, which is torque times rpm, can continue to rise just on the rpm increase.

On a "torquey" engine, the torque peak occurs fairly low down (at, say, 50 percent of peak revs), but falls slowly, so that the power peak is pushed far up the scale. This kind of performance is typical of a dirt-track engine. The Harley XR750 dirt tracker has peak torque down at 5,500 rpm, but its horsepower peak doesn't come until 9,000 or slightly above. This is a torque-to-horsepower separation of 3,500

rpm, or 3,500/9,000, equal to 39 percent. This is a wide, wide band, essential to give these bikes solid acceleration off the turns and all the way down the straightaways on a mile dirt-track, without shifting.

On a peaky engine, the torque and horsepower peaks are much closer together. On a TZ250 two-stroke road-race engine, peak torque may come at 11,000, with peak horsepower at 12,300. This is a separation of only 1,300 revs, or 1,300/12,300 = 11 percent, and it requires a close-ratio gearbox and constant shifting.

Between these extremes we could put Rob Muzzy's best 150-plus-horsepower, 1,025cc Kawasaki Superbike of 1982, whose torque peak was at 8,500, with peak horsepower at 10,250. This is a separation of 1,750 revs, giving 1,750/10,250 = 17 percent.

STOCK BIKE PERFORMANCE CURVES

The torque curves of modern, stock sportbikes are amazing. The torque they deliver and the rpm they can achieve would have been considered race-only numbers a decade ago. Yet here they are, combined in a civilized package giving a smooth, rideable curve without serious holes or spin-inducing sharp peaks. This is an engineering accomplishment.

The curves for race bikes of a decade ago weren't so flat or so rideable. That was OK because those bikes had close-ratio gearboxes and were ridden by experienced professional riders who could keep the revs up in the top 20 percent of the band. But combining that kind of torque and rpm in streetable form has given us bikes with amazing performance, yet with power flexible enough to carry a passenger, potter docilely through slow city traffic, and "speak" through a quiet muffler that summons no police.

The Daytona Superbike lap record is now just over 1 minute 37 seconds on the shortened 2.95-mile course. Top bikes in the class make roughly 200 horsepower and frighten everyone concerned by reaching speeds over 190 miles per hour. Because of that high speed, the Daytona 200 is no longer a Superbike race, but has become a kind of 600 Superbike event.

We expect high speed from modified bikes, so what is more impressive is how close the lap times of Supersport 600 bikes are to those of the modified 600s in the 200-mile race. Engine modifications in Supersport are limited to valve seats only.

BASELINE

Before you begin modifying your bike, make one or more baseline dyno runs to see what you have in the stock package. This will be your reference as you work, telling you where you've gained and where you've lost. This should be put into a loose-leaf notebook for reference. This information is power; you've paid for it, so don't lose it. Dyno runs are cheap compared with any other potential improvement. Think of them as the *cost of making things work*. Their cost is only a small percentage of what the hard parts cost.

Your relationship with the dyno operator is important. Many of these people are very experienced in sensing what engines need, and they can help you a lot. Dyno operators divide their customers into two basic groups: *(a)* the secretive "performance wizard" types who don't want any advice, and *(b)* the others who just want their engines to run at their best.

You'll learn more by belonging to the second group. Many people get into performance work with a cocky attitude, but engine development work has a way of adding humility to almost any personality. The more you learn, the more areas of ignorance previously unsuspected you will discover. A good thing, too. This way, you never have to be bored as long as you live.

GOING TO THE DYNO

Usually, you'll have to pack up your gear and go to where the dyno is, although I've heard of some operators who make house calls! Going to the dyno is just like going to the races— you end up needing the thing that's sitting at home on the bench. Therefore, make a list of what you'll need. Obviously, you bring whatever you're testing, such as different exhaust system parts, and whatever software or hardware you need to tune for best power with each test. You bring tools needed in making these changes. You bring your own fuel and oil. Assuming that you have a records book, in which you keep all your dyno and other running test data, that has to come along, too. No sense in having a baseline if it's not there to be compared. Especially if your bike has a racing-type exhaust system, bring the hearing protectors.

DYNO SAFETY

Dyno testing is a situation filled with potential dangers, because there are fuel and oil, hot parts, and lots of steel in rapid motion. People have been killed or injured in engine testing, so you should take a serious attitude toward it. I once walked into a test facility late at night to find a life-test engine cycling away in a test cell whose floor was covered with gasoline from a leak. All that was lacking was a spark. Another test setup belonging to a very respected man had a dyno control room whose only entrance was from the test cell itself. If there were a dyno fire, there would be no possibility of escape. The fuel was sitting in the dyno room, right next to the test bike, in a plastic 5-gallon can! In a test cell at a college, a U-joint failed, allowing a short piece of driveshaft to yank itself off the engine and then absolutely hammer everything in the cell before it came to rest. I could go on, but you get the idea; be careful and think about what you are doing.

There's no harm in bringing your own large, capable carbon dioxide or powder fire extinguisher and putting it where you can get to it quickly. A couple of pairs of cotton work gloves will make it easier to handle hot parts without waiting for things to cool (and for your bill to increase without limit). Locate yourself along the crankshaft centerline rather than to its side, in case parts escape at high speed from the engine. Chains and shafts deserve similar caution; it's power curves you want, not purple hearts. Be quite sure that fuel lines are properly in place. Tolerate no leaks. Have and use a drain pan when changing oil, emptying carb float bowls, etc. During rapid carburetion changes, it's tempting to just let your hands do the work they know so well. Supervise them!

A special danger in cradle-type test setups is accumulation of fuel and oil beneath the equipment, the result of many tests. Another temptation is to gravity-feed the fuel supply from up high. This is dangerous because if there is a fire, gravity cannot be switched off as a fuel pump can. Ideally, the fuel should be located outside the test cell, supplied by a pump that can be stopped if there is a problem.

If you are going to evaluate cam or ignition timing changes, you'll need the special tools for those jobs: degree wheel, dial gauge(s), and clamps to hold them in place, as well as all the hand tools required. If you have a barometer and thermometer (or air-density gauge) that you use at the track or strip, take them to the dyno as well and enter their readings with your data. Your dyno operator probably has these things, but bring 'em anyway. Remember your notebook and pens or pencils.

Think about the things you want to test, and sketch out a sequence. A little thought here can save you quite a few runs, just as clever programming saves computer CPU time.

ALTERNATIVES

Inertia dynos are convenient and easy to set up on, but often the dyno operator's experience and knowledge turn out to be as valuable as the dyno time itself. Go to the most experienced dyno operator in your area.

Before the coming of the Superflow, Dynojet, and others, there were endless arguments about correction factors, dyno methodology, and equipment. The arguments may continue, but the volume of good work being done on the hundreds of new dynos has made it all seem pretty small. Every time new equipment is adopted in some field of work, you get a chorus of complaint from the high priests of the old way, saying the new equipment and methods are inaccurate, that the old way is best, and so on. But you and I don't want to be dyno-priests muttering incantations about better correction factors. We just want useful information. And because there's so much being generated on these new dynos, we may as well accept them and their methodologies as the new standard and get on with it! Yes, errors do occur, and some of them are not accidental. When one dyno operator in a given area gives bigger numbers than the others, you can guess what happens.

CORRECTION FACTOR

Horsepower goes up and down with the amount of air an engine breathes in. Therefore, engines make a little more power when the atmospheric pressure is high than they do when it's low, a little more power when the air temperature is low than when it's high. And, yes, there's even a small humidity effect; water molecules in the air displace some oxygen molecules, leading to slightly reduced power when humidity is high.

If your data indicate a small gain or loss against baseline, you'd like to be sure it's because of tuning or equipment changes, not changes in the weather. To eliminate weather from your data, therefore, a *correction factor* is used. It converts the actual observed horsepower to *what it would have been at some standard atmospheric conditions*. These corrections are normally quite small, but they can become important when you are fine-tuning an engine. They are especially important if engines are tested and used under widely differing conditions. For example, snowmobile engines may be developed during summer, in 70 degree air, but later used at 35 below zero up in Thief River Falls, Minnesota. Kawasaki used to develop race engines in winter and used outdoor air for engine cooling in its old dyno cells: then its engineers were amazed when their engines with crew-cut cooling fins wouldn't cool properly in 90 degree weather at Talladega!

The corrections are normally made automatically by the dyno's computer, and this is the data you should look at—not the raw, uncorrected "observed horsepower." Dyno correction uses simple proportion, not advanced math. A standard atmosphere is 29.92 inches of mercury, so at 30.2 inches, there will be $30.2/29.92 = 1.00936$ times more air in every breath your engine takes—whoop-dee-doo, almost 1 percent. Power is corrected by *dividing* the observed horsepower by that factor.

Temperature correction is a little more complicated, but only a little. Dyno correction for temperature is again a simple proportion, but *absolute* temperature must be used (temperature above absolute zero). If we are correcting to, say, 60 degrees Fahrenheit, we add 460 degrees to this to get temperature above absolute zero. This gives us 520 degrees absolute. If our test temperature is 72 degrees, this gives us $72 + 460 = 532$ degrees absolute. Our horsepower would have been higher at 60 degrees because the cooler air at that temperature is denser. Therefore, we make the ratio of absolute temperatures, $532/520 = 1.023$. If observed horsepower at 72 degrees is 114, we correct it by multiplying it with the temp correction factor—in this case, 1.023, so $114 \times 1.023 = 116.6$. It's a little disappointing to think you've just picked up some power, only to find that the barometer has risen or the temperature fallen. But, as they say, that's racing.

Many tuners of the carburetor era carry and use an *air density meter*, which does this math for you, reading out in air density as a percentage of some standard atmosphere (29.92 inches of mercury and 60 degrees Fahrenheit, for example). On the dyno, you enter the current air temperature and pressure into the computer as you begin testing, and it uses this data for correction of performance to standard atmosphere until new data are entered.

Once you have the correction factor for the day's weather, you can convert (or the dyno's computer does it for you) the observed, raw horsepower and torque data into corrected horsepower and torque—as if all your tests were being made at the same 29.92 barometer and 60 degree air temperature. Compare apples with apples.

The hot new way to do this is to eliminate the correction factor by correcting the atmosphere itself. Major NASCAR and other teams have test cells in which pressure and temperature are themselves controllable.

WHAT ARE YOUR GOALS?

You know in your mind that it is acceleration that gets you to the next corner or away from the lights. But in your romantic heart, if you are at all like me, you have a special affection for the largest horsepower number that the dyno can show you. The struggle between these two can lead to errors—and reduced performance.

Race bikes often carry data acquisition systems that record such things as throttle angle, engine rpm, suspension position, and so on. One striking thing you learn from such computer data is how little full throttle gets used around many racetracks. I was once invited into the Suzuki garage at Laguna Seca, where I was shown some of the day's computer data. It showed that full throttle was being used *less than 1 percent* of the time around this course. The real game, in a case like this, is not having more power, but having the kind of power that can actually be used. This leads to some generalizations:

1. The more performance you build, the more important a smooth torque curve becomes. The more torque you have, the easier it can knock you down in a corner if it comes on too hard. What counts is how much power you can *use*, not how much you *have*. This is how Lawson, Wayne Rainey, and Muzzy beat the Honda Superbikes in the early 1980s; Muzzy gave his riders smoothed, easier-to-use powerbands.

2. Time from point A to point B is determined by averaged horsepower across the rpm range actually used—not by peak power. In drag racing, for example, there's no point in pushing up the peak if by doing so you pull a deep flat spot right at the best launch rpm. In street riding, what use is extra power up at 12,000 if guys on 60-horsepower Harleys can all pull you in a midrange roll-on? I think of the power curve as a ladder; what good are extra rungs up on top if the bottom rungs are missing so you can't even get up there?

3. There's a big difference between performance and the feeling of performance. A bike with a light-switch powerband feels fantastic—nothing, nothing, nothing, then **wham** as its power hits at 10,500. But it's hell to get off the line and useless in off-corner acceleration. The fastest machine is almost always the one that pulls like a tractor *and* has decent top-end power. Bikes with wide, smooth power *feel* less exciting because they don't hit hard, but they are usually faster because you can actually use more of their kind of power. Don't let the excitement fool you—look at the time slip or lap time.

Bear in mind that the torque curve you end up with is a piece of engineering representing choices made. As I've remarked before, the torque curve is the sum of many characteristics—of the cam timing, port sizes, the pipe, intake length, and so on. You can move the boost that each of these systems gives you, up or down in rpm to offset losses caused by other systems. The result can be a pretty smooth, usable torque curve that will leave the peakier alternatives for dead. All the power you make has to pass through that soft kiss between the rear tire and the road. A smooth, strong torque curve makes that kiss last. A peaky one breaks it.

As a specific example of horsepower versus acceleration, vintage racer/tuner Todd Henning built a Honda 450 twin up to the 60-horsepower level, with peak torque at 8,000. A tuning "mistake," made just before the 1997 Daytona vintage events, cut peak power by almost 10, but lowered the rpm of peak torque by 1,500 revs. At subsequent races, he was able to *lap faster* on the less powerful "mistake" engine, *because it accelerated off corners like a 750*. Jeremy Burgess, Valentino Rossi's engineer, points out that the last 50 meters of the straightaway—the one place where peak power counts—come once per lap. But the first 50 meters off each turn—where smooth, strong acceleration is what counts—comes many times per lap.

A USEFUL TRICK WITH CARBURETORS

Many dyno operators make use of what I will describe next, but I learned it from bike dyno and airflow pioneer Jerry Branch. He wanted a way to determine quickly if a machine was rich, lean, or correct without making run after run with time-consuming jet changes between. What he did was gather up all the float-bowl breather lines from the carbs on the test engine and hook them into a common piece of tubing running into the control room. There, he had a small pressure/vacuum pump with which he could either blow or suck slightly on that piece of tubing. This line had a bleed to atmosphere, so operation was normal when the pump was not in use. With the test engine running at a particular rpm, he'd try a little pressure, then a little vacuum, which made the engine slightly richer, then slightly leaner, and watched the torque to see when or if it rose or fell. This not only told him which way to go, but (by reading the pressure/vacuum amount from a gauge) approximately by how much, to get to peak-power mixture in that test condition. Neat.

ANOTHER ONE

One of the most valuable commodities in roadracing is so-called overrev, which is the ability of an engine to continue to pull past peak-power rpm without a drastic torque drop. Overrev provides the effect of a wider powerband, enabling an engine to keep revving when an upshift is inconvenient, or when a particular corner and the gearbox ratios you have would otherwise leave your engine breathless. One way to get this is to "fool" the exhaust pipe into acting shorter, and this is done by providing an ignition map that retards the ignition in the overrev band. This increases the velocity of sound in the pipes by dumping more heat into them, and makes them act shorter than they are. This makes the engine continue to rev when it would otherwise drop dead. The dyno is the place to work out ignition curves.

RACE WHAT YOU TEST, TEST WHAT YOU RACE

Many times I have heard from experienced engine people that it is best to test what you will race, not to rely on a test engine, test carbs, test pipes. Too many times, they say, the supposedly identical part from the machine shop turns out to run very differently from what's on the dyno engine. Kel Carruthers made this point with respect to two-stroke engines in the early 1970s, and Rob Muzzy has made it again and again with respect to four-stroke carbs, pipes, and so on. In a race team situation, it's tempting to have a dyno engine or dyno bike, and try to apply what is learned from it to the actual race bikes. Something can get lost in the translation.

CHAPTER 6
CARBURETION

I'm going to include this chapter even though the arts described herein are now largely obsolete. Until vintage racing eligibility gets deep into the 1990s, there will be some need for this information. Beyond that, in the current era ordinary tune-up procedures are easily forgotten because almost everyone leaves such things to the dealer or else doesn't even know what maintenance is.

I watched a friend having trouble starting his drag bike. It was obvious that its throttles were out of synch and that there might be other problems. I suggested that he might benefit from standard tune-up procedures. "That stuff's irrelevant," he replied, with a dismissive wave of his hand. "The moment the last yellow starts to fade, I'm on full throttle all the way."

When I offered to do the tune-up myself, he grudgingly got out his 7mm wrenches and began to synch the carbs—to make sure that all throttle slides began to lift at the same time. Then he checked the timing and reset it. And he installed a clean set of plugs.

Jet kits still exist, but the mainstream of tuning has moved on to fuel injection. This Dynojet Power Commander III is widely used to recalibrate factory fuel injection systems to work with engine modifications that would otherwise change the engine's performance enough for power to be lost from incorrect mixture. Goodbye brass jets, hello software and laptop. Software corrections for some specific exhaust pipes can be downloaded from the Internet. Dynojet

The next run was almost half a second quicker. Why? When he brought the revs up as the tree came down, all cylinders came up together, and quickly. When it was time to leave, all those cylinders kicked up to peak-torque revs without hesitation or popping, and the engine turned the tire and left. Seems that something important does happen between idle and full throttle.

My point is that many bikes run poorly, and their riders, having got used to it in small stages, don't even notice it. A careful standard tune-up would give riders free horsepower and make their bikes much easier to ride. As I also note in Chapter 2, taking excess slop and friction out of cables and readjusting hand and foot controls to comfortable heights and angles can make your bike easier to ride well. As a further example, a visitor arrived on a new four-cylinder machine and offered me a ride. As I departed, I noticed that it was impossible to feed power smoothly. It came in with a hard "clunk." When I suggested to him that this was a bother, he retorted with "this is a powerful bike and so it's going to act like it."

Wrong! I had watched Anthony Gobert at Loudon on the last of the three-injector Ducatis, accelerating from turn one. The engine came in with a whisper that smoothly grew stronger as he turned the throttle. Because his engine was so well-behaved, he was able to get on-throttle sooner than his pursuer, Mat Mladin, whose Suzuki's power came in with a visible jerk. These days, very powerful race bikes are often smoother in throttle-up than are streetbikes. They need to be!

Not all bikes of a given production run have identical carburetion requirements. Most will be at least a bit lean off the bottom, and a good many will hesitate if the throttle is moved smartly. This results from manufacturers' zealous compliance with emissions standards. Some riders move to Denver, with a 5,000-foot altitude, from some lower point, so their bikes are now drowning rich. My point is that standard carb settings can often be improved upon.

Years ago, you made these improvements by buying a range of main jets, needle jets, and pilot jets, and you changed one thing at a time to come up with improvements that were often well worth the effort. It is quite common to widen a stock powerband by hundreds of revs by carefully tailoring carburetion to that engine's special needs.

When Supersport racing began in earnest in the 1986–1987 period, constant-vacuum (CV) carb tuning became a critical

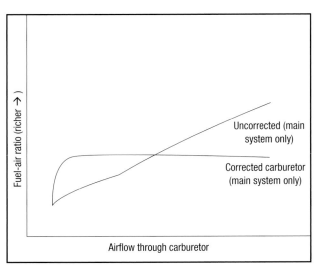

Airflow versus Mixture in Carburetors. *What we'd like is a nice, flat curve that shows constant mixture as airflow increases. But with an uncorrected carb, the natural trend is to enrich. Air correction systems exist to prevent this. Typically, the air jet is the one located at six o'clock as you look at the carb bell mouth, and it bleeds air into the needle jet to mix with fuel before emerging into the intake airstream.*

element in success. At Daytona in 1987, the paddock-area public address system was constantly barking, "Will Mark Dobeck please go to garage 36." Dobeck's Dynojet Company was a pioneer in the jet-kit field.

CV carburetion became an industry in the form of jet kits, each made to correct the problems of a particular model or, in the case of pipe/jet kits, to correct a given model's carburetor when run with a particular aftermarket pipe. You would know that you needed a jet kit when your machine, despite having had a recent and competent tune-up, would not accept throttle, hesitated, or accelerated poorly.

The basis of jet kits was to enrich part-throttle carburetion from lean stock settings. This was done either by replacing the stock carb needles with others of subtly different shape or, in some cases, by raising the stock needles with tiny, thin washers. The changes were small, but the effects could be large, which is why jet kits were so popular.

TIRESOME BUT PREDICTABLE WARNING ON SAFETY

Being a father of three boys, I feel obligated here to remind you that gasoline is, when vaporized, an energetic explosive, easily ignitable. Do not, please, ever become casual about working with fuel. Old man Hideo "Pops" Yoshimura was badly burned in a dyno fire, and others have been killed in fuel explosions and fires. I'll never understand the dad who washed paint off his children with gasoline while he smoked a cigarette.

Further, gasoline contains ring-structured aromatic compounds which have health effects on living organisms. Prolonged breathing of gasoline vapor or skin contact is

not a good habit; neither is washing parts in the stuff. That's what low-volatility parts-washer fluid is for—it will burn, but does not readily form an explosive vapor.

HOW CARBURETORS WORK

It was old Daniel Bernoulli who noticed back in the eighteenth century that air lost pressure as it speeded up. This makes sense because as air rushes to fill a vacuum, the energy to accelerate it has to come from somewhere. This energy can't come from the vacuum, which has no energy at all. It therefore comes from the pressure of the air itself.

You can think of it in terms of conservation of energy. Pressure energy in the still air is converted into velocity energy as it accelerates. When the air decelerates again—when it arrives inside an engine's cylinder, for instance—the velocity energy is converted back into other forms—pressure and heat.

A carburetor is a fancy piece of pipe placed in an engine's intake stream, designed to apply Bernoulli's Principle. As the engine pulls air through the pipe, air pressure inside the pipe falls. You poke a hole in the bottom of the pipe, stick a straw through it, and submerge the lower end of the straw in a bowl of fuel. One end of the straw is at air-pipe pressure (low) and the other end is in the fuel, which has atmospheric pressure pushing down on it (higher). This pressure difference causes fuel to flow up from the bowl, through the "straw" (main jet and needle jet), to spray out into the low pressure at the carburetor throat.

The basic principle is that simple. All the remaining complexity of a carburetor is concerned with making sure that the fuel delivered is actually in correct proportion to the airflow, with maintaining a constant fuel level in the bowl, and so on.

DESCRIPTION OF CARBURETOR SYSTEMS

Carbureted sportbikes of the 1980s and 1990s were delivered with CV carburetors, so I'll cover those first. It is interesting to note that early troubles with motorcycle fuel injection were solved by applying the CV carburetor principle of two throttles in series.

Beginning at the engine side of the carburetor, there is a butterfly throttle that rotates on a shaft, connected to the throttle cables. A spring returns this butterfly to the nearly closed position, set by a stop screw. The remaining small airway supplies air to the engine at idle, and the stop screw controls how much air is delivered. In the fully open position, the butterfly is parallel to the airflow, offering minimum resistance. This part of the carburetor is of large diameter to prevent the presence of the butterfly and its shaft from reducing airflow.

Right at the edge of this butterfly, in its nearly closed position, you will see a series of tiny holes. These supply fuel and progression air for idle and off-idle operation. Fuel for these passages is supplied through a pilot or idle jet (PJ) that is screwed into the bottom of the idle fuel passage, submerged in fuel in the fuel bowl. Air to these passages is controlled by the idle-mixture screw (AS, for air screw).

Just upstream from the butterfly, the carburetor bore decreases to form a simple venturi, and entering the bore from the top is a vacuum-controlled throttle piston. This piston in its lower position does not completely close off the bore but leaves a space beneath, where the shape of the underside of the piston forms a convergent/divergent venturi through which air can pass.

Hanging down from the center of this throttle piston is a tapered metering needle, called the jet needle (abbreviated JN in carb specs). It sticks down into a tube, whose bottom end is submerged in fuel. This tube is the needle jet (NJ). Screwed into the bottom of the passage feeding this needle jet is the main jet (MJ).

As the vacuum piston lifts, it pulls the tapered jet needle higher in the needle jet, making the fuel supply orifice larger and keeping fuel delivery in proper proportion to airflow. When the vacuum piston is fully lifted, fuel delivery is controlled by the main jet, rather than the needle and its jet.

A Rack of Smoothbores for a 1025 Superbike Engine. *All carbs for multi-cylinder engines are rack-mounted, because it simplifies slide synch, controls carb vibration, and it reduces throttle-spring tension.* John Owens Studio

The vacuum piston's motion is controlled by venturi vacuum applied above a thin, flexible rubber diaphragm located under a cap atop the carburetor. The piston lifts because the area of this diaphragm is larger than the area of the piston itself. A control orifice feeds venturi vacuum to the space above this diaphragm. What this system does is maintain a constant vacuum above the needle jet. If airflow decreases, venturi vacuum decreases a bit, which in turn causes the slide to fall. This causes vacuum to increase back to the original value, and so on. It is this vacuum which is "constant" in the description "constant vacuum."

Why bother with this complication? The reason is that fuel is 600 times heavier than air by volume. If the rider controlled the throttle piston directly and jerked it upward, air would rush into the engine, leaving behind the much heavier, slower-accelerating fuel. The momentary result would be very lean operation, with misfiring and a big stumble (vintage riders with British bike experience know this stumble well). But with the rider controlling only the butterfly, when the rider snatches open the throttle, it takes time for venturi vacuum to act on the vacuum piston, through the control orifice. The piston rises, but at a rate that keeps airflow under it moving fast enough to pick up the correct amount of fuel. The result—when everything is adjusted right—is snappy throttle response without stumble or misfire.

This relatively simple picture is complicated by a number of details. Fuel enters the fuel bowl through a float valve (FV), controlled by a pair of molded foam or hollow, soldered-brass floats. As fuel rises in the bowl, the floats rise with it, closing the float valve. As the engine uses fuel, the level falls, causing the float valve to open, and so on.

If the fuel system is gravity feed—no fuel pump—there is little pressure to push fuel into the bowl, so the float valve is relatively large (usually its size is stamped into it somewhere, in millimeters, such as 2.5). Recent bikes usually have electric fuel pumps, which supply a lot more pressure. Consequently, their fuel valves must be much smaller to prevent pump pressure from overcoming the floats and causing pressure flooding. These typically use smaller FVs, in the 1.5mm range.

The mathematics of carburetor operation calls for fuel to stand just below the outlet of the needle jet, so that very little venturi vacuum is needed to get it flowing. But the reality of vibration and vehicle maneuvering makes it necessary to set it lower than this.

It's quite common, after carburetors have been dry on the bench for re-jetting, for one or more to overflow when the fuel is turned on again. The cause is a stuck float. A sharp whack on the fuel bowl with a plastic screwdriver handle usually stops this.

IDLE SYSTEM

When fuel enters the pilot jet, air from the air screw mixes with it there to form an emulsion. This emulsion is lighter than raw fuel, so vacuum at the edge of the throttle butterfly can lift it

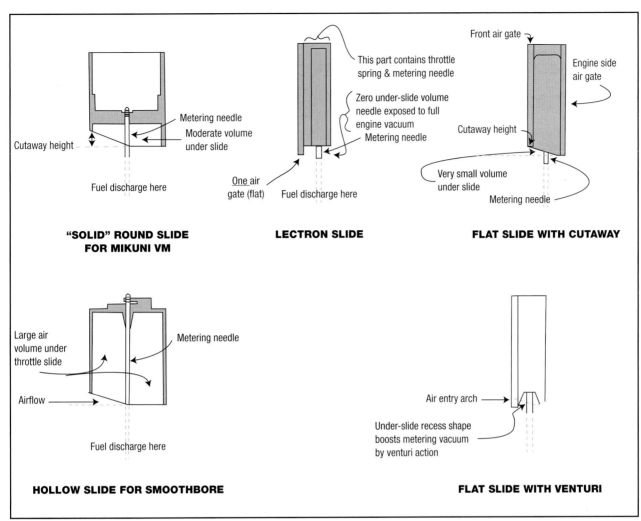

Evolution of Carb Slides. *Because people were fixated on wide-open airflow, smoothbores evolved first, but their large under-slide air volume limited the strength of the metering signal, making part-throttle performance sluggish. The "solid slide" type improved off-idle response by reducing under-slide air volume. Lectron changed everything by locating the needle in full engine vacuum. The cutaway-type flat-slide, with minimum under-slide air volume, was Japan's response. Later types contour the slide's underside to act as a venturi, creating maximum signal at the metering needle.*

more easily. The emulsion sprays out on the downstream side of the butterfly, mixing with air leaking past its edge.

As the rider begins to open the throttle, the edge of the butterfly begins to move, uncovering more tiny holes—or a thin slot—causing them to flow more fuel. This is the so-called progression system.

MAIN SYSTEM BEGINS TO FLOW

Meanwhile, the increased airflow is also moving under the vacuum piston, creating more vacuum there. This does two things: *(a)* it lifts fuel from the needle jet, and *(b)* it begins to apply vacuum to the upper side of the vacuum-piston control diaphragm.

As the edge of the throttle butterfly exposes all the progression holes, fuel delivery from the needle jet begins. If it did not, fuel delivery from the progression holes would rise to a maximum, then fall as further movement of the edge of the butterfly cut down on the local vacuum created there. As fuel flows from the needle jet, vacuum acts on the vacuum piston diaphragm, causing the throttle slide to lift, supplying more airflow. The engine accelerates.

Note that this process of progression from idle system to main system has a lot of overlap. It's not as though the idle system stops and the main system starts up. What happens is that the idle system tails off as the main system chimes in.

EFFECT OF VACUUM PISTON LIFT SPEED

Previously I noted that venturi vacuum is fed to the space above the vacuum piston's diaphragm through a control orifice. Let's consider what happens if that orifice is made larger or smaller.

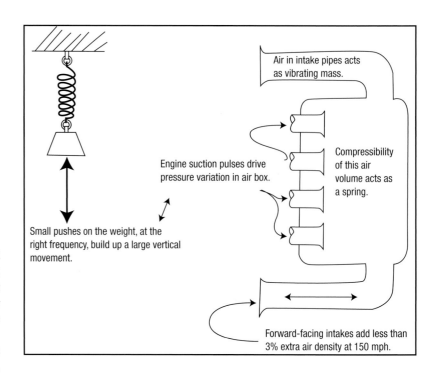

Mass-on-Spring Analogy to Resonant Air Box.
Everyone assumes air boxes work because their intakes face forward, but the ram effect is worth only 3 percent at 160 miles per hour. The real value of the air box lies in the large resonant pressure variation that can build up inside it, driven by intake pulsing. If the engine takes air only on the positive side of each cycle, it receives a useful supercharge across a range of a few hundred rpm. This can be used either to boost top end or to fill in a hole in the powerband elsewhere.

If we make it larger, the slide lifts faster, and airflow may accelerate faster than fuel flow, leading to a lean condition. If we make it smaller, the slide lifts more slowly, fuel flow keeps up better with airflow, and mixture gets richer.

Once the vacuum piston stops moving—either because it is fully open, or because the engine is now running at some constant speed—the mixture is controlled only by the orifice formed between the needle and the needle jet, or—at wide-open throttle—by the main jet itself. Thus, the speed of slide lift, controlled by the slide lift vacuum orifice, gives sensitive control over mixture during acceleration, not during constant-speed running.

AIR CORRECTION

Once the vacuum piston is fully lifted, mixture control is handled by the main jet, but there is a problem. Air is elastic but fuel is not. As air moves ever-faster through the venturi, it loses pressure, becoming less and less dense. The density of the fuel remains constant. This causes the air/fuel mixture to become richer as the engine pulls more and more air through the carburetor. This requires some kind of correction, or the engine will drown itself in fuel as it revs up.

The usual answer is to bleed a small amount of air into the fuel as it rises in the needle jet. The jet controlling this bleed air is called, appropriately enough, the air jet (AJ). As the venturi vacuum increases with rising engine revs, not only more fuel, but also more bleed air, will be pulled into the needle jet. The result, if the air jet is correctly sized, will be constant proportion between fuel and air delivered to the engine. This air jet is usually located at six o'clock as you look into the carb intake.

Air-jet tuning is usually not undertaken by many because it's a bit complicated, but it's nice to know that there is a way to change the slope of the air/fuel curve; a bigger AJ causes the curve to go leaner as the engine revs up, and vice versa. The complexity arises because a change in AJ also requires a change in main jet.

COLD STARTING

Engines require a much richer mixture for cold starting, because the cold engine can only evaporate a small fraction of the fuel. To get a rich enough fuel vapor to fire, the engine must be given lots of fuel. In car carburetors, this is accomplished with a choke butterfly, which acts like putting your hand over the carb intake; unable to get enough air, the engine sucks in a lot of fuel.

Most motorcycle carburetors use a different system. Cold enrichment is performed by a sub-carburetor, cast in unit with the main carb body, with an air passage that bypasses the slide and butterfly. Its "throttle" is a cable-operated piston, and it has a very rich main jet. In order for this starting carburetor to flow maximum air, the main throttle butterfly must be closed, so opening the throttle as you try to start a cold engine defeats the effect of the cold-start circuit.

TRADITIONAL SLIDE CARBURETORS

Although some racing CV carbs have been built, most racing carbs employ throttle slides directly controlled by the throttle cable. Carburetion works a bit differently in these units.

Idle System

Idle holes are located at the bottom of the throttle bore, right at the engine-side edge of the throttle slide. They are served, as in CV carbs, by a pilot jet and air screw.

Because slide carbs lack the CV carb's self-regulating constant-vacuum feature, transition from idle to main systems involves more tunable parts. The first of these is the throttle slide itself.

The problem is to create a vacuum under the slide that will pull the appropriate amount of fuel from the needle jet. The strength of this vacuum is controlled by the shape of the slide. In the case of a cylindrical slide, the edge closer to the engine closes almost completely, but the intake-side edge is higher than this. The lower the intake-side slide edge is made, the stronger the vacuum beneath the slide becomes, and the sooner the main system begins to flow fuel. The higher it is made, the weaker the vacuum. The height to which this edge of the slide is cut is called its cutaway (CA), usually measured in millimeters. Thus, a 2.5 slide cutaway is richer than a 3.0 (the number is stamped at the bottom of the slide).

Oval, flat, and rectangular slide carbs employ variations on this idea, but always the intent is to create just the right degree of vacuum beneath the slide as it lifts, to bring in the main system smoothly.

WHY DIFFERENT SLIDE DESIGNS?

Why the variety of slide types—solid round, hollow round, rectangular, and so on? The round slide came first because it was easy to machine and was copied from European models. Later came rectangular, oval, and other gate-like slide designs.

Here is why carb design has taken this route. When the engine's suction pulse hits the carburetor, it must sneak under the engine-side edge of the slide, then pull air out of the space under the slide fast enough to create a vacuum there that is strong enough to pull fuel.

A round slide has quite a lot of volume under it, so this requires a pretty strong suction pulse to pump all that volume down enough to pull fuel. A rectangular slide's engine- and intake-side edges are closer together, so the volume under

the slide is smaller. Consequently, the rectangular design can flow fuel in response to a weaker engine suction pulse. This makes this type of carburetor more responsive, able to continue to form a mixture even in powerband regions in which engine suction pulsing is weak.

In more recent slide designs, the underside of the slide is carefully contoured to form a venturi with the bottom of the air passage, which itself may have a special contour. This produces an even stronger vacuum, able to pull fuel in response to the weakest engine suction pulses. Grand Prix (GP) tuner Erv Kanemoto was once told by a Honda technician, "Whatever you do, don't mess with that shape. It took us six months' work to get it right."

Most of this slide development has occurred in motocross, where extreme responsiveness is essential to make use of every instant the rear wheel has traction. (Listen to the engine go "burp-burp-burp" as a bike hammers through the whoops. Every time there's traction, the rider gives the engine a shot of throttle.)

Some of these slide designs cannot be used on GP road-race bikes, precisely because they are *too* responsive. The slightest touch on the throttle in mid-corner and the engine barks strongly to life, possibly destroying rear wheel grip. Earlier round-slide carb types give a less-sudden power onset.

Throat of a Smoothbore Carburetor. *The slide and needle have been removed from this carb, but you can easily see the thin slits in which the hollow cylindrical slide rises and falls. Thanks to this construction there is little disturbance to airflow on full throttle—hence the name "smoothbore." Part-throttle carburetion is not this type's strong suit.* John Owens Studio

A Fast by Gast Lectron Carburetor. *This flat-slide carb meters all its fuel from one point—where the needle disappears into the needle orifice. There is no idle system, so there is no idle-to-main system transition. Lectrons are famous for good part-throttle carburetion and the ability to vaporize fuel even in cold engines—something that's important to drag-racers.* John Owens Studio

CARBURETION

PLAYING WITH AIR BOX RESONANCE

Making an air box work is a trial-and-error process, but the basic formula describing Helmholtz resonance shows us how to get what we want.

Resonator frequency = 5/300
Total Area of Intake Pipe(s)
[Air Box Volume] x [Length of Intake Pipe]

If you have two intake pipes, the length in this expression is the length of one, not the total of two. Area of intake pipes is total area—that is, if there are two intake pipes, each of 2 square inches area, the total is 4 square inches.

Looking at the formula, you can see that increasing intake pipe area raises the resonant frequency, and vice versa. Increasing box volume or making intake pipe length greater lowers the resonant frequency.

The basic facts about sealed and/or ram air boxes are these:

1. There are two basic kinds of intakes. One type is cut into a flat or slightly curved fairing surface, perpendicular to the direction of motion. Locating intakes at the sides of fairings will take in lower pressure air that is speeding up to flow around the bike's shape, thereby losing pressure.

The second type, the "rocket launcher," consists of a forward-facing tube, or tubes, that project forward several inches from any surface. This puts it in undisturbed airflow. You have seen these, made in black carbon fiber, on Honda NSRs and the Roberts KR3.

2. The total area of the intake pipes must be significantly greater than the total engine intake throat area.

3. The intake pipes must enlarge gradually as they approach the box, not enlarge suddenly from a small diameter. Sudden enlargements waste a lot of the ram pressure. The angle of the enlargement should not exceed 10 degrees.

4. The box must be truly sealed, meaning a rubber gasket compressed between box and cover, and each induction pipe sealed to the box positively—not just shoved through a hole. There can be no leaking holes for frame members, cables, or hoses. Current design prefers to make the intake air box a part of the engine, as they are bolted to it.

5. With carburetors, all float-bowl vents and the fuel tank vent must be connected to box pressure. Otherwise, at maximum speed there will be carb lean-out.

6. The box volume and the intake length and cross-sectional area must be chosen according to the Helmholtz formula. Check your work via the track or dyno test to put the box resonance in the desired frequency range.

Some 1980s–1990s Superbike carbs had roller-equipped slides. In the early days, engine suction pulled standard carb slides hard against the engine side of the carb, making friction that strongly resisted the rider's attempt to begin lifting the slides. This caused many an ungainly corner exit, as the rider twisted the grip harder and harder until, finally, *"Blammo!"* the slides popped loose and opened much farther than intended. The rollers—or, in some cases, plating or other friction-reducing coating—ease the roll-on.

WHAT ARE SMOOTH BORES?

Many years ago when carburetors were a lot less responsive than they have become, much smaller bore carburetors had to be used as a means of achieving good response. Such small carburetors (how about the 24mm carbs on Vincent 1,000cc twins?) created considerable flow loss, so engineers thought about ways to make them slicker inside.

One idea was to put the metering needle in a side chamber (this was done on AMAL RN and GP carbs), thus getting it out of the airflow. Another idea was to make the throttle slide like an inverted bucket, open on the bottom, sliding in and out of the carb bore through a round, narrow slit. When this slide was fully open, the carb bore was perfectly smooth—save for the narrow slit.

AMAL GP and RN carbs are museum pieces today, but in the first Superbike era (1976–1983), smoothbore carbs were still considered the ultimate. The classic Japanese smoothbore is the Keihin CR, made in several sizes. Unfortunately, the hollow slide of the smoothbore makes its throttle response inferior to that of later designs, which in turn means that it must be used in smaller bore sizes.

WHAT IS A POWERJET?

As I note in Chapter 3, engines need a correct mixture for part-throttle operation, but need an enriched mixture for acceleration and maximum power. One way to achieve this selective enrichment is with a so-called powerjet. There is nothing exotic about the concept—even VW Beetles had powerjets!

In a slide carburetor, a tube is hung down from near the 12 o'clock position, just upstream of the slide. The tube is fed through a jet, and there is a passage (often just a hose) leading to the fuel bowl. As the engine runs, the powerjet does nothing so long as the slide is closed enough to prevent fast-moving air from generating a vacuum near the end of the powerjet tube. But as the slide rises higher, high-speed airflow does rush across this tube, generating a vacuum that lifts fuel from the fuel bowl, draws it through the powerjet, and sprays it out of the tube and into the airstream. As the air velocity past the powerjet increases, so does the fuel flow.

Powerjets are tricky. Get them just right and you have a responsive midrange with adequate enrichment for strong top-end. But make the powerjet too big and your engine will drown as it revs up. One solution to this exists in the solenoid-controlled powerjets used on current Yamaha TZ250 road racers. The ignition computer turns on the jet only when needed (in the TZ's case, this is below and above the rpm range where the exhaust pipes pump strongly). Carb makers and others offer powerjet kits, but not every carburetor needs one. Some, in fact, actually benefit from high-speed lean-out.

OTHER CARBURETOR TYPES

A place of honor belongs to the U.S.-made, Edmonston-designed Lectron carburetor, for its radical design stimulated a lot of later developments from Japan. Lectrons are still available, and they are the preferred carburetor in certain drag-racing classes.

The unique feature of the Lectron is that it is a single-point metering device. There is no idle system—all fuel flow is controlled by a non-tapered, hard steel needle, working in a closely fitted hole in the carb body. There is no main jet. The needle has a single flat ground on it at a very slight angle and is installed with the flat side facing the engine. The throttle slide is a simple gate—there is no cutaway. Because the needle and fuel orifice it works in are on the engine side of the throttle gate, they are subject to full engine vacuum at all times. This gives them maximum metering signal.

The great strengths of the Lectron are:
1. Excellent part-throttle response. This accounts for its initial popularity in roadracing in 1977–1981.
2. The ability to form a good mixture even when the engine is cold. This is what makes it attractive for drag racing. Drag racers run cold because cold engines induct more air than hot ones.
3. It is easy to tune, because mixture strength is controlled by screwing the needle up or down, or by changing to a needle with a richer or leaner flat ground on it. You need no boxes of jets and slides.

Older Lectrons had no air correction system, so they enriched as revs rose. Today there is a later design offered with an air-corrected powerjet that compensates for this lack.

FUEL INJECTION

Electronic fuel injection is now the definitive fuel system for sports and racing motorcycles. Its accuracy facilitates meeting emissions regulations, and its ability to compensate for a changing atmosphere keeps mixture—and therefore power—much closer to optimum. As always, "The first instance of superior principle is invariably defeated by the developed example of established practice." Some early fuel injection systems washed the oil off cylinder walls, or produced "throttle hiccups," but these troubles were solved.

In a typical system there is an electric fuel pump inside the fuel tank, supplying a constant fuel pressure (such as 4–5 atmospheres) to the injectors. In place of a carburetor on each intake tract there is a throttle body, typically containing a butterfly valve on a rotating shaft. When automotive-inspired slide throttles were tried in MotoGP, their extra friction proved troublesome—just as it had years before in slide-throttle carburetors.

Most often there is one injector just below the butterfly to cover the range from idle through, say, 60 percent of peak rpm. As the engine revs up, injection may switch to a second, or "showerhead," injector located to spray straight into the bell mouth of the intake pipe. This is a system adopted from earlier development for Formula One and is typical on Japanese sportbikes. Ducati, after 1999, developed its solutions around a single showerhead injector.

Each injector is actually an electromagnetic valve. Early types sprayed through a single hole, but in the interest of more thorough fuel evaporation, multi-hole injectors with up to 12 tiny holes are now used. When fuel is to be delivered to a given cylinder, the computer determines when injection is to begin, and then opens the electromagnetic valve. Fuel quantity is determined by how long the injector is turned on.

Fueling information is stored in a three-dimensional "map" in electronic form, relating injector "on-time" to engine rpm and throttle angle. When a given system is described as an "n-alpha" system, "n" is rpm and "alpha" is throttle angle. The computer modifies the data it takes from the map as necessary, according to both atmospheric and engine variables. Air pressure and temperature are measured by sensors, and various means are used to compensate for the reduced fuel evaporation that results from reduced engine temperature. Some earlier fuel injection systems required use of a manual cold-start enrichment system, but newer systems perform this automatically. After years of struggling with motorcycle and car carburetors, I must confess that I love electronic fuel injection. Engines start, run, and respond regardless of temperature, cold or warmed-up. Wonderful.

Map data are originally obtained by running an example engine at many operating points on a dynamometer. This process assumes that all production engines, whether brand-new or well-worn, will be alike enough to operate well from the resulting map.

Owing to ever-tightening exhaust emissions regulations, motorcycles increasingly monitor actual fuel mixture with exhaust oxygen sensors. This permits the engine computer to hold mixture in the zone that allows the best operation of exhaust catalysts.

An early complaint against mapped fuel injection was that it had to be re-mapped each time the machine's owner made a modification, such as substituting an aftermarket exhaust system. One way around this has been the use of external electronics which fool the engine computer into supplying the desired changes. Dynojet's Power Commander III has become the tool of choice here. The modified machine, with the device plugged into its electronics, is run on a dyno while its exhaust oxygen is monitored by a sensor. Several pulls are made on the dyno, and the feedback from the oxygen sensor allows the system to learn to modify the fueling to obtain best power from the modified engine. At the 2007 Daytona event, I was told by mechanics on the Erion team that this reprogramming takes them about three hours.

It is possible to effectively build this capability into the engine control, as S&S has done on its new X-Wedge large

V-twin. Bolt on the chosen modifications, then ride the bike around your favorite road loop a few times, and the system learns what it must do to fuel the engine correctly.

Racing engine controls are computer-addressable, so that the current fuel map may be altered in detail as desired.

It may be that in future, engine controls will become completely self-optimizing, using cylinder pressure sensors to constantly measure where, in crank degrees, peak combustion pressure is reached. Such a system would do away with the ignition map by finding optimum timing continuously, and would do away with a fixed fuel map through use of oxygen sensors.

INTAKE LENGTH EFFECTS

As noted in the discussion on cam timing, when one cylinder's intake process begins, a suction wave travels out the intake valve and up the intake pipe. It is reflected from the open end with its sign reversed—the suction wave becomes a pressure wave—and it returns toward the engine. If this positive wave—or any positive wave resulting from multiple reflections—arrives just at the end of intake as the intake valves are closing, it will stuff extra air into the cylinder and increase torque. The bad news is that at some other rpm, it is a suction wave that arrives just at intake valve closure. This sucks out some of the charge and causes a minor flat spot in torque. The positive and negative effects can be quite large—as much as a 10 percent torque boost has been observed.

On the current Cagiva/MV F4 and on the last versions of Honda's RC45 Superbike, a two-length intake system is used. One length—the shorter of the two—is used to boost top-end. An added piece of intake stack is snapped into place by a servo-motor to give a boost at some lower rpm. In Fl car racing, continuously variable intake-length systems have been used.

The reason I mention this is that so-called velocity stacks are still sold for a variety of carburetors, and many riders put them on simply because the name sounds racy and/or they like the look of the shiny aluminum or plastic things. If you change intake length, evaluate the result on the dyno or drag strip! Extra intake length will lower the rpm at which intake effects boost torque; you may or may not like the result. Customizing may be a lot of fun (I haven't tried it—maybe in my next life), but don't let it determine your performance bike's intake length.

CARBURETORS AND VIBRATION

People today are spoiled, because the only carbs they have ever seen on bikes are rubber-mounted. It wasn't always so. I mention this not because the past is coming back, but because you may not be familiar with the effects of vibration on carburetion.

It occasionally happens that a carb (or carbs) is mounted in such a way that it can make hard contact with metal parts of engine or chassis. The resulting vibration can cause frothing of fuel in the bowls, allowing air to pass into main jets, leading to lean-out. I have seen fuel climb up the sides of transparent fuel bowls as engines were revved up, leaving the main jet hanging in fumes. The first version of Kenny Roberts' Modenas KR3 500 vibrated enough to ruin its fuel mixture.

THE AIR BOX AND WHAT IT DOES

Early bikes had open carb intakes. Then filters were added to prolong engine life. Finally, when new noise standards proved impossible to meet without some kind of intake silencing, air boxes came into being.

Sporting riders have always hated interference with the purity of their engines, so one of the first acts on buying a new bike was to trash the ugly, molded-plastic air box concealing those beautiful, functional carburetors. What can be more beautiful than a row of carburetor bell mouths, like trumpets upraised before the walls of Jericho? Everyone knew that this raised horsepower because it eliminated the restriction of the filter and the (usually) tiny entry leading into the box. Those who wanted filtration added sporty-looking individual "sock" filters to each carb.

Then just after the mid-1980s, riders got a terrible surprise. When they trashed their air boxes, their reward was not more power, but less. Powerbands that had been chubby and full suddenly turned lumpy—even with careful re-jetting. The problem was especially severe in Supersport roadracing, the one year when air boxes and filters were made optional. So people grudgingly put their air boxes back on, and the power came back. Something new was happening.

That something was air box resonance. Everyone has hummed or whistled across the mouth of an empty bottle. At just the right frequency, the air in the bottle resonates in step with the tone being hummed or whistled. This is just like a weight, hanging on a spring, bouncing up and down. The spring is the compressibility of the air in the bottle. The weight is the slug of air in the bottle's neck.

If a suitable volume is connected to an engine's intake stacks, it can resonate in this same way, within a certain rev range. When the box is resonating in this way, its pressure is high just as one cylinder begins its intake stroke, and this drives more air into the engine. As the engine takes air, box pressure falls, but more air is on its way in through the box's intake snout.

If everything is sized correctly, box pressure is high again just as the next cylinder's intake stroke begins, and so on. The net result is a substantial boost—like free supercharging—within a particular rev range. This can amount to 10–15 percent more power. There are always weak areas in any engine's torque curve, so engineers have tuned air boxes to strengthen those weak areas and presto—a stronger, smoother torque curve.

This is why current sportbikes—and all World and AMA Superbike racers—have sealed air boxes. They are very well sealed—with rubber gaskets and quarter-turn fasteners—because

PLUG READING

Reading spark plugs was long considered one of the tuner's black arts, but is of little used today, having been replaced by oxygen sensors. Begin with clean, fresh plugs. A dark plug will not lighten to indicate a correct or lean mixture, so used plugs are useless for mixture assessment. Also, forget all the plug manufacturer's four-color advice sheets about chocolate-brown. That is the color a plug assumes in a street-driven bike with hundreds or thousands of miles on it. The color you are looking for in main-jet tuning is white. If you make a top-speed run of 30 seconds or so and your fresh plugs come out brown, your engine is hopelessly rich.

The "reading" of spark plugs is based upon the fact that the insulator is a thermometer that can be read just like any other, except that it is not calibrated in degrees. The tip of the insulator is designed to operate—provided you are running the correct plug heat range—at a temperature high enough to prevent free carbon from sticking to it, but not hot enough to act as an ignition source on its own. As you travel up the insulator from its tip, toward the metal shell of the plug, the temperature falls until it is the same as the cylinder head metal into which the plug is screwed. That means that somewhere along the insulator, it will become cool enough that free carbon—if any—can exist on its surface.

Free carbon is an indicator of incomplete combustion, so if, at some point along the insulator's length, it is surrounded by a dark ring, this is proof that your engine is still rich. As you jet down, peak

combustion temperature in the engine rises, the plug runs hotter, and the ring will recede up the insulator and finally disappear. You don't want no ring at all, because maximum power is given at a slightly rich mixture (the physics of why is alluded to elsewhere). Nevertheless, good tuners are pretty ruthless in pushing that ring up the insulator.

They are also watchful for signs of oiling, which is usually evident in one cylinder first—the result of ring failure. Oil will darken the whole insulator, and there may also be odd colors resulting from metallic oil additives plating-out on the plug. Time—and experience—will teach you the difference.

Gadgety little combination flashlight/magnifier things are made for plug reading, but almost always the battery is half dead and the light is feeble even with a new battery. You will do better with strong sunlight and an eye loupe or a little pocket magnifier..

How can you know if your plug's heat range is correct? With a stock engine, plug heat range is determined by tests made with instrumented plugs. The goal is to achieve a desired range of operating temperature for the plug tip—the hottest thing in the engine. Look up the correct heat range in your manual. Plug makers can supply charts of equivalent heat-range plugs from the different manufacturers. For modified engines, the choice is up to you, which should be guided by your vigilance and understanding.

Obviously, if you boost your engine's power, it may need a colder plug by a heat range or so. With a 6X magnifier, examine the end of a fresh plug's center electrode—the wire that comes out the end of the central insulator, not the side wire. You will notice that it has been cut to length by some kind of shear, leaving the metal with somewhat distressed edges. If the centerwire is getting too hot, you will see that after hard use, the sharpish edges of the centerwires appear to have softened—very much like the edges of a broken-off glass rod heated by a Bunsen flame in chemistry class. That's an indication you should move to the next colder plug.

This is also a diagnostic for excessive ignition advance, so ask yourself whether your engine's timing is correctly set. If you're sure ignition timing is OK and you are getting centerwire edge softening after a bit of hard use—a number of pulls on the dyno, a few laps on the track, a few top-speed runs on your favorite, perfectly legal straight road—then you should try plugs a half or a whole heat range colder.

If an engine looks a bit rich on a given plug, it will look richer on a colder plug and leaner on a hotter one. Don't get sucked into thinking you can correct your engine's mixture by changing plug heat range. Some people still believe it, but this is about as scientific as trying to improve the weather by blowing into a low barometer.

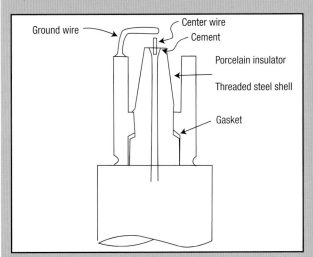

Cutaway of CV Carb. *These Keihins were the usual fit on late carburetor-era sportbikes. The rider controls the butterfly throttle, but air pressure in the carb throat controls the air slide's lift. This—when everything is tuned correctly—makes it impossible for the air to get ahead of the fuel and cause acceleration stumble.* Keihin

any serious leakage destroys the resonance, just as a leaking valve pad stops a saxophone from playing a note. They are rigidly constructed, too, because a "soft" air box would also kill the resonance, just as a flannel trumpet cannot be played. Like intake

and exhaust resonances, the air box resonance works against the engine at some other rpm range. Some modern systems are designed to prevent this. One method is to provide a large hole in the air box that is plugged by a valve at resonant rpm, and open otherwise. This kills any anti-resonances. Another method is to provide two air box intakes with valves to shift operation from one to the other. With each tuned for a certain rev range, the boost range of the air box resonance can be widened.

RAM-AIR AND HOT AIR

It was initially assumed that sealed air boxes exist just to create gains from forward-facing air intakes (I did). This was considered hot because race bikes have very visible snorkels, scoops, or other SR-71-looking air-intake hardware up front. Sadly, even if the energy of moving air could be completely converted to pressure, at 150 miles per hour the pressure gain is only 3 percent. This is fine on a Superbike racer, where it might give an extra 3 to 4 horsepower near top speed.

But ram pressure is proportional to velocity, squared. If you double the speed, you get four times the pressure. Conversely, if you halve the speed from 150 down to 75 miles per hour, you get only $1/2 \times 1/2 = 1/4$ the effect, or $3/4$ of 1 percent. This is a horsepower or less on a big engine. Not the stuff dreams are made of.

Rad-looking scoops sell bikes, but forward-facing intakes have one real purpose at less-than-race speeds. That is to prevent

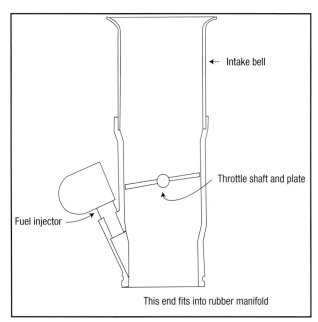

Intake bell

Throttle shaft and plate

Fuel injector

This end fits into rubber manifold

Fuel Injection Throttle Body and Injector. *The most common arrangement on Japanese bikes is butterfly throttles, with one injector below the butterfly and a second "showerhead" injector hovering over the center of the throttle body's intake bell. The lower injector supplies fuel at low and midrange conditions, with the showerhead progressively taking over at higher revs. Injectors are electromagnetic valves, typically with multiple spray orifices, opened by electric current. Instead of figuring fuel flow in terms of jet sizes, fuel injection figures it in on "time"—the number of microseconds that the injection valve is held open at a particular rpm and throttle position. Ducati, following F1 practice, employs only the showerhead in its race engines.*

hot air from the radiator, cooling fins, or hot exhaust pipes from entering the intakes, as it always used to. Air loses density when heated, so hot air gives less power than cool air. Forward-facing air box intakes exclude all hot air. Another achievement is they point intake noise in the opposite direction to exhaust noise. This is as useful in meeting noise standards as the time-honored trick of putting one exhaust pipe on each side of the bike—the noise meter can only be in one place at a time.

Electronic fuel injection has no problem with Ram-Air pressure rise in an air box, but carburetors plus very high speeds may call for some enrichment. As pressure in the air box rises at very high speeds, it reduces the pressure difference across carburetor main jets, causing lean-out. If air box pressure kept right on rising, it would push the fuel right back down into the float bowls and blow bubbles!

The simplest compensation for high-speed lean-out is to vent the float-bowl breather lines into the airbox (which is done by the manufacturers on recent carbureted motorcycles). Even with this, a 3 percent density increase will still lean out an engine, just as will a 3 percent rise in the barometer. But we're talking about legal speeds here, so we'll ignore this one.

While on the subject of venting things into the air box, I should mention the gas tank breather. As your engine takes fuel from the tank, an equal volume of air must enter the tank through the tank breather to take its place. The breather on production bikes is usually incorporated into the filler cap. On some modified bikes, it has happened that the tank breather was too small for the bike's new appetite, or got covered up by the cap gasket or such, causing mysterious lean-out only at high speeds, when fuel demand is highest.

If you have any weird symptoms like this, think about restrictions that may exist in the tank breather or in the fuel lines and petcock. I once had a bike that revved up to 8,500 down the Daytona back straight, then cut dead, coasted down to 6,500 revs, cut back in again, and so on. It turned out to be fuel starvation caused by carb float valves being a bit too small, inline gas filters, and fuel-line quick-disconnects. All this restriction was causing the fuel bowls to run dry on top, then refill at lower revs. Once I had provided enough flow capacity, the problem obediently went away. This applies to bikes with gravity fuel feed. Current fuel-injected bikes have in-tank electric fuel pumps, which are another story.

Here is a caution on operation of carbureted race bikes. Some tank petcocks leak, and so do some carburetor float valves, so when such a machine is not in use, pull the fuel line off the petcock. Leakage, given time enough, can result in a cylinder full of fuel. Ever seen those World War II airplane movies, in which two or three ground crewmen pull the prop blades around before starting up a big radial engine? They did that to be sure no cylinder was full of oil or fuel—radials have many cylinders below the crankcase—so the starter could safely turn the engine without hydro-locking a con rod. Fuel in a cylinder is just as incompressible as oil. Just one more little thing to think about.

TUNING SLIDE CARBURETORS

Carbs are complex because of their overlapping systems and their many parts. It's easy to feel it's all too complicated and just give up. But no, there's a step-by-step method. This was taught to former Kawasaki team rider Hurley Wilvert by a craggy old Australian speedman, and Hurley taught it to me.

Assume that the machine is in good running order, that the carbs are properly mounted, with consistent float levels, and all have the same tuning parts in them. Set all idle airscrews to the same setting, such as 1 1/2 turns open.

Set any idle-speed adjusters to let the slides close completely, then synch the slides to lift simultaneously. Some people will tell you to synch to make all slides reach fully open together. This is wrong, for it's much more important to have smooth power off the bottom. Since you have to do this with the gas tank off, remember that when you replace the tank, it may disturb the lie of the cables; making a cable bend tighter lengthens the housing. Recheck synch with the tank in place.

Race-only machines are not set up to idle, so their slide carbs are synched for simultaneous opening. Street machines have to idle and, for setting this, there is the method of connecting vacuum gauges to each carb and thereby equalizing all carbs' airflows.

Start the engine and warm it up. Have a friend hold it at a constant idle, as low as possible. Note the rpm and have your friend keep an eye on the tach. Now turn each idle airscrew open one-fourth turn more. If rpm falls, turn the screws back to the starting point, then one-fourth turn inward. If idle rpm again falls, the original setting is good and you can go on to the next stage.

But if idle rpm continues to climb as you adjust the idle air screws, keep going until either of two things happens: (1) you find the peak rpm setting, in which case leave it there and proceed to the next tuning step, or (2) max idle rpm requires that the idle screw be less than a half turn open, or more than three turns open. If (2) occurs, you must change pilot (idle) jets to a different size. If the best idle setting is smaller than a half turn open, install richer idle jets. If the best setting is more than three turns open, install leaner idle jets.

Continue this process until you achieve an idle-airscrew setting that gives peak rpm and lies within the range between a half turn open and three turns open. If this is a street-ridden bike, you can now set the idle speed.

The next tuning stage is selection of slide cutaway. Be sure that the engine is happy—not overheating and not fouling its plugs. With the engine idling, roll the throttle on very slightly. Does the engine follow willingly, or does it misfire or lag behind? If there is a problem, install a slide 1mm or 1/2mm richer (less cutaway). The cutaway numbers are stamped on the slide, or you can easily measure the cutaway by standing the slide on a flat surface (desperate tuners sometimes cut slides and don't change the stamped numbers!).

If the engine responds to the throttle better now, try slides that are richer yet. If the engine responds worse to the change, go the other way—install leaner slides, with more cutaway.

You may now ask if the engine is running on the needle now, and wouldn't it be appropriate to play with needle height. No, the shank of most needles is not tapered, so the first 10mm of slide lift—a lot more than we are using in this part of the tuning process—is not on the taper. Therefore, mixture at these low throttle positions is controlled by: (1) the continuing but tapering-off effects of the idle system, (2) the slide cutaway, and (3) the orifice between the needle's shank and the inside diameter of the needle jet.

The rest of the test is best performed under way, on track or secluded road. You will now perform a series of roll-ons, as before, to evaluate how the engine takes throttle.

If you can't make the engine accelerate during the first quarter of slide lift without using either a very lean or very rich slide (rich is 1.0 cutaway, and anything beyond 4.0 is pretty lean) you should think about changing the needle jet size. Sizes are stamped on the parts, for example "O-4." In this case the next richer needle jet is an O-6, and the next leaner is an O-2. Tiny changes make a big difference here.

CARBURETING FROM ZERO

Occasionally, a rider may have to adapt carburetors to a machine not delivered with them, and so lack any starting point for such things as needle type, slide cutaway, and so on. One proper response is to call friends or others who may have more experience. Another is to call the carb manufacturer's importer and ask for help there. For common machines, importers often can supply carbs with at least approximate jetting for your bike, and you can use the procedure described previously to refine this.

If you have to do the job solo, all is not lost. Size the carburetors realistically to be slightly larger than the port I.D. at the head flange and begin with middle-of-the-road slides like 2.5, midrange pilot jets (#60), and a middling airscrew setting like 1 1/2 turns. Start with some commonly used needles. What's common? The carb makers' catalogs list available needles, with diameter measurements given at a few points along the taper. Pick a type and begin. If the engine has a fuel pump, use small (1.5) float valves. Otherwise, use something good-sized, like 3.0. The tuning procedure in the previous paragraphs will get you pilot jet, slide cutaway, and needle-jet sizes that work. Now all you need is to refine the choice of needle.

Test at other needle heights. If this by itself takes care of your mid-throttle position running, you can proceed to main jet selection. But if simple changes of needle position don't do the job, you may need to change to different needles. They are supplied in a dizzying array of tapers—single, dual, and even triple—with different shank diameters as well.

Whatever your on-the-needle running problem may be, you have to determine two things about it in order to correct it. The first is to identify the throttle position when the

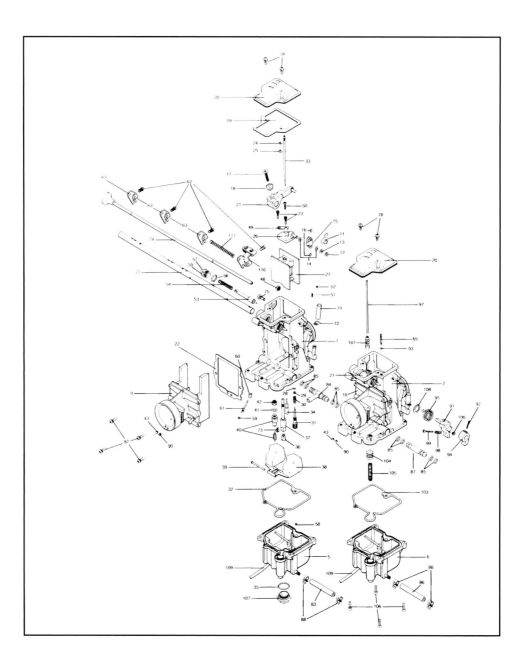

Mikuni Radial Flat Slide.

In the carburetor era , carbs like these were the preference for pure race bikes and sports machines whose users were willing to become carb experts. Don't expect smooth around-town casual use of big slide carbs. Mikuni American

CARBURETION

problem occurs. The second is to know whether the problem is richness or leanness.

One way to find out is to turn off the fuel to the carbs, and continue to run the engine until it has pulled the fuel level in the bowls down significantly. If, in this condition, your bike runs better in the problem area, you know it is rich there. Or try a little choke; if the engine picks up, it was lean in the problem area. With a little thought, you can devise a lot of little diagnostics like these.

Now identify the throttle position at which this problem occurs, and measure the needle diameter at the point that is just inside the top of the needle jet at this throttle position. Get out the carb maker's needle list and look for needles that are fatter in this area, but about the same elsewhere. If you have to

jump to a needle with a different shank diameter, you will have to redo the needle jet selection as well.

From-scratch carb tuning can be a tricky process, but motorcyclists who want more performance are highly motivated and are able to juggle tiny carb parts tirelessly and quickly. Or they can learn! As old Mack McConney—the second Triumph dealer in North America, and who lived to be 99 years old—used to say, "The human mind has created this system, and the human mind should therefore be able to comprehend it."

MAIN JET SELECTION

Some engines are quite sensitive to main jet size, while others don't seem to care too much so long as they are reasonably

62

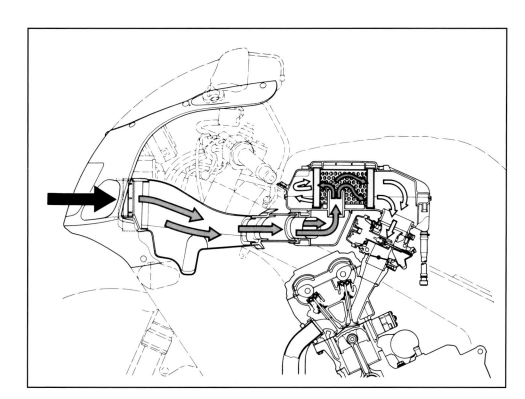

Ram Air box System. *Air enters the system and is conducted to the intake resonator tube (vertical tube at bottom of air filter), through the filter, and into the air box in which the carbs are sealed. Think of a resonant air box as a guitar body, and the resonator tube as the sound hole in that body. Pressure variation in the air box is driven, not by vibrating guitar strings, but by the engine's suction pulses. At the tuned rpm, the engine takes air from the box only when pressure inside it is positive. In the other half of the cycle, the box takes air through the resonator tube.* U.S. Suzuki Motor Corp.

close. This kind of difference often has to do with an engine's combustion chamber turbulence. Highly turbulent engines are less sensitive because turbulence substitutes for flame speed; the richer the mixture, the slower the flame travel. An engine lacking in turbulence therefore acts as though its timing is retarded when it is rich.

The old stories about carburetion going completely off because the sun went behind a cloud describe a past era of bad carburetors and half-baked engines. Things are better now. But you will find that as you make the carbs on a given engine bigger, carburetion becomes touchier. This is because engines don't run well unless they receive a fine fuel mist rather than a stream of blobs. Forming that mist depends on air velocity.

As the fuel shoots out of the needle jet into the air stream, the fuel droplets are beaten into little pieces by the impact of the air. Slow the air down by making the carbs huge and you get adequate fuel vaporization only way up at peak revs. Suddenly, pulling away from the stoplight two-up becomes a nightmare of stalling and restarting while your riding buddies disappear into the distance.

Sure, big carbs look impressive, but smaller carbs are easier to tune and more likely to stay in tune. They are less fussy on the throttle and easier all around. But jump right in if you must, and try to put giant mixers on your project bike—it'll be an education.

Main jet tuning methodology depends upon having someplace to run at full throttle in top gear, long enough to perform a simple engine diagnostic (for slide carburetors), or long enough to color a spark plug (any type fuel system). The diagnostic is to slightly close the throttle and note whether there is a slight gain in maximum revs. If there is, the engine is rich and should be jetted down.

Classical tuning relied upon plug readings, but the ultimate truth about main jet size is not the appearance of the plug, but the appearance of the tachometer. Jet for maximum speed, and do it in a place where it can be done in safety. Modern sportbikes are not touchy about main jet and don't require endless fiddling to keep them right. Better to get on with the riding than to spend your time searching for perfect carburetion, surrounded by dismantled carburetors and the smell of drained fuel. There are a lot of fascinating points in tuning that invite us to become monomaniacs, but you have to remember that we all got into this because it looked like fun.

CHAPTER 7
EXHAUST PIPES

Pipes are the most popular bike mod because they are an easy, do-it-yourself installation. They save weight and give a racy sound and appearance. Unfortunately, bikes with aftermarket pipes too often have powerbands less smooth than with the original equipment manufacturer (OEM) pipe. Aftermarket pipes may affect carburetion for the worse and usually need additional tuning work to give their best. They can be loud, too.

What can you expect from a pipe, as compared with your stock system? A lot less, unfortunately, than you could 30 years ago. Early bikes, such as the classic Kawasaki Z1 and Honda CB750, had unsophisticated exhaust systems, so a modern pipe can uncork an older bike. But recent sportbikes have highly engineered pipes. Even if you're willing to tolerate much higher noise levels, don't expect an aftermarket pipe to deliver an overall boost on a late-model bike.

What aftermarket pipes can do is relocate and concentrate your engine's torque for some special purpose, other than general street riding. A simple, four-into-one pipe, for example, will boost roughly the top 3,000 rpm of your engine's performance—but don't be surprised to find a good-sized flat spot just below that. Other pipe designs and features can alter this basic tendency, but none can completely avoid it, as we shall see.

An exhaust system is more than just tubing to carry away your engine's smoke. It is also a pump, using the energy in exhaust pressure pulses (as much as 100 psi) to help empty and refill your engine's cylinders. This pumping action has negative as well as positive effects, however. While it can create peaks on your torque curve—rpm regions in which the engine pulls more strongly because exhaust waves are pumping more mixture into the cylinders—it also generates other rpm zones, so-called flat spots, in which your engine's pull is weakened.

All production pipes have to meet sound standards, and there is only one way to do that—with plenty of silencer volume. This is why so many stock systems have two silencers, one on each side. Today, many people like the look of a Superbike-like single silencer, but killing the noise in a single silencer calls for the dimensions of an RFD mailbox. Style and legal function are thus somewhat at odds.

The general rule is, therefore, that a quiet system is a big system, while a small, racy-looking system will tend to be

Peter Doyle is one of the best-known tuners in racing today, and his work on Mat Mladin's bike has helped to earn Mladin a number of championships and countless race wins. Brian J. Nelson

loud. In World War II a common type of carrier aircraft was the "torpedo bomber," which like Buell's motorcycle carried under its belly a large, round, black, cylindrical object. In the case of the aircraft, it was a marine torpedo. In the case of the motorcycle it is the exhaust muffler. Erik Buell has started a useful trend with his "torpedo bomber,"—large, single, under-engine silencer—by putting the muffler where some bikes have the most room for it. A large-volume system can be quiet and powerful, but if a small system is corked-up enough to be quiet, it will most likely cause a power loss. The bigger and fewer the engine's cylinders, the harder their sound pulses are to quiet without loss. Twins are a case in point, needing silencers that don't package easily anywhere on the bike. Fashion can enter the discussion too, as it has with Harley's Sportster. Its traditional small mufflers have to be quite restrictive to avoid being very loud.

HOW PIPES WORK

As an exhaust valve opens, a pulse of high-pressure exhaust gas is released into the pipe. It travels down the header tube at high speed until it reaches the junction with the collector pipe. Here, pipe area suddenly expands, so the pulse expands, too. It expands in all directions, including back up the pipe from whence it came. This means that an expansion wave (suction) travels back up the header.

A 4-2-1 Pipe. *This example is an Akrapovic pipe for a Kawasaki ZX-12R. A four-into-one can give a good boost in the top 2,000–3,000 rpm, but there is often a flat spot at 7,500 revs or so. The 4-2-1 gives a smoother powerband than the old four-into-one design. Akrapovic*

If the pipe is correctly dimensioned, and the engine is operating in the rpm band for which the pipe is designed, this negative wave arrives back at the exhaust valve during valve overlap. Overlap is the period near TDC at the end of the exhaust stroke, when the exhaust valve is just closing and the intake valve just opening. During overlap, both valves are slightly open for some time period—with street cams, overlap may last less than 30 crank degrees, but with race cams, it may be 60 degrees or more.

The expansion, or negative pipe wave, travels in through the open exhaust valve, and its low pressure helps to pull residual exhaust out of the small space above the piston. Remember, this occurs near TDC, so the piston is essentially stopped for about 30 degrees at the top of its stroke.

As the suction wave pulls cylinder pressure down, it also travels out of the intake valves, into the intake tract. This causes immediate flow of fresh charge from the intake system toward the cylinder—even before the piston has begun its suction stroke. This early acceleration of the intake flow gives the intake process a valuable head-start, causing the cylinder

to fill more completely than it would if there was no exhaust pipe negative wave. This boosts torque, making a positive area, or bump, on the torque curve.

This tuning effect works over a range of rpm a few hundred revs wide because: (1) the valve overlap period has some duration, allowing the effect to work even if the suction wave is a little early or a little late, and (2) the exhaust pipe's suction pulse itself has some duration; if its leading edge arrives before overlap begins, its trailing edge can still do some good work.

Now for the bad news. At lower rpm, each revolution of the crank takes longer, but exhaust waves travel at the same speed as before. The result is that the "good" negative pipe wave now reaches the cylinder *before* the overlap period, *before* the intake valves have begun to open, thus it can't reach the intake system. Moments later, when overlap does begin, it is a positive wave that arrives, not a negative one. This is because negative and positive waves alternate in the pipe in an unending series, bouncing from end to end, just as they do in an organ pipe.

This unwanted positive wave pushes hot exhaust gas back into the cylinder, maybe all the way back through the carburetor and clear into the airbox. The result delays the intake process and dilutes it with exhaust gas. It also makes the engine run very rich (unless it has fuel injection, about which more later) in a process called multiple carburetion.

Multiple carburetion works this way. Carburetors are devices for adding fuel to moving air by use of Bernoulli's Principle: moving air has less pressure than still air. But carburetors are dull-witted and don't care which way the air is moving through them, or even whether what's moving is air or not.

So when a positive exhaust pulse blows back through the carburetor, it picks up fuel on its way into the air box. Remember, this is exhaust gas, with all the oxygen already burned out of it. It can't support combustion a second time. Once the piston gathers speed on its downward suction stroke, carburetor flow reverses, and the fuel-rich exhaust gas swirling in the air box is drawn through the carb a second time, picking up even more fuel. Pure air follows it later, but the damage is already done.

This episode of reverse flow has diluted this cylinder's charge with exhaust. It has also made it very rich—maybe

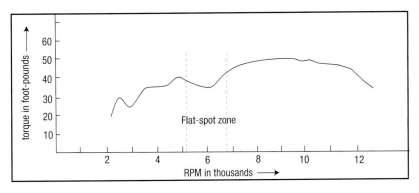

Here is the dreaded flat spot, the rpm zone in which it is a positive wave that hits the cylinder during valve overlap, pushing exhaust back into the cylinder and even right back through the intake to the air box. In the flat spot, the engine is weak from charge dilution and intake delay.

even too rich to burn, in which case the engine misfires, or at least stumbles. You, riding the bike, feel this as weak acceleration or a hesitation. Even if it doesn't misfire, the rich mixture burns poorly and with reduced effect, and cylinder filling is poor because of the delayed intake process. Torque is weak. You feel the dreaded flat spot, an rpm zone of poor acceleration. This mechanism causing momentary richness is called multiple carburetion because the charge passes through the carb more than once.

Countless riders, discovering this flat spot after fitting a new pipe, have devoted themselves tirelessly to trying to tune their way out of the hole they've made. Soon discovering that their engines are rich in the flat spot, they jet down. Power in the flat spot improves, so they jet down again. But when they check overall performance, they find that their engines are almost too weak (lean) to run everywhere else across the band.

Sadder but wiser now, they have to accept the flat spot and just ride around it—or try another pipe.

Fortunately, this is not the end of the story. Four-into-one pipes—as good as they are in their top 3,000 rpm, or "boost band"—are not the only design out there. Most production and race pipes are now of the four-into-two-into-one (4-2-1) design, and this is good medicine against the flat spot. Because the 4-2-1 pipe has two points of expansion—one where each pair of headers joins its mid-pipe, and one where the two mid-pipes join at the collector—it can send back two pulses to the cylinder.

Its basic idea is this: In the rpm zone in which the positive wave from the header end would spoil cylinder filling, the negative wave from the collector junction is also arriving. The two waves—one positive, the other negative—cancel each other, preventing formation of a full-strength flat spot. There is neither a hole nor a peak, and no multiple carburetion to make the mixture over rich, either. The engine pulls smoothly, if not maximally.

Drag racers don't care—they have their engines shrieking in that top 3,000 rpm band, so the flat spot doesn't bother them. But sport riders and road racers can't afford to have a big hole right where they may need to accelerate out of a turn.

This relationship between pipe action and valve overlap means you can change the pipe's influence by changing valve timing. In general, making overlap timing shorter reduces the depth of a race pipe's flat spot, but it also reduces its torque boost at rpm above the flat spot. What this change is doing is opening or closing the "window" through which your pipe is able to influence carburetion—for good or evil. Increasing overlap opens the window, and vice versa.

What you will want in a pipe depends upon your philosophy of riding. If you are a pure, stay-in-the-powerband madman, and don't mind "riding around" a flat spot or two by constant shifting, a properly designed four-into-one pipe may be fun. A good one can boost the top end nicely. If you prefer something more civilized, and if it's important to you not to have to use 9,000–10,000 revs to pull away from an uphill stoplight, two-up, a 4-2-1 pipe is the choice.

Only one thing is guaranteed when you buy an aftermarket pipe; it will be a bunch lighter than your stock system, which is built with heavy materials. This may be the ultimate bottom line in the pipe world; a lighter bike is a better bike, every time. In many—but by no means all—cases, the aftermarket pipe will give you more cornering clearance, too. This is something you must check out carefully; pipes by mail are convenient, but it's better to have a look at the pipe you want—on someone else's bike. That way, if it has a pavement-hungry kink in it, or if its design turns it into a passenger foot burner, you can see the problem without having to own it.

Stock pipes are heavy because they're designed to last. Heavy-gauge metal, large mufflers with complex internal flow paths, and the need for compliance with noise standards make them that way. With an aftermarket pipe, you will have to consider its little sacrifices. To be made thinner and lighter, aftermarket pipes are often made of corrosion-resistant stainless steel or titanium. Lacking a production pipe's internal tubes and baffles, your aftermarket muffler canister is going to be louder than stock—maybe too loud for even your own taste. More reasons to inspect before you buy.

Years ago, two-stroke race bikes began to sport black carbon-fiber muffler canisters, and the high-temperature resin that makes this possible is now at work making super-light four-stroke muffler shells with that trendy black textile look. I know they now make carbon fiber–look shelf paper, but when will it come out in spray cans?

HEADER TUBE SIZE

The tide comes in, the tide goes out. Years ago, there was a mad fad for huge header pipes on Triumph twins. Bigger was nastier, purer, bad. Then it went back the other way. Little teeny tubes looked sophisticated, just like the ones on Daytona-winning Triumph 500 road racers. Fashion is always there, tempting us to worship false gods—gods, that is, other than the dyno, the time slip, or the lap time.

But the option is still there; some pipes have bigger header tubes, some have smaller. Why? The answer is that header-tube size is related to exhaust valve-open area—valve circumference multiplied by max lift, times the number of exhaust valves per cylinder. Street engines have moderate lift because they are supposed to last at least as long as the payments. Therefore they have small header tubes. In modified engines with more exhaust-valve lift, bigger tube pipes can be considered.

The rule of thumb is that header-pipe inside area should be 1.16 times exhaust-valve open area.

What happens if you put on the big tubes and don't have exhaust area to match? It's just like oversized carbs; slowing down the gas speed tends to hurt bottom-end performance and may not help the top-end either. Exhaust gas must accelerate to high velocity to duck under the exhaust valve and get through the port throat. If the header-tube size is too big, the gas then has to slow down again.

If the pipe is too small for the valve area, the pipe will be the restriction. Too high a pipe velocity creates friction loss. Too low a velocity makes it too easy for pipe waves to reverse flow when it shouldn't happen.

SLIP-ONS

For the rider who wants a different look but doesn't care to wrestle with all those bolts and nuts, there is the slip-on—a replacement muffler that takes the place of the stock part. There is likely a weight saving and there may be a drop in back-pressure, but the bottom line, I fear, is: no pain, no gain. But, again, if you are just starting out with modifying, it's an easy place to start, with reversible consequences.

IS PERMANENT BEAUTY POSSIBLE?

My metallurgist friend likes to say, "Metals can hardly wait to get back to their natural state," which means they oxidize—rust—and return to mineral form. It is therefore pleasing that today's stainless-steel and titanium pipes resist such decay, and make unnecessary the primitive practices of painting and plating. Paint burns off, rubs off, and weathers off. Plating peels, chips, and discolors.

The fact is streetbikes look good only if their owners take the time to make them look good. Race bikes look good because they are frequently maintained and always indoors in comfortable shops or transporters, perhaps paid for by deep-pocket sponsors to whom appearance is important. For myself, I find beauty in a strong dyno printout. I appreciate the look of a bike that is actually ridden, with the natural grind marks on the ends of the pegs and, yes, even on the handlebar ends or fork top nuts. I happily leave the cosmetics to others.

Whatever It Takes. *The seam of a weld may not add performance, but it beats not being on the grid. A helper holds up the end of the exhaust pipe as this mechanic works into the night. The welder's drink—a remnant of tonight's trip to the local fast-food outlet—sits handy. The bike is a TZ750 Yamaha.* John Owens Studio

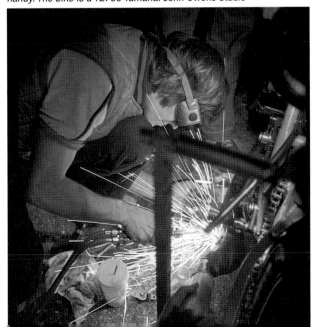

HEAT WRAP

Particularly in NASCAR-oriented magazines you will find ads for heat-wrap-insulating tape that you wrap around your pipes to insulate them. Some people find the appearance of wrapped pipes irresistibly high-tech. But the major reason NASCAR racers use this stuff is to prevent exhaust heat from overheating nearby components in the engine bay. When you ride in rain, this stuff absorbs and holds water next to your pipes, helping them to deteriorate. Meanwhile, the NASCAR racecars are safe and dry in their 45-foot transport trailers. Draw your own conclusions. John Wittner—the "Doctor John" who built such fast Moto Guzzi twins a few years back—points out that if you wrap titanium pipes, the metal oxidizes into a flaky yellow powder and falls to pieces.

INSTALLATION

It would be nice to have a set of metric combination wrenches—box and open-end—and even some sockets for tackling this job. Often, getting at the attachment of the pipes to the cylinder head requires removing the radiator or hinging it forward. Each header pipe is held in place against its exhaust port by a collar, which in turn is held in place on a pair of studs by nuts. The muffler itself is supported on brackets and detaches from the pipe system by means of a large clamp.

Find all the fasteners, then remove the muffler first. After unfastening the headers from the cylinder head, the rest of the pipe can be removed as well. Expect to hurt your knuckles—it comes with the territory. As with anything that has been together for a while, some wiggling may be necessary to free the parts. Note whether sealing washers are used between pipes and head. If new ones are not included with your pipe kit, get them from your dealer or via mail order.

Race pipes are flexibly mounted to save them from vibration-induced cracking. Instead of being held into the head by bolts, the header pipes slip into couplers that bolt to the head. The pipe ends are held into these couplers by springs. While this is racy, it also will leak slightly, giving your engine a bad case of the brown dribbles, or embarrassing backfires on deceleration. If your pipe kit is spring-mounted this way, invest in a spring hook, or make one out of a screwdriver. Many a mechanic's knuckle carries scars inflicted when trying to hook up pipe springs using only a pair of pliers.

Once you have the stock pipe removed, inspect the exhaust ports with a strong light and remove any crud that would be trapped by the new pipe and its fittings. If your pipe is spring-mounted, you can bolt on the couplers now, using whatever seal or washer is required. It's a good idea to be sure the hole in the washer is at least as big as the hole in the coupler, so there is no partial masking of the port by the washer.

On some engines, the pipe or coupler actually fits deeply into the head. This is done to make the port in the head shorter. A lot of the heat that the engine's cooling system must get rid of is picked up right here, around the exhaust port, because velocity, and therefore heat transfer, is large here. In this case, the pipe is held in place by a piece of tubing split down the middle to make a pair of collets.

To install, put in the seal washer, slip the pipe or coupler in on top of it, and then slide the pair of collets in against the back of the flange on the pipe's end. Next, slide the collar up the pipe to bear on the outer ends of the collets, and over the pair of studs projecting from the cylinder head. Put the nuts loosely on the studs to hold everything together, but don't tighten yet—everything must be lined up first.

Some pipes are welded in one piece, while others may have slip joints to allow for some adjustment during installation. If your kit uses couplers, present your pipe to the couplers now for a trial fit. On some engines, all ports face the same direction, but on others this is not so, requiring some jiggery-pokery to get everything in place. With the header pipes inserted into the couplers now, snug up the mounting nuts.

Bear in mind that 6mm studs should be tightened to no more than about 50 in-lb, or 8mm studs to 150 in-lb. It's very unpleasant to pull or break a stud on a cylinder head, because getting a broken stud out or a thread repair into a stripped hole is tricky and may require removing the head. You want this to be an easy job, so be careful when tightening!

On a spring-retained pipe, bring the pipe to its final position, and you'll be able to see if the rest of the kit—the canister and its associated brackets—is going to fit nicely in place.

If your pipe is rigid-mounted, with the pipe and flanges in place, snug up the mounting nuts to bring the pipe firmly against the head, thereby positioning the rear part of the pipe. Jiggling the pipe slightly as you tighten the nuts can help align things, and prevent binding. You can now see if everything else is going to fit nicely.

A word of caution about mounting brackets. It's common for there to be small misalignments, and the temptation is to force everything into alignment and slap the bolts through, tighten them up and forget it. But that will build tension into your installation, and the vibration of operation will add to that tension, making cracking and breaking more likely. Better to take some time making things line up, using a round file or whatever is needed to create stress-free alignment. Then you can put the mounting bolts in without having to be Tarzan. Also be sure any fasteners tighten against flat surfaces, not irregular blobs of weld.

Whatever man can put together, vibration can take apart, so at this point, you may want to consider what to do about it. Your kit may come with self-locking fasteners of some kind, which you should use. Plastic-inserted self-locking nuts may not, however, be much use on the hot exhaust flanges, so consider using nuts drilled for safety wire, and then wiring the nuts in place. (See discussion on fastener security in Chapter 21.) You may also be able to find deformed-thread nuts that work in hot applications.

If you have drained and removed your radiator for this job, refer to your service manual for the proper procedure for refilling and bleeding your cooling system. Start up the engine. Enjoy the rich, mellow sound. Investigate the possible other benefits.

Carbon fiber mufflers cut weight to the quick on this late-model RC45 Honda. John Owens Studio

But wait! You're not through yet, because most pipes require changes to what I will loosely call "carburetion." If your bike is a late-model with fuel injection, you will need a means of altering the fuel mixture to suit the new conditions. The usual way of doing this is to buy a Dynojet Power Commander III (referred to as a PCIII in ads) and either obtain the mapping for your particular pipe from Dynojet, or book in at a dyno facility that can map your system.

In former times, carburetor jet kits were the tool for this, with settings for widely sold pipes often available. There are three ways to go here. One is a full kit including new needles, needle-height adjusting washers, and possibly instructions on how to modify the rate at which the CV throttle pistons open during acceleration. Another is just needles and washers. A third possibility is to adjust the position of the stock needles by thin shim washers.

In any carburetor work, prepare to display all the patience of which you are capable. Getting at the carburetors on a streetbike isn't easy, because it involves removing layers of stuff that's designed to stay on there forever, not for easy maintenance. There are going to be regiments of resisting fasteners, knuckle-barking opportunities, and occasion to doubt the sanity of those bright young engineers who designed your bike.

All this, let me assure you, is normal, and you'll overcome it. Just keep thinking about the outcome: you want your bike to run right, and you want to learn something about carburetion in the process. These goals make the nonsense worthwhile. Soon you'll be an ace at whipping all those parts on and off.

All the foregoing is made obsolete by electronic fuel injection. Whether you use a PCIII or a laptop, your only connection with hardware is via electrical signals. Tools, jets, needles, and throttle slides are eligible for the museum now. Even our current era of ignition timing and fuel injection mapping stands ready to be swept away in its turn by the next flood of self-optimizing electronic controls.

Why, the only skill left for us to learn will be riding itself.

CHAPTER 8
CYLINDER HEAD AND VALVETRAIN

Everything comes together here—intake airflow, exhaust waves, ignition, fuel mixture, and combustion chamber shape. The sum of all things is taken here. All influences converge to produce pressure on the piston crowns.

INTAKE PORTS

An intake port is not a cylindrical tube of constant diameter, but varies along its length for a number of reasons. The overall length is determined by experiment on the dyno and is chosen to make maximum use of intake wave action. When the valve opens and the piston pulls a deep vacuum in the cylinder, a wave of low pressure propagates up the intake pipe, toward the bell mouth of carb or throttle body. It is reflected with the opposite sign at the open bell mouth and returns as a pressure wave to the engine. The idea is to have this wave (or the second or third reflection, if you have to make the intake pipe shorter) arrive just as the intake valve is closing. This stuffs in a bit of extra charge, increasing torque by a potential 5–10 percent.

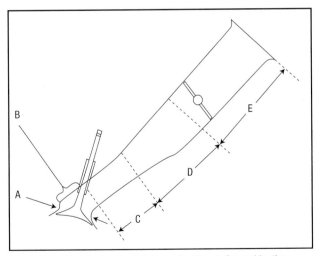

The Intake Tract by Zones. A *is the valve throat, formed by the seat insert, whose minimum diameter is always close to 0.86 times valve head diameter to smooth flow to the seat-to-valve gap.* B *is the bowl, an enlargement to slow the flow where it passes the guide and approaches the valve head.* C *is the "flywheel" of the intake flow, a high-velocity section whose energy drives post-BDC intake flow.* D *tapers to zone* E, *which is large to cut flow loss. Intake tract length is determined by intake wave tuning.*

Sometimes, to tune in a particular wave, the resulting intake system will be either too long or too short. As an example of a long system, look at the right side of a Harley dirt-tracker, whose intake pipes turn aft, putting the carbs behind the rider's right calf. The other extreme is current MotoGP four-strokes, whose heads are counterbored to allow the closest possible location of throttle butterflies. To avoid such extremes, the designer may tune to a different intake reflection.

Air friction is proportional to the square of velocity, so where possible, the port is made large. The intake bell and throttle body or carb are therefore made as big as function permits. Because the metering signal (the partial vacuum in the carb throat that causes fuel to be drawn into the airstream) becomes weaker as the carb throat is made larger, the development of the carbs once used in Superbikes was a remarkable accomplishment.

Back in 1950, a 15/16-inch (24mm) carb was considered possibly too big for road use on a 500cc cylinder. A decade later, the 500cc Manx Norton single raced with a 1 1/2-inch (38mm) carburetor. At the end of the carburetor era a substantially bigger carb (39 or 41) was used on a 187cc cylinder, making almost as much power as the 500cc cylinder of 1960, so the carb size similarity was no accident.

Today engine performance has been set free of the size limits of carburetors. Electronic fuel injection needs no venturi signal because its control arises from stored information, not from intake vacuum. Injection throttle bodies have therefore become quite large—those on twins being typically considerably over 2 inches.

If your engine is carbureted, the limits remain. It is almost invariably true that the smaller the carburetor, the easier its tuning is. This is because a strong signal is easier to work with than a weaker one.

As flow leaves the injection throttle body or carburetor and enters the vibration-insulating rubber manifold, the port diameter decreases, and this decrease may continue a distance into the cylinder head. There is a reason for this diameter reduction. The restricted portion of port upstream from the valve guide is the intake charge's flywheel, a piece of port in which velocity is made high by small diameter. This gives a limited volume of moving charge the inertia to keep on filling the cylinder after BDC. Because a likely maximum ABDC flow is 20–25 percent of the cylinder volume, this small-diameter part of the port is long enough to contain that volume. Think of this piece of port as the "piston" that will perform the inertia supercharge after BDC.

Unfortunately, in older motorcycle engine designs, this small-diameter part of the port was compromised by packaging considerations. Most commonly, the port was bent down to allow carburetors to fit under a traditional flat-bottomed fuel tank, or bent inward to make room for the rider's knees. The problem with a bend is that it causes so-called secondary flows, which are flows across the port rather than along it. Secondary flows often complicate what happens downstream, at the guide and valve. The high-speed part of the flow moves to the outside of the curve, while on the inside, the flow decelerates and may at some point downstream separate or even flow backwards.

Straight intake ports have become the rule today, when much of the volume above the engine has become the intake air box, containing near-vertical intake stacks.

Even a day spent playing on a flow bench teaches useful lessons. Without that experience, it's easy to become fixated on obvious things, like the slight mismatch between carb manifold and port, or on the pebble finish inside some ports. But the flow bench shows that these things have little effect; it's what happens at really high velocity between the valve and seat that counts most. There are engines in which the valve seat rings form ugly step-reductions in port diameter of 3mm or more. The air hardly cares; its problem is getting between valve and seat. An example would be the Suzuki Katana 600s of 1988, which looked as though some production engineer had just put smaller seat rings into a 750 head and called it a 600. Never assume that your eye tells you all you need to know about an airflow situation. Maybe I should qualify that. The late Keith Duckworth, inventor of the modern turbulent flat four-valve combustion chamber, liked to say that he could tell more about airflow with his forefinger than others could learn with full instrumentation.

FUEL WASH

Air is not the only thing flowing in the intake port. This air contains fuel vapor and fuel droplets, and it is also sometimes pushing a layer of wet fuel along the port walls. Sudden enlargements and changes of direction can cause evaporated fuel to condense again or fuel droplets to centrifuge out onto port walls. Liquid fuel is 600 times heavier than air, so the air can turn corners while fuel tends to go straight. This adds another reason to prefer small- or moderate-sized ports; they keep fuel in suspension better, and their high rates of turbulence contribute to mixing on the way. Early fuel injection systems were among the worst, with single-hole injectors blowing out fat droplets that formed a heavy wall wash. Liquid fuel could in some cases make it all the way to the cylinder to splash onto its walls. It was then scraped down into the crankcase where it made the oil level rise. This was a major reason for the next step—adoption of multi-hole injectors with 8 or 12 tiny orifices.

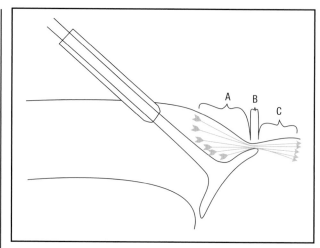

Detail of Valve and Seat. *In zone* A *the flow is guided by the shapes of valve and port throat to approach the seat restriction,* B, *in near-parallel streamlines. Velocity is very high at* B, *which is why it's important to decelerate (diffuse) the flow smoothly in zone* C *by using the cylinder head surfaces as half a diffuser.*

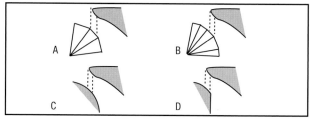

Various Valve-Seat Cutting Treatments. A *is a three-angle seat, typical of many as-manufactured valve seats.* B *more closely approximates a smooth curve by having five angles.* C *is a so-called blend seat, cut with a formed cutter or by one of the new CNC seat cutters. Seat* D *is ported right to the inner edge of the actual valve seat, with no smooth approach. In my time as a tech inspector, I saw all four types of seats in the winner's circle. Put this book down and go learn to ride!*

NASCAR racers in particular study the movement of wet fuel. One pioneer in this respect was Jack Williams, an Englishman who showed great resource in developing the AJS 7R single-cylinder race engine in the 1950s. His method was to put a cylinder and head with carburetor onto his homemade flow rig, with blotting paper lining the inside of the cylinder. With the air flowing, he would pour a spoonful of dyed water into the carb's empty float bowl. This would spray from the needle jet and, by marking the blotting paper, show the flow path of wet fuel in a running engine. The goal of such studies is, so far as possible, to keep fuel in suspension rather than let it wash into the cylinder along port and head surfaces. Any fuel on the head surface has only a poor chance of taking part in combustion. Such fuel wash is the cause of the black streaking that you will sometimes see on the combustion chamber or piston crown. Since this fuel doesn't

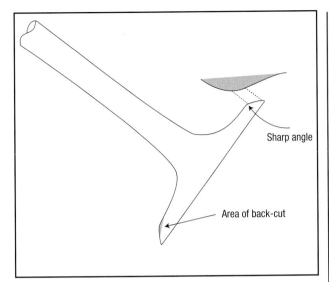

In some older engines, the back side of the intake valves may be almost flat, forming a sharp angle to the 45 degrees of the seat itself. Because it's hard for the fast-moving air to make this sharp turn, you can often achieve a useful low-lift airflow gain by softening this sharp angle by a back cut of 30 degrees or less. When I looked at an intake valve from a Ducati D16RR, there was the 30-degree back cut.

participate in combustion, you have to run such an engine richer to compensate, and the unburned fuel acts as a damper on normal combustion, causing a power loss.

Engine people the world over have written software that attempts to predict the flash evaporation of liquid fuel on port walls during the intake stroke. Automakers need to meet mandated fuel consumption standards, and bike engineers know that the axe that hits Detroit will hit them five years later. There is good practice for this development in MotoGP roadracing, where fuel tank size is limited.

BOWL AND THROAT

In the intake port region around the valve guide, where the port turns down to the valve head, the diameter usually enlarges. As airflow veteran Kenny Augustine says, air doesn't like to turn corners when it's going fast (neither do motorcycles, so it all makes sense). This enlargement is often called the *bowl*. Then at the seat, diameter decreases again to form a flow-enhancing *venturi throat* that will guide air as it approaches the gap between valve and seat. Here, the minimum diameter will be something like 0.85 times valve head diameter.

If you prepare a variety of valve throats of different I.D. and take a flow-versus-lift curve for each, the 0.85 throat will generally show the greatest total area under the curve. A 0.9 throat may show more flow near full lift, but it shows less at mid and low lifts. As a one-time AMA tech inspector, I sometimes saw Supersports engines ported right to the edge of the 45-degree valve seat, but it was clear this had not helped performance. The value of the 0.85 throat has been known since at least the 1930s, when aircraft engine development uncovered the relationship. It was "rediscovered" in the 1960s. If you look at a cross-section of valve and seat at moderate lift, the value of the 0.85 throat is apparent. It helps the air to approach the gap under the valve smoothly—as a bell mouth guides air into a carburetor. At higher lifts, this becomes less important.

SEAT PREPARATION

Leading the air to the gap under the valve is crucial to flow, which is why this area gets so much attention. If you do nothing else to your cylinder head, contour the valve seats. As delivered from the factory, the seats usually have a three-angle valve job. One of the angles is, of course, the 45-degree seat itself. There is also an inner cut (about 70 degrees) and a top cut. A five-angle valve job comes closer to producing

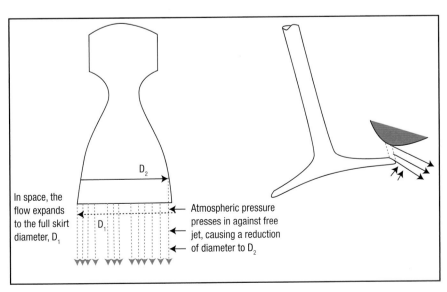

In space, the flow expands to the full skirt diameter, D_1

D_2

D_1

Atmospheric pressure presses in against free jet, causing a reduction of diameter to D_2

Why There are Flow Losses in a Free Jet. *The left-hand figure shows a rocket motor. In space, the exhaust expands fully, delivering maximum thrust against the expansion skirt. But in the atmosphere, air pressure can press inward against the high-velocity, low-pressure flow (remember Bernoulli), preventing full expansion and pinching the free jet. In the right-hand figure, a free jet is formed as high-velocity airflow emerges from between the valve and seat. Again, as with the rocket motor operating in the atmosphere, the surrounding air can reach the jet, pinch it where its pressure is lowest, and both dilute and restrict the flow.*

a smooth venturi for the airflow, and some engine builders still use it. Smoother yet is the blend valve job, performed with either a formed cutter that is smoothly radiused to shape the seat in a single operation or by a single-point cutter that forms the desired contour under computer direction.

Busy shops perform full blend valve seats, but smaller outfits still cut multi-angle seats, using single or multi-edged cutters. The craftsman uses a magnifier and scale to ensure that each cut is made to the desired width.

The wider the 45-degree valve seat and its contact with the matching part of the valve, the longer the seal will last, with some penalty in increased flow resistance. In race engines, the intake valve may simply be ground to kiss a blend seat, making a very narrow contact ring. Power and longevity are always two sides of a tough compromise. Ask your engine builder's advice, after telling him what kind of use your bike will get. Supercharged engines, endurance engines, and equipment bound for Bonneville need wider exhaust valve seats and other special treatment.

DOING IT OVER AND OVER

If you are preparing an engine for Supersport racing, or just for higher performance, you'll want to begin with appropriate valve seat preparation, as noted previously. But as your engine piles up the hours, it will begin to leak everywhere and become soft or baggy. Then it will need to have its top end freshened up by having the valves and seats re-cut and/or (depending upon the taste of the person doing the work) the valves ground to the seats. Ideally, if you cut just the seat, it will grow wider and restrict flow slightly, so all angles should be cut again for top results. You decide how much of a maniac you want to be about it. The better the seal, the more power an engine will make. As with anything else, you do what you can. Some riders can't afford the time or money for constant freshening-ups, so they just ride harder and hope it all comes out even. These details matter less when you're just starting out, because as you learn to ride, you gain speed more quickly from personal software improvement than you ever could from more power. Time and again, I have seen low-hours riders *go slower* with more power than they did the week before with less. Think about that for a while.

DOWNSTREAM FLOW LOSS

In the manual that comes with a Superflow flow bench, it mentions that about 40 percent of the flow restriction of an intake valve and port occurs as an exit loss, *after* the air emerges from under the valve. The implication is that nothing can be done about this loss. That's not quite correct, as many Superflow users well know. The loss occurs when high-speed airflow emerges into the cylinder as a so-called free jet. It is carrying a lot of energy, but that energy is not smoothly converted into pressure in the cylinder. Instead, the free jet creates a turbulent mixing zone in which its energy is largely wasted—like squirting water from a hose into a pond.

Another kind of free jet is formed when you flow-test an exhaust port, blowing air from the combustion chamber, out through the valve and port to atmosphere. Now comes the interesting part. Note the flow in cfm (cubic feet per minute, the measure of all things in the airflow business) with the bare port, then roll up a piece of paper to make a crude megaphone, whose small end just fits in the port. Now when you put the megaphone into the port, note that the flow increases about 30 percent. Why? You have eliminated most of the expansion flow loss by using a megaphone to more efficiently convert velocity into pressure. This conversion of velocity into pressure is called *diffusion*, and the device that does the job—the paper magaphone in this case—is called a *diffuser*. The flow increase occurs because the diffuser prevents atmospheric pressure from pinching the jet where it is fastest, and its pressure the lowest. The paper diffuser in our example allows it to expand and flow more freely. Take the megaphone away and just put the back of your hand up to the flow, so it travels along your skin. Again, the flow increases, but not by the full 30 percent. Your hand is now acting as a part of a diffuser.

We can apply this principle to the problem of intake valve exit expansion loss by contouring the valve seat into the combustion chamber. The idea is to make the inside surface of the combustion chamber, around the intake valve(s), act as half of a diffuser, guiding the attached flow and preventing local atmospheric pressure from having access to one side of the jet.

THE EXHAUST PORT

Because exhaust valve cooling takes place mainly through contact between valve and seat, the exhaust valve seat has to be wider than the intake. Modern exhaust ports are pretty good, but still on the low side for my taste. You have to look at real race engines to see exhaust coming out at a natural high angle. I think Japanese engines continue to have sharply downward-curved exhaust ports chiefly because the stylists think an engine would "look funny" with the exhausts emerging at less than 90 degrees to the cylinder axis.

I once received an improved exhaust port over the telephone. Calling airflow specialist Kenny Augustine, I asked him what to do about a Honda 450 exhaust port.

He replied, "Do you notice the irregular sound it's making on the flow bench?"

I did.

"That's the flow unable to decide whether to fill the whole port, or unstick from the floor. Start filling the floor with modeling clay, and you'll see the flow go right up. The roaring will stop. Keep filling it until the gains stop—maybe 15 percent. Then start adding material under the head of the valve—tulip it right out. You'll see another 15 percent gain from that."

I went back to the flow bench and did it, and it worked. You may have seen or heard about D-shaped exhaust ports—flat on the floor, rounded on the roof. They result from this filling process.

I also spoke to West Coast porting pioneer Jocko Johnson, who said that years ago, he'd noticed swirly marks

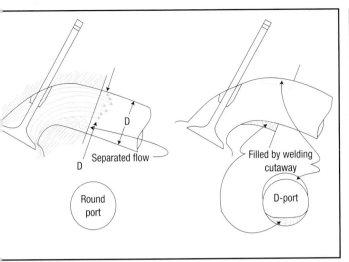

Floor Separation in an Exhaust Port. *Because the high-speed exhaust flow can't make the tight short side turn, the flow separates from the port's floor. The actual flow is occurring up against the roof of the port, with reduced diameter d, of much less area than the port outlet and header pipe of the full diameter D. For many years, cylinder head modifiers have added material to the floor and/or raised the port by cutting the roof. Both operations reduce the sharpness of the exhaust elbow and may thereby increase flow. Today many production heads use such D-shaped ports.*

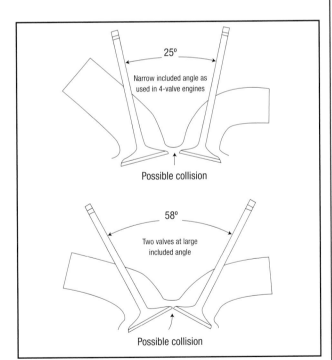

Will Valves Collide during Overlap? *Liquid-cooled four-valve engines normally have a small valve included angle, so valves approach each other slowly as lift increases. Air-cooled two-valve engines need a larger valve included angle to get cooling air to the fins between the cam boxes. This larger angle makes the valves approach each other faster, placing a limit on overlap valve lifts.*

on the floor of a Mopar exhaust port, but straight streaks on the port roof.

"It looked to me like streambeds, or sand dunes, there on the bottom. It looked like the flow was even going backwards. But up on the roof, it looked like high-speed flow, So I just started cutting to raise the roof, and when I had room, I brazed up the floor—straightening out the port as much as I could [these were iron heads, and this was the origin of the "raised and brazed" exhaust treatment]."

The result was a new drag-race record for the class.

The late Jim Feuling made a good living from such exhaust port "smallifications." He described sitting in Detroit meetings across a conference table from engineers who tried to deny what they were seeing in test results. He showed them that conventional exhaust ports are much too big and much too curved. His designs left more room for bigger intake valves and made exhaust valves and cylinder heads run cooler. To get an idea of a progressive exhaust port, have a look at a Ducati Testastretta head, with its updraft exhaust ports.

Often people reason that, with only the atmosphere's 15 psi to push the intake process, and with end-of-stroke exhaust pressure of maybe 100 psi to push out the exhaust, the intake should get all the development work. Yet some engines have such poor exhaust ports that they lose power from having to *push* the exhaust out on the exhaust stroke, rather than just letting exhaust pressure push most of itself out right after the exhaust opens, before BDC. They also run hotter because of their poor ports. Good exhaust ports make power because *(a)* less push is required on the exhaust stroke to pump out residual exhaust gas; and *(b)* less hot exhaust gas is left in the cylinder to take the place of, and preheat, the fresh charge.

This is particularly important in air-cooled engines. Get the exhaust out early and be rewarded with a lower operating temperature. Who knows, maybe sufficiently lower to permit some extra compression? Everything is interrelated.

ABOUT REVERSION AND REVERSION BARRIERS

It's a good idea to pay attention to what the NASCAR people are doing, because they know an enormous amount about 355-cubic-inch Chevy V-8s. In this connection, you'll hear about reversion barriers, which are steps or cuffs that face any positive wave returning from the exhaust pipe to the cylinder. Their purpose is to prevent much of that wave from entering, and these devices are reported to have doubled horsepower at lower revs—like from 30 horsepower to 60 horsepower at 3,000 rpm. How much time do you spend at 3,000 rpm on your bike?

Lots of motorcycle people have tried to make this idea show gains on their engines, largely without success. As a NASCAR stocker tries to accelerate out of pit lane, positive waves from the exhaust blow back through the cylinder and screw up the carburetion. This is made worse by having to use long cam timing so the heavy pushrod valve gear, fighting million-pound valve springs, can reach full lift without rocket assist. That means long overlap, giving more opportunity for those nasty positive waves to get into the cylinder. These engines need reversion barriers. But your overhead cam, six-speed engine, with its four valves and matching short-duration cams, probably does not. All you see on your torque curve, as evidence of reversion, is the usual pipe-induced flat spot. The two usual tools for dealing with this are the 4-2-1 pipe and limited valve overlap.

VALVE SPRING CONCERNS

Every time a valve seat is re-cut to restore the original seal, the valve sinks into the head slightly and sticks out of the valve guide farther. This, if not compensated for, will reduce the valve spring pressure. Consequently, each time a cylinder head is assembled, it's a good idea to measure the distance between the head surface, where the bottom of the valve spring sits, and the underside of the spring retainer, assembled onto the valve stem with its collets. There will be a specification for valve spring installed height, whether your springs are original stock or aftermarket. To get the correct height, you add special valve spring shims under the spring.

How do you know if your springs are tired? Often, the service manual will give a free length, and you may work to this spec (reject if shorter than such-a-number) or compare it with a new spring. How much pressure loss is there in a spring 2mm too short? With a bathroom scale on the table of a drill press, compress a stock spring to be as short as the sagged one, and read the pounds off the scale. Head shops use a proper spring pressure gauge, measuring each spring to see that it delivers the correct seat and open pressure. Obviously, if the springs sag, they may no longer be strong enough to make the valvetrain follow the cam lobe. Bounce and irregular action will follow.

Back in 1964 I shared a Honda 305 Super Hawk with a friend, and we noted that with new springs, the engine would rev to 10,200 or a bit more. But after two weeks of being ridden by crazed young men, the springs would sicken and gradually the rev ceiling would fall toward 9,500. Then it was time for new springs again.

Springs and spring materials have come a long way in 40-odd years. Fancy valve springs today are made from special high-purity steel that has been re-melted twice under vacuum, allowing foreign matter to vaporize and be pumped away. The material is drawn into wire, wound into springs, the ends are closed and ground parallel, and then the wire is shot-peened to put its surface into compression, further ensuring against cracking. In addition, the springs may be made smaller at the valve retainer end, this being called a "beehive spring." This shape not only lightens the moving end of the spring, but also makes it stiffer, preventing some of the normal pile-up of coils against the underside of the retainer as the cam sharply accelerates the valve off its seat. This coil pile-up is the first step in the generation of "spring surge"—the rapid, Slinky-like bouncing of wave motion between the two ends of the spring. This motion causes variations in the pressure available to control valve motion—possibly enough to result in premature valve float.

Various techniques are used to damp this spring vibration or to make its frequency too high for the engine to excite. These waves greatly increase the number of fatigue cycles that the wire experiences, hastening its failure.

Often the spring is progressive-wound, like a front fork spring, with the coils pitched closer together at one end than at the other. The end with the closer coils goes against the cylinder head. As the valve lifts, the closer coils begin to coil bind (close against each other), and this damps vibration. Or the spring may be made with so few coils that its natural frequency is too high to be excited by the cam. For many years, springs had five or more turns of wire, but racing springs often have only three and a half. This increases spring wire stress, so good materials are essential. Or nested springs may be used, wound in opposite directions so the coils rub on one another slightly, providing damping. Alternatively, a flat-wire damper may be nested inside the outer spring.

Some current motorcycle valve springs are made of oval wire, and there has even been discussion about the means of making hollow wire, whose stiffness-to-weight ratio would be unusually high.

The fit of the spring retainer collets into the valve stem's groove(s) should be checked before assembly to be sure all parts are indeed compatible. Sometimes the collet angle differs from that in the retainer, resulting in a retainer that teeters uncertainly. Prepare for frustration as you may drop or even lose the tiny collets. The collets in Ducati's $72,000 D16RR MotoGP replica are titanium, so if you drop them, magnets will not save your bacon.

PREVENTING COLLISIONS

Valves can hit each other, the piston, or the spark plug(s), depending upon the geometry, the cam timing, and valve lift. All these possibilities have to be checked by trial assembly in any modified engine. Four-strokes are a lot of work! Check valve-to-valve on a bare head by setting a pair of valves at their overlap lifts. Valves on late-model sportbikes have little problem here, because their valve included angles are so small (as little as 20 degrees in recent designs) that the valves hardly approach each other at all as they lift. But on older two-valve engines, the included angle is large (60–80 degrees) and so are the valves themselves, therefore valve-to-valve clearance has to be carefully checked. If the valves come closer than 0.040 inch, your options are either to time the cams to move the valves apart or cut the seats, "sinking" the valves away from each other. This set of problems can become a real poser on racy two-valve engines with big valves. In extreme cases, adventuresome workers have relocated the valves with oversized offset or angled valve guides or by welding up the guide holes and starting over again. Pick your poison. If you love the calm, reflective life of the machine shop, here's your excuse to stay there.

Valve-to-piston clearances are checked by assembling the head with light springs (or just the inners), putting it

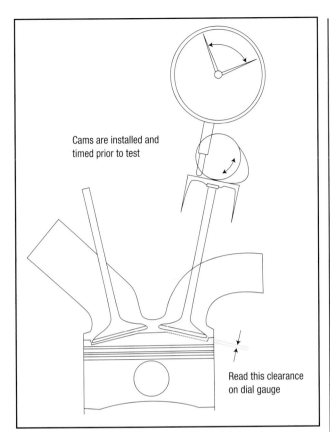

Cams are installed and timed prior to test

Read this clearance on dial gauge

Checking Valve-to-Piston Clearance. *With a dial gage against the tappet, or another part of the valvetrain that travels the same distance as the valve, and with light "checking springs" on the valves, roll the crankshaft through overlap while pushing the valve down against the piston—tap, tap, tap to find the point of closest approach. If it's too close for safety, you can* (a) *shift the cam timing (quickest way, but compromises timing);* (b) *sink the valves by cutting their seats deeper (bad); or* (c) *mill the valve clearance pockets in the pistons deeper (best).*

on the engine with standard gaskets and torques, timing the cams, and then rotating the crank through TDC/overlap while pushing the valves down repeatedly ("tic-tic-tic") to feel for the minimum clearance to the piston. Measure each with a dial gauge and write down the minimum numbers on a chart. If the exhausts are coming closer than 0.040 inch or the intakes 0.030 inch to the piston, you will have to re-cut the piston's valve reliefs. Different people have different limits here, and they will be bigger for big engines, smaller for small ones. You need some clearance because at high rpm, valve motion is not exactly what the cam is asking for, and you have to allow some room for these "position errors." At one time in NASCAR, five valve bounces after seating were considered marginally acceptable, but this has since been reduced to three. There's a lot of action in a valvetrain! Pushrod engines will need more room, while shim-under-bucket engines will need less, because the valvetrain in the first case is more flexible, in the latter less so.

VALVE MASKING

Big valves can be a problem. Even stock valves are sometimes located fairly close to the cylinder wall or other obstruction. It's worth doing a flow study on a junk head to determine the value—if any—of removing the obstructions or grinding away part of the cylinder wall (no further down than the upper edge of the top piston ring at TDC, obviously). Vintage Honda racer Todd Henning has found that often, big valves can be most useful in restoring a good relationship between head diameter and throat diameter.

MAINTAINING AIR MOTION

Engines need mixture turbulence to speed flame propagation, and the major source of this turbulence is intake flow velocity. As the intake stroke ends, the cylinder is full of whirling air. As the piston rises on compression, this rotary motion breaks down into smaller and smaller scale turbulence. In a good design, there is enough of this turbulence left at the ignition point and thereafter to produce rapid, efficient combustion.

Sharp edges or other obstructive features on head or piston should be smoothed off, as they serve to slow down air motion as the piston rises, causing rapid turbulence decay. During my last brisk official trot through the Ducati racing department I chanced to see the piston crowns of a just-assembled Superbike engine. They were perfectly smooth—no cuts, no edges. Everyone has to go through the stage of being excited by the rad look of high-dome pistons, then later discovering that smoothing off the fence-like rough edges, and even reducing the compression ratio by doing so, gives better performance.

Here, let your engine's best ignition timing be your guide. If the engine needs as much as 40 degrees or more to develop best power, suspect that something is slowing combustion. When that something is identified and fixed, your best ignition point will move toward TDC, indicating faster combustion. Usually in such cases, more power is the result. There's not a lot of point in developing outstanding intake and exhaust flow, only to lose from slow, inefficient combustion.

SWIRL

One way to store air motion energy in the cylinder during compression is to give it rotary swirl *around* the cylinder axis. It is to produce such swirl that intake ports on two-valve engines have been offset (as viewed from above) to make the flow enter the cylinder more on a tangent, rather than on a diameter. Many, many two-valve engines employ such offset ports.

DOWNDRAFT ANGLE

Picture a vertical engine cylinder, with the intake port entering from the left. If the port axis is essentially at 90 degrees to the cylinder, it is called a *flat port*. This design persisted a long time because it made carburetors fit under the gas tank (not up inside it, as at present). The flat port sends its flow *across* the valve to emerge mainly from the far side, with very little flow, if any, emerging from the near or short side of the valve. One major trend of design in flat ports has been to raise the port, thereby removing some of the sharp bend made at the turn-down to the valve. As long ago as the 1930s, practical tuners saw that raising the intake port could have the effect of preventing intake flow from being partly lost by shooting straight at the opposite (and, during overlap, still slightly open) exhaust valve. Such raising of intake ports is what caused certain Velocette and Norton bikes to have their gas tanks notched to permit the higher carburetor position.

TUMBLE

Later, especially with the coming of four-valve engines, intake ports have assumed higher downdraft angles, and this affects in-cylinder air motion. In a four-valve, short-stroke engine, a new type of air motion called *tumble* has taken the place of swirl. In tumble, air enters the cylinder, travels down the far-side cylinder wall, back across the piston, and up the near cylinder wall in a rotary motion, like that of the crankshaft. A lower downdraft angle favors the creation of strong tumble, while a higher angle favors flow at the expense of tumble. Classic Cosworth four-valve race car engines favor a 30-degree downdraft angle (60 degrees from vertical, in other words), but Japanese bike engines display higher angles. The designer chooses based upon the expected application. Just as Harry Ricardo measured swirl rpm in the 1920s with his "swirl meter" (a little anemometer placed inside the airflow test cylinder, with means of measuring its rpm), so today Ducati measures tumble motion with a similar device. A race or pure sport engine would receive a higher downdraft angle than would a utility engine that needed best performance in lower or middle rpm ranges. A high-speed engine gets its combustion-speeding turbulence from high intake velocity, but if midrange is needed, tumble may be called upon to provide it.

COMPRESSION COMPROMISE

Drag engines need a lot of compression to "turn the tire," but they usually pay for their tight combustion chambers with top-end power drop-off, as combustion can't burn the chamber in the short time available at higher revs. This is a good compromise for the quarter-mile, but not for the sports or road race application, where both acceleration and top-end are needed. Extremes are attractive, but consider compression ratio in light of what it can do to combustion. Often the lower compression setup outperforms the tightly squeezed one. Keep an open mind.

If you can get some pourable rubber molding compound, it's instructive to take a TDC cast of your combustion chamber, then section the cast to see where the charge is really located. The desirable goal is to push charge in as close as possible to the spark plug(s) and reduce to a minimum the volume contained in outlying areas and squish. In a 72x44mm cylinder, with a 13:1 compression ratio, if the combustion chamber thickness was uniform all over the piston, it would be only 44/12mm thick = 3.7mm. Not much charge motion can survive, squeezed to the thickness of two 50-cent pieces between piston and head. Therefore, the chamber is made roomier in the middle by bringing the piston very close to the head everywhere but in the valve clearance pockets and under the spark plug(s). Because the valves make up about 40 percent of the bore area, putting almost all the chamber volume under them allows the chamber height to be doubled there. This gives more room for turbulence to persist and is a key to quick combustion.

Squish regions are reduced to a TDC thickness that is basically the mechanical limit—around 0.025 inch in four-cylinder engines. Measure the clearance in your engine by making a trial assembly with standard gaskets and torques, and with either solder or modeling clay on the squish regions. Be sure to place the measuring medium symmetrically, or piston rock may give you a false measurement. Turn the engine through TDC, tear down, and measure the clay or solder thickness.

Squish is another key to rapid combustion because it re-agitates the mixture around TDC, when the combustion space is at its smallest.

Lift and Velocity Curves of Valve Motion. *The lift curve begins with a clearance ramp, then quickly rises to a smooth peak and reverses. The velocity curve (the double-humped curve) shows valve velocity rising early to a maximum as the cam lobe accelerates the valve upward. Then velocity falls as the valve decelerates to zero velocity at maximum lift. Valve acceleration is the slope of the velocity curve. Note that the cam-controlled part of the velocity curve has a slope much steeper than that of the spring-controlled part. This is because the cam can exert much more force than can the spring.*

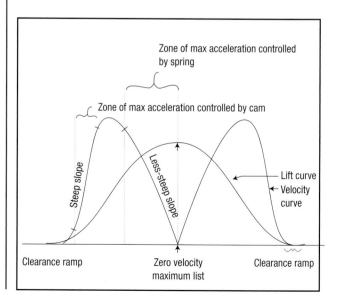

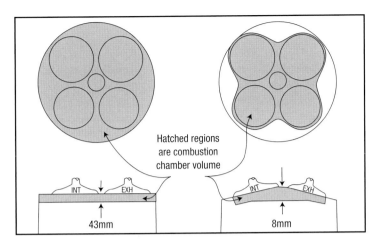

Volume Distribution in Combustion Chambers. *In the drawing on the left, the combustion chamber volume giving 12:1 compression ratio is distributed uniformly, resulting in a chamber only 4.3mm high. This "low ceiling" quickly kills mixture turbulence as the piston nears the cylinder head, slowing combustion. In the drawing on the right, the valves have been tilted slightly, and the piston has been notched for valve clearance, while the non-hatched region has been made into squish. These three measures concentrate the chamber volume under the plug, giving an 8mm thickness there—almost twice the headroom. This gives turbulence the room to survive all the way to TDC and thereby speeds combustion.*

VALVE MECHANISMS

For years manufacturers went back and forth on just what is the best valve drive system. Kawasaki, Honda, and Ferrari have announced the lightness of the pivoted-finger cam follower, only to go back to the inverted bucket type in the next engine. Lately, the choice has gone to the finger follower if design flexibility is required, because it is easier to re-design for increased valve lift with that system. Drag racers know that increasing lift with bucket followers requires boring the head for larger buckets—and finding suitable buckets—as a means of keeping the higher-lift cam's lobes from overhanging the bucket. Bucket tappets are most reliable when the clearance-adjusting shim is underneath, not resting in a shallow recess on top. With pivoted fingers, it's comforting to have the clearance-adjusting function at the pivot or in the form of a lash cap atop the valve stem. In older designs, clearance-adjusting screws madly leaped up and down at the valve end, constantly threatening to come loose.

DESMODROMIC VALVES, ETC.

Back in the 1950s, valve springs were a weak link. Existing materials developed fatigue cracks and failed. This caused Mercedes-Benz to develop its Z-drive, or desmodromic valve system. This opens the valve by action of one cam lobe and closes it by action of a second, complementary lobe, operating through a forked closing rocker. In the middle 1960s, vacuum-remelted steels of high purity became available, and valve springs made of such stuff worked a quiet revolution in engine design, being able to tolerate increased stress and operate reliably for extended periods. For many years this seemed to make desmodromic valve operation no more than a historic curiosity. With Ducati's success in MotoGP racing, that company is entitled to its claim that desmo is the equal of any other system.

Metal valve springs have departed from the highest levels of motor racing, with pneumatic springs taking over the task in F1 roughly 20 years ago and with Yamaha, Kawasaki, and Suzuki having now adopted them in MotoGP.

One possibility that gets little notice is titanium valve springs. Titanium is not only lighter than steel (one-third to half the spring mass is considered part of the moving mass of the valvetrain), but it has a higher fatigue limit. That means that, for a given amount of material, you can work titanium harder. There has been at least some testing of titanium springs in NASCAR, and I wonder why there hasn't been more use of them in motorcycle racing.

VALVES

Valves in production engines are just good enough to work. The intakes are made of carbon steels, while the exhausts often have stainless heads (magnet does not stick) and carbon-steel stems, friction-welded together. One-piece stainless valves are often preferred by engine builders because they have no welds. For higher temperature applications (air-cooled engines, or heavily supercharged or turbocharged) there are more highly heat-resistant exhaust valve materials, some containing cobalt and being related to turbine blade materials. BSA had problems with valve stretch on its historic Gold Star single, largely solved in 1952 with the gas turbine alloy Nimonic 80. Another Nimonic material was later used by Honda in its air-cooled racers of the 1960s. Titanium valve technology has advanced to the point that many production engines now employ them—at least on the cooler intake side. Fifteen percent lighter yet is titanium aluminide, an intermetallic compound. It has been used in valves and wrist pins.

Production valves are often lightly hard-faced on the seating surface, to prevent valve recession (loss of clearance as material erodes from valve and seat). Sometimes this material is so thin that a routine regrind will cut through it, and new valves will be required.

Small-diameter valves in water-cooled engines have a pretty cushy life, which is why titanium can be used as valve material (only 60 percent the weight of steel, recall). Great big valves in auto engines are sometimes, in aircraft style, made hollow and partly filled with sodium metal. When the valve gets hot, the sodium liquefies, then sloshes from end to end, tending to level the temperature spikes that would otherwise exist (makes the hot parts cooler, the cool parts hotter). A sodium-filled valve may, however, bring so much heat to its stem that lubrication problems develop there. Some of the last great air-cooled aircraft radial engines "solved" this problem by flooding their rocker boxes with oil!

VALVE SEATS

Production valve seats are made of sintered iron or other iron-based material. Changing valve seats is a demanding operation of extracting the existing seats, boring the head at the correct angle and dimension for a new seat, then using temperature difference to shrink and press the new seat in place. Sometimes you may have to resort to this to save a good head with one or more damaged seat rings. Then you must find a shop that regularly does this work. Beryllium copper (Be-Cu) seats are preferred for titanium valves.

During one-year-and-a-half period in AMA Supersport racing, it was legal to install "pop-up" seats, which pushed the valves toward the piston. This was simply a technique for boosting compression ratio.

Quite often, factory race engines will have bronze seat rings, the basis for which is improved heat conductivity and the fact that a steel valve on a bronze seat may suffer less valve recession (that's why bearings are often made of bronze—steel and bronze get along).

When unleaded fuels were mandated at the pump, there was a panic over the possibility that without lead as an anti-seize agent between valve and seat, older engines would consume themselves by seat recession. Many a Harley owner had the valve seats replaced with super-hard ones. It turned out to be much fuss over little; unless an engine is on heavy throttle most of the time (marine, aviation) its valves don't run hot enough to be in trouble.

ABOUT CAMDRIVES

Every imaginable device has been used to drive overhead camshafts. The Norton Manx used a towershaft and bevels, later employed as well on a bygone generation of Ducatis. The AJS/Matchless singles had chains, used today in most production overhead cam-shaft (OHC) engines, often in the noise-suppressing tooth-chain style pioneered by Morse. The great Italian multis from Gilera and MV had trains of spur gears, adopted by Honda after a brief 1959 hiccup with towershafts, for its classic four-stroke racers of the 1960s. NSU used quartered connecting-rod drive, which some folk termed "locomotive rods." Most recently have come the variety of tooth forms and belt constructions, lumped under the name tooth belts.

Every drive has its special strengths and problems. Towershafts can compensate handily for engine heat growth by having a splined slip joint in the shaft, but there are all those gears to be precisely located with little shims. Chain runs will vibrate if they are not made to run against curved and well-lubricated damper strips faced with rubber or plastic (the British term is "Weller blade"). The multitude of parts wear and the chain grows longer. But chains are cheap and their tension can be looked after by automatic spring-loaded or hydraulic tensioners. Trains of spur gears are precise (the more so, as there are fewer gears in the train) and fairly rigid, but you can hear them—the 1990s race-kit camdrives from Kawasaki and Suzuki had their special whirring noise signatures. Tooth belts are popular solutions in automotive work because they are both quiet and cheap, but they require changing from time to time. Automakers show their distrust of these belts by designing what they call "free spin" engines—those with so much piston-to-valve clearance that belt breakage damages nothing but your mobility. Yet perhaps, being organic-based, they contain valuable damping.

Every new high-performance engine design has some kind of development trouble with its camdrive. Crank speed variation, any torsional vibration, plus the lumpy torque requirement of cams conspire to impose load spikes on the drive that break parts. Engineers get busy and try to find the problem There are torsional absorption devices in many race car engine camdrives—effectively a very short torsion bar somewhere in the drive, built in unit with a miniature clutch. The torsion bar allows some compliance, and the clutch stack prevents any buildup of cyclic motion. Camdrive problems happen to everyone.

Part of this problem is really crankshaft dynamics. Note that often, the first version of a company's four-cylinder inline has the camdrive taken from crank center. The supposition is that this is a nice quiet place to put the drive, while the ends rattle and twist. Later, as the engineers are looking for bearings they can eliminate in their search for lower friction, this center camdrive gets moved to the crank end. The crank is forcibly spun by a series of very firm pushes—the combustion events. The lighter the crank, the more moment-by-moment speed variation and crank wind-up this produces. If you put the camdrive where a lot of this action is located, it will try to make the cams dance to the same tune. This is when the fun starts. One maker's experiments showed that its crank was twisting back and forth 6 degrees at one particular speed, as measured from one end to the other. This confuses the camdrive.

Why am I mentioning this, when you aren't planning to design your own engine? With the cams' rotational speed varying in this way, valve float may take place prematurely. I think especially of the new, no-flywheel 450 four-stroke singles, whose crank speed variation must be extreme. Just keep the possibilities in mind.

If you decide to run nonstandard cam timings in your engine (it's always a good idea actually to know what the best timing is by experiment), you'll be running adjustable timing sprockets with slotted bolt holes. The bolts will come loose unless (a) they are really, seriously tight; or (b) they, and the threads into which they screw, have been degreased

VALVETRAIN ELEMENTS REVISITED

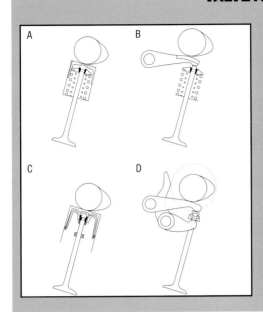

A. Inverted bucket tappets have been with us since 1916. They're reasonably light, extremely direct, and exert zero side force on the valve stem. Many engines still use them despite a current consensus that lever followers are lighter and accommodate lift increases more easily.

B. The pivoted finger, so often in and out of fashion, is currently "in." It carries a hard radiused pad against which the cam lobe operates. Fingers do produce stem side-force, increasing as lift is increased. Fingers do not limit spring size.

C. Pneumatic closers were invented by Renault for its F1 auto engines. They are not yet used on any sportbike, but now dominate MotoGP. Here, what was formerly the spring retainer grows into an umbrella shape as the seal carrier, nested inside the normal inverted bucket tappet. Gas pressure under the seal carrier closes the valve.

D. The fabled desmodromic (Greek roots meaning "chain-operated") valve gear uses one lobe and rocker to open the valve and another complementary lobe and rocker to close it—there is no spring. Ducati's racing success has confirmed its claim that the desmo system is the equal of any other.

and dried, then the bolts have been drenched in thread-locking compound before insertion.

Obviously, to avoid losing the correct timing once you have it, remove one bolt at a time for the degreased thread-locker, insertion and torquing treatment.

Four-stroke engines have a discouraging number of parts, and sometimes it seems that the number of trial assemblies, measurements, and fiddlings-about involved in a good build will break your resolve to become a high priest of internal combustion. Don't worry. It will become second nature quickly, and it all makes sense. When I was first tackling the family lawnmower engine, my dad would say to me, "What makes you think it's ever going to run again?" My somewhat cocky answer was, "It has to run. When it's put together right, it has no choice."

As the cam rotates with the valve closed, the first part of the opening process is the approach of the *clearance ramp*, which is a gradually lifting part of the profile intended to take up operating clearance in a noiseless, shockless way. Once the clearance ramp has picked up the tappet and valve slightly, the actual lift profile takes over.

Early cams had mathematically simple lobe shapes that were easy to make, but were very hard on valvetrain parts. If you are planning to push the neighbor's car to get it started, you don't back up and take a run at it, but that's effectively what these early cam forms did. Hitting the tappet hard, they applied the lift acceleration almost instantly, resulting in extremely high peak forces. After whacking the valve open, they also tried to decelerate it as suddenly at the top of its lift. The result was that the valve sailed on, "floating" above the cam lobe until spring pressure finally stopped and reversed its motion. Then

it snapped hard onto the cam profile again, bounced, bounced again, and was then delivered with equal violence onto its seat. At lower rpm, all was well and such a cam, if properly timed, might make excellent torque. But as soon as the revs rose, all sorts of dismal results accumulated, such as damaged tappets, broken springs, and hammered valves.

When physics-minded people looked the situation over, they realized that valve accelerations and decelerations would themselves have to be applied progressively, loading up and unloading the parts at rates their materials could accept.

Thus, when you push your neighbor's car, you approach the bumper slowly (clearance ramp). Then once contact is made, you open the throttle slowly to get both vehicles moving (buildup of acceleration off the seat). As a result of such rationally designed cam profiles, valves can now be opened and closed at very high peak acceleration rates, but without impact damage to parts. In some cases, the cam is made to take account of the flexibility of parts such as rocker arms and pushrods, to "tune out" parts vibration modes that would otherwise cause float and bounce.

Always remember that the cam profiles are designed as though the camshaft were attached to an infinitely heavy flywheel, so that it rotates at a uniform rate. Because of crank and camshaft torsional vibration, and the flexibility of camdrive elements, this is rarely the case—sometimes so much so that float and bounce show up at rpm lower than the cam designer expects.

When you graph out valve lift versus crank degrees, then convert this lift curve to a velocity curve (velocity is the *slope* of the lift curve at each point), and finally convert the velocity curve to an acceleration curve (acceleration

Honda NR750 Oval-Piston Engine. *This $60,000 curiosity shows how far manufacturers are willing to go in pursuit of an idea. Honda wanted to achieve four-stroke GP racing success in a two-stroke era. Rules said no more than four cylinders, but the engineers knew they'd need eight cylinder's worth of valve area. So they made oval pistons, each served by eight valves. Peak version of the NR500 finally made 136 brake horsepower at 18,000–19,000 rpm. An endurance-racing 750 was later built, but the real payoff was Honda's long line of round-bore V-4 engines.* American Honda

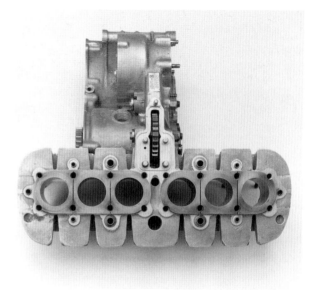

It's routine today, but it wasn't easy then. This is the one-piece upper case and cylinder casting for a Honda RC166 six-cylinder 250 racer from 1964. Making this in one piece gives the part greater beam-bending strength and eliminates cylinder-to-case oil leaks. Crank-driven flex makes cases writhe, thus testing the base gaskets of engines with separate cylinder castings. The fix for some is a solid-copper base gasket. Many modern production inline fours employ one-piece case/cylinder construction. Iannucci Collection/John Owens Studio

is the slope of the velocity curve at each point), you will find something very interesting. The acceleration applied to accelerate the valve upward initially and, at the end, to decelerate it onto its seat is much greater (typically three times) than the acceleration that slows the fast-lifting valve, stops it, and then re-accelerates it back downward. Engineers thus say that "cam-controlled acceleration" can safely be much higher than "spring-controlled acceleration." It makes perfect sense because, while the force of the spring is limited, the cam can exert much greater force.

AIR-COOLED HEADS

When you pick up an air-cooled head, the first thing that strikes you is its weight. These things are *heavy!* In contrast, a water-cooled head is very light. The reason for the difference is that, in the first case, the heat path is made of aluminum, which weighs three times more than water. An air-cooled head has to directly conduct heat away from the hottest parts (around the exhaust valve/port, and above the combustion chamber) to someplace where fins can be constructed. Making the heat path thick enough to do the job is heavy.

Sit awhile with your air-cooled head, perhaps with a cup of coffee. You may notice that there are places where the spaces between the fins are partly blocked by casting flash. There may also be cooling air holes here and there, intended to bring air to the very hot region between the cam covers, directly over the combustion chambers. These holes (not all engines have them) are commonly full of casting flash, enough in some cases to block them completely. Take the die grinder or file and remove all obstacles to flow.

CHAPTER 9
TRANSMISSION, CLUTCH, AND FINAL DRIVE

GEARBOXES

Power passes from your engine via the primary gears (older engines used chains) to the gearbox, where it passes through another pair of gears to reach the output sprocket. A chain drive takes power to the rear wheel. Each mesh of gears, and each chain drive causes a typical loss of 2–3 percent, so we have a 6–10 percent power loss from the engine to the rear wheel.

The purpose of the gearbox is, of course, to allow the engine to operate in the rpm range in which it makes useful power, while vehicle speed covers the range from zero to some highly illegal top speed. As engines have been progressively tuned to make more power over a narrower range, and as top speeds have risen with increased power, there has naturally been a need for more gearbox speeds. Early bikes had one speed, and two speeds arrived in last century's teen years. Three speeds were usual for American motorcycles for decades, while European types, driven by taxation and fuel cost to smaller, higher revving engines, normally had four speeds until the 1970s. Race bikes have been built with as many as 12 to 18 speeds, but the Federation Internationale de Motorcyclisme (FIM) decided at the end of 1968 to limit all to six speeds, and as a result, production bikes, too, have settled on that number. That's pretty much where the matter rests at the moment. Because bigger engines generally have wider power, 1,100-class machines occasionally have only five speeds, but six is the common number today.

RATIO SPREAD

You can get some idea of the intended use of a given transmission by computing its ratio spread. To get this number, divide sixth ratio into first. Roadracing gearboxes will typically give numbers between 1.9 and 2.25. Sporting road-bike gearboxes extend from the 2.25 range upward, with bigger engines getting smaller numbers and smaller engines getting bigger numbers. Big engines with their generous torque don't need as much reduction in first gear to pull away from a stop.

Wide-ratio gearboxes, with ratio spreads up around 3.0, are found in trials bikes, which have to spin their engines at useful speeds at a slow walk, so they can do amazing things like climb over house-sized boulders yet still offer a reasonable road speed.

Some tour bikes will have an abnormally large spacing to top gear, which is intended to reduce engine revs significantly, easing the pain of droning across Nebraska or similar stretches.

Sportbike gearboxes have successively smaller splits all the way up the gearbox. This is because aero drag is large near top speed, so engine revs can't be allowed to fall far enough so that there isn't power to accelerate in the next gear.

HOW GEARBOXES WORK

Almost all modern motorcycle gearboxes operate on the indirect, constant-mesh principle. Indirect means that power enters on one shaft and exits from the other, always passing through one of the five or six gear pairs. Constant mesh means that all gear pairs remain in mesh. Selection of a particular pair to carry the drive is accomplished by making that pair the only pair in the box, both of whose gears are locked to their respective shafts. Of the pairs not engaged, one gear is always free-spinning on the shaft. Shifting is not accomplished by cramming precisely formed gear-tooth profiles into and out

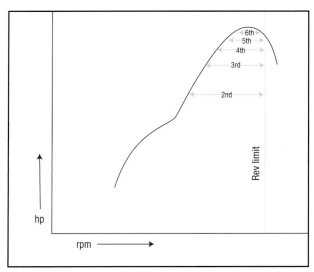

Gearbox Ratio Separations. *This is a typical power curve, showing how the wider ratio separations of the lower gears pull engine revs and power down further than the closer separations of the top gears. If all ratios were as close as fifth and sixth, average horsepower would be higher in all gears, but you would need more gearbox ratios to cover the speed range from clutch start to top end. Why not? Racers would if the rules allowed it, but on the street, you'd never stop shifting. Also, the bike needs maximum power most near top speed, so the ratio separations are made narrower as you go up the gearbox.*

of mesh. Instead, the end-faces of gears are provided with rings of heavy pegs, called dogs. Thus, the ends of gears resemble the crenelated towers of medieval castles. Of any given meshing gear pair, one gear will be free-spinning, and the other splined. To select that pair to transmit power, the free-spinning gear must be dogged to the shaft by sliding an adjacent splined gear or dog-ring against it, so that their dog sets engage. The gears that slide in this way do not move far enough for their teeth to go out of mesh with their mating gear—the motion is only 5mm or so. Now both gears are locked to their respective shafts, and power can be transmitted through them, from the clutch shaft to the output shaft.

Naturally, only one pair can be permitted to engage at a time, otherwise the dreaded double engagement could occur and lock the transmission. Professional riders dread transmission problems, especially on a speedbowl, because such a lockup cannot be released by pulling the clutch.

The engagement and disengagement of all gears is taken care of by a shift drum or plate with wiggly slots milled into it. As this drum or plate is rotated from one detent position to the next by the shift linkage, it drives shift forks this way and that by engagement of their guide pins into the wiggly slots. Because of the way the slots are cut, it is normally impossible for two gears to be selected at once. To hold the transmission in a given gear, the shift drum or plate is equipped with a detent device. This usually takes the form of a circle of bumps machined onto one end of the shift drum, or onto a detent ring attached to the drum. They are engaged by either a spring-loaded plunger or pivoted arm. The act of shifting causes the shift linkage to rotate the drum or plate from one detent position to the next.

Early shift drums rotated metal-to-metal in bored holes in the cases, but recent designs invariably incorporate rolling bearings to reduce shifting friction. There is one detent position (valley) for each gearbox ratio, and there is an extra but shallower detent for neutral, normally located between first and second (normal or racing-style). If the clutch drags (warped plates, insufficient lift), it is typically quite hard to select neutral with the engine running as you dab up and down, with the shift drum jumping between two deep detents, never stopping at the shallow neutral detent between them. Frustrating.

GATE VERSUS SEQUENTIAL

Traditional manual-shift auto transmissions are of the so-called gate type, which means that the shift lever moves not only back and forth, but also sideways, as in the "H-plus reverse" used on a typical four speed. With a gate shift, you can shift directly from any ratio to any other—what computer people would call "random access." Motorcycle transmissions and the latest auto-racing gearboxes, however, are of the sequential type, meaning that to get from first to sixth, you must shift through every ratio in between (serial access). The advantage of a sequential gearbox is that you have only two possible motions—upshift and downshift—and this makes

Gearbox, Shift Drum, and Forks. *This gearbox is a real antique (Kawasaki H2R race bike, 1972–1974), but the principles are timeless. Each shift fork is driven by a wiggly track in the drum, via a peg or pin. Each shift fork controls the position of a gear that can slide endwise on the shaft's splines. All gear pairs are constantly in mesh, but only the pair that is driving has both of its gears locked to their respective shafts. Free-spinning gears are engaged by moving the dogs of an adjacent splined gear into engagement with its dogs.* John Owens Studio

shifting faster. When you release the shift lever, it always returns to the same position.

The motion of the motorcyclist's foot acts on a shift pedal, which is connected to the shift shaft either directly, or through a linkage. Direct is nice because it is simple and there is no linkage either to fall apart or be maladjusted so it binds. Unfortunately, the rider's toe isn't always within range of a shift pedal of reasonable length, so linkage is usually used, especially now that vertically stacked gearbox shafts have pushed the shift mechanism—and the shift shaft—to a high position. Long direct shift pedals can sometimes vibrate so badly that they either break off after a while, or break off the shift shaft (especially likely if there is a circlip groove in the shaft). Very commonly, the shift pedal or the linkage is loose on the shift-shaft's spline. When this is so, engine vibration plus dirt act together to make the connection looser and looser, so your shifts become sloppier over time. Keep the connection tight. On occasion, homemade shift linkages have been made so heavy that when the bike hits a good bump, the pedal inertia shifts the gearbox. As our Japanese technician at Kawasaki used to say: "Bad effect."

The shift shaft is always returned to its position by a scissor spring inside the case. The pedal always returns to the same place—it doesn't have a different position for each gear. When you move your foot and the shift shaft rotates slightly, this motion is transmitted to the shift drum by either an arm with a hook on the end of it, engaging a ring of pins on the end of the shift drum, or a sector gear and a ratchet that fits *into* the end of the shift drum. Both systems and their variants can be made to work well. There are stops provided in the mechanism, such that only enough motion is permitted to index the shift drum by one detent position. Obviously, if this travel-limiter feature gives too little throw, the shift drum won't reach the next gear, and if it gives too much, a vigorous shift may whack the drum *past* the next position. Typically, the correct amount of shifter travel brings the drum *almost*, but not quite all the way, to the next detent position, allowing the detent to complete the last millimeter of motion. If the shift mechanism pulled the drum all the way to the detent position, there would be no deceleration zone in which the momentum of a fast shift could dissipate, and such a shift might then whirl the drum past the detent position into a false neutral beyond it.

A good many shifting problems arise from external linkage—either because it is in an awkward position for the human foot, or because the linkage binds before the shift drum has completed its movement. Common sense rectifies such troubles after inspection.

Other kinds of trouble can be fixed by attending to the mechanism inside the primary cover, which transmits the motion from shift shaft to shift drum. Unfortunately, still other kinds of shifting trouble require splitting the cases to

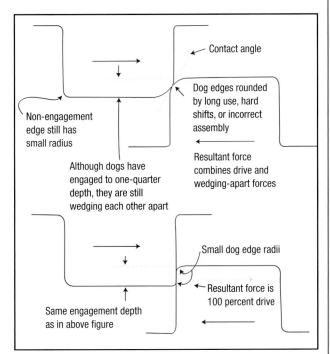

Gearbox Dog Engagement. *In the top figure, dogs with rounded edges hit each other at a large contact angle, showing that they are generating a strong wedging-apart force even when engaged to one-quarter of their total depth. This tries to kick the gears apart, making the gearbox "jump" rather than complete the shift and transmit torque normally. Jumping further damages the dogs. In the bottom figure, engagement depth is the same, but with unrounded dogs the contact angle is zero, indicating zero wedging-apart force. This shift is transmitting torque.*

get at the gears themselves. I don't intend this section to be a how-to, just an appreciation of what causes what and how it all works. Don't read it if it makes you nervous.

Inside the gearbox itself lie other mysteries. The free-spinning gears are located on the shafts by means of circlips and selective-fit spacer washers of various thicknesses. The idea is to locate the gears and shafts endwise so that:

(a) when in neutral, even if you pull the closest pair of dogs toward each other, taking up all clearances, they still miss, and

(b) when in any gear, the engaged dogs can be bottomed against each other without exerting pressure on the shift fork that is involved.

Item *(a)* ensures that you cannot have a double engagement, and item *(b)* ensures that full engagement can occur without the gear pulling on the shift fork and possibly friction-burning it. Many, many streetbike transmission shift forks are found to be burned and/or bent.

How can a gear pull endwise? Street transmissions usually have straight dogs that do not pull when they are transmitting torque, but racing and some sports gearboxes have *undercut dogs*, the intention of which is that they will pull themselves into engagement once they make any contact during a shift. Undercut *dogs* will pull, which is why it's important that mating pairs be able to bottom without bearing hard on a shift fork as they do so. One item usually found in a factory race shop is a set of cases that have been cut away so that gear dog engagement depth can be checked visually. Some aftermarket outfits offer a dog undercutting service.

An experienced gearbox specialist can usually make a balky transmission shift slickly, but there aren't too many people who want to tackle this kind of work. Suffice to say that everywhere in the shifting mechanism where there is friction, surfaces get polished. Dogs get surfaced to prevent tool marks on their ends from locking a gear pair together during a shift. If, during the shift, the dog sets hit dog-to-space, you get a good shift, but if they hit dog-on-dog, those tool marks may prevent the dogs from sliding off each other and dropping into engagement (half-shifting). Racing gearboxes are remarkably loosely fitted, to allow the parts to "seek their own positions." To this end, gears are often lapped onto their shafts with abrasive powder, eliminating tool marks and reducing shifting friction.

Gearbox shafts are located endwise by the drawing-up of the nuts holding on the clutch and the output sprocket. If either nut is loose, a shaft may move endwise, carrying all the free-spin gears on it to new, accidental locations, while those locked to the shift drum by shift forks stay where they are. The result can be incorrect dog engagement depths and bad shifting. It sometimes happens that as an engine is assembled, the builder fails to check for normal shifting at every step. Then as the sprocket or clutch nut is tightened, the gearbox suddenly fails to shift normally—and the engine must be completely disassembled again to correct the problem. I really hate it when I hear the first birds begin to chirp at 4 a.m.

How Gears Are Located on Transmission Shafts.
Only three gears are shown for clarity, but three types of location are illustrated: (a) *On the far right, a free-spinning gear is located against a shaft shoulder and shim on its left face, while its right face bears against another shim and a shaft-support bearing that is pegged or snap-ring located to the crankcase. The gear's longitudinal position can be adjusted by changing the thickness of the locating shims.* (b) *In the center is a gear splined to the shaft, located longitudinally by the shift fork, riding in the groove shown.* (c) *On the left is another free-spinning gear, located between shaft circlips and selective-fit shims.*

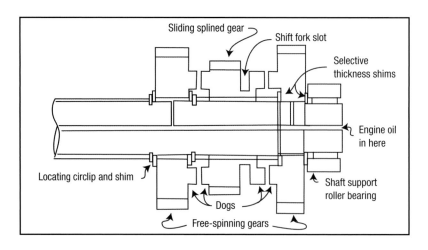

If a bike has been crashed (always assume any used bike has been), there's a good chance that the end of the shift shaft has taken a whack and is possibly bent. This can, on occasion, make the shaft hang up or be stiff somewhere in its travel. Check this by moving the shifter with your hand, which is more sensitive than your foot. Don't expect the gearbox to shift nicely when the engine and rear wheel aren't spinning, because some dogs will hit dog-on-dog.

GEARBOX FEAR

It's normal to regard the gearbox as a bit of a mystery, something better left to the experts. But if you are going to have your engine apart yourself, you might as well take this valuable opportunity to examine the gearbox for the most common faults. First of all, when you drain the oil, display normal curiosity as to how it looks. The last thing you want is shimmering layers of tiny metal particles in the drain oil, or chunky bits on the drain-plug magnet (if any). As you remove the gearset, be careful that no shims, bearings, or gears drop off the shaft ends. Let the assembly drain for a while, then take it to a strong light. Slowly turning the shaft, look deliberately at each tooth face. Normally, in a run-in gearbox, they will be reasonably shiny and smooth, but may show some tool marks parallel with the shafts. What you don't want to see are pits—areas in which the tooth surface has crushed off, leaving irregular cavities.

Usually, first gear pair is at one end of the shafts, second at the other. On the countershaft, second gear will be the second-largest gear on the shaft. Look with special care at the dogs that engage second (they are on the free-spin gear of the pair). If the dog corners look reasonably square, like those on other gears, well and good. But if they are getting round and shiny, think about how your bike has been shifting; has it refused second, or jumped in and out of second? The first-to-second shift is the most likely to produce problems, but the other dogs should get scrutiny also.

Eyeball the circlips and shims holding the gears in position on the shaft. Are any burnt blue or coned? Now examine the shift forks in the case half; dark discoloration indicates an abnormal thrust condition.

Free-spin gears should turn easily on the shaft, and splined gears should slide endwise without resistance.

Many are those who have reassembled their own engines without being sure that all gearbox bearings are properly oriented, located on their C-rings or fitted over any anti-rotation dowels that may be present. When the case bolts are done up, the dowels deform the bearings and the gearbox becomes stiff. When they find out what they've done, they almost can't believe it. This is worth avoiding. There is no dishonor in having and reading the service manual. Common sense and a careful last look before closing the cases prevent most screw-ups.

TRANSMISSION BACKLASH

A common complaint of magazine editors is "too much transmission backlash." These comfort-oriented persons seem to want to be able to roll the throttle on and off without feeling a big *clunk* as the angular dog-to-dog backlash is taken up, forward and backwards. But a sports or racing gearbox needs to have big spaces between dogs to increase the chance that, during any shift, the engagement will be dog-to-space, allowing the shift to be completed quickly. Such gearboxes, therefore, typically have three dogs per set, while street boxes will have five or six, with little narrow spaces between, barely big enough for the dogs to engage. In fact, for many years, racers converting street equipment for competition typically used to cut out every other dog, using an abrasive cutoff wheel, to make their gearboxes shift faster. Therefore, don't be a moaner. If you want low backlash, buy a gross touring bike and spend your time rolling the throttle on and off so you can enjoy it. Otherwise, know that backlash is part of having a fast-shifting gearbox.

The all-this-and-heaven-too people have an answer to this. Some street gearboxes are made with six dogs, but with every other one cut down to half height. This allows a big space for rapid engagement, but small backlash once the dogs are fully engaged.

Back in the 1930s some motorcycle gearboxes were made in the so-called sliding-gear style, in which gear teeth did actually crash into and out of engagement—effectively using them as dogs. That was probably OK as long as riding was a calm and gentlemanly undertaking, and shifting was performed with a hand lever. Not any more.

Even with proper dogs, problems can arise. If engagement depth is too little or the shifting is done sluggishly, as the dogs hit corner-to-corner, enough rounding-off can occur that eventually the dogs will jump once or twice before they engage. As you ride, this process rounds the dogs more and more, so the jumping gets worse until, finally, the box won't stay in that gear on full throttle any more. If you have *any* jumping, especially on the difficult first-to-second shift (difficult because it has the maximum speed difference, so the shift is most likely to give trouble), attend to it at once rather than waiting for it to get worse and worse. Dogs jumping past each other generate enormous end-thrust, the common result of which is to burn the shim washers that are locating the gears and even pop their circlips out of their grooves, or bend the shift forks. Fixing any of this is split-the-cases time. It won't fix itself.

As options, there exist close-ratio gearsets and various kinds of drag-racing gearboxes. Close-ratio gears are for roadracing and achieve their closeness by raising the lower gear ratios. The result is a much taller first gear than you'd find in a street transmission. This is a pain on the street, perhaps too much to bear. The drag trannies may have beefier gears with fewer ratios, intended to prevent failures with big modified engines. They may also include an "automatic" feature, in which the next gear pair can be engaged *without* first disengaging the pair that are driving. This is accomplished by cutting the backsides of the gear dogs at a 45 degree angle, so that when back-torque comes on the pair that is no longer needed, the pair kicks itself out of engagement automatically. The shift drum is slotted to permit this auto-kick-out action. The idea is to save the time that would otherwise be wasted while waiting for the disengagement to be accomplished by the shift drum. Obviously, such a gizmo is out of place on the street, where it would be kicking itself out of engagement every time you rolled off the throttle. But you see wheelie bars and slicks on the street, so I'm sure somebody, somewhere, is running a drag automatic on the street, too.

Race bikes began to employ "cassette" gearbox construction in the 1960s. This allows all gearbox internals to be removed from one end without splitting the engine cases, as well as relatively quick trackside tailoring of individual

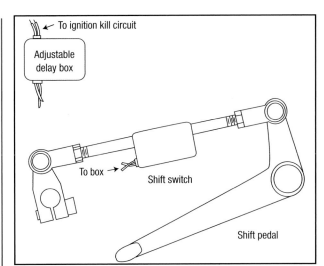

A Shifter Switch. *For years, time-conscious riders have upshifted without the clutch, sometimes easing the engagement with the kill switch, sometimes not. A shifter switch is a fancy automatic kill switch that triggers a timer (often adjustable), which cuts off the engine's ignition for a certain number of milliseconds during upshifts. Makers and some users claim such devices, correctly set, can save two or more tenths of a second per lap in circuit racing.*

ratios to the needs of a given rider or circuit. Today, some premium sports motorcycles have this feature as well. Giacomo Agostini became accustomed early to being able to alter any ratio by as little as 150 rpm, as a means of tailoring the gearbox to the needs of acceleration off particular turns. Racers dislike hovering just below the power for three-quarters of a second in some corner, just because one gearbox ratio forces them to do so. Cassette construction also enables your transmission to cost beaucoup bucks, too, because three to six alternate ratios for each of six speeds cause the bottom line to grow. All in the name of fun.

CLUTCHLESS SHIFTING AND POWER SHIFTING

For many years it has been standard practice in roadracing to make upshifts without the clutch—just dab the shifter with perhaps a slight wrist motion to relieve the engine torque enough to let the gears move more easily. Some people used the kill button for this function. The idea was to save time and, in some cases, to save clutches that were shaky. Today, we have the shifter switch. As your foot begins the upshift motion, a switch in the shift linkage turns off the engine's ignition for a programmed length of time—just long enough to bang through

A Spalled Gear Tooth. *Why do experienced builders look at every tooth of every gear? To find things like this. This condition will only get worse, leading to complete failure. Remember that pulling the clutch doesn't release a gearbox lockup. This condition began with a little row of pits along the pitch line of the tooth—a line parallel with the shaft and about two-thirds of the way down from the tooth tip. Sometimes the pits polish out, sometimes they get bigger and the part has to be replaced.* John Owens Studio

the shift. Nearly every race bike now uses such a switch.

Power shifting is the antique practice of using the clutch for the upshift, but without closing the throttle or using the kill button during the shift. This causes the engine to rev up momentarily as the shift is made. Will this float the valves? Will it get you into the rev limiter? The idea of this is to keep engine power on, not wasting the power it could make during the time the throttle is snapped during the upshift. By keeping the throttle open, engine power goes into the flywheel mass of the crank and is then, so the theory goes, applied to the rear wheel when the clutch engages again. I think it's stupid, personally, having the engine sound go "weeoo" between gears, indicating extra, unnecessary strain on valvetrain and clutch. You decide.

FINAL DRIVE

Yes, you can often give your bike more out-of-the-hole grunt by use of a smaller front sprocket or a larger rear one—but it causes your engine to spin proportionally faster in all gears. Choice of gearing is always a compromise. At Daytona, for example, you might expect race bikes to be geared to produce maximum bowl speed at peak-horsepower rpm. This is not usually done because acceleration through the infield can benefit lap time much more. The fastest lap time (as opposed to radar-gun speed) is achieved with a gearing that overrevs the engine somewhat past start-finish, in return for that acceleration improvement in lower gears.

Likewise, you can gear your bike up and may achieve a slightly higher top speed by doing so—provided there isn't a headwind the day you try it.

What will you get from a gearing change? Suppose you change from a 16-tooth countershaft sprocket to a 15. This will reduce top speed by straight proportion—in this case 15 divided by 16, which is 0.9375. If your previous top speed was 140 miles per hour, your new speed will be of the order of 0.9375 x 140 = 131 miles per hour.

Or you can estimate these things in your head with fair accuracy. A 1-tooth change out of 16 is 1 part in 16, or about 7 percent. Now 7 percent of 140 is about 10, so the speed reduction by this rough method would be 10 miles per hour, to 130. Pretty close.

Same rules apply at the back. Suppose you have a 46-tooth rear sprocket and your current top speed is 140, but you want to estimate what your speed would be at the same engine rpm, but with 2 fewer teeth (44). Two parts in 46 is 1 in 23, or about halfway between 4 percent (1 in 25) and 5 percent (1 in 20), so a 4.5 percent speed gain would be 4.5 times 1.4 miles per hour, or about 7 miles per hour (actual answer is 146.36 miles per hour).

If you don't enjoy such games, just drag out the trusty calculator and get the exact answer by proportion. Remember that you won't get exactly the changes that you calculate in most cases, so umpteen-decimal-place accuracy is beside the point. Often, for example, a stock bike will be geared to keep the engine well away from the rev-limiter and the warranty department when maxed-out in top gear. It may turn out that, by putting one more tooth on the back, the engine will rev up to where it can make more power and will actually go faster, not slower as the numbers would indicate. It all depends on where you are beginning. Experiment is the order of the day.

Never underestimate the wind. When Kawasaki read the AMA rule book in 1975, it said nothing about number of gearbox speeds, so the Akashi company built a seven-speed gearbox for its KR250, just for use at Daytona. The idea was that as the Florida land-breeze/sea-breeze duel made up its fickle mind, the rider could pull sixth against the wind, and seventh with the wind. The two ratios were only 3 percent apart.

When thinking about gearing and speed, remember that power requirement goes up faster than does aerodynamic drag. Aero *drag force* increases as the square of the speed, but the *power* to push that drag includes another speed factor, making power requirement increase as the *cube* of the speed. That being so, in still air, to boost the speed of a correctly geared machine making 140 miles per hour by 5 miles per hour would require 11 percent more power (145/140 cubed). It's hard to just pull another 11 percent more peak power out of a jet change, but it is very common for the wind to change that much between one practice and the next. Many a dismal ride at Daytona or other high-speed tracks has been caused by estimating incorrectly the possible effects of wind changes. When you're geared wrong at Daytona, you're *really* wrong—having to change down to fifth upwind, being lost in the infield, and so on.

What is top speed? We all went through the stage of being fascinated by the gearing on our bicycles—gosh, if I keep putting smaller and smaller sprockets on the back, and bigger ones on the front, I could go a hundred miles an hour! The fallacy in this reasoning is that the enthusiastic child pushing the pedals around can produce only so much horsepower, and that power can only push the vehicle so fast.

The same is true of a motorcycle, even though its power is much greater; gearing up beyond the maximum attainable speed just pulls engine rpm down, causing you to go slower than before. The vehicle's resistance can be shown as a rising curve that, at any point, is the sum of aero drag and rolling resistance. At the same time, we can also make graphs of the rear-wheel thrust produced by the engine in each gear. At some point, the resistance curve and thrust curve cross (become equal). This is the maximum speed attainable. Below the crossing point, there is an excess of engine thrust after resistance is subtracted. This is the net power available to produce acceleration—and it can be pretty small at high speed, which is why you can stare at the tach for long seconds near top speed, unsure as to whether or not it is still creeping upward. If you have a headwind, this raises the resistance curve—perhaps enough that the engine can no longer pull sixth gear, and you must shift down.

In practice, people don't consult resistance curves, they just try a little taller gear the next session to see if the engine will pull it. Here another word of caution; even at Daytona with its high-speed bowl, the peak revs you see as you brake

Aftermarket Sprockets. *This nice-looking color-matched sprocket and chain is on Roger Lee Hayden's Kawasaki. Stock sportbike chain is often a heavy 630, and switching to the GP bike 520 size saves weight. After installing sprockets and chain, always spin the back wheel to check for out-of-round sprockets; the top chain run should not move up and down. Check for out-of-line by laying a straightedge against the face of the rear sprocket; it should slide right onto the face of the front sprocket.* Brian J. Nelson

for turn one or for the chicane are not just the result of the power of your engine and the gearing you have chosen. The competitive edge depends upon how fast you get launched out of the chicane or . . . what are they calling it now? Turn eight? Anyway, the new left onto the back straight. A sluggish corner speed or late acceleration will show up as a several-hundred rpm deficit at the far end, and you'll be looking at a lot of seat backs. Engines are great, but they need all the help you can give them. High exit speed and strong early acceleration give you a boost that helps all the way to the next brake point.

Another gearing question revolves around which gears to use on tracks that don't use all six (except for the start). In this case, you might have a choice of gearing to use first through fourth, second through fifth, or third through sixth. The farther up the box you go, the closer the ratios are to each other. Now how do you decide? You sit and think about your revs coming out of each corner. The most crucial thing is never to allow yourself to sit in a corner, stuck just below the torque threshold, with your engine making a sickly moan, while others, geared to spin in their powerbands, easily leave you for dead. Another consideration is the number of shifts per lap. Every shift entails a time loss, so the fewer the better. Sometimes the closer, upper gears give you a better match, while other times the wider spaced, lower gears do the job. Sometimes, a particular gearing puts one or more shifts where you can't make them—with the shift pedal on the ground. This requires thought, too. Is it better to scream the engine by holding the lower gear (Freddy

Spencer style), or to upshift early and take the penalty of lower acceleration? It depends on who's paying the bills.

Sometimes gearing and riding style are mingled. Gary Nixon, on shorter tracks, liked to gear short, then rush up beside other riders on the inside, pushing them off-line and taking away their concentration. Then he would brake to a lower speed, turn sharply, and recover on the superior acceleration that his short gearing gave him. This might not be the fastest way around the *track*, but he often made it the fastest way around *other riders*. There are quite a few riders whose style is based upon not having to race with anyone—they draw these beautiful high-speed lines in corners and gear for that high speed. Then along comes the Gary Nixon style and messes up all that beautiful geometry with actual in-your-face *racing*.

Dale Singleton expected that, in the heat of battle, he would drop 1 1/2 seconds off his lap time. To compensate, he would intentionally overgear with the expectation that in the race and running faster, his off-corner acceleration rpm would be about right. It is professional to be able to run race speeds in practice, but not everyone can do this at will, so the idea is presented for what it's worth. Once, at a backwards Loudon AMA National (the so-called Noduol events), Singleton overdid it and spent the race droning, trying to get off corners with his engine turning just below the torque threshold.

Another possible application for overgearing comes when you know your bike is down on horsepower but not so far down that you can't stay in the faster machines' draft. You may therefore gear for the draft and hope you aren't dropped by the fast guys and have to run on your own. Sometimes it works.

Sprockets and chains are discussed elsewhere in this volume. A lot of force is exerted in first gear, and this large force can cause front sprocket nuts to loosen and rear sprocket bolts or studs to stretch and become loose. Inspect these heavily loaded parts from time to time. I have seen loose sprocket bolts break as a result of assuming they were tight.

Chains used to be a high-maintenance item in racing, but the coming of "permanently lubricated" (O-ring-sealed) chain has helped a lot. Despite this, race teams replace chains often. All riders should keep track of chain mileage and be on the lookout for the kinking that indicates a chain is stiffening up.

CLUTCHES

Sportbike clutches are multi-plate, made up of a stack of alternating steel plates (steels) and plates faced on both sides with some kind of friction material (frictions). The frictions have driving tabs on their outside diameters (OD) and are driven by the clutch outer basket, which is connected through the primary gear to the engine. The steels have driving splines on their inside diameters (ID) and engage similar splines on the clutch inner hub, which is secured to the gearbox input shaft. The plate stack is compressed by either a circle of small coil springs or a single diaphragm spring. The clutch spring(s) exert their pressure against a pressure plate, which takes the form of the top plate in the stack. A throwout mechanism is provided to lift the pressure plate against spring pressure, decoupling the engine from the gearbox. You will notice that the plates are radially very narrow. The reason is the same that causes front brake discs to have the same appearance. If the OD is much bigger than the ID, the heating rate there during slip will be much higher than it is at the ID, and the plates will strongly tend to cone. Since spring pressure is trying to hold them flat, coned clutch plates respond by either dragging or cracking. Having more but narrower plates, of larger diameter, has made clutches more durable.

With the engine running and gearbox in neutral, steels and frictions spin together, held against one another by the springs. When you're ready to go, you pull the clutch lever, lifting the clutch pressure plate a millimeter or so. Then you clunk the gearbox into first. You hear a noticeable "chunk" as you do this, because the spinning mass of the clutch steel plates and the clutch inner hub is suddenly stopped by being locked to the countershaft by the engagement of first gear. Indeed, if the engine is cold and the plates are stuck together with gooey oil, the act of engaging first may even stall the engine because the plates don't unstick easily. On some engines, steel or rubber springs separate the plates when the rider pulls the clutch lever in order to prevent this.

The outer basket, carrying the friction discs, is now spinning, while the inner hub, carrying the steels, is stationary. There is some friction-to-steel drag nevertheless, because the plates are so close and the assembly is exposed to oil. This generates heat the longer you hold the clutch disengaged—sometimes enough in competition situations to cause the plates to expand, drag even more, and begin to drag the bike forward. This is why it's a good idea to avoid holding the clutch lifted, with the transmission in gear, any longer than strictly necessary.

The clutch has to transmit engine torque, multiplied by the primary ratio, with some safety factor. The springs are fitted at a certain free length and installed height, giving a certain design pressure against the pressure plate. This pressure drops over time because:

1. The springs lose free length, especially if the clutch is severely overheated.

2. As the plate stack wears, it becomes thinner, allowing the springs to expand slightly, again losing pressure.

To complicate the matter, some owners adjust their clutch levers to disengage very high (early in the lever pull). When parts expand with heat, this may result in the throwout exerting pressure even when no fingers are grasping the lever. The result is some loss of clutch grip, or slippage. This is why a clutch play adjuster is normally located at the hand lever—so you can, if necessary, adjust this on the fly. Another possible grim development is that, as a result of wear or fitting incorrect clutch plates, the plate stack may become so short that the pressure plate sinks low enough to contact the face of the clutch inner hub. This, obviously, causes loss of spring pressure on the plate stack, and loss of torque capacity.

When you soup up your engine, your clutch may get left behind by the increased torque. Clutch slippage is felt most prominently in top gear, where you will hear the engine note

rise unnaturally fast, then drop as you roll off throttle. A variety of kits and other parts are made to correct this problem:

1. Stronger clutch springs, which may or may not be objectionable to your left hand.

2. More durable friction plates, possibly faced with material of higher friction coefficient; in years past, some streetbikes have been fitted with plastic friction discs that broke up under hard usage.

3. A complete clutch stack, whose individual plates are made thinner so that one extra friction disc can be fitted; since a typical clutch has six friction plates or so, this gives a 17 percent improvement in torque capacity, even with stock springs.

Stock clutch throwouts are sometimes pretty basic—just a rod and ball pressing against the pressure plate pusher (I call this part the "mushroom"). Rotation is accommodated at the ball, which survives in engine oil, at stock spring pressure. But with stronger springs, these parts love to weld together (I've seen astonished novices pull out their entire throwout stack—rods, ball, and mushroom, all friction-welded into a rapier-like stick), so the aftermarket offers roller throwout bearings that are more durable.

In some cases, the clutch outer basket splines are made as free-standing fingers, and engine torque tends to spread these fingers. The aftermarket may supply a band to enclose and support the tips of these fingers, or even whole baskets of greater strength, to contain the power of up-rated engines.

HYDRAULIC CLUTCHES

Many sportbikes have been built with hydraulic, rather than cable-operated, clutch throwouts, but so many riders dislike the feel of the hydraulic type that the aftermarket now makes cable conversion kits. If you have difficulty getting smoothly off the line with a hydraulic setup, consider a cable conversion.

CLUTCH INSPECTION

When disassembling a clutch, I like to inspect all the plates for warping, cracking, or breakage. As I take the plates out, I stack steels and frictions separately, then solvent-clean all. Taking a pair of steels, I hold them between thumb and forefinger at one point. If I see no light between the discs, I turn over the top disc and try again. This is the test for coning. A coned disc will stand away from the disc with which it is paired. Go through the pile in this way, inspecting visually at the same time. Take frictions in both hands and twist slightly. This reveals cracks as the crack edges make a sound when twisted. Inspect visually for missing friction material and discoloration. When a wet clutch is used hard, most of the heat goes into the steels, because the frictions are insulated by their organic facing. Thus, it is the steels which become heat discolored (blue or actually black). If the plates remain flat, they may be used again. If they are coned, they will cause clutch drag and/or slippage.

Look up the spring free-length spec in the manual, then measure your springs. There may also be a clutch stack thickness spec. Be sure when putting the clutch back together

A Slipper Clutch. *Here you are looking at just the pressure plate of a back-torque-limiting clutch. In a normal multi-plate motorcycle clutch, one set of discs is splined to the clutch outer basket driven by the engine, while the other set is splined to the clutch inner hub, which drives the gearbox countershaft. This plate stack is forced together by springs as the rider releases the clutch lever, transmitting engine torque to the gearbox countershaft. In a back-torque-limiting or slipper clutch, there is an added element—a ramped device resembling a one-way clutch, concentric with the shaft. When the engine drives the rear wheel, the drive is solid. When the rider closes the throttle and the rear wheel drives the engine, the resulting reverse torque causes the ramped device to expand, exerting force that lifts the clutch pressure plate and softening the connection between engine and rear wheel. This prevents the dragging, hopping, or sliding-out of the rear wheel that otherwise might result from engine braking.* Hinson Clutch

that there is clearance between the pressure plate and the face of the inner hub.

DRY CLUTCHES

For many years, the dry clutch has been commonly used on roadracing machines. Because it is external and requires no oil drain for service, it is convenient. Because its release is very clean rather than viscous and resisting, it was ideal in the days of push-start races (which at GP level ended in 1984).

SLIPPER CLUTCHES

When you close the throttle on a big four-stroke as you brake for a corner, you are reversing the normal relation between engine and rear wheel. Under power, the engine drives the rear wheel, but with throttle closed, it is the rear wheel which drives the engine. The engine resists being turned in this way because it has mechanical friction—typically 15 percent of power at that rpm.

This adds up to quite a few horsepower—enough to sometimes drag the back tire, cause rear wheel hop, or make the back end of the bike slide out as you lean over into the turn. The

Pinch Test for Coned Clutch Discs. *Take a pair of plates and pinch each plate at one point. If both plates lie flat, turn over the top one and pinch again (if they are both coned the same way, they will lie flat one way and stand apart, as in this photo, when one disc is flipped over). If they lie flat both ways, they are flat. Check for cracking and blue discoloration as well.* John Owens Studio

bigger the engine, the bigger this engine braking problem becomes. It was the biggest single problem that riders and engineers faced in the first two years of MotoGP racing under the 990cc formula.

The first technology for dealing with this was the back-torque-limiting, or "slipper," clutch, developed in the 1980s for Honda's special FWS Daytona V4, and has since been widely adopted in Superbike. In the most common type, a ramped coupling—looking much like a one-way ratchet—connects the clutch inner hub to the gearbox countershaft. When the engine drives the rear wheel, the drive is solid. When the rear wheel drives the engine, the ramps are driven apart by relative rotation, and this motion is used to unload the spring pressure from the clutch stack.

More and more sportbikes have such clutches as stock.

Slipper Clutch Problems

Production bikes have electric starters, so the following is irrelevant but interesting. When the ramp angle is 45 degrees, the engine can be easily push-started or started on rollers. If the angle must be made smaller, such starting becomes iffy as the clutch self-releases. This is why some MotoGP bikes are started with an external starter, inserted through a door in the fairing—typically into a square socket in the crankshaft end.

Because the gearbox is between the rear wheel and the ramps, the force required to lift the clutch becomes greater the lower the gear you are in. This is why MotoGP bikes also have a second system to deal with engine braking—the "throttle kicker." This is a motorized throttle positioner that is controlled by the engine computer and can open the throttle to the right amount to cancel any engine braking that the slipper can't deal with. Ducati tested a system that would de-clutch when the throttle was closed and let the engine go back to idle. It would then smoothly hook up and go when the rider began to feed power. It was abandoned as unready.

The ramps of wet slipper clutches are nicely lubricated, but some dry types exist that operate through rollers. Others must be re-lubricated manually between events.

Where there is friction there is heat, so conversion to slipper operation may either shorten component life or require increased clutch capacity.

CHAPTER 10
IGNITION

Engine lore is filled with tales of secret ignitions, coils, or spark plugs that mysteriously produce massive extra power. But the fact is that a match burns the house down as well as a blowtorch. The power is in the air/fuel mixture, not in the spark. If that mixture is correct and well-mixed, it requires only a minimal spark to light it. As the late Bobby Strahlman of Champion Spark Plug liked to say, any time you get more power by changing ignition components, means you had a bad ignition to begin with. Two examples:

1. The first Femsa electronic ignitions made less and narrower power than the terrible racing magnetos they were designed to replace. Why? The magnetos' spark *duration* was too short to reliably find an ignitable zone in the mixture swirling past the plug points. Longer spark duration made the Femsa a great replacement for the mag, with much more consistent spark timing.

2. Honda's first electronic system for its big double OHC (DOHC) fours was weak. It worked best with a feeble 0.014-inch plug gap. An updated system was able to fire a 0.024-inch gap without misfire.

On my old AJS 500 single, I had to manually retard the ignition timing before kick-starting to avoid a kickback. On British twins of the 1950s and 1960s, a centrifugal advance performed this retard automatically, then advanced the timing normally once the engine accelerated. Most four-strokes ran with 36–38 degrees BTDC ignition timing.

FOUR DECADES OF IGNITION DEVELOPMENT

Ignition has come far since magnetos and points-triggered battery systems, both of which suffered from bad spark scatter (inconsistent timing caused by shaft wobble, points bounce, and rubbing-block wear). Because some early systems produced weak sparks, they tended to work best when timed to fire too early; the closer the piston comes to TDC, the higher the compression pressure, and the higher the voltage required to break down the plug gap. The next step was simple transistor-triggered systems with accurate but fixed timing (Honda adopted this in its RC-181 500 GP bike of 1967). Transistor systems sparked at the same place within a degree or less.

But as noted previously, the point of best ignition changes with throttle position and rpm. This led to development of vacuum-advance systems and, later, simple electronic ignition

Spark Plugs Large and Small. *On the right is a standard 14mmx0.680-inch reach plug, like those found in older motorcycles. The tiny item on the left is an 8mm plug developed by NGK for the extremely small cylinders of Honda's famous 250cc six. Note its heat range; in the NGK system, a No. 14 is extremely cold to compensate for the engine's high cylinder head temperature.* John Owens Studio

"curves." These came closer to an engine's real requirements, providing retarded spark to make starting easier, then bringing in necessary advance, and advancing further yet for efficient cruise during high-vacuum (part-throttle) operation. Most recently, computer-controlled ignitions can match ignition advance to even the smallest details of an engine's power curve. This is done with a so-called map. This map is electronically stored information obtained during dyno testing. Minimum timing for best torque (MBT) is determined at many rpm and load points, and the resulting data are stored on a computer chip. The disadvantage of mapped systems is that if you modify the engine, the map is no longer correct. Currently, devices like the Dynojet Power Commander III make reprogramming possible.

Modern ignition works like this. A hundred times a second or so, the ignition-control computer monitors basic variables such as engine rpm and throttle angle via a throttle position sensor (TPS). With this data in hand, it then looks up the correct ignition timing for those conditions on its

SPARK PLUG GAP TYPES

| Standard | Projected tip | Fine wire | Retracted gap | Surface gap |

(a) *Standard plug found in most applications;* (b) *projected tip exposes the gap to combustion chamber turbulence, increasing the chance that an ignitable mixture element will pass through the gap during the spark;* (c) *fine wire electrode sometimes widens the engine's firing range by reducing the voltage required to break down the gap (the same reason lightning rods are*

sharp); (d) *the R-gap plug gives the least electrode exposure, and so gives maximum insurance against preignition from an overheated plug—now used mainly in fuel dragsters;* (e) *the surface-gap plug is sometimes used with fast-rise-time ignitions because it gives best protection against gap growth as a result of spark erosion. This is the coldest of all plug constructions.*

stored map. When the crank brings a given piston to a fixed point BTDC, the computer is informed of this by a crank position sensor—but it doesn't fire the spark now. Instead, it begins counting as the crank continues to turn, until the map-specified firing point is reached. Then it fires the ignition, producing the spark. The crank position sensor is a multi-toothed wheel with a reluctance pickup that reports the passage of the teeth. Irregularities of spacing enable the computer to "know" where the crank is in its rotation. Early systems also used a cam sensor to tell the computer which cycle the engine was on. Today, this can be done by measuring the difference in crank speed between exhaust and compression, thus eliminating the cam sensor.

Not all ignitions are equally complicated. Late-model igniters have all the features, but earlier mapped ignitions monitor only rpm.

SPARK PLUGS

If the tip of the spark plug's centerwire, or the insulator nose, runs too hot (1,600 degrees Fahrenheit) during operation, it can act as an ignition source, igniting the charge before the spark (preignition) and causing engine damage. But if the porcelain insulator runs too cool (under 600 degrees Fahrenheit), carbon will accumulate on it, causing it to conduct and short out the spark current, leading to misfire. It is to avoid these two extremes that spark plugs are supplied

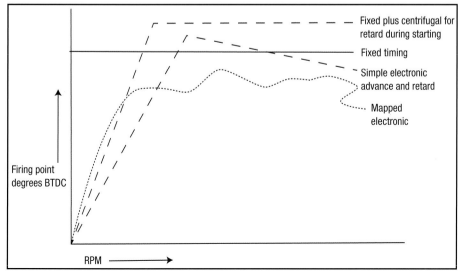

Firing point degrees BTDC

RPM

- — — — Fixed plus centrifugal for retard during starting
- —————— Fixed timing
- — · — · Simple electronic advance and retard
- ········· Mapped electronic

Evolution of Ignition Curves. *A simple magneto or points ignition had a fixed advance—same timing at all rpm—but suffered from spark scatter. To ease the starting of larger engines, a centrifugal advance unit was added next. This retarded the timing during starting to make kickback less likely, then quickly brought in full advance to hold a fixed timing out to maximum revs. Since the 1970s, simple electronic advance-retard curves have arrived, which better approximated the engine's needs. Today we have the computer-controlled mapped ignition, which supplies the engine's needs in the finest detail and with accuracy. Self-adaptive systems are next.*

Spark Discharge. *Voltage rises until the gap breaks down and begins to conduct. This is the rise time of the ignition. The prompt energy release is the so-called capacitive portion, meaning that this is energy contained in the capacitance of the ignition wire and plug. During this phase, voltage drops steeply. If there is no resistor in the plug or ignition wire, the discharge will thereafter continue at a much lower voltage (like 40 volts), operating on the inductive energy stored in the ignition coil's secondary winding. Because this phase radiates radio frequency energy that can interfere with soaps on daytime TV, resistor plugs or wires are employed to kill this long-duration part of the spark discharge.*

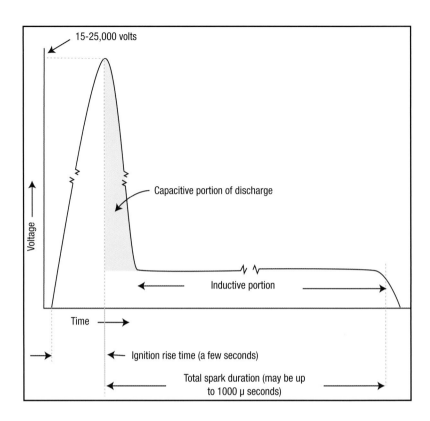

in various *heat ranges*. A hotter spark plug's insulator runs hotter in a given engine than does that of a colder plug, and you can see why—the hotter the plug, the longer and/or more slender are the insulator and centerwire, and vice versa. The farther the tip of the centerwire is from the cooler plug body, the hotter it will run in operation. To postpone centerwire overheating and broaden the heat range, the centerwire may have a copper or other highly heat-conductive core. Because sparks jump more easily from a sharp edge, some plugs are made with fine-gauge centerwires of heat-resistant materials, like platinum or iridium (nickel is standard), and you pay extra for this.

The plug recommended in your owner's manual is of a heat range worked out by experiment, but if you modify your engine, you may need to run a colder heat range to compensate for hotter average conditions in the engine (more compression, racing use, etc.). Examine the end of the centerwire with a low-power magnifier (6–10X). A new centerwire has a sheared-off end that is a bit jagged. If you see this jaggedness begin to soften at its edges after use, rather like a glass rod softens in a Bunsen flame, this indicates you should go to the next-colder heat range (and, of course, check that your timing isn't too advanced).

My vintage-racing friends have reminded me of the special plug problems of air-cooled engines. In a water-cooled engine, the spark plug has a constant heat range because it is screwed into a piece of metal (the head) that is cooled to a constant temperature. But in an air-cooled engine, the head temperature goes up and down with the air temperature and inversely with the flow of cooling air. For this reason, it may be necessary to run a colder plug heat range on a hot day than on a cold one.

Various gap designs exist for different applications. Projected-tip plugs have their gap protruding into the combustion chamber, where it can be scavenged by fresh charge. Such a plug may interfere with pistons or valves in

some engines, but its purpose is to assure clean firing and foul-resistance. A contrasting design is the old retracted-gap (R-gap) plug, formerly universal in racing. In an R-gap plug, the sidewire is either flush with the end of the shell, or is pushed radially inward through a hole in the shell, making its gap to the centerwire down inside the shell at some depth. These plugs may still be used in special applications, such as top fuel drag racing. Putting modern projected-tip, fine-wire plugs into vintage race engines that used to use R-gap plugs really wakes up their throttle response. There is progress.

New bikes tend to have stick coils that are part of the spark plug cap. Because everything that could emit radio frequency is buried down in the plug tunnels, there is no need for other measures. Older bikes needed suppression devices. Plug wires act like antennas, and spark current sends a strong signal. Many older ignitions used resistor spark plugs—plugs with an internal gap or resistor that stopped current from flowing in the ignition circuit, after the initial discharge. Only the so-called capacitive portion of the discharge was allowed to reach the plug—no long-lasting arc at the plug, driven by continuing inductive current in the coil output and plug wire. In some cases, switching from the original, stock resistor plug to a non-resistor plug will bamboozle the ignition box (Honda CBR600 F1, for example). Refer to your owner's manual for this information.

Will multiple-gap or other "trick" types of plug give dizzying performance and economy gains? No doubt a set of sharp, new trick plugs will work better than a high-mileage stock plug set, with its gaps all rounded off from thousands of miles of spark erosion. So would a new set of stock, conventional plugs. Many comparison tests are based on this illusion. Some models of Suzuki come with twin-gap plugs. Are they therefore best for all engines? Aircraft spark plugs have triple gaps; are they 50 percent better again? You know better.

Conventional plugs cover a range of prices. Why? The expensive plugs are the ones with the rare-metal fine-wire gaps, or they are plugs made in low volume for a special application. An example of the latter would be the "shorty" race plugs made for Yamaha and Honda 250 two-stroke racers, at something like $30 a pop. Otherwise, it's off to the auto-parts store where you'll pay a low, fair price for what is really a commodity item.

IGNITION ADVANCERS

There was a fad for ignition advancers. These were ignition trigger wheels for modern bikes, shifted slightly (typically 5 degrees) from stock, to advance engine timing. These often did nothing but cause hotter running—especially of spark plugs. They were based on the fuzzy idea that bigger is better, but the germ of truth in them was that stock timing at peak torque is often retarded from MBT by 1/2 degree in the interest of making spark plugs last longer. Power varies little in the close vicinity of MBT, but plug life is inversely proportional to something ridiculous like the fifth power of electrode temperature, so a little retard makes the plugs last much longer and loses almost no power. Do your own research. If it makes significantly more power on the dyno, shows quicker lap times, or ETs better at the strip, by all means use it. Speed is truth. But if it doesn't, it's just kinetic art and doesn't belong on your bike.

Drag racing may be a legitimate application for timing advancers, if the bike's compression ratio has been raised. Normally, other things being equal, a higher compression ratio would speed up combustion, but in an engine with an already fairly tight combustion chamber (modern four-valve sportbikes), the tighter combustion space produced by higher compression pistons will burn more slowly. More timing may be necessary to restore peak pressure to its proper place, about 14 degrees ATDC. Drag racers, remember, are trying very hard to get the jump in the first 50 feet, and that calls for a big tire and the torque to turn it. Compression is the key to that torque.

Back in the days of points ignitions, you set ignition timing with timing marks or with a degree wheel or piston motion gage. Then along came ignitions with a built-in advance-retard curve. You couldn't change the curve, but you could change its starting point, just as with points. When Ducati brought out its 851 twin, timing and fuel injection maps were recorded on Erasable Programmable Read-Only Memory (EPROM) chips. The stock chip came with a map that passed emissions and made decent power. For the fortunate few, there were better chips for competition-only use. Then the later in 1990s, racing systems became addressable, whether with a special box or with an ordinary laptop and USB cable.

To make your own fuel and ignition maps used to require long dyno running, holding at each 50-rpm step to find MBT and best fueling. Such information was gold! But then came such systems as Dynojet's Power Commander III, which allows this mapping process to be shortened to a few dyno pulls with the right equipment in place.

The aftermarket supplies a lot of ignition updating parts for popular older bikes. A favorite cost-cutter for production engineers is to specify dinky coils with the minimum of copper in them, so aftermarket coils wake up some of these machines. Poor or flaky coil grounding remains a fertile source of ignition mysteries. As with any computer system, connectors breed troubles. On older machines, connector pins and sockets can develop insulating corrosion layers. If, heaven forbid, your older bike's ignition is triggered by mechanical switches (dignified by the obscure name "points"), you can narrow its spark scatter a lot by finding an electronically triggered system for it.

Old ignition wires crack and some of the spark intensity may get lost along the way. Sometimes it's educational to run an engine in darkness, revealing any arcing. Another diagnostic is poor starting and operation in wet weather. Time for new wires.

Current ignition boxes include a rev-limiter function, intended to prevent mechanical damage. Engines modified to operate at higher-than-limiter speed will require that the limiter be bypassed, or that the ignition be replaced with one having its own adjustable limiter. The limiter doesn't protect you against everything. An overenthusiastic downshift will still send the revs soaring. Well-equipped dealers will have an ignition test module that simulates the engine's ignition trigger, checking your box up to limiter rpm. It also checks limiter function.

Now a word of tiresome advice, learned the hard way. If you decide to modify your bike's wiring for any reason, do the following:

1. Preserve the original color-coding by using colored wire available at any auto-parts store; I have tried to trace enough problems on bikes rewired with all-black wire.

2. Use enough length so that wired-in items can be removed and inspected.

3. Make connections with solder and shrink-tubing, or with some kind of reliable connectors; you will have nothing but grief from hastily twisted–together wires insulated with wads of electrical tape.

4. Duplicate the gauge of any wire to which you are splicing, and don't use little skinny stuff that will overheat, then melt onto the wires next to it in the bundle; no mechanic likes to see "replace and repair wire harness" scribbled on the work order, and he will get even with you if you make him do it.

5. If you are doing anything at all confusing with wiring, make notes in a notebook (not on junk mail or nearby cardboard boxes, as I do).

6. If you are removing items like headlights, disconnect wires at existing connectors if possible. That way it's much

easier to put it all back to stock when you decide to sell the bike. If the bike will be raced in some stock class, it's also much easier to explain your changes to the tech inspector (or to replace anything he says the rules require). Resist the temptation to just hack off everything (gimme those cutters!). How heavy is a little wire, anyway?

PROTECT YOUR ELECTRONICS

Anything with semiconductors in it prefers life at less-than-boiling-water temperature. It also does better away from high-frequency vibration. Even coils respond to TLC. Therefore, electronic components should be kept away from heat and vibration. It has even happened that electronics have been damaged by welding on an assembled bike.

Sometimes one thing leads to another. For example, in one case, vibration slowly destroyed the spark plug caps, which responded by developing internal arcing. This, in turn, reacted back up the line to cause coil failure. The coil failure then passed the buck (more like $300, actually) to the ignition module, causing it to become flaky. Then, of course, the sky's the limit. What are the module failure modes? Does it, for example, fail by switching mysteriously to full advance, thereby pushing your engine into detonation? The people who design these things have no idea what troubles they are foisting upon an innocent world. You just have to learn your bike's symptoms, either through bitter experience or from veterans. One of the early TZ250 Yamahas, for example, might finish a race running strong, yet absolutely refuse to start next time. In this case, a low-speed charging coil is the culprit, necessary only at lower rpm. As the coil failed, the bike ran fine on the high-speed charge coil, "proving" that nothing was wrong with the ignition, yet it then failed to start the next time. With ignition problems, you sometimes have to sit down in a quiet place and think through all the symptoms to get to the cause.

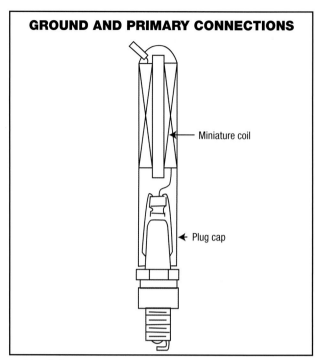

GROUND AND PRIMARY CONNECTIONS

Miniature coil

Plug cap

Ignition Coil Integrated into Plug Cap. *Recent engine designs are adopting unit coil or "stick coil" design. By eliminating radio-frequency emission from non-existent plug wires, this allows use of both capacitive and inductive portions of the ignition discharge.*

Four-valve engines have their spark plugs in the right place—the center of the combustion chamber—but two-valve engines from the 1970s and vintage bikes have often been modified with twin ignition. Addition of a second plug often allows shortening the combustion time and can set free some useful power. Look for a shop that has done the work before. You'll need double-ended coils made for just this application.

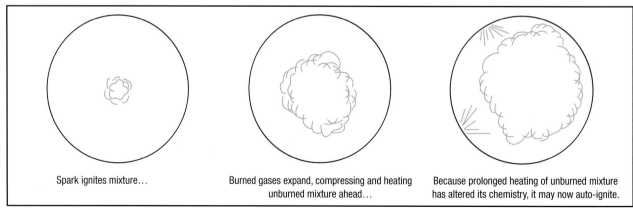

Spark ignites mixture…

Burned gases expand, compressing and heating unburned mixture ahead…

Because prolonged heating of unburned mixture has altered its chemistry, it may now auto-ignite.

Where Detonation Occurs. *Detonation is not preignition. A detonating combustion cycle begins normally with spark ignition, followed by normal flame propagation. The still-unburned fraction of the charge, heated by contact with hot engine parts, compression, and then by further compression ahead of the expanding burned gas, undergoes pre-flame chemical reactions. If this chemistry goes far enough, the altered end-gas (last part of charge to burn) can auto-ignite, or go off by itself. In its altered, hair-trigger state, it burns at the local speed of sound (very high in the hot combustion gas), generating shockwaves that we hear as knock and see on parts as detonation damage.*

CHAPTER 11
THE ELECTRONIC MOTORCYLE

LESSONS FROM MOTOGP

Let's get one thing straight before I begin: I am in favor of the use of electronic controls on both racing and production motorcycles. They are a natural continuation of technologies like electronic fuel injection and three-dimensional mapped spark advance. These systems break compromises to keep systems operating closer to optimum more of the time. They also increase rider control by instantly coping with disturbances such as wheelspin, wheel stands, and abrupt power application that would upset the motorcycle.

There's talk of banning or limiting electronics, as has been done in other motor sports. The claim is that this will keep spectator interest (by ensuring there are more crashes?) and keep racing a noble contest of human beings, rather than a sort of BattleBots contest where winners are determined by which team's eggheads can best apply the latest technology.

Sorry folks—the damage has already been done. Most motorcycles already use computers to monitor fuel injection systems to balance emissions control and performance.

Even if we hadn't already crossed the electronic bridge, what's the point of drawing a line in the sand, claiming that real racing is on one side of that line and electronic robots are on the other? Where in the broad sweep of history should we draw this line? 1950? 1980? Oops, electronic bike ignitions appeared from 1969 (also the first year for VW's electronic fuel injection). Today's electromagnetic fuel injector traces back to Italian Ottavio Fuscaldo in 1940, and his injectors were tested by Guzzi in the early 1950s. The last of the four-stroke 500 MV GP bikes employed data acquisition systems in the early 1970s, and they became standard equipment on Japanese 500 GP bikes from 1989 onward. Mapped ignitions arrived on Yamaha GP bikes in 1988. Are computer engine controls too modern? In a glass case at Munich's Deutsches Museum, you can see BMW's Kommandogerat from 1941, a hydro-mechanical computer controlling mixture, ignition timing, and supercharger boost.

Where can we draw the line so all the pure, honest, true technology is on one side, and unsporting modern "nonsense" is on the other?

This consideration is complicated by the fact that racing is the major laboratory which the factories use to develop the technologies that will sell their future production bikes. Set racing's technological date back to 1970 and that is taken from them. Will they continue to participate?

Bear in mind that motorcycle racing is not directly comparable to four-wheeled motor sports. Formula One and even the fairly low-tech NASCAR racecars are custom-built machines that bear little or no resemblance to their street-going counterparts. This is a dramatic contrast to racing and production motorcycles, which closely resemble one another in both appearance and function.

Nicky Hayden at speed on the 2007 800cc Honda RC212V. In the early years of MotoGP, the closer a rider was to the front, the more in control he looked. The reason? Passive torque smoothing (from trackside ignition and fuel injection mapping) tailored engine torque to available grip, enabling riders to use additional power more confidently. Today, active torque smoothing is in use, in which engine throttles are rapidly moved by the ECU during off-corner acceleration to plane down torque spikes and fill in flat spots. Brian J. Nelson

Modern racing motorcycles are developing "nervous systems" of sensors to measure suspension travel, wheel and vehicle speeds, front and rear brake line pressures, and GPS position on the racetrack. Here, a mechanic adjusts wiring details while the ever-present laptop stands ready to enable further "conversation" with the machine. Brian J. Nelson

If motorcycle racing technology is artificially set back to some past date by well-intentioned but restrictive tech rules, production bikes will quickly catch up and surpass race bikes. Then where would we be? Race bikes would become like bowling balls, a generic part of the sport made distinct only by paint color and subtle variations in fit.

Another distinction between auto and motorcycle racing is determined by traction. Racing cars have abundant traction, thanks to wide tires, but grip is always very limited on bikes. Should we ban technologies that give the rider more secure and confident use of that limited grip?

THE UNIQUE TECHNOLOGY NEEDS OF MOTOGP

The premier motorcycle racing class has had some challenges that new technology has been particularly well suited to address. Most of these dealt with the switch from the 500cc two-stroke engine to four strokes in 2002. From 2002–2006 MotoGP displacement was 990cc. Race engines that have big displacement have big engine braking—twice as much as the engine braking that made life so hard for the MV 500s in the early 1970s (they were the only four-strokes left in 500GP then). In early testing, prototype 990s dragged and hopped their back tires on closed throttle, and they slid out unpredictably during corner entry. Something had to be done to handle these problems.

Aprilia's 990 triple was designed using F1 technology such as pneumatic valves. The power delivery was so abrupt that early versions were unrideable. The other manufacturers' early four-stroke GP bikes had similar problems, moderated by their greater two-wheeled experience.

The problem was inherent to the new formula. Race engines have steep torque curves with a lot of ups and downs. A nearly 1000cc race engine with such an alpine torque curve was a loss-of-traction accident-in-the-making in every corner.

Famous and highly capable organizations (BMW, Ilmor, etc.) took turns applying F1 engine technology to motorcycles. Their reward was stunning horsepower output, but with a violent power delivery that led to a spree of high-side crashes during test sessions. What to do?

The problem was simply physics. MotoGP bikes are extremely light and have short chassis. When these very powerful bikes have good tire grip and accelerate, they wheelie. When they brake, they stoppie. The tires lift quickly, and usually where you least want it to happen—during corner exit when you'd like to keep on steering, or just before corner entry, when wobbling in on just the front wheel is a ticket to a quick flop on the ground. These tendencies were accentuated by the strong off-throttle engine-braking produced by large four-stroke engines. The result was braking instability and—all too often—crashing on corner approach/entry.

The MotoGP rules makers further complicated things when, at the end of the 990 formula, the fuel allowance was dropped from 24 to 22 liters, and then further to 21 liters as the 800cc formula began in 2007. This made it difficult to combine the power to win with the economy to finish—kind of like real life these days. More had to be extracted from less and less fuel.

MOTOGP SOLUTIONS

The challenges presented by the new MotoGP engine format required the development of electronic controls that would make the new horsepower controllable. These new developments are making their way to production bikes. Perhaps the naysayers will feel differently about the application of technology on the racetrack, if the advances save them from high-siding their new sportbike during a Sunday ride on their favorite winding backroad.

ENGINE BRAKING

Lots of automobile engines and a few bikes have what are called "throttle positioners," which are little electric motors that the computer can use to reset the idle speed stop. This is the technology that has given fuel-injected autos their excellent idle stability, banishing the old start-and-stall cycle of lean carburetion.

Turns out there are other uses for this system called, in F1 racing, "throttle kickers." As you close the throttle, the system "knows" there will be engine braking and sets the idle up to cancel it. Engine management software can be easily programmed to cancel any desired percentage of engine braking, from 0 to 100 percent. Such a system is even simpler to implement if two or more of the engine's throttles are directly controlled by the computer. For a time, Yamaha's MotoGP 990 throttle kicker operated on one cylinder only, making it sound like a low-revving single during corner entry.

Before the special problems of MotoGP arose, engine braking was dealt with by use of back-torque-limiting slipper clutches. Since the adjustment of these must somehow cover all six transmission speeds, a slipper clutch is an inadequate solution for extremely high-performance machines.

TORQUE CURVE AND TIRE GRIP

Years ago, tuners learned that tire traction set limits to engine tuning. Kevin Schwantz once described how one of his 500cc two-stroke Suzukis had such a steep torque onset that he was at first opening the throttle during corner exit, then quickly *turning the throttle back* as engine torque rapidly climbed. If he didn't do this, the engine would have kicked the rear tire right out from under him. As Valentino Rossi has said, this you can do for one or maybe a few laps, "but twenty-four laps are another story."

Give a four-stroke enough valve overlap and the chiming-in of exhaust pipe wave action can likewise build torque faster than a rider can modulate it. In modern times, engineers have developed systems to do something about this.

In the early days of MotoGP, the simple way to make engine power more usable by the rider was *passive torque smoothing*. All this meant was that:

(1) The engine was designed to have a smooth torque output, thanks to moderate cams and moderate dependence on rpm-sensitive intake and exhaust tuning.

(2) Trackside engineers could change engine characteristics by *trackside engine mapping*. Up to the present, the very smooth torque curves of production sportbikes have been developed by passive torque smoothing.

Honda engineers were the leaders in trackside mapping, and Valentino Rossi and Jeremy Burgess later brought the technique to Yamaha in 2004. As an example of how this works, consider this situation. The rider may say, "It's getting away from me a bit on the exit of turn three." He and his crew chief work out the rev range in question, then pull down the ignition map and retard the timing a little just in that range. At the next practice,

We can't know what they are actually doing here, but they could be downloading data from the last practice session, uploading a modified fuel map, or adding a "patch" to an existing program that will deal with something special that has just come up. Plug the cable into the machine's USB port and start "talking." Brian J. Nelson

the rider finds he can now use the throttle more confidently and smoothly off turn three, and his lap time has dropped a quarter- or a half-second.

Now that MotoGP teams are openly admitting that they use GPS technology (it's just another chip on the board now), the rider and engineer can program their ignition to be retarded in this way in specific corners.

Passive torque smoothing uses extra fuel because retarding the ignition reduces fuel efficiency. The mandated cuts in MotoGP fuel tank capacity forced the teams to experiment with throttle-by-wire systems so that they could achieve their goals by *active torque smoothing*.

Active torque smoothing (also known as traction control) means the engineers write software that directs the computer to vary throttle angle rapidly as the engine accelerates, so that its torque increases *smoothly and predictably*. The system actively smoothes the bumpy torque curve of a highly tuned engine. Without this system, such an engine would be nearly useless, and therefore would not even be built. But with it, engine state of tune can be sharpened considerably. Traction control is what has permitted the steady power growth from the sharper engine tuning that we have seen in MotoGP.

Traction control is the mirror image of anti-lock brake action.

(1) The first-level system simply measures the rear wheel's rate of acceleration, and if it exceeds a certain level, the computer closes its two throttle butterflies just enough to bring the wheel's acceleration rate back to the desired level.

(2) The second-level system compares the surface speed of the front and rear tires, taking care to compensate for various special cases, such as wheelies, stoppies, and so on. Sharp-eyed fans can spot toothed wheels and speed sensors on the wheels of bikes so equipped.

(3) A third-level traction-control system further refines the data by continuously monitoring vehicle speed so that rear wheelspin can be compared with something more accurate than front-wheel speed. Cars have used Doppler microwave devices to measure pavement velocity, but bikes aren't a good platform for this. Instead they use GPS—provided adequate satellite coverage is available. We can imagine a future rider in scuffed leathers, limping back to his pit, saying, "I was just about to nail Pedrosa when my system dropped a satellite."

More than one GP rider has said he has seen the Ducati men simply snap their throttles to the stop and "let the system handle it." Other riders say the system on the machines they are riding cannot do this. The system on Ducati's Superbike homologation special, the 1098R, has eight activation levels. Each level permits a specific level of excess rear-wheel rpm. On a racing system, it is easy to imagine this being set on a corner-by-corner basis. I have spoken to Honda riders who have referred to setting up their anti-wheelie and traction-control levels, track section by track section, indicating this is now a routine setup task, like the choice of gearbox internal ratios has been for 40 years.

HARDWARE?

"What does this have to do with me?" I can hear you saying. This technology is not just coming to you soon—it has arrived! Back in 2006, Yamaha's 600 sportbike was given motorized throttles. Then the company offered an optional traction-control box for competition use at about $1,300. Don't have a Yamaha? Ammar Bazzaz of Bazzaz Performance has released a system of original design that adapts to a variety of bikes. And these are just the beginning, as 2008 has brought several 1000cc production bikes with simple traction-control systems, thinly disguised with names like "spark management system." On the 1098R, Ducati bravely named its system Ducati Traction Control. The times they are a-changin'.

WHEELIE/STOPPIE CONTROL

It's easy to fall when the back end snaps around hard as you brake on the front wheel alone. Would it be a better, fairer, manlier contest if this remained forever a lively possibility? Don't try it—I've seen the result and you won't like it. Since race bikes already carry a full suite of suspension motion sensors (linear potentiometers with A-to-D converters to digitize the data), it's easy to add software to use their data to control wheelies and stoppies. Like traction control, these functions can be set at various levels from 0 to 100 percent.

BRAKING STABILITY

A severe problem in the first two seasons of MotoGP was braking stability. The damping force that controls a motorcycle's two modes of instability—wobble and weave—comes from the tires. Any time a tire's contact with the road is reduced, instability is a possibility. This happens when accelerating out of turns, as the front tire is unloaded. Honda's classic four-stroke racers of the 1960s had this problem. Instability also commonly occurs as a motorcycle is leaned from one side to another, as it does navigating an S-curve. As the bike rolls rapidly from turning one way to the other, centrifugal force unloads both tires as the machine passes through the vertical. You could see this just after Laguna's Corkscrew corner, especially on Kawasakis (always set up for quickest response, and therefore closest to instability). Anthony Gobert always paused just an instant at the vertical, making the maneuver look like an airplane doing a hesitation roll. When asked about it, he said, "The bike gives a big shake if I don't do that." His pause allowed it to settle slightly on its tires, whose damping then suppressed incipient weave.

Because of these effects, some MotoGP bikes would wag their rear from side to side when riders braked hard with the rear wheel very light. This effect was further accentuated by the bike's engine-braking problem. In the worst cases, the weave built up fast and threw bike and rider on the ground. You can see the beginnings of this instability in videos of Ben Bostrom braking on Superbikes. The rear of his bike swings from side-to-side at the characteristic weave frequency of two to three cycles per second. This instability recedes as use of throttle kickers and slipper clutches soften the engine-braking problem. This is because a tire that is turning has directional control, but as it begins to slide it loses that control and will just as soon slide sideways as straight ahead. The problem returned for Honda when it switched to a higher-power, shorter-stroke engine in 2005—probably because its increased fuel consumption kept technicians from setting the throttle kicker high enough to fully cancel engine-braking.

FUEL MANAGEMENT/CONSERVATION

The current 21-liter fuel allowance in the 800cc MotoGP formula has required major development. This technology is important to future production motorcycles, for as fuel price rises fuel economy must be combined with traditional motorcycle qualities. Much has already been accomplished, as the current 800cc bikes are lapping quicker on their 21 liters of fuel than did the original 990s on their 24 liters—better performance on 12 percent less fuel.

How is this accomplished? Ducati's Claudio Domenicali said to me recently, "we have implemented fuel conservation measures in all regimes of engine operation, from idle to top-end." He said that although the engine as a whole might need only 0.42 pound of fuel per horsepower per hour at its best point of operation, it could easily need twice that at other rpm and load. Finding out why has been one key to fuel conservation.

The details are complex, as intake and exhaust pressure waves push some mixture out the exhaust at times, and at other times intake blowback, or "stand-off," pushes fuel into the intake airbox. Some liquid fuel is usually creeping along the inside walls of the intake pipes; when intake valves open and air rushes in, some fraction of this wall fuel flashes off, adding itself to the fuel coming from the injectors. Making sure that each cylinder receives no more fuel than it needs is complicated. While a given cylinder is receiving extra fuel from another cylinder's stand-off, it may be losing some to the exhaust and gaining other fuel from wall evaporation. Improving fuel conservation at this high level becomes a very detailed research project.

Honda is known to be putting major engineering resources into this problem, for at least twice in 2007 Honda MotoGP bikes have run out of fuel on the cool-off lap. All teams use the fuel consumption technology found on most new cars. The computer system adds up the time each fuel injector is activated to measure directly the fuel used. The car's dash display shows miles per gallon for the current period, and estimated range with the fuel on board. It is a short step from this to writing predictive software that estimates from current per-lap fuel use whether the bike can finish the laps remaining, or further economy measures must be taken—such as leaner operation on part-throttle, with extra ignition advance to compensate for the resulting slower flame speed. In practice, these machines are leaned-down as much as is tolerable, given the need for throttle response and power. At least one rider—Loris Capirossi—found that while he was as fast as ever on unlimited fuel, once the "economy program" was in place, he was unable to match his usual quick lap times.

MotoGP riders have been heard to complain that a mid-race drive was stopped by the engine "going lean." This doesn't mean what it did in the previous era, when a change in the weather could make a carbureted engine change its state of tune. It simply means that because the bike used so much fuel in the early laps, the computer switched to the first level of its fuel-saving program to be sure it had enough to finish the race.

NEW PERSPECTIVE ON FUELS

Electronics have solved the problems created by the demands on fuel in MotoGP. The new regulations have made it imperative that the bikes squeeze as much horsepower as possible out of the fuel. The simplest solution is to run high-compression ratios. Fuel efficiency is directly related to compression ratio—the higher the better.

At high rpms, high-compression engines run fine on nearly any type of fuel. Honda research discovered in 1964 that an engine's octane requirement *declines* beyond 12,000 rpm, and that up at 27,000 rpm, even a horrible 37-octane fuel would not knock. Why is this? It takes time-at-temperature for the chemical reactions leading to knock to be completed. This being so, a higher-revving engine can "outrun" detonation—and thereby safely operate at higher compression, higher temperature, or on lower-octane fuel.

A high-compression engine will still require high octane fuel at lower rpms. This is a problem because the anti-knock qualities of racing fuel in international classes are set by regulations. But the methods used to measure fuel octane number were developed in the 1930s by fuel pioneers who never dreamed of 20,000-rpm engines.

Fuel suppliers can use the rules to their advantage by repeating the classic 1930s knock-measurement experiments of Dr. Graham Edgar, but this time using a test engine capable of very high rpm operation. Maybe this research has revealed certain fuel components that do not exceed the FIM's 1,300-rpm knock standard performance just happen to be remarkably knock-resistant at higher rpm. Now we make ourselves special fuels that pass the FIM fuel spec, but which also tolerate lots

of compression up at higher revs. Could it be that this very research has already been performed in spades by F1 fuel suppliers, such as Shell and Mobil?

In the end, our electronic friends accomplish what the fuel suppliers cannot. The certainty that such fuels *will* detonate at lower revs (say 5,000 or 10,000) is no problem because we can just map the ignition timing to deal with it. The engine is rarely operated at these low rpms during a race, so the efficiency loss is minimal.

NASCAR restrictor engines use high 18:1 compression ratios and suffer similar problems without the benefit of electronic controls. If the driver accelerates too hard out of the pit lane, the high-compression engines will blow up due to violent detonation.

ENGINE COOLING AND AERODYNAMICS

Clever engineers find other solutions to the fuel problem. Could a special fuel somehow reduce aerodynamic drag? Here's how it could work. We could use the extra knock-resistance of our trick-but-legal fuel to tolerate a higher-than-usual combustion chamber surface temperature. This would allow us to push up our coolant temperature, which would mean we could use a smaller radiator, thereby cutting aero drag slightly. The reason is that less power is required to flow a given mass of air around the outside of a vehicle than to push it through the resistance of an internal flow path. World War II fighter aircraft could close their radiator shutters to reduce drag enough to either close with, or break away from, an opposing machine.

The hotter radiator dissipates the same heat as before, but now by heating a smaller flow of air to a greater degree. In case the "ban all new technology" faction decides to include this concept, it should know that it was a major tech initiative of the U.S. Army Air Corps, 1923–1930.

GASOLINE DIRECT INJECTION

Ultimately spark-ignition engines may switch to the new gasoline direct injection (GDI) fuel system, just now being introduced in Detroit on Cadillac's V-6 CTS. Fuel is injected

Racing success is ultimately about confidence. Going to the limit, as we see here, requires extreme consistency from all aspects of machine performance. When electronics are handled well, riders gain confidence. But when they are handled poorly riders get spooked and take time to recover lost confidence. Suzuki

directly into the combustion chamber, increasing volumetric efficiency because the vaporizing fuel is no longer competing with air for space in the intake flow. Because such injectors can be aimed directly at the spark plug, fuel-saving ultra-lean stratified-charge operation is possible at part-load, even with conventional ignition. The injection technology for GDI is based upon the high-speed, fine-particle-size injectors originally developed in 1987–1991 for the highly fuel-efficient direct fuel injection (DFI) two-strokes, then being considered as possible future auto powerplants. We live in a world of rapidly changing acronyms, and it's not always easy to keep up.

As noted before, once you have the computer on the bike, it's not hard to find work for it. This is so much the case that processing speeds of production bike computers have steadily increased, along with leaps from 8-bit to 16-bit to 32-bit computation. Currently Yamaha's Marelli race electronics make use of sub-processors to handle some of the tasks.

NOT THE END OF HISTORY

Don't fall into the trap of thinking we are living at the end of history—what we know today is just a snapshot in the midst of an endless process of development. Right now, automakers are installing combustion pressure sensors in certain advanced models. Such sensors were $8,000 laboratory specials just a few years ago, and were fragile and vulnerable to high temperature. Once their price has been driven down by volume production, and their reliability has risen because of accumulated field experience, these sensors will make all the seemingly high-tech fuel and ignition mapping of today as obsolete as manual spark and throttle levers. Engines will become truly self-managing, as they automatically seek optimum operation on a wide range of fuels.

Ignition timing becomes self-managing as soon as the ECU can "see" the pressure-volume (PV) curve of combustion. Then it can instantly put peak pressure where it has to be—at about 14 degrees ATDC. Poof—no more ignition map needed. Quickly finding the area under the PV curve (engineers and mathematicians call this "integrating"), the ECU computes the indicated total mechanical energy output from that combustion cycle. Now it can update its fueling experimentally by supplying slightly more, and then slightly less, fuel on successive firing cycles. If there is a trend of increase in one direction, the ECU will follow it to its peak. It may do this continuously or it may just periodically update a fuel map.

Some present-day fuel systems—those equipped with oxygen sensors—can learn in a related way, continuously updating the system's knowledge.

Direct torque measurement technology exists that will provide data allowing closer control of anti-spin systems. We all know, having driven cars of various ages, that there has been an increase in the sophistication of anti-lock brakes on cars. Early systems operated slowly in a jerky lock/unlock cycle, but more recent ones cycle faster, becoming smoother and more transparent in their operation. Similarly, early anti-spin systems were simple, but have become more effective with development. This will continue.

OTHER SYSTEMS, OTHER EXPERIMENTS

Some systems which have been tried give us an idea of the kinds of things the future may shortly bring. Before the MotoGP era, the Italian electronics firm Marelli made a motorcycle version of its Selespeed automated clutch/gearbox/throttle control system. As MotoGP began, Yamaha and Suzuki fielded similar systems. Development was too demanding for them to be immediately successful, yet heavy trucks routinely employ such systems.

Selespeed was developed for F1 and high-end production autos. At idle, the operator selects first gear and the system declutches automatically. When the throttle is opened, the car moves off, clutching and upshifting as required. It is easy to see how a launch control would be a natural outgrowth of this. Selespeed was tested on a Ducati Superbike in the late 1990s but not adopted. In MotoGP it was hoped that such an automated system would permit control of problems like engine braking and braking instability. Yamaha dropped its system early but Suzuki persisted, enduring a period of non-competitiveness as a direct result.

Ducati actually began the 2006 season with a concept that declutched during braking, allowing the engine to go back to a fuel-saving idle. In the corner, the system selected the right gear for acceleration and, as the rider turned the throttle, smoothly re-engaged the clutch, allowing corner exit to proceed. Ducati failed to make this system workable in the time available and it was withdrawn. What it put in its place in the 2007 season was outwardly conventional, yet allowed the company to combine the highest power in the class with race-finishing fuel economy.

At the end of the 2006 season, the new Ilmor 800cc transverse inline four appeared at the Valencia test. Before starting the engine, the crew plugged a circulating water heater into its cooling system. A crewman explained that if you wish to use a close piston clearance in operation, there may not be enough clearance to safely rotate the engine when cold. This is probably another symptom of the change to lower-viscosity lubricants. The same practice is seen in F1 but, so far, mainstream MotoGP engines don't require this.

Production sportbike engines spin on plain bearings implemented as precision steel-backed insert shells, giving great flexibility in setting clearance during assembly. Such bearings are normally cooled by pushing a substantial excess flow of oil through them. This conflicts with the modern trend toward friction reduction by use of lower-viscosity oils with reduced bearing clearances, as cooling oil flow is reduced.

Where can the excess heat go? In some branches of motor sport, design has returned to the antique practice of plating bearing material and soft overlays directly into the con rod and cap—eliminating the imperfect heat transmission of the normal insert-to-rod fit.

The most important data channel is the human one, the one which all other channels must serve. Here Yukio Kagayama uses the classic rider hand gestures to add to the equation. Something is being decided—the Pirelli engineer nervously clicks his pen, a technician with a data folder stands by, and in the background men toil with laptops. Suzuki

Think of the problems of designing a detachable cylinder head. Yes, it's convenient to be able to remove the head for service, but this requires extra metal—a system of bolts or studs and nuts to provide the clamping force to seal it reliably against combustion gas pressure, cooling water, and lube oil. The steel fasteners are heavy, as are the substantial bosses into which they screw or against which they bear. So is the extra material at the parting line, necessary to support the large forces there. It's tempting to do away with all of it. Now that strokes are so short and valve included angles are so small, straight-on valve seat machining and service through the cylinder bottom are quite practical. If desired, cylinder finishing can be made easier by screwing the liner into the head. This was standard practice in large aircraft piston engines and has now been adopted in some F1 designs. Just for comparison, under the 3-liter V-10 F1 formula, some engines were as light as 220 pounds, but produced more than 700 horsepower.

CHASSIS EVOLUTION

Since motorcycles first were built, chassis rigidity steadily increased until a point near the end of the 500cc two-stroke era. At that point, the chassis became too rigid to act as supplemental suspension when the machine was at high lean angle. The initial response of cutting chassis or swingarm crossmembers soon gave way to formal studies of just what kinds of chassis flexibility were needed. In the process many mistakes were made in the late 1990s, but the current response is to maintain high chassis twist resistance, while allowing both the swingarm and the forward part of the chassis to deflect laterally. The motions permitted are of the order of a few millimeters—just enough to clip the tall spikes off of tire force transients—but are evidently enough to be useful.

This is far from an ideal solution. The more mass that must move with the wheel over bumps, the more sluggish and slower the response. Yet here we are, expecting the front wheel, the brake system, the entire fork with its steering-head, and the laterally flexing forward third of the frame to rapidly follow road texture at high lean angles. That this helps at all is amazing.

Any flexibility added to the chassis runs the risk of provoking weave instability or chatter, and undoubtedly slows steering response slightly. Only the best-considered compromises can work. Getting the chassis to flex in desired ways, while preventing it from flexing in undesired ways, is like trying to get a majority vote in a parliament with ten warring political parties. Good luck!

A THOUGHT EXPERIMENT

Now imagine what might happen if some innovation made motorcycle tires capable of the same grip levels as race car tires. How would you use it? The first thought is to go around corners faster, but that would require higher lean angles, which in turn would require engine and footpeg heights to be raised (or narrower engines designed). The need for "sideways suspension" would increase as the machine's attitude in corners became more and more horizontal.

Or maybe we could use the higher grip to accelerate harder. Having raised the engine, and likely the rider, to permit higher lean angles, our bike now wheelies and stoppies more easily than ever because of its higher center of gravity (CG). That means *reduced*, not increased, accelerative and braking performance.

If we compensate with a longer wheelbase (like dragsters have), our steering slows down and our riders complain. If we move the engine forward to help acceleration, we go straight back to the situation of the 500s in the late 1980s—of having to cut a big slot in the radiator for the front wheel, plus having no room for exhaust pipes. Also, moving the CG forward causes the brakes to pick up the rear wheel more easily, extending braking distances. The resulting bike scores on the way out of corners, but gets nailed on the way in.

Fortunately, we don't have to deal with this imaginary huge grip increase, but every year tire grip does go up a notch, so we face all of the above problems in small periodic doses. We're stuck in the above compromises, too—like being at the bottom of a deep hole in sand. Is it possible to dig out? In any direction that you dig, the sand begins filling in behind you.

So far, the gains in tire performance help the motorcycle mainly between the extremes, which are upright braking and acceleration, and mid-corner, full-lean turning. This is the region of combined accelerations—carrying braking during corner entry, and feeding throttle on exit.

When I look at a MotoGP bike, I see wiring and sensors everywhere, as if the machine is turning into a living organism with a nervous system. Will this mean endless complication for production bikes, and prohibitive expense? Maybe not. The coming technology in automobiles is to put all accessories on a power bus, but not wire the switching back to the computer or instrument panel. Rather, each power user—such as headlights or sunroof motor—will have a simple local computer that keeps in touch with the engine control computer and driver's panel by coded signals transmitted on the power bus. When the local computer receives its coded "on" signal, it connects its accessory to the power bus. This is expected to greatly simplify what would otherwise be a mad rush to wrist-sized wire bundles and million-pin connectors, with all their problems with vibration and corrosion.

At present, MotoGP electronics uses military spec (mil-spec) connectors and wiring technique as a means of achieving an acceptable standard of reliability. This is both expensive and heavy. We hear of fly-by-wire aircraft failing to respond to pilot commands—as in the 777 that landed short after failing to throttle up, and the Airbus that ignored pilot actions and went into the trees. Is this to be the motorcyclist's fate?

Just after World War II, a common form of commercial aviation accident was a crash during landing in low visibility. Radar-based instrument landing systems were rapidly developed, but then as now there were traditionalists who objected, "Who, me? Bet my life on a #@*&ing vacuum tube? No way." But the systems were made reliable and landing accidents subsided. Electronic development is not that different from engine development—significant development expenditure takes place *after* certification, in response to the failure modes that the engineers failed to anticipate.

Motorcyclists had similar, if less consequential, experiences with early fuel injection. The calibration of some systems was incomplete, ignoring the many special cases that really annoyed riders. Occasionally, even today, a new bike will have such problems. Over time, however, fuel injected bikes have become the paragons of responsive performance, and the passing of carburetors has been unlamented.

REVOLUTIONARY CHANGE?

I ask myself, how have we continued to use the spark-ignition internal combustion engine at its dismal 25 percent efficiency for more than 100 years? First, it has been a practical solution to the problem of portable power. Second, we've had cheap fuel during almost all of those 10 decades. We could afford to throw away three-quarters of the fuel's energy, because it was always cheaper to buy more fuel than to significantly improve efficiency.

Not any more. As China, India, Indonesia, and others industrialize and provide their peoples with cell phones, refrigerators, and motor vehicles, our choices are either to accept a smaller energy share or pay a higher price. That can't go on forever. How will we manage?

Small turbo-diesels are a real step up in fuel economy. There's much talk of electric vehicles, but the efficiencies of electricity production, transmission, and application haven't improved any more than those of the spark-ignition engine. Electric vehicles are ultimately powered by coal, oil, gas, or nuclear.

Hydrogen fuel cells? Hydrogen is not an energy source—it is only an energy *carrier*. To liberate hydrogen from water, we must put in roughly twice as much energy as we will get back from its conversion to electricity in a fuel cell. If we take

Step by step, systems become more sophisticated. Adjustable traction control allows the rider to dial in the amount of difference between front and rear wheel speeds that the system will permit. Add GPS to the package and you can now set traction control for individual corners (routine in MotoGP 2007). Add an inertial measuring unit and you can add lean angle data and measure yaw and roll rates. Brian J. Nelson

Ben Spies and crew chief Tom Houseworth look for clues to a problem. Fortunately, they have more accurate means than the arm-waving of the past. Hard data allow careful thought to lead to understanding. Piece by piece, these men will assemble the capability for fast, consistent laps. Brian J. Nelson

hydrogen from fossil hydrocarbon sources such as methane (natural gas), we must throw away, or otherwise deal with, that fraction of the hydrocarbon's energy associated with its carbon content. Liquefying hydrogen for compact storage reportedly adds another 40 percent to its energy cost.

Alternative energy? If all the farmland in the United States were planted to corn, which was then fermented to alcohol, the result would not fuel all the vehicles in the nation. There would also be the nagging problem of nothing to eat.

For the moment, we're stuck with the systems already in place, and I suspect combustion engines—continually improved by small degrees—will be with us as long as there is fossil energy to fuel them.

CHAPTER 12
TURBOCHARGING, SUPERCHARGING, AND NITROUS OXIDE

Turbocharging doesn't really fall within the confines of sportbike technology as I see it, but I know there are lots of people who yearn for the rush of throttle wheelies above 130 miles per hour. Turbocharging is the way to get them.

You know that horsepower goes up and down with barometric pressure, so at equal air temperature, a given unsupercharged engine will make 40 percent more power in Death Valley, 600 feet below sea level, than it can atop Pike's Peak at 12,000 feet above sea level. Anything that increases the density of the air/fuel charge going into your engine will increase power.

A supercharger is one device for pushing more mixture into your engine than the atmosphere can, but it requires mechanical power to drive it. The Roots-type blowers used on AA fuel drag cars consume several hundred horsepower, just as one example.

Turbocharging works differently, by a bootstrap mechanism. As you know, when the exhaust valve opens on an engine running on full throttle in its powerband, a pressure pulse of more or less 100 psi is released into the exhaust pipe. This energy is virtually useless to the piston—that's why we don't open the exhaust valve later, after that 100 psi or so has done a little more expansion work. But there is useful energy in the exhaust pressure pulse, and what a turbocharger does is to put it to work driving a supercharger.

The reason it can be put to work is that while the piston is a pressure machine, the turbocharger is more like a velocity machine. There's not enough pressure left in the exhaust gas to drive a piston efficiently, but the gas entering the header pipe is really moving—doing 1,700 feet per second or more. Anything that plans to use this kind of energy has to be really moving, too.

That something is the radial-inflow impeller of the turbocharger. The fast-moving exhaust gas is ducted to the OD of the turbine through a snail-shaped duct. Whirling around this duct, the gas moves radially inward because it has no place else to go. As the whirling gas hits the turbine's vanes, its velocity is converted locally into pressure, which pushes the wheel around. The spent gases exit at low speed from the center of the wheel to the exhaust duct. To move at a velocity close to that of the exhaust gas, the small turbines used on motorcycle-sized engines must spin extremely fast—200,000 rpm or so. This sounds terribly impressive, but in small scale such as this, the resulting stresses aren't too bad. The radius of the turbine is only an inch

or so, which limits centrifugal loads. The bearings are very small, which limits their rate of oil shear, and so on.

Because high-speed gears are prohibitively expensive, whatever kind of supercharger this turbine is to drive must couple directly to it and run at the same rpm. The only choice is the centrifugal compressor, which works in the opposite sense to the radial-inflow turbine driving it. Air to be compressed approaches the center of the compressor rotor, along its shaft centerline. The center of the impeller has curved inducer vanes, and the air then turns outward and is sharply whipped around by the radial vanes of the impeller, whose tip speed is 1,500 feet per second or so. The air emerges from the impeller's OD moving at this speed, but is immediately decelerated as smoothly as possible to convert its large velocity energy into pressure energy. Complete, 100 percent efficient conversion of the energy of air moving above the speed of sound, into pressure, yields 1.86 atmospheres, or 12.6 psi above atmosphere.

If this pressure was delivered to a 100-horsepower engine's intake, and the operation of the turbine did not reduce power by adding back pressure, the engine would then produce power in the ratio of intake pressures; with 1 atmosphere of intake pressure, the engine made 100 horsepower, so with 1.86 atmospheres of intake pressure, it will produce 186 horsepower.

This, as the British love for understatement would have it, is "a useful increase."

None of our manmade devices is or can be 100 percent efficient, however, and the choice of compressor wheel tip speed in our example is also arbitrary. It can be higher or lower, depending on design. Even with that assumption, however, consider that turbine and compressor efficiencies are generally in the 80–85 percent range, and that efficiencies multiply. Therefore, we can multiply 0.85 by 0.85 to get an overall turbocharger efficiency of about 72 percent. Now to find a rough idea of a realistic discharge pressure, we multiply this overall efficiency times the boost (pressure above atmosphere). This is 0.72 x 0.86 = 0.62 ata, or about 9 psi above atmosphere. This gives us an intake total pressure of atmosphere, plus this 0.62, or 1.62 ata total. Thus, our horsepower will be 162. Useful. I can feel that front wheel getting light.

In the early days of turbocharging, people thought they were doing well having the compressor output pressure be as high as the exhaust back pressure created by the presence of the turbine. This was partly because they were operating the turbine

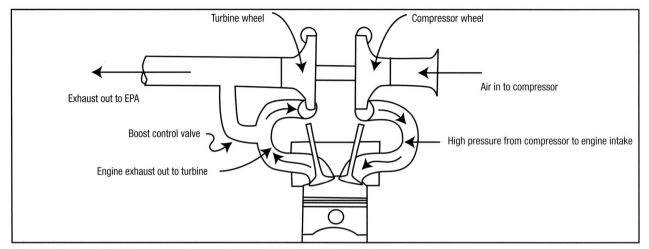

Basic Turbo Operation. *Exhaust energy is used to drive a radial-inflow turbine, spinning it to 150,000–200,000 rpm. It drives a tiny centrifugal compressor that supplies pressurized air/fuel mixture to the engine's intake. To keep intake pressure from rising high enough to make the engine detonate, a boost control valve called a wastegate is used, operated by intake pressure acting against a diaphragm (not shown).*

in "pressure mode," meaning that they treated the exhaust from the engine as if it were compressed air. High-velocity exhaust gas was decelerated in the manifold to make pressure, and this pressure was led to the turbine, where, in the turbine's nozzle and scroll housing, it was reconverted into velocity to spin the turbine. This conversion from velocity to pressure and back again creates a lot of back pressure, which acts against piston motion on the exhaust stroke, eating horsepower and pushing extra heat into the cooling system.

More recently, turbines are operated in "blowdown mode," which means that the high velocity that the exhaust gas reaches on its way out the valve is not decelerated until it reaches the turbine rotor. This creates almost no back pressure against the pistons, but suffers some efficiency loss at the turbine because the exhaust hits it in the form of a series of pulses, rather than as a smooth, steady flow. Nevertheless, blowdown operation has the higher overall efficiency.

Another temptation of early turbo workers was to put the turbo where there was room and then run the necessary pipework to it. It turns out to be more efficient to keep the exhaust pipes as short and streamlined as possible, which puts the turbo just behind the front wheel, ahead of the crankcase, on transverse inline-four engines. Often, smaller pipe works better than larger ones, the reason being that you want as much as possible of the total gas expansion and deceleration to occur in the turbine, not in oversized plumbing.

The first problem with turbocharging is that the compression ratios of stock engines are designed to be efficient and detonation-free in normal operation. But blowing extra mixture into the cylinders is not normal, so even moderate boost is enough to push a stock engine into detonation. The direct reason for detonation is cumulative overheating of the air/fuel charge. Turbocharging heats the air by compressing it, so this is pro-detonation. The usual answer is to reduce the compression

ratio of the engine when the turbo is added, and then to have some kind of controls to keep detonation at bay.

A turbocharger is a bootstrap device; the more charge it sends to the engine, the more exhaust volume there is, making the turbo blow even harder, and so on. Were there no control in this cycle, it would push your engine straight into detonation and failure. The usual control device is called a boost regulator. It measures the boost pressure going to your intake manifold. If that pressure exceeds some set point, the regulator opens a valve that diverts some exhaust gas flow around the turbine, straight to the exhaust tailpipe. This reduces the boost back to the set point, preventing overboosting. The valve is called a wastegate.

To allow use of significant boost without detonation, turbo engines typically have their compression ratios reduced to the range of 8:1 or 9:1. An associated problem is that this lowered compression makes your machine less responsive during off-boost operation. When you turn the throttle, your engine will initially feel soggy because of its lowered compression ratio, but in a little while, the turbine will spool up and massive horsepower will appear. Away you'll go. This spool-up time is called turbo lag, and it is a problem that has only partial solutions.

First, though, let's consider this compression ratio business. The more horsepower you want, the more boost you'll have to use, and the more you will have to reduce compression ratio to run knock-free when on-boost. The lower the compression, the soggier your bike will feel when it's off-boost.

Car turbo systems often employ an intercooler to reduce the temperature of compressed air coming from the turbo. This staves off detonation, allowing the system to operate with either a higher compression ratio or higher boost than would otherwise be possible. It's harder to find room for such gadgetry on a bike than on a car.

Before you decide to go ahead with high-boost turbocharging, you should know something else; highly turbocharged engines blow up instantly if they miss a shift and there isn't a fast-acting rev limiter. All the torque from burning all that charge will cause an engine to rev up so fast that the valves, pistons, and other internal parts will blend into expensive modern art instantly.

Turbo lag is caused by the rotational inertia of the turbine and compressor rotors. When you open the throttle, exhaust volume increases, but is at first only that of a non-turbo engine. This much exhaust begins to accelerate the turbine, whose inertia resists this, so it takes time. One method of shortening the lag is to use an intentionally undersized turbocharger, because rotational inertia decreases rapidly with diameter. The trick is to size the turbo to the engine so that it's working pretty hard to produce the highest boost you need. This makes it a small unit that will accelerate more quickly than would a bigger turbo that could blow more peak airflow into your engine.

On very large engines, such as in cars, faster response can be achieved by using two small turbos in place of a single, larger, slower-accelerating one.

Lighter turbine and compressor wheels can also shorten spool-up time. Turbines made of light, temperature-resistant silicon nitride ceramic provide hope for the future

Another possibility is to use a turbo with a variable-area turbine entry nozzle. Standard turbos have fixed nozzles, so gas velocity is low when exhaust flow is low. But with a variable-area turbine nozzle, the nozzle control closes down at low boost, raising the velocity of the gas as it enters the turbine. This extracts more energy from the low exhaust flow, thereby accelerating the turbine wheel faster. Think of it like putting your thumb over the end of the garden hose to make the stream squirt farther. When the boost set-point is reached, the turbine

TYPES OF SUPERCHARGERS

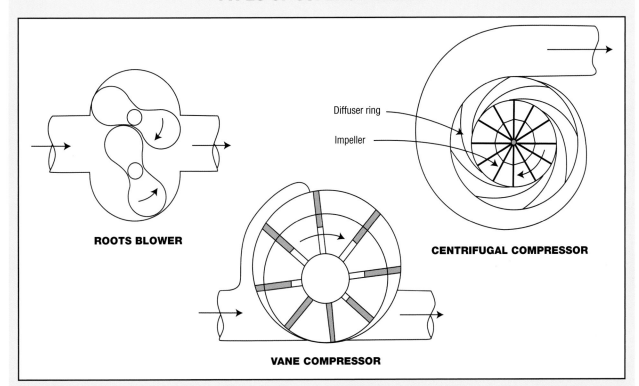

ROOTS BLOWER

Diffuser ring
Impeller

CENTRIFUGAL COMPRESSOR

VANE COMPRESSOR

Roots Blower: The Roots blower is a kind of glorified, powered turnstile, whose rotors sweep air around from one side of the casing to the other—without any internal compression. These are the big blowers you see on AA fuel drag cars, driven by wide cog belts. Smaller versions are made for bikes. Typical blower speed is crank rpm plus some fraction.

The Eccentric-Vane Compressor: Air taken in from the left is compressed as the space between rotor and outer casing shrinks and is delivered to the right. As with the Roots, rotor speed is moderate—

approximately equal to crank speed. Because it has internal compression, a vane blower is more efficient than the Roots.

The Centrifugal Compressor: Air enters at the center and is then accelerated outward to the vaned wheel's tip speed, typically close to or above the local speed of sound. This fast-moving air is then decelerated in the expanding passages of the diffuser ring, converting the air's velocity energy into pressure energy. Centrifugals have to turn extremely fast, and work best in constant-speed applications (aircraft engine).

entry area opens up, cutting energy transfer to the turbine wheel, and limiting boost to the set-point.

Only you can answer the question of whether to go for response or for brute horsepower. If straight-line performance is your meat, go for the power. But if it's a dual-purpose bike you want—part streetbike, part missile—go for the compromise with the higher compression ratio and lower boost.

During World War II, supercharged aircraft engines faced a similar dilemma, but with different variables. Lots of power was needed for take-off and for combat, but most flying was in cruise, when a higher compression ratio would give range-extending good fuel economy. Thus, a bomber or transport engine might be given a higher compression ratio and lower maximum boost to give cruise economy, while a fighter might be given a lower compression ratio so it could stand more boost and make more peak power, without detonation.

For a bike, it looks a little different, but the underlying variables are the same. You want a lot of power, because that's fun and it's impressive. That tempts you to go for the low compression ratio so you can use the big turbo. But unless you are a pure drag-racer, most of your riding will be off-boost. The lower your compression ratio, the less snap your bike will have in this condition. The bigger the turbo, the longer the lag time, making your bike doubly unresponsive. What use is power that arrives after your opponent has already won?

This is why so-called street turbos are small and give only enough boost to make the bike really strong on top, but not enough to make the 500 or more horsepower that the drag-bikes have. This requires less lowering of compression ratio, and it works with a turbo small enough not to be too irritating in its turbo lag.

Still, even with the compromise finely drawn, don't expect your turbo bike to be much use in sportbike-type canyon racing. It's primarily early throttle that wins in that arena, not top-end power, and that's not the turbo bike's strong suit. On your turbo bike, you'll find yourself turning the throttle, waiting, and wondering if you should turn it some more when, "Wham!" too much power arrives, and you have to shut down or head for the weeds. Meanwhile, your buddies on their 12:1 compression stockers will have smoothly fed in just what their back tires need and they'll be gone. But if you can anticipate accurately the moment when you need lots of power, as you can at the strip or in heads-up roll-ons, the turbo can make power like nothing else.

Basic Nitrous Oxide System. *The essential point about nitrous is that both fuel and nitrous oxide gas must be injected simultaneously and in correct proportion—enough fuel to exploit the extra oxygen released as the gas breaks down in the combustion chamber's heat. Early systems were single stage, but because a bike can use more power as its speed rises, nitrous systems with two or more boost levels have been developed, better matching power to speed.*

During the turbo era in F1 auto racing, some fantastic power was made during qualifying. On one occasion, one of these 90-cubic-inch engines made 1,300 horsepower.

I watched a regional open-class road race a few years ago, in which two turbo bikes were entered. The announcer prattled on about the massive, pavement-wrinkling horsepower we would soon see in action, and the flag dropped. The turbos shot away, leaving everyone for dead, and the noise died away in the distance. We all stared at the exit of the last turn. Presently the non-turbo field hove into view, snaking out of the turn, and came past start-finish. Two very chastened high-tech turbo enthusiasts came trundling slowly along behind them, looking crestfallen after their terrifying experiences trying to exit corners with all that now-you-see-it, now-you-don't horsepower. Give it a try—it might be fun!

The turbo-bike world has a day shift and a night shift. The day shift comprises the card-carrying event drag racers and the compromising street riders. The night shift is a dead-serious crowd who race for dead presidents or pink slips, when all but the most hardcore lawmen are fast asleep. They ride built-to-the-limit, mile-long bikes that somehow have license plates on them.

SUPERCHARGING

Supercharging, as noted in the first paragraphs, is a way of generating boost mechanically, rather than through application of exhaust energy. In return for the power they consume, mechanical superchargers offer instant boost, which is why they are offered on some sporting autos. Several types of compressors exist.

Roots Blower

This is a relatively inefficient pump but a popular device in some kinds of drag racing. Some small units are made suitable for bikes. The problem is taking the drive off the engine someplace that isn't too much in the way. This blower is like a very simplified gear pump with its "teeth" evolved into just two or three lobes

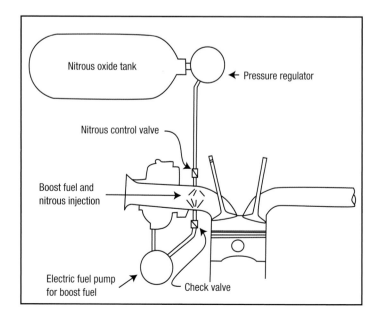

Nitrous oxide tank

← Pressure regulator

Nitrous control valve

Boost fuel and nitrous injection

Electric fuel pump for boost fuel

Check valve

on a pair of counter-rotating impellers that sweep air into the intake manifold in chunks. It's inefficient because the air isn't compressed in the blower, but is compressed by the air already in the manifold, rushing back into each of the blower's lobe spaces to squeeze the atmospheric-pressure air contained there. If the blower shoves enough such pieces of atmosphere-pressure air into the manifold, something's gotta happen. The first drag bike ever into the sevens used a blower of this type.

Vane Blower

This one uses a single, slotted rotor carrying several spring-loaded vanes, which are pushed outward against an outer housing. Since the rotor is off-centered in the housing, the space between vanes gets bigger and smaller as the rotor turns. By locating ports in the right places, a compressor is made. Vane blowers are eminently practical because they don't turn very fast (close to crank speed, depending upon size and desired boost) and are efficient.

Centrifugal Blower

This is the type used on the compressor side of a turbocharger. In order to achieve significant compression, this blower must spin fast enough to reach an impeller tip speed at or above the speed of sound. The problem with using it as a supercharger is that crank speed must somehow be multiplied to blower speed through some kind of step-up drive. Difficult.

As with turbocharging, these forms of power-boosting push your engine closer to detonation, so there may be a need to reduce the compression ratio and/or intercool as you increase the boost. There's power to be had. Can you use it?

NITROUS OXIDE

Engine power depends upon the mass of fuel you can make react completely with oxygen, per unit time. Unsupercharged engines attempt to increase mass flow by revving higher, performing more pumping strokes per minute. Supercharged engines boost mass-flow by cramming mixture in at higher density.

There is a third way to increase power, and that is to inject oxygen-rich substances, along with enough extra fuel to react with the oxygen they release. Nitrous oxide is one such substance. (There are many, and therein lies a tale!)

Nitrous oxide, sometimes called laughing gas, is usually a colorless, odorless gas, and it's stable at room temperature—some of the other potential oxygen-donor substances are emphatically not. When injected into an engine's intake stream with the corresponding quantity of extra fuel, it breaks down during combustion, releasing its oxygen and burning the extra fuel. As much as a 40 percent torque increase can be produced in this way, simply by triggering the flow of gas and fuel when that power is wanted.

The gas is supplied from a pressure bottle, and its expansion into the intake manifold has such a cooling effect that detonation is generally suppressed. The method was pioneered on British aircraft during World War II as a means of either closing with, or breaking away from, enemy aircraft in combat.

Simplicity. *This is a nitrous oxide setup from NOS, showing how little you need to get a big power boost—but for a time limited by how often you want to refill that green bottle.* NOS

Naturally, the bottle is soon empty and your bike turns back into a pumpkin, but the mad rush of acceleration is such that you hasten back to the nitrous dealer, fanning large bills, begging for more. You get the picture.

Nitrous systems are made up as kits, with a bottle, pressure regulator (without it, the gas would come out at a higher flow rate when the bottle is full than when nearly empty), fuel pump, valve, and plumbing. The proper result is that, when triggered, the gas valve and fuel pump/spray nozzle deliver the two substances in correct proportion. There must also be a convenient trigger to switch on the flow. Finding room on the bike for the bottle is your problem, as is the prickly question of just how often to let yourself return for more such bottles.

Because drag bikes need more horsepower the faster they go, staged nitrous systems have been developed to approximate this changing need. Without a staged system, fixed-rate nitrous injection either produces too much power for your tire to handle at lower speeds, or else not enough for the desired effect on top-end.

You'll see ads showing, one the one hand, a pile of speed parts requiring considerable mechanical skill to install and adjust, and on the other hand, the fascinating green bottle and its modest pile of accessories. It's very compelling. You will quickly notice that, once installed, the speed parts are always ready to boost performance, while the bottle has to be kept full. You choose.

The nitrous system is only used on demand, so it doesn't affect bottom-end and midrange performance the way a turbo or speed parts will. It also doesn't compromise the way your machine comes off corners. Indeed, a nitrous system was used many seasons ago to boost a two-stroke TZ250 road racer, running in the old Formula USA race against things like 1100 Suzukis and 1000 Yamahas. The little TZ retained all its agility in corners, yet gained useful full-throttle acceleration from the nitrous system. It's just too bad that the neighborhood gas station doesn't stock the stuff.

CHAPTER 13
HOW SUSPENSION WORKS

At the 1991 U.S. Grand Prix at Laguna Seca, Eddie Lawson repeatedly brought in his 500 Cagiva from practice, making the international rider sign language for front end push, followed by tuck. "Speaking" to his Italian mechanics, Eddie's hands mimed first the twisting throttle, then the slow turn of the bars into the corner as the bike pushed (understeer), heading for the outside, and the rider scratched for grip to make it steer—and then the sudden tuck as front grip peaked and let go. This kind of problem is what so often stands between a talented rider and the fuller expression of his talent. Problems like this also slow the learning curves of beginning and intermediate riders. Riders often try to improve by "trying harder," but this often just takes the form of emphasizing their mistakes, not fixing them. When you fix the specific problems that are holding you back, you go faster, or you go with more control and confidence.

This is why there is so much emphasis on suspension and chassis questions today. Technology can give us pretty much all the power we want, but it's useless unless the rear tire is in firm contact with the road and the front tire is steering.

Tire chemistry is fragile. So often in races, the early leader fades out and doesn't even get on the box at the end. Later he says, ruefully, "I got the suspension setup wrong and burned up my tire." If the rear tire is sliding around or bouncing, or the bike is wallowing, the rear tire burns up instead of hooking up. Hard use fatigues rubber, and when it loses a few percent of its properties, the rider has a simple choice: slow down or pile up. Five-time 500cc world champion Mick Doohan spoke of trying to develop enough lead while the tire is working so he could survive "the last ten laps of sliding around."

Having the right suspension setup means that the tires will spend maximum time hooked up. The bike won't nose-down extravagantly under hard braking, tending to lift its rear wheel. It won't waste time wallowing and plunging as its rider tries to flick it over. Curing such problems takes observation, some skills, and a willingness to spend time testing and thinking about what the symptoms mean. Chassis and suspension are where the big gains are made today. Engines remain important, but because they are so well-understood now, there is less to be gained from increased power.

In racing, the practice sessions are a race to achieve a good setup in the very limited time available. On the street as on the track, riders go only as fast as their confidence allows them. A good suspension setup is the best possible confidence-builder because it lets the rider know, not just guess, what will happen next. Fast riders go fast because they want to, and because they have learned how. Riding harder—that is, leaving more to chance—just makes lap times erratic.

THE BASICS

As a vehicle without suspension moves over a rough surface, the whole vehicle rises and falls over every bump. The faster it moves, the more rapid becomes this up-and-down motion. Bumps hit at speed can kick the vehicle up pretty hard, but it can't fall back any faster than gravity pulls it. Therefore, at some moderate speed, the wheels will leave the ground over the tops of bumps, just as a floating valve will fail to follow the contour of the cam lobe at excessive rpm. A tire in the air has no grip, so when this happens in corners, the vehicle will jump sideways,

Attitude Change! *Ultimately, the two reasons for seeking a good suspension setup are (1) to generate as much grip as the tires can give, and (2) to ensure that this grip is balanced, front-to-rear, so that the motorcycle is controllable. Always remember that there is a difference between performance—which is the* magnitude *of some measure of vehicle behavior—and handling—which is the degree to which that can be controlled.* Brian J. Nelson

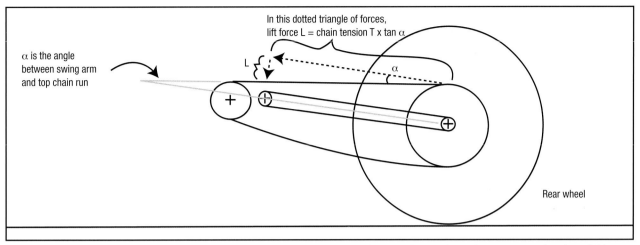

In this dotted triangle of forces,
lift force L = chain tension T x tan α

α is the angle
between swing arm
and top chain run

L

α

Rear wheel

How Drive-Chain Tension Generates Lift Force. *The chain does not pull parallel with the swingarm, but rather at some angle to it, and this produces a force tending to extend the rear suspension. This lift force is handy because it can be used to prevent bikes from squatting at the rear as they accelerate. Squat, by taking weight off the front tire, can cause a bike accelerating off a turn to push the front end.*

or "step out." The faster it goes, the more time it spends off the ground. This is the opposite of what you need, which is more grip and control the faster you go.

By placing a spring between the wheel and the vehicle (load), this situation is changed. Let's see why. A typical wheel weighs 30 pounds, while one end of a loaded, fueled sportbike weighs perhaps 300 pounds. Now we have a 30-pound wheel

being pressed against the pavement, not by gravity alone, but by a spring carrying a 300-pound load. We can figure the acceleration rate of an object by dividing the driving force (F) by the mass (M) of the object being accelerated. Therefore, in this case, we can have as much as 300/30 = 10 G of vertical acceleration to push the tire back down against the ground. This is a huge increase in vertical acceleration over the first case, in which we had only

SINGLE-PURPOSE SETUPS

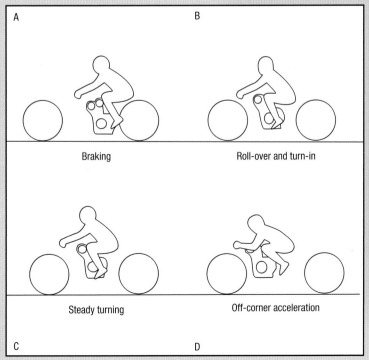

A

B

Braking

Roll-over and turn-in

Steady turning

Off-corner acceleration

C

D

A. If Braking Was Your Bike's Only Job
To keep the rear tire on the ground and the bike steering controllably, major masses are moved rearward and lowered. Front suspension is stiff to carry close to 100 percent of weight. Front tire is large for traction. Wheelbase is extended to prevent stoppies.

B. If Corner Entry Was Your Bike's Only Job
Masses are centralized to speed roll and turning. Rigid suspension eliminates suspension delays. Front tire is of knife-like profile for quick response. Wheelbase is minimized to speed steering.

C. If Steady Turning Was Your Bike's Only Job
Engine and rider are raised for cornering clearance, while suspension is supple to maintain maximum grip. Front & rear cycle tires are equal sizes to carry equal loads.

D. If Off-Corner Acceleration Was Your Bike's Only Job
Major masses are moved forward but not lowered (cornering clearance is needed initially). Wheelbase is long. Front suspension is soft to exploit grip with very light load.

gravity (1 G) to pull the whole vehicle back to earth after each bump. This translates to ability to keep the tires in much better contact with a rough road, up to a much higher speed.

This 300/30 ratio of wheel mass to load carried is what the suspension engineer calls the sprung/unsprung weight ratio, and it defines the maximum rate of vertical acceleration the suspension can achieve in following the bumpy road contour. In other words, the lighter the wheels can be made in relation to the load they carry, the faster they can track the surface. This is why it's desirable to reduce unsprung weight to the lowest value possible, and therefore part of the reason for mag or carbon racing wheels, carbon brake discs, and tubeless radial tires.

SPRING RATE AND BUMP ISOLATION

Look at the problem another way: from the standpoint of how much upward shove a vehicle gets from a bump. With no suspension (what old Mickey Thompson called "Rigidamatic"), even a pretty ordinary bump can put you in orbit, but as we soften the connection between wheel and vehicle with springs, the vehicle becomes increasingly isolated from the bump's effect. This brings us to the idea of *spring rate*, which is the number of pounds it takes to compress a spring 1 inch. For a helical spring with constant spacing between coils (spring pitch), this rate will be constant. A spring with a 100-pound rate will get 1 inch shorter for every 100 pounds of load we add to it—up to the point that it becomes coil bound.

If we have a 100-pound-per-inch spring directly supporting the front of our vehicle, when we hit a 1-inch-high bump, the spring will be momentarily compressed 1 inch as the bump lifts the wheel. Compressing a 100-pound-per-inch spring by 1 extra inch increases its pressure by 100 pounds, so our vehicle feels only

this extra 100-pound force as the effect of the bump (neglect for the moment the inertia of the upward-moving wheel, which must also be stopped). How much vertical acceleration does this extra 100 pounds produce? We've already said our bike has 300 pounds on each of its wheels, and acceleration is driving force, divided by the mass of the thing being accelerated. Therefore, we have 100/300, or roughly 1/3 G. This is a great improvement over the rigid case, in which upward acceleration can easily be *several* G. Using the spring achieves a great reduction in vertical disturbance.

Now note the trend of improvement as we reduce the spring rate to 50 pounds per inch; vertical acceleration drops to 50/300 = 1/6 G. I am noting this particularly because there are so many riders who seem to believe that stiffer springs are somehow racier. Stiffer springs have their uses, yes, but they do increase the severity of the upward impulse that any bump gives to our machine.

SIDE EFFECTS; ATTITUDE CHANGE

Absorbing bumps is only one of the suspension's jobs. In the course of absorbing bumps, suspension adds new problems: unwanted machine attitudes, altered weight distribution, and loss of ride height.

As we make the springs softer in hope of getting better isolation from bump upset, the machine assumes ever-more extreme attitudes (tilts) during braking and acceleration. Suspension is compressed during cornering—possibly leading to grounding. This is because a soft spring compresses more under a given load and extends more when load is removed, which means a bike on soft springs will dive more at the front during hard braking, and rise farther at the rear. The result is a strongly nose-down attitude that transfers extra weight to the front wheel. This nose-down, tail-high attitude causes the rear wheel to lift off the ground under braking sooner than it would if the machine had no suspension and remained level. This is the reason why, in the early 1980s, there was a brief flurry of interest in anti-dive devices that used brake torque to jack the front end up and pull the rear end back down. But those devices interfered with suspension action (consider what happens when tires skip over bumps, and brake torque spikes violently) and were gradually dropped.

A similar situation exists during acceleration, complicated by the existence of chain force reaction on rear suspension. It is very undesirable for the rear of the machine to squat as the rider attempts to accelerate out of turns. This transfers extra weight to the rear, possibly unloading the front tire enough to make it stop steering. This problem I call "squat and push." The front end "pushes," or fails to steer in proportion to the steering angle the rider gives it, so the bike runs wide out of turns, forcing the rider to use less throttle. Making rear suspension travel shorter minimizes these problems, but obviously absorbs bumps less well.

In cornering, soft suspension becomes a problem when centrifugal loading pulls the machine down on its suspension so far that pipe and pegs hit the ground. This can't be tolerated, so the

DRY FRICTION LEVER DAMPER

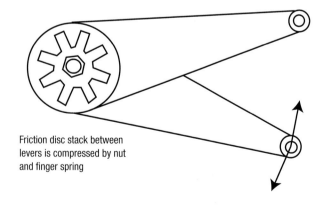

Friction disc stack between levers is compressed by nut and finger spring

How It Used to Be. *This is a scissors-type friction suspension damper (sometimes called a "Hartford"), as used on many prewar motorcycles and cars. Dry friction damping force was too large at low speed, too soft at high speed. Complicated devices for adjusting damping "on the fly" were developed. Race bikes built before 1970 used steering dampers of this type, with a wing nut atop the steering head for adjustment.*

rider jacks the machine up by adding more preload to front and rear springs. But making it taller increases weight transfer during acceleration and braking, and may affect the way the bike rolls over for turns. Ground clearance problems go away with stiffer suspension—but so does bump isolation. Poor bump response means the tires are off the ground more of the time in turns. This makes the machine run wide and not hold line.

Therefore, motorcycle suspension spring rates are a compromise, soft enough to give useful bump isolation and good grip, but not so soft as to permit wild attitude changes that limit performance. Touring and sports/touring machines are not ridden to 100 percent weight transfer (wheelies, stoppies) and can therefore be biased in the direction of comfort, with longer travel and softer springing and damping. In racing, this compromise is redrawn at every circuit. If the circuit is smooth, less bump isolation is needed, and benefits can be had from firmer setup, permitting less attitude change and faster response. If the circuit is bumpy, the suspension will have to be softened up and the bad side effects of this accepted—up to a point.

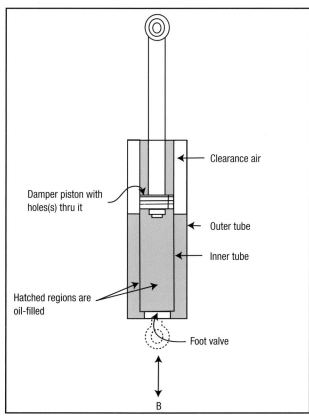

Simple Hydraulic Damper. *The simple hydraulic damper with a constant-sized damping orifice has limitations in how it absorbs impacts; because its damping force increases as the square of the piston's speed through the oil, it is too soft at low speeds, yet damping force quickly becomes far too much at higher speeds. Fluid friction is smooth, but a sharp impact like an infield-to-banking pavement transition will make an improperly designed or wrongly valved hydraulic damper act essentially rigid!*

The sports motorcyclist wants to do the right thing, but simple fables often push aside common sense. Too often, magazine reviews say things like, "When we got to Willow, we cranked up the damping at both ends to full-rigid with max spring preload, and got down to some serious lap times." This implies that it's always best to run the hardest possible settings. Reverse logic also implies that if you run hard settings, you must be a good rider. Like it or not, we're all a bit status conscious, so this kind of thing sucks us in. Believing that harder is better, all these riders are jolting around this nation's highways with their suspensions set on magazine-max, when in fact they would benefit from considering the word I used above: *compromise*. You need traction to go fast, and on any but the smoothest surfaces, that means the suspension has to move.

Stuart Shenton, crew chief of Suzuki's MotoGP team, said once that riders really needs four separate motorcycles. During braking, they need a machine with its weight to the rear, to allow the full grip of the front tire to be used without lifting the back wheel, with firm enough front suspension to keep from bottoming. During turn-in, they need a machine with a very short chassis for quick steering, with no suspension at all to delay the action. In the turn, they need balanced weight distribution that does not overload either tire prematurely. They need ground clearance, but with suspension soft enough to maintain tire grip. When acceleration begins, they need a chassis with its weight forward, to keep that front tire loaded enough to steer without pushing. There is no way to combine all these separate and conflicting requirements in the motorcycle as it now exists.

There is no simple rule that reveals the best compromise, which is why assertions like "harder is better" are nonsense. The more you work with suspension, and the more combinations you try, the more you will learn about how to achieve a compromise that works.

DAMPING

Adding springs only brings us up to the horse-and-buggy era. There's a problem with this simple mass-and-spring system; it's an undamped oscillator, just like a child on a playground swing. If you pump in energy in step with the system's natural frequency, the oscillation will build up without limit. As we ride our bike with sprung wheels down a washboard road at just the right speed, the bumps kick the suspension again and again, building up the bounce until the wheels are hopping right off the road, and directional control is progressively lost. Likewise, in sudden maneuvers, undamped suspension wallows and plunges—the exact opposite of the stable platform riders need. We need something to stop oscillations and other unwanted movement in the suspension system. We need to provide a "leak" through which unwanted energy can be bled out of the moving suspension.

That something, that energy leak, is damping—the fancy engineering term for friction. A ringing bell is silenced by placing a soft thumb on the vibrating metal. A rearing, plunging vehicle is stabilized by its dampers, or "shocks." In this book, I am going to refer to any device that supplies damping as a damper, although I could use the common terms "shock absorber" or just "shock." I like the word "damper" because it accurately describes what the device does. If you find that stuffy and professorial, go right ahead and use the good old, all-American term "shocks."

In early autos, damping was provided by a scissors-link arrangement, with a stack of clutch-like friction discs at its pivot. Suspension worked the scissors, producing friction at the pivot, which could be adjusted by a large wing-nut or some more complex remote adjuster. But this dry friction damping technology provided too much damping at low speed and too little at high speed, so constant adjustment fiddling was needed.

HYDRAULIC DAMPERS

Just before and during World War II, oil-damped telescopic aircraft landing gear struts were developed, and soon cars and bikes adopted similar telescopic hydraulic dampers. A telescopic damper employs a piston working inside an oil-filled cylinder. The piston rod is attached to the vehicle, and the cylinder is attached to the suspension. Bump and rebound suspension motion causes the piston to cycle to and fro in the cylinder. The oil being forced back and forth through holes in the piston resists this motion, because high-speed motion through damping orifices converts suspension energy, first into the kinetic energy of the fast-moving oil jets, and then into heat, thereby generating the damping force to control the motion. Making the holes bigger reduces the damping force by accelerating the fluid less, and making them smaller has the opposite effect.

A simple hydraulic damper is practically useless because it has the opposite characteristic to dry friction dampers; it has too little damping at low speed, rising rapidly with increasing damper-rod speed, to infinity at high speed. This would lead to wallowing at low speed, changing to bone-jarring rigidity at high speed. Fluid forced through an orifice resists in proportion to the square of the velocity. Pushing the piston through the oil twice as fast generates four times as much resistance. The graph of force-versus-velocity curves upward quickly toward infinity! Any hydraulic damper whose damping quickly approaches infinity is said to be "orifice-limited." We'll return to this problem in a moment.

When the vehicle hits a bump, the bump not only compresses the suspension spring, but it also must also move the damper piston through the oil. If the hole in the piston is correctly sized, the resistance will bring the suspension motion to a quick stop after a bump impact, with no nodding up and down afterwards. This condition is called "critical damping." It will also prevent buildup of hop on washboard roads. Now we have achieved a desirable result—a stable vehicle.

THE NEED FOR CORRECT PROPORTION

Always remember that spring stiffness and damping force must exist in proportion. Too much damping overcomes the spring, slowing suspension response, making the ride too firm, and reducing the wheels' bump-tracking ability and grip. Too little

damping is overcome by the spring, and the vehicle oscillates after every disturbance.

Damping has an undesirable side effect. With damping plus spring, any bump gives the vehicle two upward shoves—one from the spring, the other from the resistance in the damper. This extra push is unfortunate because it somewhat increases the bump's disturbance to the vehicle.

In the early days of hydraulic motorcycle suspension dampers (early 1950s), this bump disturbance was minimized by installing a one-way valve on the piston. Now the damping operated only during the extension (rebound) stroke, as the one-way valve opens during compression, preventing much compression damping force from being produced. Now, when we hit a bump, we get only the upward push of the spring, without the extra push from the compression damping force. We have zero damping on compression, 100 percent on rebound. Since we've lost all damping on compression, we'll have to increase rebound damping to restore control and adequate damping—the situation in which the machine doesn't keep nodding after it hits a bump.

Motorcycle dampers today aren't this extreme. They are designed to produce only about one-fifth as much damping on compression as on rebound. As with rebound damping, it is made proportional to velocity, but only up to a point. To prevent further growth of compression force at higher speeds, the force is "plateaued," or limited to a maximum value, by a blow-off valve. Small amounts of compression damping, correctly engineered, can be very useful in preventing bottoming, but the basic principle remains true: we keep compression damping to a minimum to limit the upward disturbance to the vehicle. Most of the damping acts on rebound because that disturbs the vehicle less.

This short description updates us from horse and buggy times to the 1930s (or to the miserable level of front fork dampers up to the mid-1980s). The next problem was how to provide damping that was truly proportional to the speed of the suspension motion. Recall that a simple orifice hydraulic damper (a steering damper is made this way) provides little damping at low speed, building rapidly to too much or even infinite damping (damper becomes rigid) at very high damper rod speed. This would produce a vehicle that nodded and wallowed at low speed, handled middle suspension velocities well, then became harsh or rigid at high speeds. The curve of damping force versus velocity—called the damping curve—would then be exponential, curving upward steeply in proportion to velocity, squared. In a word, useless.

This was the problem of *orifice limitation at high damper speeds*. Now the challenge was to change this exponential damping curve into a nice sloping straight line—with damping directly proportional to speed. This would supply enough damping at low speed to stop wallowing, yet also prevent damping force buildup from making the suspension rock-hard at high speeds. In this case, the winning idea was to use variable damping orifices. At zero speed, the damping orifice would be very small, close to zero area. The faster the piston was driven through the fluid, the bigger the damping orifice would get. There are various ways to achieve this, but I will describe just two.

Coning Washers

The first is bending-washer technology, used in Fox, Ohlins, Showa, and other dampers. In a simple implementation of this system, the piston has a ring of holes through it, and the holes are covered by a thin washer. The washer is held against the piston by either its inner or outer edge, with the other edge free. Stacked on top of this washer, there may be other washers or spacers to modify its stiffness or limit how much it can flex. As the piston is driven faster through the oil, the pressure developed pushes against the washer, lifting it off the ring of holes and deflecting it into slightly conical form, thereby allowing fluid to pass through the damping holes and out from under the deflected edge of the washer. Think of this washer as a kind of stiff reed valve, made in circular geometry. The faster the piston moves, the more the washer stack deflects, increasing orifice area.

As an arbitrary example, imagine that a thin washer covers the ring of holes and is backed by a small-diameter spacer, then a second washer. As the damper piston accelerates, the thin washer deflects easily at first, but as it bends up more, it contacts the second washer. This stiffens its resistance. Various combinations of washers of various thickness and diameter, with spacers, can be used to make damping closely proportional to velocity.

Unfortunately, this proportionality doesn't extend smoothly down to zero velocity. To handle low-speed oil flow, therefore, a separate, adjustable orifice is provided. This orifice is adjusted by screwing a tapered needle into or out of it, and this screw is held at the desired setting by a spring detent. As you rotate the screw, you will feel the detent click. This is the "clicker," or external adjuster, on your damper.

Balls and Springs

The other system, used on Works Performance and possibly some Kayaba dampers, covers each damping hole in the piston with a tiny ball, backed by a spring. By choosing the rate and preload of these springs, these ball valves can be made to open in sequence, producing the desired curve of damping versus piston velocity.

THE BIG PICTURE

Now look at how the system works. The clicker orifice is set to give good motion control at low speed, preventing wallowing. As the piston moves faster in response to higher speed bump motions, this orifice would quickly go into orifice limitation, but it doesn't matter now because the washer stack or ball valves begin to open up more oil flow area and take over the control of damping.

Why is the clicker even there at all? It serves to adjust low-speed motion control and acts as a trimmer or fine adjustment on higher speed damping. Think of it as an adjuster that can *slightly* raise or lower the whole damping curve, but cannot change its shape. Clickers are useful because they give you adjustable control of low-speed motion and they let you adjust higher speed damping slightly, which can be useful as a diagnostic.

Always remember that many damping problems lie outside the clicker's range of adjustment. When this

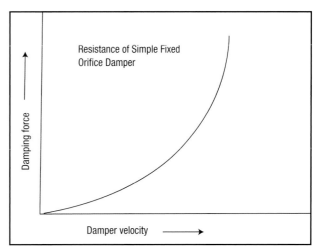

Orifice Limitation. *This shows how damping force rises exponentially with velocity when a simple orifice is used. When you double the damper-rod velocity, you get four times the damping force. A damper based on this behavior is useless because it becomes rigid in response to sharp movements.*

happens, the only remedy is professional help. A qualified person depressurizes the damper, drains its oil, and then disassembles it. He then restacks the compression and/or rebound washer stacks to change middle- or high-speed damping characteristics as needed. Recent developments in damper design—such as Ohlins' TTX series—have brought increased consistency, reducing the number of re-stacks required to achieve a good setup.

Never try to disassemble a pressurized damper without first depressurizing it! A typical nitrogen pressure is 275 psi, which, acting on a typical-sized damper piston, would produce a 350-pound accelerating force. Anything in the way of that piston, suddenly released by an unthinking person, would suffer serious misfortune.

The limitations of the clickers are why you cannot take a shock, set up for one bike, and retune it for use on another bike of different characteristics, simply by twiddling the clickers. Their fine adjustment doesn't have the range to make large changes in middle- or high-speed damping, and cannot change the shape of the damping curve. Yes, when you test damping by the time-honored push-down-on-the-seat method, the clicker makes a lot of difference. But the "seat-push test" checks only low-speed damping—you can't hit the bike the way the bottom of the Corkscrew at Laguna will hit it.

Remember that compression damping is normally much less than rebound in motorcycle dampers. This was not always so, for in the 1970s, suspension engineers didn't know how fast damper pistons really move. When the suspension moved sharply, as it does when bikes hit a pavement change at high speed, early dampers were driven straight into compression orifice limitation. Even with all orifices wide open, there wasn't enough area to handle the flow, and the dampers locked up, causing hopping and wobbling.

The story is told that Kenny Roberts, testing in Japan, was so annoyed at the continued compression rigidity of the test dampers that he asked the technicians to disassemble a rear damper.

"Which of these parts controls compression damping?" he demanded. They pointed it out. "Can you assemble the damper without it—just get rid of it?" he asked. "Wellll . . . I sink not possible," was the cautious reply.

Kenny put all of his considerable force of character to work on the problem and it suddenly became possible. When the damper was reassembled, the next test showed vastly improved performance! Eliminating the upsetting effects of compression orifice limitation improved the lap times.

Honda discovered the problem in a different way. When an instrumented motocross bike showed how fast damper rods actually move, a faster test machine was constructed to reproduce such high velocities. When existing dampers were tested at such speeds on this machine, they broke just as they had been doing in field operation. The fix was to design compression orifice systems that were not driven into compression orifice limitation by high damper-rod speed.

On many dampers, the rebound functions are built into the piston, while the compression functions are built into a valve stack that communicates with the reservoir. Therefore, the rebound clicker is found on the end of the damper rod, while the compression clicker is located at one or the other end of the reservoir hose.

As the piston rod enters the cylinder, something has to accommodate its extra volume. You can't push a big piece of steel rod into oil without something getting out of its way. The oil flow that the rod displaces from the cylinder into the reservoir has been used to control compression damping. This is a much smaller flow than that controlled by the piston, but compression damping is normally only about 20–25 percent of rebound damping, for the reasons given already. In more recently designed dampers, a larger compression flow is used.

Until the mid-1970s, almost all dampers were of so-called atmospheric construction. As the damper rod enters the damper cylinder, something's gotta give to allow its volume to enter. To provide this give, dampers were built as two concentric tubes, with the piston stroking inside the inner one. The inner tube was completely filled with oil and communicated with the surrounding outer tube only through the compression valve, located at the bottom of the tubes. The outer tube was filled half with oil, half with air or other gas. It was the compressibility of this "clearance gas" that allowed the damper rod to move in and out of the inner cylinder.

It worked—sort of. But when the action got heavy, the violent motions of the piston and the bike itself entrained air into the outer-tube oil, from which it was drawn into the inner tube, forming an air/oil mixture (emulsion) that reduced damping force and made the damper springy (air makes a good spring—consider pneumatic valves). Racers just had to accept that their suspension would work well only for a couple of laps, then deteriorate as their dampers entrained air.

The first answer was to put the clearance air behind a sealed piston, or into a plastic bladder, but even this didn't do the whole job. As the damper piston worked vigorously back and forth, it could move faster than oil could flow in behind it. The result was cavitation, which became more likely as temperature rose. When this happened, the damper cylinder failed to refill completely, and the next stroke had no damping at all. This gave harsh, erratic suspension action.

The final answer was to pressurize the clearance gas which, to prevent reaction with hot damper oil, had to be inert nitrogen. Such gas-pressurized dampers can be built in any of several forms. An older type has a separate reservoir, located at the far end of a hose. This reservoir is what hydraulics people call an accumulator. The oil and clearance gas are separated by a sliding piston—oil on one side, high-pressure nitrogen on the other. Shall I tell you about the father-and-son motocross racers who repressurized their damper, not with inert nitrogen, but with what they happened to have on hand—oxygen? Imagine the explosion as the oxygen first deteriorated the seal, then joyously united with the hot damper oil.

Damper and accumulator may be built end-to-end, as they were in the first Yamaha Monoshocks. More recent constructions eliminate the hose and separate accumulator, and integrate the damper body and reservoir, resembling a "blaster" from a space western.

The dominant damper construction of the 1990s and early twenty-first century has placed the rebound adjuster on the damper piston rod (at the top) and the compression adjuster between damper body and accumulator. The newer Ohlins TTX (TT stands for "twin tube") series of dampers has no valving on the piston, and both adjusters are now located at the base of the damper body. In some Ohlins' recent forks, compression damping is in one fork leg and rebound in the other. This allows a one-way valve to be placed inline with each adjuster, preventing either adjuster from acting as a leak that interferes with the function of the other.

ABOUT SUSPENSION SPRINGS

All the springs currently used in motorcycle suspension are cylindrical, helical-wound, round-wire metal springs (OK, there are exceptions, like a few applications using torsion bars). Front springs are long and floppy, and of diameter small enough to fit inside the fork legs. Rear springs for single-shock suspensions are short and stiff, like car suspension springs. There are reasons for the differences.

Front springs must be able to support the vehicle's whole weight during hard braking, but they must also be soft enough to give good compliance during acceleration, when the front wheel is very lightly loaded. This determines two things about front springs. One, they have to be long because part of the fork's ability to carry heavy load lies in its abundant travel of 4 inches or more. Two, they are usually *progressively wound* to give them two or more spring rates: soft near full extension, and much firmer near full compression. A simple progressive spring has its coils wound at

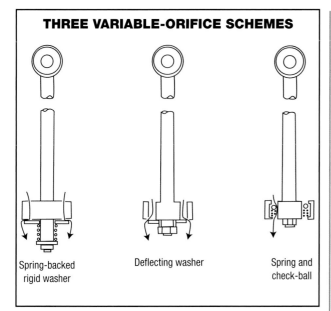

THREE VARIABLE-ORIFICE SCHEMES

Spring-backed rigid washer

Deflecting washer

Spring and check-ball

Avoiding Orifice Limitation. *To prevent damping force from increasing to infinity at higher damper speeds, the damping orifices are made variable, becoming larger as pressure across them rises. On the left, the orifices are covered by a spring-backed washer that rises with pressure. At center is the deflecting washer scheme, in which the washers themselves become the spring. Resistance can be tailored by stacking on combinations of washers and spacers of various thickness to obtain almost any damping curve. On the right is the multiple check-ball and spring system, in which orifices are made to open in sequence as damper velocity rises, by use of different spring rates and/or preloads.*

two different pitches. At light loads, all coils are in action and the spring is soft. At some heavier load, the closely wound set of coils bottoms, leaving only the remaining, wider spaced coils in action. A spring's rate, in pounds per inch, is inversely proportional to the number of coils in action; the fewer the coils, the stiffer the rate. If this seems backward to you, recall that you can more easily bend a 6-foot piece of 1/4-inch steel rod than you can a 6-inch piece.

Other progressive schemes are possible. Springs can be wound with more than two pitch zones, or the pitch may vary continuously along the spring's length, making its rate increase smoothly rather than in steps. Or the zones of differing pitch may be wound on separate springs that are then stacked one on top of another into the fork.

In modern front forks, there is a threaded adjuster bearing on the top of the spring. By screwing this in or out, the front of the bike can be raised or lowered. This is called a preload adjuster, but its real job is to set the height at which the bike sits. Preload is the degree to which the spring is compressed when the fork is fully extended, and may be zero or even negative, but is usually positive—that is, the spring is slightly compressed at full extension. To determine the existing preload, back out the preload adjuster, counting the turns, until it no longer puts pressure on the spring. Screw it back to the original position

and write down the number of turns. Check the other fork leg to be sure the numbers are the same.

Front-end height can be adjusted independently of preload by loosening the fork clamps, sliding the tubes up or down, then retightening the pinch bolts.

A fair number of people intuitively believe that increasing preload makes the suspension stiffer. It does not! All the preload adjuster does is raise or lower the point at which the bike rides on its suspension, by setting the load on the spring with suspension fully extended. People *feel* that preload makes the spring stiffer because it's harder to push the bike down when the preload is increased. But the only way to make the spring stiffer is to replace it with a stiffer spring.

On older forks that lacked a threaded preload adjuster, the preload was adjusted by replacing a preload spacer with one of a different length (PVC pipe, cheap, easily sawed to length, and lightweight, was the usual choice) or, for finer adjustments, by stacking washers on top of the spring. Because few of us carried many washers of the right diameter, quarters were often used, and people would figure preload in dollars and cents.

FRONT FORK OIL LEVEL AND AIR PROGRESSIVITY

Because front fork legs are sealed, they derive another kind of support by compressing the air trapped above the damper oil inside them. This kind of air spring is quite progressive, which is good because it's just what front forks must deliver. Unfortunately, you can easily overdo air-spring progressivity, as follows. With any front fork, there is a specification given for oil quantity or, preferably, oil level. I say "preferably" because, when you have drained your fork oil, there is still a lot of oil inside, clinging to the parts and trapped in all the nooks and crannies of the damper mechanism. If you refill using a fixed quantity as your standard (it was, for example, 6 1/2 ounces for the classic 35mm Ceriani. Was it an accident that this was exactly the volume of the old five-cent Coke bottle?), you may very well overfill the fork. Well, you may object, why worry? So long as the damper is covered by the oil, it's harder for it to suck air, so what's the difference if there's an ounce extra?

The difference is that the more oil there is inside the fork leg, the higher that leg's "air compression ratio" rises. Under heavy load, the fork compresses and the high oil level tries to cram the clearance air above it into an impossibly small space. The air resists, making the last bit of fork compression undesirably stiff. You may, in fact, believe you are bottoming when this happens, or you may develop front-wheel chatter. Therefore, keep this relationship in mind and refill each fork leg to a standard level, not a standard quantity.

You do this by supporting the front of the machine, then pulling both fork top caps, spacers, and springs (have a basin ready to hold these drippy things so they don't pick up shop dirt from a bench top—you don't want dirt plugging any damping orifice). With both legs fully extended, refill each with oil sufficient to cover the tops of the damper tubes. Now stroke the sliders up and down to expel air from the dampers. Once the dampers are just covered and air is no longer coming up as you stroke, finish adding oil until the oil level measures the specified distance (given in your owner's manual) down from the top of the fork tube. It's handy to have one of those tiny pencil-sized flashlights for this, and a millimeter tape measure (the oil level is invariably given in metric).

If all this is somewhat confusing, remember that the goal is clear—let that be your guide. What you want to end up with is a front end that can carry the 100 percent plus braking load without bottoming, yet still be soft and compliant enough to hook up near zero load during acceleration.

REAR SPRINGS

On single-shock bikes, rear springs are short, straight-rate (non-progressive) and very stiff. This is because the single rear spring carries its load through a linkage that multiplies the force at the axle by two or three times. Rear springs are straight-rate because any desired progressivity can be designed into the linkage. Where a pair of front springs may add up to a total spring rate of 80–100 pounds per inch (40–50 pounds per inch, per spring), the rear spring is commonly in the range of 275–400 pounds per inch. It takes hefty wire to give this rate, so the resulting spring weighs several pounds. One can only hope that the ex-Soviets, burdened with all their titanium production capacity, will realize our profound need and hit the market with low-priced titanium suspension springs.

At the rear, it is often possible to change ride height and spring preload independently. Preload determines how much pressure is needed to make the suspension begin to compress. For example, if the threaded collars on the damper body are adjusted so that the spring is exerting 180 pounds with the rear suspension fully extended, and the linkage ratio is three to one, that translates to 60 pounds at the axle. Thus, it will take 60 pounds of force to make this setting begin to compress. By adjusting preload, we are setting the distance into the suspension travel that we will compress the suspension when we get on. But for various other handling-related reasons, we may want to raise or lower the back of the bike—without changing the preload. To make this possible, there is often a threaded length adjuster on one end of the damper. Changing this allows the damper's eye-to-eye length to be changed without changing the amount of suspension travel used up by the rider's weight.

REAR SPRINGS ON TWIN SHOCKS

Older machines had two rear spring/damper units, and for these there is still a wide range of spring rates and types—including progressive-wound. In the early 1970s it was common on the 750 Kawasaki H2R to use 60/90 progressive springs on flat circuits, and 100-pound straight-rate springs on banked tracks like Charlotte or Daytona. The soft initial rate (60 pounds per inch) gave good bump isolation, and the 90 took care of occasional higher loads. The 100s carried the added centrifugal loads imposed by banked turns.

Lighter bikes used lighter rate springs. It was common for older bikes to be over sprung, and good improvement could be had by replacing harder springs with softer ones. Use your judgment

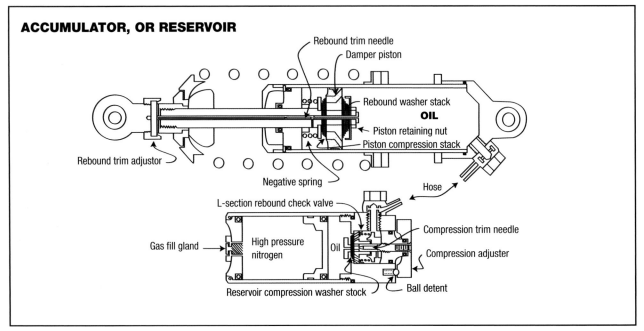

ACCUMULATOR, OR RESERVOIR

Rebound trim needle
Damper piston
Rebound washer stack
OIL
Piston retaining nut
Piston compression stack
Rebound trim adjustor
Negative spring
Hose
L-section rebound check valve
Compression trim needle
Gas fill gland
High pressure nitrogen
Oil
Compression adjuster
Reservoir compression washer stock
Ball detent

Rear Suspension Damper with Reservoir. *This gadget looks complicated but the ideas behind it are simple: oil is pumped by suspension motion through combinations of fixed and variable orifices to give a desired curve of resistance versus velocity. To achieve consistency and accuracy, the quality of the parts must be very high. The shapes of the damping curves for compression and rebound are built into the washer stacks covering piston and reservoir orifices.*

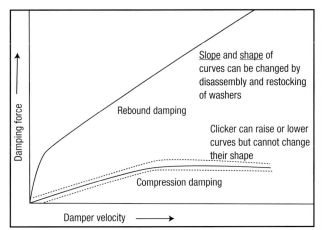

Damping Curves in a Modern Damper. *Rebound damping is roughly proportional to damper velocity, with extra stiffness at the bottom to prevent wallowing. Compression damping begins with a linear rise, but is then chopped off at a plateau level because beyond some force level, further rise would upset the bike. The clicker can raise or lower either curve slightly, but cannot change their shape. This is why you usually cannot make a damper stacked for one bike work on another just by twiddling the knobs.*

and experiment. The damper bodies carried ramped collars, allowing three to five steps of preload adjustment. With lighter springs, the adjustment could be made by hand, but heavier ones required a paint-gouging set of slip-joint pliers or the right tool, a hook or pin spanner. Although length-adjustable twin dampers have been made, such height changes usually had to be made by getting longer or shorter dampers. Accordingly, they have been made in a variety of lengths. Alternatively, a variety of mounting points were sometimes provided along the swingarrn.

Most twin-shock bikes are made with the lower shock eyes directly above the rear axle. In this case, a 100-pound-per-inch spring will give a 200-pound-per-inch rate at the axle (two springs, remember?). But as the lower eye of the shock is moved farther forward along the swingarm, you have to apply the fairly obvious arithmetic of proportion to convert spring rate to axle rate. Whole books were written in the 1970s on the subject of forward-mount and lay-down shock suspension. They await your further curiosity.

One more point on twin shocks. One of the reasons that older bikes often handled poorly was the early design of their rear suspension dampers. Consider upgrading an older bike to gas-pressurized dampers of modern design—unless something contrary to common sense, like vintage racing rules, forbids it. Even then, who's to know what's inside the antique damper bodies?

ABOUT LINKAGES

In the mid-1970s, Yamaha introduced the Monoshock—a single rear damper linked to a triangulated swingarm at a 2:1 ratio. For every inch the rear wheel moved, the spring/damper moved 1/2 inch. This concept eliminated effects from differences between twin shocks, and the triangulation stiffened the swingarm against twist and moved the damper/spring unit's mass forward, toward the machine's mass center. The other makers soon had their own proprietary linkage systems, most with what is called rising rate. This meant that suspension became stiffer in rate as it compressed. At the start of its travel, the ratio between rear axle and suspension unit might be 3:1, then rise as the suspension compressed to become more like 2:1 at full compression. The idea was to put more load-carrying ability into a limited amount of travel, but because each manufacturer had a different rising-rate scheme, a suspension unit sprung and damped for a given model would turn out to be much too stiff or too soft for another model. Countless hours have been wasted by riders who have tried to transplant bargain-purchase suspension units from one bike to another, hoping they can readjust the unit by changing preload and clicker settings.

The early thinking about linkages was that, by using a rising rate, they could absorb more bump energy in a given travel. This looked like an advance over the first (1974) long-travel setups, which, with 6 inches of travel front and rear, allowed machines to wallow uncertainly and dive severely during braking. Riders like stability because they need a firm platform from which to launch maneuvers. Shorter travel, combined with rising rate, looked like the best of both worlds. Every company had its own patent system, with a painful acronym to call it by.

This entire development course—from short to long travel, through rising-rate, and back to linear rate with shorter travel—has been driven by one fact. That has been the original excessive firmness of compression damping, a situation allowed to continue because the damper testing machines of that day operated too slowly to reveal the problem. Long travel appeared to make things better by reducing spring and damping rates. This meant reduced compression damping, and that in turn meant ability to travel faster over rough surfaces without excessive disturbance. The added travel allowed at least as much bump energy absorption as with the previous stiffer setups.

The problems of 135–150mm of long travel, such as exaggerated pitch and weight transfer, pointed development toward rising rate. Yet rising rate had its own special problem; knees in the curve gave the same impression as premature bottoming. Meanwhile, the coming of improved dampers with intelligently designed compression circuits allowed rising rate to be gradually abandoned. This brings us around almost to the starting point in terms of rear suspension travel, but we have gained enormously in rear damper performance. One by one, rising-rate curves with knees, bumps, or dips in them have been found to cause racing suspension problems, and special aftermarket linkages have been marketed to linearize (straighten) them.

ANALYZING LINKAGES

Those interested in analyzing their suspensions' rate curves can do so by moving the axle in small steps and measuring how much each step compresses the damper (with the spring removed, naturally). Graph the results, suitable for framing. Race teams have employed specialists, using linkage analysis computer programs, to do the same, and this method has the advantage of being able speedily to run through many variations in a short time.

No computer skills? Have no fear; the same results can be reliably obtained by building a two-dimensional model of the suspension on a drawing board, using tag board for the swingarm and links, and thumbtacks as the pivots. I've used this method more than once myself. You draw out the arc of travel of the rear axle and divide it into equal steps. Then you measure the compression of your cardboard damper as you compress your suspension in 1/2-inch steps. Graph the relationship of the two. Lo and behold, you have the suspension linkage curve. As an example, the curve of the 1988 Suzuki GSX-R1100's rear suspension is smoothly concave upward, its rate rising about 25 percent from full extension to full compression. Rider Dale Quarterley reported that this curve made his bike pop up suddenly as he got on-throttle to accelerate from turns. Through the miracle of cardboard and scissors, he was supplied with a design for a linear linkage that he liked better. Computers have impressive capabilities, but plenty of good work can be done without them.

OLDER FORK DAMPERS

In older bikes of three or more decades ago, the front fork dampers are very simple devices, located at the bottoms of the fork sliders and held down by Allen bolts, whose heads can be seen from below by removing the front axle and wheel, and looking up at the bottoms of the sliders. These are simple, rebound-only dampers. Their important parts, therefore, are the rebound orifice(s), the check valves, and the much larger compression orifice(s).

These dampers live in the bottom of the fork, with the springs perched on top, so it's essential that there is enough oil in the fork to cover the tops of the damper tubes with the fork at full extension. To make matters worse, instructions for such older forks usually call for a quantity of oil instead of a fill level—and in some cases the fill quantity doesn't even cover the tops of the damper tubes! When the fork begins to operate, the dampers soon suck in air from above and make foam. Small surprise that such springy stuff doesn't damp well.

On the really early fork dampers, compression oil flow shoots up out of the top of the damper tube. This carries the oil up into the spring, from which it takes time to drip and run back down. In the meantime, the damper cylinders lacking enough oil to cover themselves have sucked air, and the same evil process goes to work, ruining your front-end

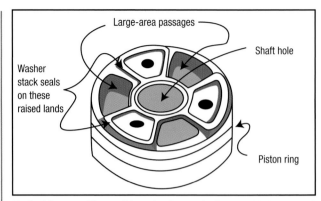

Typical Damper Piston. *When the damper is disassembled to restack the washers, the piston is revealed as a very complex casting with large ports in it, which are big enough to flow damper oil past the washers without orifice limitation. The recent Ohlins TTX construction is different, using a solid piston. TTX units can be revalved without complete disassembly.*

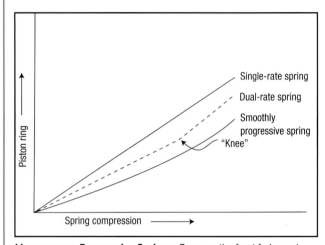

Linear versus Progressive Springs. *Because the front fork must support 100 percent of the machine's weight during braking, but must also be light and sensitive during off-corner acceleration to maintain front grip and steering, the fork springs may have to be progressive— to have their rate rise as they are compressed.*

damping. Later, engineers saw the light and put a fitting atop each damper tube that directs the compression flow *sideways* instead of straight up.

Usually these early dampers also include a hydraulic stop to cushion the impact of bottoming. This takes the form of a tapered piece on the bottom of the damper tube, below the compression orifice(s). As the fork compresses, oil is displaced through the larger compression orifice in the damper tube. But close to bottom, the damper piston slides past the compression orifice, thereby closing it off. The only escape for the oil now is between the hydro-stop cone and the inside of the fork tube, which has now slid down over it. In this way, compression damping is made to increase steeply, preventing hard, metal-to-metal bottoming. This feature is falling out of use in the latest forks, which use a shaped cone of rubbery material as a bottoming cushion instead.

In this same early era, dampers made for race bikes such as Yamaha TZs have one more feature—a footvalve. This is just a one-way valve implemented with a captive washer, made in unit with the hydraulic bottom stop. Its purpose is to unlock the system so the fork isn't held down after bottoming by the very force that cushioned the blow. The footvalve also provides extra flow area through which the damper chamber can be refilled during the rebound stroke. Often, aftermarket dampers for earlier bikes, such as Kawasaki Z1, have such footvalves.

The limiting feature of these early forks is that they are fixed-orifice, atmospheric dampers. Having fixed orifices means that their damping goes up steeply with damper speed, and this makes such forks potentially harsh in compression. Usually, to avoid this problem, they are given such big compression orifices that there is virtually no

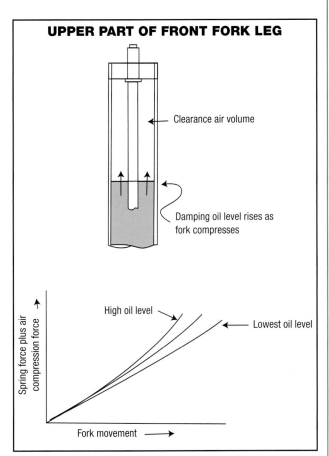

UPPER PART OF FRONT FORK LEG

Clearance air volume

Damping oil level rises as fork compresses

High oil level

Lowest oil level

Spring force plus air compression force

Fork movement

How Front Fork Oil Level Affects Spring Rate. *The top figure shows how damping oil compresses the air above it as the suspension is compressed. The higher the oil level, the smaller the space into which this air is compressed. The lower figure shows the result of various oil levels; the higher the level, the more progressive is the support the fork gives.*

compression damping at all. The rebound orifices are one or two little holes, drilled up high into the damper tube. In fact, much of the "orifice" exists in the loose tolerances with which these fork dampers were made. Even with the holes welded up solid (and ground smooth so the mating parts will slide past easily in use), some of these forks have little damping unless filled with something really gooey, like maple syrup. Likewise, many of the early "adjustable damping" production forks show little change in damping as you turn the adjuster from minimum to maximum.

You can learn a lot about a fork damper by stroking one leg held in a vise without its spring. You will feel the one-way valve open and close, and you will hear the rush of oil (and any entrained air) through the damping orifices. It's a good practice to stroke a completed front end through its full travel, with its wheel bolted in, but without springs, on the bike. Any alignment problems will instantly show up as drag or irregular action. Quite often, wheel spacers are the wrong length, causing the fork to bind as it nears full compression. Hydro-stops are sometimes misaligned, causing drag near full compression. Slightly loosen the damper hold-down bolts, bottom the fork, and retighten. This may allow them to recenter and stop dragging. Better and easier to discover nonsense like this in the shop than out on the road or track.

Since these early fork dampers are atmospheric, the damping oil is unpressurized and is in contact with air. That means the oil can be pulled apart—cavitated—by sufficiently vigorous riding and mixed with air. This can lead to irregular damping. Many good riders went very fast on this kind of primitive equipment, so it can be made to work. Recent racing forks from makers like Ohlins and Showa are now pressurized, preventing cavitation. You can see the pressure accumulators as small cylinders, parallel with the fork tubes and attached to the fork bottoms.

For earlier technology forks, Paul Thede made a little device he called "the gold valve," which is a compression valve made to sit atop the damper tubes, under the spring. They allow an early type of fork to have compression damping without orifice limitation at high speed.

INSTABILITY: WOBBLE AND WEAVE

We have to talk about this somewhere, the dreaded word that no manufacturer wants to hear: instability. All types of vehicles—cars, airplanes, artillery shells, motorcycles—display one or more types of instability. Motorcycles have three types: the capsize, wobble, and weave modes.

The capsize mode is just a fancy way to say you'll fall over if you don't pay attention and steer. Capsize is the mode you fought as a kid, when you were trying to learn to ride a bicycle.

The other two are caster oscillations, which are just like the wobbling of a caster wheel on a shopping cart. One vehicle dynamics researcher has characterized the motorcycle as two casters—one short, one longer—hinged together. The "length" of the front caster is the steering trail, while that of the rear caster is essentially the wheelbase.

The wobble mode is rapid fluttering of the front caster, in a speed range of 8–10 cycles per second or so. Riders often encounter it when accelerating or decelerating through the speed range of 35–45 miles per hour, with their hands off the bars or in light contact. Wobble occurs in this speed range because wheel rotation frequency comes into step with wobble here, allowing any wheel imbalance or out-of-round to drive the oscillation (the same thing, in the same speed range, can be seen in older cars with loose suspension or steering joints). The damping force of your hands on the bars is usually enough to prevent wobble, and natural damping for wobble increases with speed. A steering damper is effective against wobble. As the steered mass of wheel, fork, bars, and brakes is decreased, wobble is damped more strongly. This is one attraction of the so-called forkless front ends, as on bikes like the Bimota Tesi.

The weave mode is a slower oscillation of the rear caster, in the two to three cycles per second range. Because its damping *decreases* with increasing speed, there is some speed high enough to make any machine display weave—if it'll go that fast. This is an especially dangerous mode for a couple of reasons. First, it's slow enough to tempt the foolish to think they can steer out of it, but the usual result is to make it worse. Second, a steering damper isn't much use against weave, and may even make it worse. Experienced test riders on instrumented bikes test for weave stability by striking the handlebar. This activates the mode, just as an aircraft test pilot may give a "stick pulse" to evaluate pitch stability, while instruments record how long the resulting oscillation takes to die away. It's desirable to have the oscillation end in a couple of cycles. When there is a stability problem, the oscillation may take many cycles to cease, or may continue at a steady amplitude. The worst condition, of course, is that in which the weave "diverges"—its amplitude increases with time.

Weave is only seen very occasionally in racing, and always arises from some abnormality. In the early days of aluminum chassis, Kenny Roberts' quite flexible OW53 once developed a weave at 150 miles per hour that was violent enough to deflate a tubeless tire. Sometimes a bike will weave for one rider, but not for another. The rider who "freezes" on the controls is generally the one who gets the weave. Eric Bostrom's first Daytona 200 ride on a Kawasaki took place right on the weave threshold—if he sat down, he said, "The bike started that pumping." So he essentially stood up for 200 miles. As with fighter aircraft, the setup offering quickest response is right at the edge of instability. Quite often, European Ducati teams at Daytona have weave in the first practice—simply because their usual setup becomes marginally unstable at Daytona speeds. They have dialed it out by second practice.

If you encounter instability, look for sources of lost motion, such as loose steering-head or swingarm pivots, worn wheel

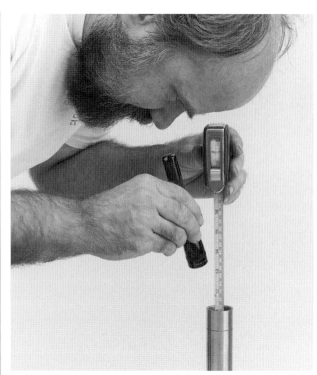

Setting Front Fork Oil Level. *On older bikes, the fork oil spec calls for an amount, but it's more accurate to set the level the modern way, by peering down into the fork leg with spring and spacer removed, fork fully compressed, and using a penlight and millimeter tape measure to measure the oil level as a distance down from the top of the tube. Do this with the fork on the bike—the fork leg in this illustration is removed from the machine only for clarity.* John Owens Studio

bearings, loose spokes, chassis or swingarm cracks, or loose or missing engine bolts—anything that can introduce abnormal extra motion or flexibility. Suspect also failed suspension dampers or chassis members bent in a recent crash. The use of smaller wheels or lighter tires reduces natural gyro stability. If you make such a change, don't be surprised if your bike feels twitchier afterward. Where there is a choice, load forward, not to the rear, as rearward weight bias makes weave more likely by acting as a "heavier pendulum." This is why European road riders prefer a tank bag to any form of rear bag. Never load anything on your machine that can wiggle or oscillate, like a heavy pack on a flimsy luggage carrier. Police bikes with heavy radios on tubular steel mounts used to be great weavers.

Because the damping that provides stability comes from the tires, there can be tire pressure effects. More pressure reduces footprint area and damping force. Because tire construction and tread profile strongly affect stability, some tire combinations just don't work on some machines. Indeed, some bikes are placarded for certain tires only, or not to be operated above particular speeds. Therefore, if you have instability, consider any recent tire changes you have made. Worn tires can also lead to instability.

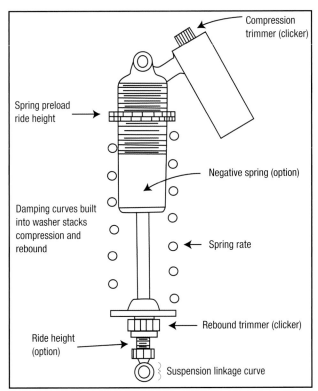

Rear Suspension Adjustments. *Each of these options has a place in your plan for control of machine attitude and rear wheel motion. The number of alternatives is large, but once you understand how the system works, it all makes sense.*

Labels in figure:
- Compression trimmer (clicker)
- Spring preload ride height
- Negative spring (option)
- Damping curves built into washer stacks compression and rebound
- Spring rate
- Rebound trimmer (clicker)
- Ride height (option)
- Suspension linkage curve

STEERING DAMPERS

As noted previously, steering dampers are effective against wobble, but they may actually make weave worse. This is part of the reason why Honda's electronically controlled steer damper was developed. Damping can be low at low speeds, permitting accurate traffic maneuvering, and then can increase in the speed range of wobble and decrease again at higher speeds. The mounting of steer dampers is a serious business—the forces involved can be quite high—so flabby clamps and poor maintenance won't cut it. Mount the damper to go full-stroke if you want full effect. Currently, a popular mounting is crossways, ahead of the fork and attached to the front fairing mount, or behind it and attached to the frame.

One thing you must have from any damper is smooth, stiction-free operation. Some older adjustable dampers have seals that stick quite hard, so test before you buy.

Damper adjustment is a matter of taste. Big hefty riders like the late Gregg Hansford, with the strength to bulldog wagging handlebars, often set their dampers at minimum. Eddie Lawson was famous for his rock-hard damper setting. That molasses-in-January steering damper was probably responsible for much of his legendary smoothness—it left him no choice!

Critical parts that stay on the bike, as opposed to being frequently serviced, can become loose from vibration over time. Therefore, check bolt tension on steering damper mounts from time to time.

ANOTHER UPSETTING SCENE: CHATTER

If you ride hard on good tires, you eventually encounter chatter, most likely at the front. Chatter is a high-frequency bouncing of the tire, typically occurring during hard cornering, as veteran Mick Grant once concisely put it, "under conditions of heavy load and high grip." The underlying phenomenon is coupling between two oscillations. One is the back-and-forth bending of the front fork, and the other is the tire's vertical bounce mode. If the damper is ineffective or the fork locked or greatly stiffened by stiction, this bounce can develop to the point where the harder you try to ride the bike, the more it tries to make you see double and run off the road. The chatter frequency is typically in the range of 20–25 cycles per second—too fast for most damper technologies to stop it. Why does chatter occur mainly at the front? Forks are less stiff than swingarms, so their natural frequencies are lower.

As with the common cold, there is no simple, universal remedy for chatter. Sometimes a small reduction in tire pressure helps, or a change to a tire of somewhat different construction. Be sure your fork is not overfilled with oil—high air compression progressivity can act like a very stiff spring and overpower the damping in the fork. Some dampers don't respond well at higher frequencies—they cavitate the damper oil or their valves become confused. If your fork has sluggish heavy oil in it (15, 20, etc.), it may be that lighter oil will work better. In general, fork dampers made to tighter tolerances, running thinner oil, do a better job in controlling chatter. Suspension pioneer Geoff Fox once said that were it not for water's ability to promote rust and corrosion, it would be a nearly perfect damping fluid! Sometimes chatter can be detuned by a change in front wheel mass—such as changing from one brake disc to two, or from a mag wheel to aluminum, etc. Because chatter is concerned with the flexibility of the front end, anything that changes front-end stiffness has some chance of changing or controlling chatter. This includes fork tube stiffness and steering-head stiffness. Don't always assume that more stiffness is better. Nothing is *always* better!

If you consult the G.M.D. Computrack people on chatter, you may be told that chatter results from fork binding, caused by incorrect steering-head angle. Mr. McDonald's views are highly influential these days, and are certainly to be considered. No matter whose advice you seek, you are in charge of your program.

Consider that many bikes will chatter on the way into corners if the rider simply rolls, decelerating, to the apex, but may stop chattering if the rider enters less hard and gets on the gas earlier. Earlier I quoted Mick Grant about chatter occurring during "heavy load and high grip." If you get on the gas, the front tire load becomes less, so the chatter may die away. But sometimes, the harder you try to push, the worse the chatter gets.

Upside-Down Fork? *I disagree. According to common sense, this type of fork is right-side up, and it's the older type that is upside-down. I call this a male-slider fork, and it makes sense because it places the larger, outer tube at the top, where the bending load is greatest. These forks contain so-called cartridge dampers, which are essentially tiny, self-contained damper units located inside the fork legs. Earlier fixed-orifice fork dampers have all the sophistication of screen-door closers.* Ohlins

The need to make forks stiffer as a means of avoiding chatter has taken us from 36mm tubes in 1980, to the present norm of 43–50mm. The switch in the 1990s to so-called upside-down construction has provided much more stiffness by placing the larger tube at the top, where the greatest bending moment is. As you might expect, the chatter frequency has risen as well.

REAR CHATTER

Rear chatter is much less common. It can, however, occur during braking as a hammering of the lightly loaded rear wheel against the suspension's top stop. Be sure that the damper is in good condition; if it has depressurized or inhaled gas, it can become bouncy. Also look for lost motion in rear suspension linkage. Support the machine on a centerstand, then lift the rear wheel to check for such looseness. Sometimes a "negative spring" has been used to control rear chatter. A negative spring is located inside the rear suspension unit, between the piston and the rod seal, and prevents hard topping.

When the throttles of a big four-stroke are closed for corner entry, engine braking can cause dragging or hopping of the back tire, or loss of rear grip as the machine leans over into the turn. The old-time medicine for this was to just set the idle speed up, but the current solution is a "slipper" or back-torque-limiting clutch.

CONCISE DICTIONARY OF SUSPENSION JARGON

It would be grand if we could use the language of Shakespeare to talk about suspension, but we need some special words here, for special jobs.

Acceleration Limit: The maximum rates at which a motorcycle can be braked or accelerated (assuming sufficient brake torque or engine power) are determined by how easily the bike can do wheelies or stoppies. The acceleration rate at which wheel lift occurs is determined as shown in the drawing. Moving CG forward increases the acceleration limit, but decreases the braking limit, and vice versa.

Attitude: The angle at which the chassis sits, determined by the front and rear ride heights. Attitude controls steering-head angle, a major variable in steering/handling. Roughly speaking, raising the rear ride height 1 inch decreases the steering-head angle by 1 degree—and vice versa. Raising the front ride height 1 inch increases steering-head angle about 1 degree. Another powerful attitude effect is on weight distribution. Tipping the bike forward slightly increases weight on the front tire, decreasing it on the rear—and vice versa. Extreme attitudes cause extreme weight shift. For example, a bike that dives rapidly under braking is more likely to pick up its rear wheel than is a bike that dives less rapidly.

Available Suspension Travel: This is suspension travel, minus sag. It tells you how much travel is available for use in absorbing bumps.

Bottoming: Compressing the suspension until it reaches its stop. This is upsetting to the bike because it is the same as a sudden large increase in spring stiffness. When the bike bottoms, the motion of the bike on its suspension is suddenly stopped, delivering a blow to the tire that tends to break traction. Bottoming, especially in corners, is to be avoided.

Bump: See Compression.

Center of Gravity (CG, or Center of Mass): This is the point at which the machine's total mass, including fuel and rider, appears to act. If supported at this point, the machine would not rotate in any plane—it would be balanced around all axes. On a typical sportbike, this point is located about 24 inches above ground, near halfway between front and rear wheels.

Chain Tangent Force: This is the force, tending to extend rear suspension, caused by the fact that the top (tension) run of the chain is at some angle to the swingarm's plane. This force is proportional to chain pull, so it's largest in first gear and less with every upshift. For street riding, this has a very small effect, but it has become more important in racing because tangent force can be used to prevent squat and push. Anything that increases the angle of chain to swingarm increases this tangent force, so smaller front sprockets, larger rear ones, increased rear ride height, or a higher swingarm pivot position all increase the force. Life gets complicated at the top! Some teams, finding that changing sprockets alters anti-squat geometry, have resorted to changing overall gear ratio with alternate primary gears!

Compression: Sometimes called "bump"—this is suspension motion tending to push a wheel up, compressing its suspension.

Damping: Friction, applied to an oscillating system such as a motorcycle's suspension, for the purpose of limiting or controlling motion.

Dive: Compression of the front suspension during braking.

Linear: In strict proportion. As applied to rear suspension linkage, it means a constant linkage ratio, as opposed to a rising rate.

Linkage Ratio: The ratio between rear axle movement and damper movement. In old twin-shock setups, linkage ratio is 1.0 when the shocks are vertical and mounted directly above the rear axle. On single-shock bikes, this ratio depends on the details of the linkage used, is usually in a range of 2–3:1 and can vary with suspension position. The graph of linkage ratio versus suspension travel is called the suspension curve, or rising-rate curve.

Offset: Imagine that you could pass a plane down through the centerline of the front axle, parallel to the steering axis. Offset is the distance from that axis, to that plane. On most sportbikes, the fork tubes are also in that plane, so for them, offset is the distance from steering axis to a plane drawn through the fork tube centerlines. Offset determines trail. More offset reduces trail by putting the front wheel farther forward, and vice versa. Race teams typically carry sets of fork crowns made up in different offsets, in increments of 2mm or 5mm. Choice is a matter of rider taste.

Pitch: Rotation of the chassis to a new vehicle attitude. Applying the brakes produces forward pitch. The shorter the chassis and the higher the center of gravity are, the greater pitch is. The more the machine pitches, the greater the weight transfer becomes, up to the point that it picks up the front or rear tire, so excess pitch is always a potential problem.

Preload: See Spring Preload.

Progressive Spring: A spring wound in such a way as to become stiffer (higher rate) as it is compressed.

Pumpdown: Pumpdown, or ratchet effect, is what can happen when you ride through a bumpy corner, using a lot of rebound damping and little compression damping. Each bump easily compresses the suspension, but the rebound damping holds the bike down so much that there isn't time for it to fully extend before it hits the next bump, and the next. As a result, the bike ratchets itself down on its suspension, losing ride height and possibly resulting in grounding.

Push: Any condition in which the front wheel gives reduced steering effect. This can happen when accelerating out of a corner; acceleration makes the front wheel light, which reduces its grip. As a result, the machine runs wide. It can also happen during corner entry, caused by excessive weight transfer to the front, overloading the front tire. Thus, braking to the apex can often cause pushing.

Rebound: The extending motion of a suspension.

Ride Height: This is the height at which the machine sits, front or rear. Measuring to ground is hard because machine tilt causes errors. Therefore, measure from an axle end to some point directly above it on the machine. Write the numbers down so you don't have to remeasure too often.

Rising-Rate Suspension: Any suspension whose rate or linkage ratio rises (becomes stiffer) as it compresses. This is accomplished through linkage whose mechanical advantage changes as its links rotate. A rising rate was thought to be an advantage in the period 1978–1985, but the recent trend has been back toward linear (constant rate, as on a twin-shock bike) rate. I expect twin shocks to be "reinvented" any day now.

Sag: This is a very important concept related to ride height. Sag is the distance that a bike settles when normally loaded with fuel and rider, measured from the fully topped height. Measure the topped height with a friend holding the machine up enough to top the suspension. When you set sag, you are determining how much suspension travel will be available for bump absorption. Sag is typically set at one-fourth to one-third of total travel.

Spring Preload: This is the pressure a spring is exerting when the suspension is fully extended (topped). It is typically adjusted by screwing the spring's upper rest up or down. On a front fork, the preload adjuster is a screw, one end of which projects through the top of each fork leg. On a rear suspension, one end of the spring bears against a threaded collar, usually with a lock ring to prevent unwanted movement. The collar is wound up or down by use of a special spanner or hook wrench. When thinking about preload, always remember that adjusting preload up or down simply changes the height at which the bike rides. It does not make suspension stiffer or softer. The reason many riders intuitively feel preload changes adjust stiffness is because a bike with a lot of preload does not move as easily when they sit down on it. It takes more pressure to begin to compress the suspension. This is not the same as a stiffer spring! A stiffer spring is made with either thicker wire (a few thousandths of an inch in wire diameter makes a big difference in spring stiffness) or fewer coils.

Spring Rate: This is the measure of a spring's stiffness, given either as pounds per inch or kilograms per millimeter. For example, a 60-pound-per-inch spring will compress 1 inch under a 60-pound load, 2 inches under a 120-pound load, and so on. By fitting a stiffer spring, you make it take more load to fully compress the suspension. By fitting a softer spring, you make it take less load to compress it. One hundred pounds per inch equals 1.79kg/mm. For some reason, front spring rate is often given as the total of two springs. For example, the old Kawasaki KR750 front springs were rated at 1.5kg/mm, or about 84 pounds per inch total (42 pounds per inch per spring). Spring rate depends very strongly on wire diameter and coil diameter. Rate rises as the fourth power of the wire diameter; if a wire that is 10 percent thicker computes as $1.1 \times 1.1 \times 1.1 \times 1.1 = 1.46$, the spring becomes 46 percent stiffer! Two springs that look very similar can have very different rates. Some people make the mistake of thinking that cutting a spring shorter will make it softer. The reverse is true, for spring rate is inversely proportional to the number of coils.

Squat: Any tendency for the rear of the machine to settle under acceleration. In well-designed motorcycle chassis, chain force reaction cancels squat. During in-corner acceleration, squat tends to make the front end push.

Squat and Push: As a rider begins to get on the throttle to begin acceleration in mid-turn, rearward weight transfer—if not opposed by chain lift force—tends to make the bike squat. This takes a small but crucial amount of weight off the front tire, possibly making it push. The harder the rider tries to get on the gas, the worse the bike steers. The rider tries to "dig in" the front end (steer it more sharply into the turn) to get more steering force, but continuing this just makes the front end tuck.

Steering-Head Angle: The angle between the centerline of the steering shaft and the vertical. Roll the machine onto a level surface and lay a carpenter's angle gauge on a fork tube. Be careful to distinguish between loaded and unloaded values. Typical values are between 30 (very vintage!) and 22 degrees, with older machines having more, later machines less. In general, as steering-head angle is reduced, steering becomes quicker but the machine may become less stable.

Stepping Out: Jumping sideways in a corner, caused by too-stiff suspension keeping the wheels from tracking the bumps. Each time a wheel is knocked up off the pavement, centrifugal force drags the bike abruptly sideways.

Swingarm Droop Angle: If you raise or lower your rear suspension's ride height, you change the angle the swingarm makes with the horizontal, which is its droop angle. This angle helps to determine the lift force that the drive chain generates at the back of the machine; the greater the droop, the higher the lift force. This force is useful in preventing squat as the machine accelerates out of a corner.

Topping: Topping is hitting the suspension's stop at full extension. This may happen at the rear during hard braking; the front end dives, and the rear end rises and tops. Hard topping tends to pick up the wheel. Topping the front suspension during hard off-corner acceleration, if it picks up the wheel or almost does so, can interfere with control. Occasionally, rear suspension will hop during hard braking, banging hard against its top stop. Sometimes a negative spring (one placed inside the shock, acting to prevent topping) is used to control this.

Trail: Imagine you could look down through the center of the steering shaft, through the tire and wheel, to the ground. The spot on the road where you are looking would be the projection of the steering axis. Trail is the distance from this point, back to the center of the front tire's contact patch. Look at trail as being the lever arm by which the steering is able to center itself after any deflection. Trail is generally between 3 and 4 inches. More tends to make the machine more stable, but makes steering heavier. Less has the reverse effect.

Travel: Travel is the full stroke of a suspension, from fully extended (topped) to fully compressed (bottomed). Travel is measured by removing the spring(s) and manually moving the wheel through the full stroke. The advantage of long travel is that it gives plenty of stroke in which to absorb bumps, but its disadvantage is that it can permit extreme attitudes (for instance, very nose-down during hard braking). Typical front travel for a telescopic fork–equipped bike is 130mm (5 inches). Typical rear travel is in the range 110–130mm (4.3–5 inches).

Weight Transfer: The shift of load from one end of a bike to the other, caused by acceleration or deceleration. Brake and engine forces act on the bike at ground level, but the center-of-mass of machine and rider is about 2 feet above ground. Acceleration therefore tends to drive the rear wheel out from under the center-of-mass, putting more weight on the rear wheel. Braking does the reverse—the extreme being a stoppie. Even closing the throttle causes a marked increase in front-end load—often enough to cause the front to push as you enter a turn.

Wheelbase: The distance between front and rear axle centerlines. This is a primary variable because it limits maximum acceleration, controls steering response speed, and has some stability effects. Intuition suggests that we use a long wheelbase for high-speed stability, and a short wheelbase for quick turning in lower speed going. Actually, what works is the reverse; at high speeds, gyro effects slow the steering down, so we need a short wheelbase to make the bike steer. High-speed circuits require taller gearing, which prevents the bike from wheelying much even with the short wheelbase. On lower speed going, a longer wheelbase is useful to allow use of more acceleration without lifting the front wheel. This is why big-engined sportbikes have longer wheelbases.

CHAPTER 14
SUSPENSION TUNING

People want different things from their suspension. Most riders are happy simply to make their bikes comfortable, to have the kind of ride and feel they want. Standard suspension, adjusted up or down in damping and/or ride height, will usually provide this. Trick parts and sophisticated attention to damping and springing have little advantage for riders who have no interest in sliding their tires.

For those who ride more aggressively, appropriate aftermarket dampers and springs will better handle the increased loads from higher grip tires and more aggressive cornering. Fancy suspension exists to help good riders hang onto the ragged edge. Further back from the edge, it may be no use at all, except as art.

As a rider's skills improve, and he or she pushes tires harder, all suspension variables become more sensitive. This goes beyond ride quality. What's needed now is balanced grip front and rear, to keep the machine controllable as it slides in turns. At this level of riding, questions of machine attitude and suspension damping begin to emerge as controlling variables, where at lower levels they have little influence.

Remember this refreshing, democratic fact about motorcycles—the rider makes the machine, not the other way around. When Americade founder Bill Dutcher was in college, he rode a clapped-out Honda Dream 250 with bald tires. When a classmate with a racy Ducati Diana 250 sneered at the Dream, Bill challenged him to a duel at the nearby Elliott traffic rotary. Bill's hard, sideways riding got the wallowing Honda around the rotary 10 times to the Diana owner's 8. All the fancy suspension parts in the world won't magically put you ahead of a determined, better rider. They will make it easier for a good rider to go fast. Skill is primary. Trick parts are secondary.

THE FIRST LEVEL—ADJUSTMENTS WITHIN STOCK PARAMETERS

When you've bought a late-model bike, with all its confusing adjustments, you have to learn how to use them. The way to begin is with the standard settings—so much preload front and rear, so many clicks of compression and rebound. These standard adjustments assume you are an average rider with average requirements. But in fact you may be:

1. Heavier or lighter than average (or planning often/never to carry a passenger)
2. A more or less vigorous rider
3. Riding on rougher than average road surfaces
4. Short of stature

If you are lighter than average, the stock ride height adjustments may hold the bike up too high off the ground. Suspension will not have enough sag, so it will ride too close to full suspension extension. It may top often. Your feet may not reach the ground confidently when you stop. If this is the case, you will need to reduce preload to bring the bike back down to a more comfortable height, with more suspension sag. For a heavier rider, increase preload to restore the desired ride height.

Setting Ride Height

Setting ride height determines how much suspension stroke will be available for absorbing bumps that push the wheels up, and how much will be reserved to allow the wheels to drop to follow a hollow in the road contour. From the ride height point to full suspension compression is called "available suspension travel," and the distance from full extension to the ride height is called "sag." Sag is generally one-fourth to one-third of suspension total travel.

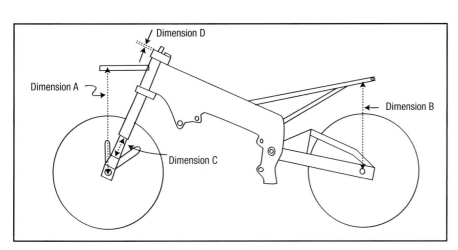

Setting Front and Rear Ride Height.
You'll need a way to hold the bike upright, loaded, while a helper performs these measurements. Race teams use ride height gages. One end plugs into the hollow axle and the other is a millimeter scale, read from a hard point on the chassis above.

Dimension D

Dimension A

Dimension B

Dimension C

Determine total travel by either reading it from your manual, or removing the springs and measuring the actual travel (if non-stock components are in use). If total travel is 120mm, for example, sag should be in the range of 30–40mm, leaving an available travel of 80–90mm.

To set ride height, you'll need to measure sag. At the front, you can simply put a tie-wrap around one fork tube. With the front suspension fully topped (use the centerstand, or pull up on the bike to top the suspension), slide the tie-wrap up against the fork seal. Now sit on the bike in normal riding position with a friend to keep you from falling over. The tie-wrap will be pushed along the tube to a new position. Top the front suspension again and measure from fork seal to tie-wrap. This number is the front sag.

Now top the rear suspension and measure from the rear axle center to some fixed point vertically above it on the chassis. Now sit on the bike while wearing your typical riding gear and repeat this measurement. Subtract the second measurement from the first to get the rear sag.

Now it is a simple matter of resetting front and rear sag to any number with which you choose to start.

If you ride harder than average, especially on high-grip tires, your extra cornering speed will generate more centrifugal force. This will compress suspension more than normal—possibly causing pipe and/or footpegs to ground. You could add preload to counter this, and it will work within limits, but it will also make your bike ride higher. To keep stock ride height *and* sag, the more vigorous rider will require higher rate (stiffer) springs. This means you should read the next category on Supersport suspension mods.

Damping

Now think about suspension damping. Damping is just friction, added for the purpose of snubbing the motion of the chassis. You need just enough to keep the chassis stable. Damping must always be in proportion to spring rate; if you switch to a stiffer spring, you'll probably have to increase damping to match. Excessive damping will make the suspension too stiff to do its job of keeping tires on the ground over bumps. Your bike will begin to "pump down," hop, or otherwise act up.

To take some of the mystery out of suspension adjustments and what they do, try this. Slack off front and rear compression and rebound adjusters to minimum damping, and then ride your bike (carefully) around a familiar and safe piece of road. You'll notice that the bike bobs up and down after every bump—the prime symptom of too little damping. All this large, undamped motion produces large peak forces at the ends of the motions. You may also notice that small bump impacts are hardly felt at all. This is because zeroing-out your compression damping removes much of the impact force that might be transmitted through compression damping.

I suggest that you write down your impressions of each of these tests in a large, hard-to-lose notebook. Don't become one of those riders who tries to describe what's wrong with the bike

Beginnings. *Whether you are riding a factory Superbike or a 10-year-old sportbike, the starting point in your quest for suspension perfection is to work with your stock settings. Set the sag, check the ride height, and be prepared to spend lots of time experimenting with damping adjustments.*

by waving his or her hands and searching for words. Write it down—and think about it later. This is the beginning of your "dictionary of symptoms" for your later suspension work.

Now dial in about half the clicks between zero and the standard settings, on rebound only. Ride the bike around the same piece of road. Notice that the bike is now under better control, but still tends to wallow and nod more than you'd like for best control. Over a series of bumps, there is less confusion because the wheels are bouncing less now.

Increase rebound damping, front and rear, again and test. Work your way to the standard settings, then beyond, to see what happens with more-than-the-recommended damping. You may like it, you may find it harsh, but you'll know what it's like. That's self-education.

At this point, with rebound damping only, and close to the recommended settings, you may encounter the ratchet effect, or pumpdown.

The Ratchet Effect

Consider what happens in a bumpy corner with rebound-only damping. Each bump you hit compresses the springs, but the rebound damping doesn't let them extend all the way before they hit the next bump. The farther you go around this bumpy corner, the more your bike pumps down on its suspension. Putting all the damping on rebound makes your suspension work like a ratchet, pulling the bike lower and lower until the pipe or footpegs grind against the road—or you run out of suspension travel and bottom. Either way, it's unpleasant and limits your speed and/or control.

Adding some compression damping helps overcome this ratchet effect. It also helps over waves and dips, when low-speed rebound damping wouldn't be enough by itself to keep the bike on an even keel. It absorbs small, lower-speed motions that could otherwise be upsetting.

Now dial in the recommended compression damping and test again. Some parts of your ride will feel a bit harsher than before, but there will be added control.

If this procedure seems elaborate, that's because it's an education. What I am suggesting is that you become a suspension expert in your own right, by testing the alternatives and learning what they do on your bike. This will dispel the fog of unknowns that stops many people from playing with their suspensions.

THE SECOND LEVEL — SUPERSPORT SUSPENSION MODS

Supersport roadracing rules permit a rider to alter front and rear spring rates, and to replace the rear suspension unit with an upgrade.

Suspension, tires, and riding style are all interrelated. Stock bikes come with compromise tires that give moderate grip. If you replace them with higher grip tires, you can go around corners harder. This, in turn, generates higher centrifugal force that compresses your suspension more, possibly causing pipes or pegs to ground out. When you brake hard with better tires and higher grip brake pads, your bike may dive more—even bottom—and this, too, calls for more support.

If you ride very hard, or enter races, you will be hitting bumps at higher speeds, and this will demand increased bump-absorption ability—maybe more than your stock suspension has. Suspension components will work hard enough to heat up—and cost-cutting stock parts may fade.

As a first thought, you could increase spring preload to carry this increased load, but there is a potential problem here. Screwing down on the springs more and more causes there to be a lot of load on the springs, even when the suspension is topped. During rebound (as when the front fork extends during hard acceleration), this heavy load will still be pushing hard to extend the suspension just as it reaches its full extension. The result is that the heavy preload makes the suspension hit full extension with a sharp thump. This is upsetting in itself, and if it is the front wheel, it makes it more likely that the wheel will be yanked up off the road. This is fine if wheelies are your intent, but unintended wheelies usually spell trouble for a machine accelerating out of a turn. When the front tire stops steering, your bike heads for the outside.

Therefore, it's better to increase spring rate to carry the heavier suspension loads, and not have to screw down so much preload. This is why the aftermarket offers stiffer front and rear springs for sports/racing use.

Back in the 1980s, a Japanese engineer was quoted as saying that the stock rear damper on a production machine had an OEM cost of $20, but the damper used on that company's 500cc GP bike cost 100 times more than that. What's the difference? The cheap damper provides damping that approximates what is needed and is consistent enough for street operation. The race damper provides the damping needed in detail and is extremely consistent in operation. It is made to high standards of precision. When you order a rear suspension unit, give the make, model, and year of your bike, the type of riding you plan to do, and your weight. The damper will arrive valved more or less for your application, with a more or less appropriate spring rate. You have to get from this shot-in-the-dark to an optimum setup, and the experience will be a valuable one.

Now another of my lectures. You will meet people who believe that the stiffer the suspension, the racier it is. Therefore, such people reason, if your suspension is on the soft side, you are a wimp or a squid. Not true! Suspension is there because it makes any speed more controllable. You can go faster over rough pavement if some good fairy lets just the wheels move up and down, while the chassis remains stable. But if you make it too stiff, the chassis gets hammered, the tires skip and lose traction, and you slow down because you are losing control.

Let the suspension do its work, and don't assume that any one idea or concept is always better. Mike Baldwin's advice to riders confronted with suspension adjustments is what I suggested previously; slack off all adjustments to minimum, then bring in enough rebound damping to make the machine stable, to prevent it from making large, undamped motions. Then bring in compression damping a little at a time, evaluating each adjustment with a couple of test laps. This reasonable procedure will familiarize you with how the damping adjustments work, and with how the bike feels when it has too little or too much of either rebound or compression damping.

The Clickers Can't Do It All

When your suspension is giving you trouble, keep in mind the fact that the damping adjusters are only trimmers. They are analogous to the idle mixture screws on carburetors. They cannot adjust damping all the way up the suspension speed range, and they can't change the shape of the damping curve. Think of the clicker's action as being like a thin spacer under the damping curve. Turning the clickers raises and lowers the whole damping curve, *but cannot change its shape.* Even if you slack off your compression adjuster all the way soft, a high-speed bump can still knock your tires loose if your high-speed compression damping is too hard. It may be that your damper will have to come apart to have its compression stack—the stack of washers that controls flow through the compression damping circuit—altered. So remember, if your bike is having trouble with pavement transitions or other kinds of sharp bumps, you may be bottoming or you may have too-harsh high-speed compression damping.

Some dampers exist that feature external adjustability of low-, medium-, and high-speed damping, but this is not necessarily better than a properly valved, conventional damper.

As with any other system that has a lot of variables, think carefully before twiddling the knobs, and do write down your initial settings. Riders (and, yes, professional race teams, on occasion) get into trouble they can't easily get out of by changing several things at once. By writing down what your starting points are—so many clicks from full soft—you can at least get back to your starting point. More than one suspension specialist, upon taking work with one of the major teams, has found suspension linkage parts scattered, information about them lost, and a lackadaisical attitude prevailing. Suspension tuning success, above all, requires that you keep good records.

Suspension Revalving Services

The back pages of the sportbike magazines are full of ads for damper revalving and rebuilding services. In many cases, particular machines have well-known problems for which fixes exist, and it can be cheaper to have your stock parts modified than to buy fancier replacements. A common failing with older suspension, for example, is harshness on compression. Many rear units are simply worn out. They need to be competently rebuilt, refilled with fresh damper oil, and repressurized. You send in your fork dampers or rear unit, tell the technician your problem or what you want, and you get your stuff back modified or fixed.

Some problems can't be solved in another zip code, which is why suspension makers provide trackside service. Experienced technicians, working out of well-stocked cube vans, talk to riders and service suspension on the spot. GP teams happily pay the approximately "N" dollars a year that these services cost. They provide access to technology, experienced consultation, and up to five damper restacks per meeting.

Chassis Alignment and G.M.D. Computrack

Computrack is a commercial service that will accurately measure your chassis, find any misalignments, correct them, and make recommendations as to chassis setup. Other devices of this kind are also in use in the automotive world. Computrack's service is available in several places in the United States and is based upon a laser theodolite, which is an accurate sighting device, coupled to a computer operating with a geometry software package. The operator sights at your axle or pivot ends from different positions and the data are used to define those points in space.

This has been tremendously useful because heretofore, chassis measurement has been pretty primitive outside the factory. You will still see people trying to line up wheels with string or 8-foot fluorescent tubes, or by bending over and sighting backwards between their legs at the bike. Modern measuring systems give you real information. Make up your own mind, and don't blindly accept any advice without comparative tests. There is no "last word" in suspension. If there were, there would be no more suspension problems. Ha!

Think of Computrack or other such services as being like going to the dyno. The dyno gives you information, and the dyno operator may make useful suggestions. But the choice of what to do with the information is still up to you.

A fair number of sports motorcycles have adjustable swingarm pivot height now. This can be useful in cases in which otherwise good anti-squat geometry would conflict with the machine attitude that gives best steering geometry. In the past, bikes lacking pivot adjustability might squat and push during off-corner acceleration, and in the absence of pivot adjustability, the frequent "cure" was a rear spring stiff enough to prevent the

squat on its own. Of course, the over-stiff spring also made the bike skate in bumpy corners, but such compromises sometimes had to be accepted. Honda, for example, has believed that its MotoGP team will work best with the smallest number of adjustments—but on occasion this policy has risen up to bite the company. Ducati is known for pivoting its swingarms directly on its engine cases, making squat/anti-squat tuning dependent on rear spring rate. Yamaha, on the other hand, tends to make everything adjustable. All three have won championships.

Some riders place so much value on a working squat/anti-squat setup that their teams will not even change gearing because that alters the angle of the chain's top run to the swingarm. At least one team carries multiple sets of different-ratio primary gears to allow ratio changing without change to the rear setup.

Machine Attitude

Competition riders often find a need to adjust machine attitude as well as ride height. As an example, consider that for every inch you lower the front of your machine, or every inch you raise its rear, you are decreasing steering-head angle by about 1 degree. This gives you some control over the nature of your machine's "steering feel" and can be a valuable tool in setup. Go carefully here; big changes can bring big results. To maintain ground clearance, lower one end and raise the other by equal amounts to make steering-head angle changes.

Changes in machine attitude also affect weight distribution to a small but often useful extent. If, for example, a machine is pushing and the rider is already compensating by pulling his or her own weight forward as much as possible, it may be effective to lower the front of the machine. This puts a small extra load on the front—maybe just enough to make the desired difference.

Changing Offset

In the course of all this suspension tweaking, it sometimes happens that a bike feels either too heavy-steering or too twitchy, and it's impossible to cure this and still retain the advantages of

"I'm sorry, Mr. DuHamel is not available, he's in conference. . . ." Which tire combination, which suspension setup? It all has to be decided. Note the stopwatch board, inscribed with the raw material of truth. John Owens Studio

your setup. The answer can sometimes be found in a change of offset, which is how far the steering pivot shaft is offset from a plane drawn through the center of the front axle, parallel to the steering axis. More offset decreases steering trail, tending to make steering lighter but possibly twitchier—and vice versa.

Offset is changed by either substituting other fork crowns with the desired offset, or using crowns with variable offset.

Adjustable Steering-Head Angle

Today, a few sportbikes (and nearly all pure race machines) are built with steering-head bearings carried in machined inserts that slip into a large steering head. By changing inserts, the steering-head angle can be changed. In some cases, significant fore-and-aft movement of the whole steering axis is possible as well. Some Ducati head angles can be varied between 23.5 and 24.5 degrees. The more adjustments there are, the more ways you can get lost in all the combinations, and the more important it becomes to write down all the changes you have made. Both Honda and Yamaha have built adjustable steering-heads that can move the whole front end through 10mm forward or back.

Wheelbase

The range of wheelbase adjustment is small, but the effects can be useful. When you accelerate in lower gears, especially with short-course gearing, it is the lifting of the front wheel that sets the limit on how much throttle you can use. Making the wheelbase longer makes the bike resist wheelying a bit more, so you can accelerate a bit harder. Conversely, too long a wheelbase can make the rear tire spin instead of push the bike ahead. Tucking the rear wheel forward a bit can stop this spin-out tendency. What you can do in these ways is, of course, limited by the range of available sprockets, the desired gear ratio, and your chain.

Beyond the Valley of Supersport Mods

If Supersport-type mods—altered front fork springs, upgraded rear damper, and careful suspension tuning—don't do it for you, there's a whole world of beautiful and expensive alternatives. Throw away your present front end and replace it with an Ohlins, Showa, or WP Suspension upside-down race fork. Don't forget that beyond the $4,000 race fork there are other, fancier options. Think you need different fork trail? Any number of CNC shops will make up works-appearing fork clamps for you in any offset you want. Trash that compromise rear suspension linkage in favor of a new linear-rate link. While you're at it, get your old swingarm braced above or below, or replace it with a part from the aftermarket.

Reduce unsprung weight with lighter wheels, brakes, and tires. Add carbon-fiber fenders (I love the fronts used with upside-down forks—put one on your head and it makes you look like a Star Trek extra).

Now you enter a wider world of choice. Like great international MotoGP and World Superbike (WSB) stars, you can begin to sound like Goldilocks at the Three Bears' house: "This one's too soft. That one's too hard. Let me try the Showa

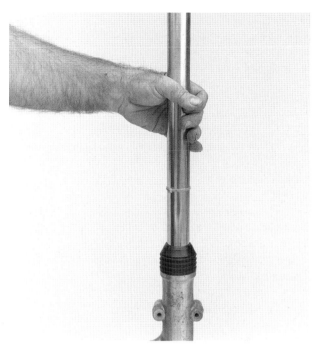

Using a Tie-Wrap to Measure Fork Travel. *It's often useful to know how much fork travel you are using (not everyone has onboard computer data-logging). Fasten a tie-wrap around one fork leg (shown removed from the machine for clarity), and push it down to the top of the slider (or, in the case of male-slider forks,* up *to the bottom of the outer tube). As the suspension works, the tie-wrap will be pushed to the extreme position and will stay there. It's up to you to figure out how far this is from bottoming!* John Owens Studio

. . . I mean the Ohlins, or . . . ." Drive yourself—and your crew—crazy. Each whim can cost thousands of dollars.

Despite the potential for social complications, there is progress. Serious work yields bikes that give their riders the confidence they need to do what must be done. People who try to understand suspension and gain the necessary experience by sifting through mistakes to get at the truth are rewarded.

Some Simple Suspension Diagnostics

When you feel harshness, the first question to solve is whether the machine is bottoming. Harshness under braking, or at maximum side-grip in mid-corner, is especially suspect situations because the suspension is already highly loaded. Ask yourself whether the harshness is preventing you from doing something you must do (like get on the gas early), or if it is just something you are noticing.

The late Bob Wakefield was racing at Laguna years ago, and while he was wrestling with his bucking TZ750 ("fighting for control" was his phrase), here came Gary Scott on the old two-stroke 500 H-D, cruising smoothly around the outside of him at a much higher speed. Wakefield was puzzled. Is this man God, or do I have a problem? How could one bike be so fast and in control, while the other, obviously at its limit, was slower? I asked him where his front preload was set (Bob was a big man), and he replied, "Standard." Standard is minimum, so Bob's TZ had been bottoming its front end, delivering jolts that were overworking his tires and giving him the impression he was at the very limit of traction.

"But I wasn't bottoming," he continued, "Because the tie-wrap wasn't up all the way."

Racers put a tie-wrap tightly around the fork tube or damper shaft, knowing it will be pushed to the furthest movement the suspension makes. Because his tie-wrap wasn't quite at the end, he'd concluded he wasn't bottoming. Yet all older fork dampers have internal hydraulic stops near the end of their travel, to ease the sharpness of bottoming. He hadn't been hitting absolute bottom, but he had been hitting the hydro-stops. Their increased resistance was knocking his front tire loose.

If your bike misbehaves under heavy suspension load (in turns, during hard braking, or particularly if you are heavier than average), always consider the possibility that it is bottoming. When your bike bottoms, your suspension becomes rigid, and that knocks your tires loose. Tires grip best under uniform pressure, and bumps disturb that with high peak forces. But when suspension can move, it lets the bump push just the tire, which takes less force than pushing the whole bicycle. That's good for grip.

Travel versus Stability

If you are like me, you have read sporty-car books about suspension, looking for useful tidbits. One that I picked up was the idea that you should use all your suspension travel, adjusting spring and damping rates until you just barely bottom at one or two places on the circuit or usual "racer road." This seems attractive because it offers a way of using all the suspension travel to isolate the machine from bumps. I tried this idea on Eddie Lawson one afternoon at a Willow test day, and the vehemence of his reply really surprised me. He complained that, no matter what settings he worked out at a given circuit, by the time he got to the next GP, Yamaha engineers had softened everything back up again, and he had to start over. "You can't flick the bike over if it's that soft," he said. "All that suspension movement delays you."

I thought about this. A bike is not a car. When you steer a car, it begins to turn, but on a bike you have the delay of having to first roll the machine over. The softer the suspension, the longer it takes for the machine to absorb the new forces you have put into it. Riders need a stable platform more than they need the ultimate in bump absorption.

If more preload or a slightly stiffer spring doesn't stop a bottoming problem, move your suspicion to high-speed compression damping. At low and medium suspension velocities, compression damping is, like rebound, made closely proportional to speed. But above some set velocity, compression damping is normally set to plateau, or level off, as a large-area blow-off valve opens. This is to prevent high-speed compression rigidity, the thing I have already lectured about in this section.

If compression damping can be so upsetting, why even have it? It's true—early bikes had almost no compression damping for this reason. But there are situations in which *controlled* compression damping can do something that nothing else can. At Laguna Seca's famous Corkscrew corner, bikes come down a short, steep hill that turns hard right while leveling off at the bottom. This high-G pullout combined with turning squashes the suspension. One way to carry this load is to use higher rate springs. But no, those springs will just make the bike too stiff over

Losing Grip. *When riders are really trying, they reduce their margin of safety to the point where mistakes become possible. You can see this on the stopwatch, as a rider who is pushing hard no longer laps as consistently as before, because the small mistakes the rider is now making take time to correct and "gather up." Here, Mat Mladin is closely pursued by Jason DiSalvo, who has made a mistake he can't gather up. A major goal of good suspension setup is to increase this margin of safety.* Brian J. Nelson

G.M.D. Computrack. *This system uses a laser sighting device (laser theodolite, common in the aircraft industry) to measure precisely your bike's geometry, making it possible to know what you have, in detail. Advice comes with the measurements. Although it's a little-known fact, many chassis are only approximately on-dimension, with deviations as large as 11mm from spec. Crashes make this much worse (or maybe better—who knows?).* G.M.D. Computrack Network Boston

the ripples in other turns—the bike will step sideways because the wheels will be in the air half the time. But adding some low-speed compression damping offers a solution. The leveling-off at the bottom of the Corkscrew isn't a sharp impact like a bump. Some low-speed compression damping will slow the suspension movement enough to prevent bottoming. You don't have to use a too-stiff spring to do the job. This is "dynamic support."

The major suspension makers have acquired their own separate traditions in such matters. Long-serving veteran race engineer Warren Willing has often referred to Showa as "the rigid suspension." This is because Showa prefers to support loads and control motions with spring stiffness, while Ohlins tends to seek softer spring rates while controlling motions dynamically with damping. Each methodology has its strengths and weaknesses. Both companies remain on the scene.

If harshness is interfering with what you must do, and it turns out not to be bottoming (or grounding of parts of the machine—look for fresh grind marks on pipes or pegs), try reducing your compression damping. If this helps (it may hurt elsewhere, but this is just a diagnostic), proceed to the trackside suspension truck (or functional equivalent) to have your high-speed compression stack redone appropriately.

When there is too little damping altogether, the machine waves up and down, plunging yet being brought up rather sharply at the tops and bottoms of the motions. It is these sharp halts that you must avoid, for they cause high peak forces on the tires. They don't like that—tires thrive on constant forces. Crank in more rebound damping until the motion comes under control and stops being free plunges with sharp fetch-ups at top and bottom.

When there is too much damping, the ride feels excessively firm, as though there is a lot of friction in the suspension (there is—that's what damping is!). This prevents the wheels from moving freely and, again, results in high peak forces being applied to the tires. Hopping and stepping-out result. This is what snaps them loose, and you don't want that. Slack off until the bike feels more comfortable, but not the slightest bit wild.

When the bike grounds something in a corner, consider where in the corner this occurs. If it happens early in the corner, and/or the corner is very smooth, the cause is most likely that you just have a clearance or ride-height problem. Crank in more ride height or relocate the offending component. But if the grounding occurs late in the corner, and the pavement is bumpy, you may have a suspension pumpdown problem. This means either that excessive rebound damping is acting as a ratchet, or that insufficient compression damping is being overpowered by a normal amount of rebound.

Remember, spring and damping always have to be in proportion. If, for some special reason, you have to increase rebound damping a good deal, it can overpower the spring; the damping slows the return of the suspension, resulting in pumpdown. When a rider upgrades tire grip and begins to ride harder, he or she is also going to need higher spring rates—not just harder preload and damper settings. Don't put off testing with stiffer springs just because it's a job of work, and messy, too. Getting to success is messy.

PUSHING THE FRONT

A very common handling problem is push. You flick your bike into a turn and everything's fine until you begin to twist the throttle. When you do, the bike heads for the outside. The more you gas it, the worse it steers. You try to dig in the steering to get more steer angle, but the front end just tucks when you overdo it. Today, many riders call this "not finishing the turn."

The cause is insufficient front-end grip during acceleration, usually because of wrong weight distribution (too little front load—hence, getting on the gas transfers even more weight off the front, so it pushes).

There is more than one way to get more weight on the front.

The simplest is to pull yourself forward, and you can see top riders doing this all the time—with arm strength. This is part of the reason for getting, and staying, in top shape yourself. The people below the top four or five are happy to ride with their arms straight and their butts far back, and they do this because they are not in good physical shape, and the tension of holding themselves forward in the "acceleration position" on the bike makes them feel weak and wobbly after just a few laps. Look at any video of top riders in a lower gear corner and you will see them scoot forward so there are inches of daylight between their butt and seatback. Their elbows are bent because they are holding themselves forward against the acceleration force they are about to apply, maintaining load on that all-important front wheel.

When that doesn't work, you have to consider mechanical causes. Eliminate the obvious stuff like wrong front tire pressure or bad front fork action (a fork can work fine under load, but patter and skip when only lightly loaded). A standard method of shifting weight forward is to change the machine's attitude, tilting it forward by lowering the front and/or raising the rear. This has become so standard an approach that it has morphed into fashion; people like the nose-down look so much that some will do it just for looks. Examine your own motives and remember that a 5mm ride height change is an appropriate place to begin.

Another question is, how much do you weigh? A heavier-than-average rider can overpower the rear spring, its rate chosen as it is for average riders. Then the chain's lift force is unable to prevent squat. If you're big, you may need more spring.

You can also shift forward heavy components, such as the battery, and if room permits you can add an inch or more of padding to the seatback to keep yourself farther forward.

Certain design features make it hard to ever achieve adequate load on the front. Chief among them is V-engines, especially the 90-degree twins of Ducati. With its front cylinder almost horizontal, such an engine pushes the heavy crankcase and rear cylinder rearward, and may also require use of an abnormally short swingarm. The V-4s of Honda and Ducati likewise present special problems for this reason—note the forward location of the seatbacks of Honda riders Dani Pedrosa and Nicky Hayden, put there to compensate.

All these approaches tackle static weight distribution, but dynamic effects can also cause push.

A USEFUL SEMI-SECRET ABOUT REAR SUSPENSION

Many riders and tuners don't know it, but when a chain-driven bike accelerates, chain force tries to *extend* its rear suspension. We are used to cars, which dip at the front under braking and squat at the back under acceleration. We assume bikes squat in the same way, but they don't. The tension in the drive chain, acting at a slight angle to the plane of the swingarm, exerts a downward force that tends to extend the suspension. Chain force is greatest in lower gears, and the lift it generates can equal or exceed the bike's normal tendency to squat under acceleration. Go and watch bikes coming off a first-gear turn and see them lift, or even top, their rear suspensions as they hit second gear. Or watch a bike on a rear wheel roller dyno, rising at the rear as its power comes on.

The existence of this chain "tangent force" is the reason for all the current interest in adjustable swingarm pivot height for Superbikes. Chain lift force is determined by the angle between the taut upper chain run and the swingarm, and by the swingarm droop angle. The bigger the angle, the greater the lift force that will oppose squat. Raising the pivot height increases the lift force, and lowering it reduces it. Even changing rear sprockets changes this lift force somewhat, by changing the angle of the top run of the chain to the plane of the swingarm. This fact complicates changes to ride rear height—one more thing to think about.

Now consider what happens in a turn as you begin to get on the throttle. Being in a turn, and subject to the increased load from centrifugal force, the suspension is compressed more than when the bike is upright. This, in turn, reduces swingarm angle. As the bike begins to accelerate, there is the natural transfer of weight from the front to the rear, tending to make the bike squat. But because swingarm angle is reduced by suspension compression, the chain tangent force is now too small to counter the squat, so the bike squats down at the rear. This rearward attitude change somewhat unloads the front wheel. If at this point you are near the traction limit, the result is that the front end pushes and you and your bike head for the outside. To stay on-line, you roll off throttle. Everyone passes you. Humiliation.

It is to prevent this squat and push that race teams sometimes play with swingarm pivot height.

Squat and push has an opposite number, which is called "kicking out." If the rear suspension geometry is such that, even loaded in a corner, the rear suspension tries to extend strongly as the rider gets on-throttle, this action may make the back end break away. As it slides, the suspension unloads, the tire catches again, and the cycle slowly repeats. Adding low-speed rebound damping can stop this by reducing the chain pull's ability to kick the suspension out. A better fix would be adjustment of swingarm angle to reduce the chain pull's effect.

These are small points that will be of academic interest only to the street rider, but you never know how far your madness will

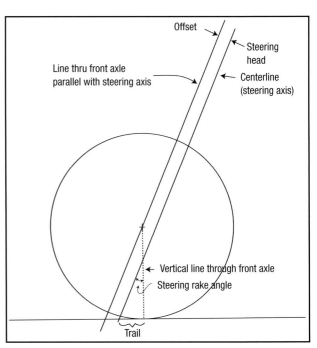

Steering Geometry. *Rake is the angle between the vertical and the steering axis. On most bikes, rake is also the angle of the fork tubes to the vertical (a very few special front ends have been built with their tubes not parallel with the steering axis). On most bikes, offset is the distance from the steering axis to a plane drawn through the fork tubes (but if the front end has an offset axle, this offset distance must be figured in).*

take you. Just as your employer offers you a lucrative partnership, with a company car and four weeks of vacation, you may decide to chuck it all and go racing. Then you may need this stuff. Besides, I find it interesting, and you may, too.

ENTERING THE TURN

As you approach a particular turn faster and faster, eventually you get to a point where the front end feels uncertain and you expect the worst if you go any faster—loss of the front end. Yet despite this, others are diving past you, as calm as Zen masters. Your bike is near its limit of front grip, but theirs are not. You have to find out why.

The classic is the rider who can't decide when he or she's finished braking, so the rider holds the lever while flicking the bike in. This adds weight to the front end, overpowering the grip of the small front tire. I have seen riders who could shred a brand-new front tire in just 5–10 laps of practice, by braking hard all the way to the apex. Tires *can* do two things at once, but will do neither of them well (jack of all trades, master of none). The more brake you hold, the less side-grip you will get. Many riders are still braking fairly hard as they begin to roll the machine over, and then brake less and less as lean angle increases. The obvious goal is to use 100 percent of front tire grip all the way in by just changing the ratio of braking force to cornering force to keep their sum constant.

At his peak, Spencer would rush up to a corner, nose-down on brakes, then simultaneously release the brakes and begin the

When Stock Won't Do. *The aftermarket is more than willing to take care of your suspension woes. The best in the business supplies much more than parts—you get the benefit of an experienced tuner who can help you identify and solve your suspension problems. Beware, however, that the tuner's help is limited by the quality of your feedback. Spend plenty of time evaluating before throwing money at suspension tuning.* Lindemann Engineering

Plenty to Think About. *Randy Mamola has just come in from practice at the French GP in 1984. He's had his conference with the mechanics (you can see veteran George Vukmanovich getting right to work in the background), and now he's ready to ponder the big question: why is this more powerful four-cylinder bike slower than the previous year's triple? Note the cooling slits in the "fuel tank"—this is the ELF-inspired machine that carried its fuel tank under the engine, with the exhaust pipes looping up through a dummy gas tank. Innovations don't always work!* John Owens Studio

Wheel Alignment. *Some people believe the little marks stamped into their swingarms. I like to lay a long straightedge (or fluorescent tube, piece of straight tubing, etc.) along the rear tire—first on one side, then on the other. If the rear wheel is straight, the straightedge will clear the front brake discs by equal amounts on both sides. One hand holds the bar against the rear tire (contact in two places), while the other supports the front of the bar. Eyeball is usually accurate enough, but measure if you like.* John Owens Studio

flick. The instant the bike reached full lean, you'd hear the sound of the engine coming back on-throttle. This calls for fine judgment and complete confidence in your conclusions. Think about it. Holding the brake on is sometimes necessary, but many riders use it as a security blanket to cover their anxiety over just what is the correct entry speed. Instead of choosing a speed, slapping the bike over, and finding out for sure if the entry is too fast or too slow, they prefer to hang onto a little of everything. The result is a slow performance and bad push going in. If the front tire's doing only one thing, it can do it much better. If it's not overloaded by your weight forward, it can do it better yet.

Likewise, the more you nose your bike over with ride height changes, hoping to get stronger drives off the corner, the more weight there will be on the front going in, tending to make the front push. Compromise!

KING OF THE LATE BRAKERS

Still on the subject of push going in, consider that a great many riders go though the "King of the Late Brakers" stage.

"Wow, I just outbraked Bloggs, and he's supposed to be really good on brakes . . . ," our low-hours hero babbles delightedly.

"Yeah, but who was first out of the corner?" asks the skeptical old-timer. Good point. The late braker has committed a classic mistake, that of blowing the corner compromise by concentrating on just one activity to the exclusion of all others. Hard on the brakes, with the front tire squashed out flat and hunting uncertainly all over the road, the rider arrives at the insertion point with his or her bike barely in control. The rider must then work very hard in the turn, cleaning up all of these mistakes, hoping to wobble around on the outside while everyone passes on the inside. The rider's brain is working overtime ("I am sorry, all circuits are busy. Please place your call again later."), and he or she still can't keep up with events. Other riders welcome this as a free gift.

Therefore, if you find your bike pushing on the way in, candidly examine your style as well as the obvious bike setup variables. You might even ask your fellow riders their opinion. Do you find yourself working ever harder, with excuses to yourself as to why the other guy got the drive, even though you were first into the turn? If so, you may be King of the Late Brakers and need to reconsider your corner-entry compromise.

Here is the underlying truth: Front-heavy bikes, like those of the present era, are more stable on acceleration than on brakes. This is because acceleration puts the load on the bigger rear tire. Therefore, working on the acceleration phase of cornering will pay bigger dividends than trying to get in deeper and deeper on the brakes. Early acceleration adds extra speed that stays with you all the way down the next straight, whereas late braking adds only a few extra feet of top-speed running. Yes, you can pass people on brakes, but that often leaves you vulnerable to running wide and being passed on the inside. To keep up, you have to do it even harder at the next turn. Eventually, your back

The Other Part of the Equation. *Your front end pushes and no matter how much you tune, it won't stop. Move up on the bike and put weight the front tire. Your form may never rise to match Doug Chandler's, but body position and suspension performance fit hand in glove.* John Owens Studio

Steering dampers can tone down headshake. Damping is typically adjustable. Street & Competition

wheel lifts and starts to snap around, giving you a deep gut scare just when you need to concentrate on corner entry. A vicious circle of error.

It's hard for riders to change their style, because style is every rider's security. So many times I have seen older riders, whose riding style has been left behind by changes in motorcycles and tires, trying to set up their new bikes to work with their old style. It works for a time, but the stretch becomes tougher and tougher until it no longer works. It's better by far to cultivate some versatility as you develop, so that you can overcome bad habits and exploit the advantages of new developments in equipment. Many top riders, nearing the end of their careers, spend too much time trying to make new bikes handle like bikes used to when they began racing 15 years ago. It can't be done—tires, chassis, and ideas have moved on.

CHAPTER 15
CHASSIS

Options for chassis improvement depend strongly on the era of the machine. Late-model bikes have such good chassis to begin with that choices are limited to things like improved rear suspension links and upgraded forks. The chassis of older bikes look pretty terrible to us now—just as today's chassis will look to our children in 20 or 30 years (if they can tear themselves away from their video games). Chassis of 1950s–1970s bikes are flabby tubular structures, often weak to the point of lacking straight-line stability! Many riders of older machines want to graft on a Suzuki GSX-R fork, or stiffen the chassis with plates or tubes, or upgrade to a fancier swingarm. This work is very rewarding because the older bikes, being as awful as they were, are easier to improve in ways you can actually feel. Look at photos of late-1970s Superbike chassis, with their steering-head tubes all sheeted-in and swingarms reinforced.

Changes to the chassis call for experienced help or a personal ability to do a bit of analysis. As I've said elsewhere in this volume, just putting wider rims and big tires on a flabby old chassis can result in an unrideable machine.

SWINGARMS

In the early 1970s there was a fad for longer swingarms. Then it was lighter swingarms, made of spindly round or rectangular tubing. Later, in the 1980s, it was braced swingarms, stiffened by triangulated structures built either above or under the arm. There was a real reason for each of these trends, but over time, the real reason seems to have gotten lost, and what is left is fashion. Fashion can be hard to ride.

There are two basic categories of reason for building a bike: *(a)* you need it for a specific performance, such as racing, or *(b)* you want it for any other reason.

I try to provide a basic understanding of how things work for the *(a)* people because they need it. But I don't disapprove of the person who wants a bike with, for instance, eccentric axle adjusters like those used on early Kawasaki Superbikes or the factory MVs of the early 1970s. This rider likes the look, and that's OK. At the same time, the rider should know that eccentric adjusters are now less used in racing because they not only change wheelbase, but they also alter ride height at the same time.

In olden times (1970), chassis constructors were caught between conflicting requirements, and their response no longer appears rational to us today. In the era then ending, light weight was a major goal, for with limited horsepower, acceleration could only be improved by mass reductions. Because suspensions of the time had short travel and poor action (damping force not proportional to velocity), it was impossible to perceive any gains from increased chassis stiffness—even though such stiffness had already been proven to work well in auto racing. Even steering geometry was controversial; a chassis that was light and limber was liable to suffer from steering oscillations, such as high-speed weave. This was a major problem for motorcycle chassis designers in the 1960s, and they tackled it in two basic ways. First, some builders moved engines forward in response to engineering tests that finally proved that this worked. Practical men such as Rex McCandless (designer of Norton's Featherbed) had long known the value of forward weight placement, but the idea that rear weight would help traction died slowly. Late-1960s single-cylinder Ducatis had forward-placed engines. Japanese engineers learned the stability value of forward weight from rolling-road tests,

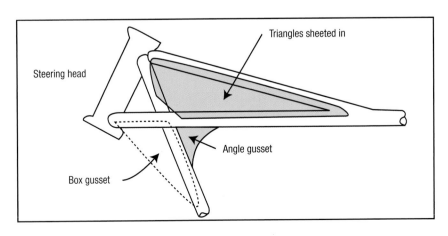

Over-flexible pioneer Superbike tube chassis were frequently reinforced by adding welded or bolted-in plates and gussets. In the mid to late 1970s, the Japanese fours had the power, but wouldn't go straight, while the European twins were more stable but less powerful. Each group won its share.

which were published in the *Journal of the Japan Society of Mechanical Engineers* in the 1960s. Didn't Japanese engineers read it?

The second approach was to employ high-stability steering geometry—high steering-head angles around 30 degrees and large trail in the vicinity of 4.5 inches. This made flabby-framed bikes stable, but slowed their steering and made it heavy. This was also, incidentally, the origin of "raking-out" in choppers. When stock bikes were modified in the 1950s for drag or Bonneville use, they weaved dangerously at high speed unless given more steering rake and trail. People liked the look, so raked-out front ends have persisted even though there is no longer any physical reason for them. Fashion rules.

Another stream of chassis-design thought I will call the "lost chord theory." It was striking that when the first Japanese race bikes encountered less powerful Western opposition, the Asian machines were often defeated, mainly in the handling area. Honda's early four-cylinder racers weaved on corner exit, and the later Honda 500 GP bike, RC 181, was unable to defeat the less-powerful Italian MV triple, to a large extent because of instability. Handling was a mystery no one seemed to understand, so it was common to ascribe good handling to the knowledge of ancient wizards. The theory was that, if you could just get the right combination of rake and trail, any old pile of tubing could become a race winner.

WEIGHT DISTRIBUTION

Some excesses were committed in trying to implement this "idea." Ducati's 750 towershaft twins, with the engine weight set so far back, had too little weight on the front tire for good stability with quick steering geometry. Therefore, to make stability adequate, the front end was raked out at a huge 31 degrees, with 4 1/2 inches of trail. This made the steering heavy and slow, even with little weight on the front tire. Some will argue that this was done in ignorance, but history shows that the nimble single-cylinder 350 and 500 racers of the 1950s and 1960s were often given steering-head angles of 24 degrees or even less, by private tuners. The value of quick geometry was well-known by professionals, but production bikes were given heavy steering as the easiest way to prevent high-speed instability. At the time, this heavy steering was praised as giving the feeling of "being on rails." What that phrase really meant was that these bikes steered like railway locomotives, which actually were on rails. They just followed the tracks and could not be steered, once committed to a line. High stability means high resistance to being deflected by any disturbance—even ones caused by the rider's efforts to steer.

The Trend of Weight Distribution. *As tires have gained grip and engines power, weight has had to shift forward to keep the front wheel steering. In the 1950s and 1960s, designers put multi-cylinder engine cranks at the wheelbase midpoint, even when this obviously did not work. What silly, obvious mistakes are we making today?*

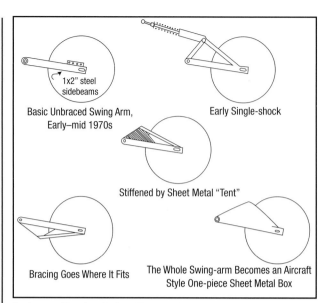

Swingarm Bracing Styles. *Early bracing was just a tubular triangle to drive a single damper, and cracking was frequent. More triangulation stiffened this up, but a lighter solution was to build the brace as a tent-shaped torque box with bracing struts running back to the axle area. This could be located either above or below the arm— wherever there was room for it. In the most recent types of MotoGP and WSB bikes, the entire swingarm is fabricated as a sheetmetal box. A tunnel provides drive-chain clearance.*

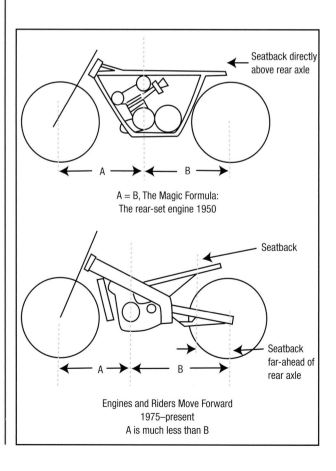

Bikes were designed with too little weight on the front wheel for a suite of reasons:

1. Honda seemed to have decided in the early 1960s that the crankshaft centerline must be at or near the midpoint of a line connecting front and rear axles. With light 50 and 125 engines, and to some extent with 250s, this worked. But when more power made front ends lighter during acceleration, stability became margin al or even negative. Have a look at YouTube footage of Mike Hailwood on the RC 181 Honda 500.

2. Ducati, rationally wanting the low vibration of the 90-degree V-twin engine layout, packaged the concept in a way that pushed the engine's crankcase mass far back. This, by reducing front tire load, reduced stability. It then had to be restored by raking out the front end, Bonneville style, and using a mile of trail.

3. Because the hard-rubber era of tire design was only to end after 1972, the designers of super-power Japanese two-strokes naturally put engine weight where their intuition and contemporary history told them it would do the most good—on the rear tire. Have a look at pictures of Ing. Remor's first MV 500 of 1950. Its engine is hard against the rear tire, with a huge space between the front tire and the front of the engine. More powerful engines pulled ever-more weight off the front tires, causing instability. Only when tire grip improved enough to work with a forward engine did rear weight bias finally lose its grip on design.

All these changes moved very slowly, because it was impossible to identify any one thing that worked by itself. Erv Kanemoto built a stiff chassis for his KR750 Kawasaki in 1976, but Yamaha in the same year showed that longer suspension travel with softer rates would make a small-tube chassis work just as well. Nothing was proved, so nothing was learned.

CHASSIS STIFFNESS

As tires improved, off-corner drives became stronger, and chassis windup became a problem. With first-gear chain pull force very close to 2,000 pounds, even the best multi-tube chassis were deformed. Cracking was a constant chassis problem through the 1970s, showing that parts were indeed bending.

Everyone knew that quicker steering, if there were a way to combine it with adequate stability, was a benefit. More than one maker of the early 1970s had tried to use steering-head angles under 27 degrees, only to be punished by marginal stability.

Gradually the fog of chassis ignorance has lightened, but we are all still surrounded by the swirling mist. The light, multi-tube chassis concept evolved during the late 1970s and 1980s, into the twin-large-beam concept of Spaniard Antonio Cobas, who must be regarded as the McCandless of the present era. The rising stiffness of such chassis made it possible to use quicker steering geometry, without provoking instability. Simultaneously, the shift of weight forward encouraged the use of such quicker geometry, because more weight on the front end would otherwise make steering heavier.

Why so little use of carbon fiber in primary structure? Japanese teams explain that metal, being easily cut and

Good Idea, No Takers. *This is the special C&J big-tube chassis, commissioned by Erv Kanemoto for his 1976 Kawasaki KR750. The builders didn't want to do it, saying the 1 3/8-inch (35mm) tubes would "look funny." The bike was built, but the coming of long-travel suspension made its value invisible. Truly stiff chassis had to wait another 10 years, but this was a historically important step. Gary Nixon rode this machine from August onward in his nearly successful bid for the 1976 World F750 title.* The Coy Collection

welded, is best for experimental chassis that must be changed and updated. Cagiva and a few others have built carbon chassis, but the costs are high.

Doing the most to bring advanced chassis concepts to production has been the new thin-wall aluminum casting processes, such as the Yamaha/Hitachi and Honda Fine Die-Cast. These, by excluding air from permanent molds, have been able to create large, complex chassis parts that greatly reduce the expense of chassis construction and provide near-forged material properties. Current Yamaha chassis are said to require only four welds for their completions.

A CHANGE OF MATERIAL

To arrive at the present, a jump had to be made from steel to aluminum. The bending or torsional stiffness of a tube increases strongly with increasing diameter, even at a constant weight per foot. But as a steel tube becomes very thin, it becomes liable to fail by buckling (see this by bending or twisting a drinking straw), and it becomes all but impossible to attach things like engine mounts to it without cracking. Aluminum, because it is only one-third the density of steel, has three times the wall thickness for a given diameter and weight of tubing per foot. This increased thickness gives the aluminum tube greater resistance to buckling, allowing the tube to be safely made bigger (and therefore stiffer) for a given buckling resistance.

Steel has what is called a "fatigue limit"—a level of stress below which the material can withstand unlimited cycles of stress without crack propagation. Conventional aluminum alloys lack such a fatigue limit. Because of this, aluminum chassis—especially those fabricated by welding—must be protected from

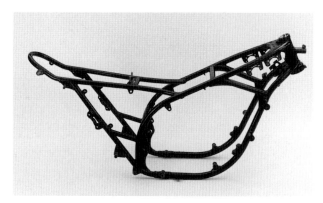

This small-tube chassis is from a Yamaha TZ750. The design is right at the cusp of possible versus impossible; this is a C-model with twin shocks and short suspension travel—and it was a handful with 100 horsepower. The following D-model was a Monoshock design, and its softer suspension action took some load off this spindly chassis, making it rideable. Riders who had thought their careers over because they couldn't ride the 100-horsepower twin-shockers were "born again" when the Monoshock arrived. Jeff March Collection/John Owens Studio

vibration if they are to survive. That required engines either to be rubber-mounted (which prevented using their stiffness as part of the chassis), or have their vibration quelled by design (inline sixes are inherently smooth) or by counterbalancers.

Early aluminum chassis looked just like the twin-loop steel units they replaced and, while light, they cracked constantly (as in every day). Gradually designers learned that chassis members had to blend into each other in organic curves, with much longer weld lines. As a Ducati engineer said recently, "Small welds break." Age-hardening materials were adopted from the railcar and aviation industries. After welding, their strength is low, but over many days, strength gradually rises. This makes it unnecessary to heat-treat complete frames (as would be necessary with our common weldable alloy, 6061). This eliminated problems of sagging or deformation.

The majority of sports or racing motorcycles are made with a twin-beam aluminum chassis, with a weight distribution of roughly 54/46, F/R, and a steering-head angle in the 22.5–24.5-degree range.

A NEW REASON FOR HIGHER STIFFNESS

Toward the late 1980s, tire engineers discovered how to achieve extremely high peak grip. As riders sought the traction limit during corner exits, this type of tire responded by sudden breakaways, followed by equally violent re-hook-up. The best result was a fast but frightening corner exit in a series of slip-and-grip oscillations, each of which provoked chassis weave. The worst case was a violent high-side.

Now the development of stiffer chassis became mandatory, because the stiffer the chassis, the shorter the period of weave after each slip-and-grip cycle. Stiffer meant more stability, better able to maintain high acceleration *and* control.

END OF A TREND?

But as true believers so often discover to their sorrow, no concept is a "final answer." In 1993 Yamaha redesigned its 500cc GP chassis to be stiffer than ever, using extruded beams with internal stiffening webs, like those on Honda NSRs. When this chassis was practiced at the Australian GP in that year, it would not hook up. As rider Wayne Rainey said at the time, "We have chatter, we have hop, and we have skating."

This outcome had been predicted by English chassis-dynamics researcher Geoffrey Rowe. He had noted that, when leaned over, a motorcycle's suspension becomes less and less useful, as the bumps act vertically, but the suspension operates only at the lean angle. At present, with lean angles of the order of 60 degrees, suspension would have to move more than 2 inches to fully absorb a 1-inch step in the road. Chassis flex, Rowe noted, is the silent partner of the movable suspension. Fork-tube bending, steering-head twist, and swingarm deflection absorb a multitude of small bumps. Yamaha had finally made its chassis so stiff that it could no longer absorb such bumps, which were then kicking the tires loose in "chatter, hop, and skating."

SIDEWAYS SUSPENSION BECOMES LEGIT

Since that time, there has been a more or less mad scramble to decipher the mystery of chassis flex. How much, and of which kind, is good? How much leads instead to the instability of the past? In 1997 Honda plunged in, making its factory 250 so flexible that it was unstable in a straight line—but nothing ventured, nothing gained! Frame cross-tubes and even swingarm braces were sawn through in an effort to recover some of whatever it was that was lost as stiffness was increased.

All speculation came to an end when Honda clearly designed its 2002 MotoGP chassis to de-couple the engine from the steering head for lateral motions only. Resistance to twist and longitudinal bending remained strong. Other makers quickly followed suit. At the rear, swingarm beams became very deep vertically, yet thin (typically 30mm) laterally—a combination that strongly resists twist but permits some side-to-side motion. The lateral motions permitted in these ways are of only a few millimeters, but are sufficient to make a large difference in grip on unsmooth surfaces.

In the past, four-stroke chassis were joined to the cylinder head as high up as possible to sensibly minimize the duplication of structure. Now, a single spar on each side drops down to join the front of the engine crankcase or the base of its cylinder. These long vertical spars allow the engine to stiffen the steering head against twist, while still permitting limited side-to-side motion of the entire front end—fork, wheel, and brake system. One by one, all makers have adopted this concept: Yamaha first, Ducati for the 2005 season, and most recently Kawasaki. Engineers will very reasonably point out that such flexibility is a spring without a damper, so the result could be unlimited oscillation. One step at a time.

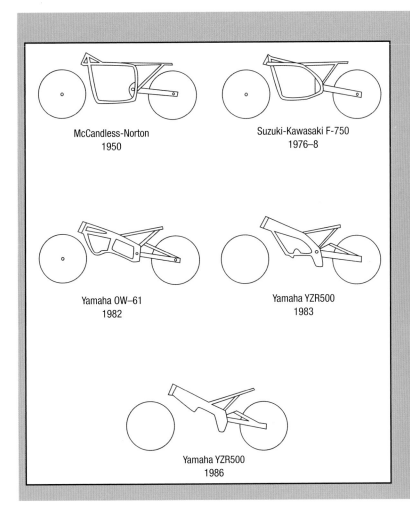

McCandless-Norton
1950

Suzuki-Kawasaki F-750
1976–8

Yamaha OW–61
1982

Yamaha YZR500
1983

Yamaha YZR500
1986

McCandless Twin-Loop, or Norton Featherbed,

of 1950: copied by practically everyone from the 1950s through the 1970s.

Suzuki-Kawasaki F750: Disc brakes put more bending load into steering heads, so designers brought points (a) and (b) together to achieve better triangulation. The load path from steering head to swingarm pivot was also shortened.

1982 Yamaha OW61: Aluminum arrives. Now the upper and lower steering-head tubes of (3) have grown into a Y-shaped aluminum beam that extends down to the swingarm pivot, but a remnant of the twin-loop chassis remains as a perimeter-style engine-hanger.

1983 Yamaha YZR: The next year (1983), Yamaha made the Y-shaped steering-head support beams into a pair of massive, full-depth torque boxes.

1986 Yamaha YZR: The engine-hangers have finally atrophied away to nothing, leaving a Cobas-style twin-aluminum-beam chassis of the modern type. The scene was set for big-beam chassis to move into production motorcycles.

In the process of getting to this "solution," there was much experimentation with fork tube diameter, swingarm dimensions, chassis design, and tire variables. The outcome of all this is the MotoGP chassis of today, whose technology is being busily moved into production bikes.

Having to move the mass of the entire front end of the machine sideways for bump compliance is far from ideal, so I believe that the flexure will move closer to the road in time—being built into either the tire or the wheel.

Therefore when you have grip or feel problems in corners, and the suspension and tire people can't help, think about the

Too Much. *After years of chassis stiffness growth and world 500cc titles, Yamaha built the supremely stiff 1993 YZR500. It was so stiff that it wouldn't hook up in corners. The ad hoc solution was falling-rate race-bike rear-suspension linkages, supplying the lost compliance. Today, chassis and swingarms are deliberately designed to be flexible laterally, providing the necessary degree of lateral suspension when the machine is at high lean angle in corners.* Yamaha Motor Corp.

The main thing these devices have to offer is less "stiction" (resistance to beginning to move) than conventional telescopic forks, of value especially during braking. Another advantage is low steered mass; the equations governing steering wobble show that lower steered mass equals higher potential stability. Each approach to the problem offers certain advantages. These drawings are conceptual only, and are not to scale.

Britten: The late John Britten wanted a supple suspension that mimicked the feel of a telescopic over much of its travel, while resisting dive in the latter part of travel. Late in travel, the shorter link at the top rotates far enough to begin to push the front wheel forward, leading to an anti-dive characteristic.

BMW Telelever: This design (similar to British Motodd) reduces stiction by having long engagement of tube and slider, and the support of the bending load immediately above the front tire, rather than higher, at the level of a conventional lower fork crown. Most riders like this system because it doesn't feel weird.

Hossack: This is obviously a predecessor of Britten's fork, but with slightly different aims. Hossack wanted constant wheelbase and trail, so this design is, as Hossack says, "non-dive." Many races and championships were won by Hossack bikes in the 1980s, but no one took a commercial interest.

RADD-Yamaha: James Parker is the designer of this system which, like the French ELF, employs a deep-dish wheel with all the suspension components entering from one side only. Steering takes place on the upper and lower ball joints, with the upright carrying a stub axle on which the wheel spins.

Bimota Tesi: This is a true hub-center system. The front swingarm supports a short stub kingpin at the center of its non-rotating axle beam. A kingpin drum rotates on this kingpin to provide steering, while a pair of large-diameter ball bearings on the drum carries the wheel itself. The extra pair of arms reacts brake torque, allowing any desired characteristic from pro-dive to the far side of neutral. Some riders praise it to the sky, others disagree.

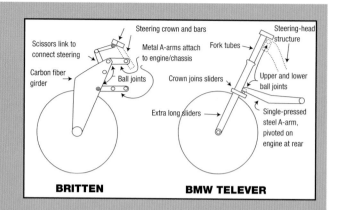

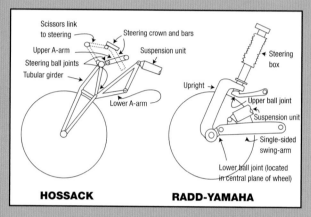

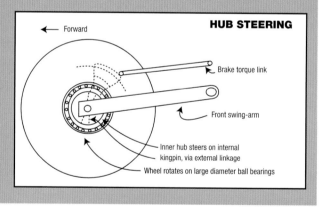

above. In the 2002 World Superbike season, Colin Edwards' Honda RC-51 was made less stiff in stages, and it worked.

POWERBAND AS PART OF CHASSIS DESIGN

It's always good to be aware that engine powerband is a part of handling and chassis design. By 1989 500cc GP engines had become very powerful. To prevent front tires from being jerked off the pavement by their sudden torque rush, their chassis were designed with absurdly forward engine placement—enough to negatively affect braking performance (too-easy stoppies). The coming of electronic engine controls the next year allowed engines to move back again. The world has moved on from two-stroke problems. Now riders need perfectly smooth throttle-up with no "thump" as primitive fuel injection "clicks-on," and no points of steep torque rise as the engine accelerates. Creamy-smooth four-stroke response—or an electronic facsimile—is the key to off-corner drives.

RACING VERSUS PRODUCTION

Manufacturers are currently generously ladling MotoGP technology and looks into production bikes. On both street and track, engines need more of the volume that used to be occupied by fuel as intake airbox. Gas tanks are assuming a flattened "Z" shape, extending back under the rider's seat. This, in turn, takes

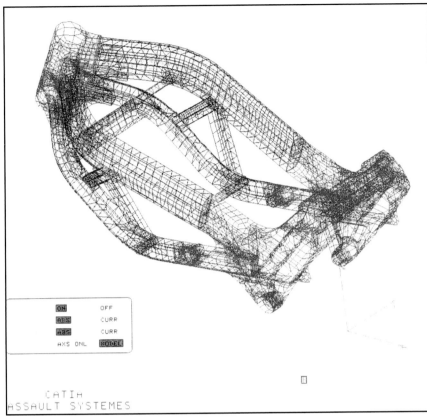

CATIA
ASSAULT SYSTEMES

room formerly occupied by the top of the suspension unit. Now the suspension unit has to be pushed down through a big hole in the front of the swingarm, with its linkage underneath it. Street and race chassis look a lot alike now.

When thinking about chassis matters, have respect for your own experience and opinions. When you think of something, don't fall into the syndrome of saying, "Well, if my idea was any good, the Japanese teams would already have tried it." Factory engineers are as easily swayed by fashion as anyone else, and they can make mistakes and overlook the obvious, too. A few years ago, one team drilled hundreds of holes in their fairings, hoping this would make the bikes easier to flick from side to side. Once they realized this did nothing, the embarrassing fairings disappeared. Very few engineers are good at seeing beyond present trends to what they imply for the future. This is because they are busy trying to optimize the currently accepted way of doing things. Real innovation often comes from the small firm or from individuals unbiased by formal engineering education. Think of Erv Kanemoto, think of the late John Britten, think of Dr. Wittner.

Because of the inertia of taste and finance, the mainstream of design changes only slowly. Tires are designed for the chassis that exist, and perhaps novel chassis work less than optimally with such tires. It is only when a single concept directs the whole design that much can be achieved—and that is rare.

What about forkless front ends, two-wheel steering, and all the other innovative but so far uncompetitive projects? Alas,

it isn't time for the suspension makers to scrap the big centerless grinders that make millions of fork tubes. It's true that sliding-pillar front suspension (telescopic fork) is pro-dive and prone to binding under the side-loads of braking, and it's true that pivoted-link front suspensions (like the Britten girder, the Tesi's forward swingarm, or the Hossack girder) shorten braking distances somewhat over rough pavement. But telescopic forks continue to provide the best of damping technology with improved anti-friction coatings and seals, while the alternatives have failed to show clear superiority. So matters rest. BMW has shown some innovation in suspension, but short of actually racing its three-cylinder 990cc MotoGP prototype, has failed to prove it superior.

Even the late John Britten felt obliged to give his girder suspension the "feel" of a telescopic fork over most of its travel. This is the social aspect of engineering. Users accustomed to a certain feel will identify other kinds of feel as not only different, but also bad. This is because they have learned to read the cues in the existing technology, but cannot yet read the behavior of the new device. Any device that makes you feel safe is good; any that makes you feel uncertain is bad. This is a difficult obstacle to overcome, and it can imprison a rider in an unchanging style.

If you have not yet seen the Britten videotape, do so. If after seeing it, you feel that you have ideas, energy, and drive similar to his, you may want to express your innovations in metal and carbon fiber as he did, and then not only make them work, but show them in all parts of the world. But if you find yourself more comfortable working one shift, rather than Britten's two to three shifts, I fear the telescopic fork/swingarm bike is with us for a long time to come. Now, if Bill Gates got interested in motorcycles . . . .

CHASSIS

141

CHAPTER 16
TIRES

Tires are the motorcycle's "feet," transferring all the forces of acceleration, braking, and turning to the road surface. The rubber tread grips because it is soft enough to mold itself to the road surface, keying itself to the tarmac like a micro-toothed gear. On the atomic scale, rubber sticks to the road by molecular forces. In the wet, and when a tire is actually sliding, a third mechanism of traction—hysteresis, or lack of perfect elasticity—comes into play.

Grip also depends on the area of rubber in contact with the road. Because of their flexibility, tires flatten against the road to form what is called the tire's footprint or contact patch. Obviously, the stiffer the tire's structure, the less flattening there is, but a rough idea of footprint area can be figured by dividing tire load by inflation pressure. For example, if a tire inflated to 30 psi carries a 300-pound load, its theoretical maximum footprint area would be 300/30 = 10 square inches. Increasing footprint area by decreasing inflation pressure has been a major development trend in roadracing tires since the 1990s.

Heat is a tire's greatest enemy, because the rubber and adhesives in it degrade at high temperature. As tire rubber rolls through the contact patch, it is bent in the process of flattening against the road, then unbent when the tire picks it up again—hundreds of times per minute. Rubber is not perfectly elastic; if you stretch or bend a piece of rubber with 100 units of energy, when you let it snap back you may get back only 65 units of energy. The missing 35 units have turned into heat. The faster you ride, and the more weight you carry, the hotter your tires run.

Heat generation is proportional to the amount of rubber being flexed, so the thinner the tire, the cooler it runs. Likewise, the less inflation pressure in the tire, the more the rubber is bent in passing through the enlarged contact patch, and the greater the heat generated. This is why a low tire runs abnormally hot, or may even disintegrate if run underinflated long enough and fast enough. In a Dunlop survey taken at a road riders' rally, 40 percent of machines inspected had underinflated tires.

A tire is much more than just a flexible rubber bag inflated with air. It has a molded-in, internal structure called the carcass, made from layers of high-strength cord fabric. Cord fabric is made of only parallel fibers, not crisscrossing and interwoven like the fabric in a shirt. The tire's shape and

the vehicle's stability depend upon the carcass fabric being tensioned by inflation air pressure. In this way, a tire is like the Atlas launch vehicle, which collapses if its ultra-thin metal-foil fuel tanks are not pressurized. If tire inflation pressure is too low, the tire will be too flexible, and the contact patch may buckle and lift up from the road surface locally. Valentino Rossi has had just this difficulty with recent low-pressure race tires, saying that at full lean angle "when I touch the throttle, the bike jumps sideways."

The carcass is kept on the wheel rim by having its cord plies wrapped around two rings of steel wire called the beads. Their tensile strength keeps the inflated tire from climbing the rim flanges and popping off the wheel. Anyone who has seen burned tires has seen bead wire.

Fifty years ago, all tires were inflated with tubes, but today tube use is rare and tubeless fitment is standard for all but traditional wire-spoked wheels. Obviously, tubeless motorcycle tires had to wait for the coming of cast wheels, for otherwise every one of 36 or 40 spokes would have had to be sealed to its hole in the wheel rim. The advantage of tubeless tires is the reduction in the amount of rubber flexing as the tire rolls, and the increased safety brought by combining the air retention function with the whole structure of the tire. A tubeless tire therefore runs cooler than the same tire with a tube in it. Tubeless tires hold air because they are lined with a thin layer of low-gas-permeability butyl rubber. They are inflated through a separate tire valve, set into a hole in the rim.

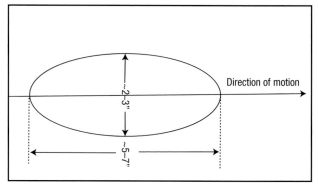

Tire Footprint. *All the forces of braking, cornering, and acceleration have to pass through two elliptical areas like this one, formed as the tire flattens against the road.*

Race Tires Are Fragile. *This one has been blistered by over-heating on Daytona's banking. Note that the damage is in a narrow band on one side of the centerline—right where the tire runs on the banking. Volatile constituents in the tread compound (oils or waxes) have boiled, generating bubbles that expand, causing loss of material from the tire. The rider senses this as unusual vibration at high speed. Tires are designed close to the edge to deliver both necessary grip and life. Sometimes the engineers get it wrong, and the tires are too hard (1979, which riders remember as the year of the "cement tire"), or a tiny bit too soft, as here.*

Early tire carcasses were made of woven cotton fabric, like that in a shirt, but tire flex made the interwoven fibers saw each other apart. The answer was to use unidirectional cord fabric, impregnated with rubber and then applied in layers, one angled 30–45 degrees to the right of the tire centerline, the next to the left, and so on, until the necessary number of layers needed for strength had been reached. These angled—or "biased"—layers gave strength in all directions and protected the fibers from sawing at one another. Tire carcasses made with such crisscrossed layers of cord fabric are therefore called "bias-construction" tires.

A long-running trend in tire construction has been to use fewer and fewer layers of ever-higher-strength cord fabric. Remember, a thinner tire is a cooler-running, longer-lasting tire. It seems paradoxical, but today's one-ply or two-ply tires last several times longer than did the six- and eight-ply tires of the 1940s.

The radial-ply tire was invented almost 60 years ago—an idea so simple, no one could think of it. The carcass of a bias-ply tire is relatively stiff because of the multiple layers of angled reinforcing fibers in it. This stiffness reduces footprint area and also increases heat generation as the tire flexes. Radial construction in its simplest form uses a single carcass ply, set at 90 degrees to the tire centerline. No fiber crosses another, so flexibility is at a maximum, and thickness at a minimum.

Unfortunately, a pure radial tire is useless because it's too flexible to be steered. This problem is solved by wrapping the simple radial carcass with a circumferential, or near-circumferential, reinforcing belt(s) under the tread area only. This leaves the radial-ply sidewalls very flexible, allowing the tire to deform easily as its tread-belt region lays down a footprint like the laterally rigid metal-link track of a tank or bulldozer. The tread area, braced by the belt(s), offers little resistance to rolling but is strongly braced against sidewise forces. This makes it possible to steer. Some bias-ply tires also use belts to stabilize the tread, but this does not make them radials.

Simply put, a radial tire combines a tread region of great lateral stiffness with very flexible sidewalls. The virtues of radial construction are these:

1. Cooler running because the tire is thinner and its sidewall carcass fibers do not interfere with each other, which leads to longer life.

2. More grip because the more flexible tire doesn't strongly resist spreading out into a maximum-area footprint—this is why all-season radial tires are accepted as auto snow tires in many states.

3. Reduced tread wear because a radial tire's more rigid tread simply rolls onto the ground; it does not "parallelogram" or "squirm"—which also creates heat—in the process of being laid down or picked up from the road.

A bias-ply tread region can deform in length or width as its crisscrossing plies scissors across each other, allowing the contact patch to scrub or twist against the road.

SPEED RATINGS

Every tire has a speed limit—a speed above which it generates more heat than it can dissipate. Running a tire above its speed limit is an invitation to heat-induced, catastrophic tire failure. For this reason, tires are manufactured to speed ratings, and it is a safety fundamental that a motorcycle should wear tires whose speed rating exceeds the machine's maximum speed.

Laboratory speed testing of tires is carried out against a spinning drum, and the speed is raised at a given load until the test tire shows signs of distress. This takes the form of a standing wave, forming where the rubber lifts up from the footprint. This standing wave is analogous to the wake of a boat, and because it subjects the rubber to extra flexure, it quickly overheats the tire, defining its upper speed limit. Tire speed ratings are molded into the tire sidewall.

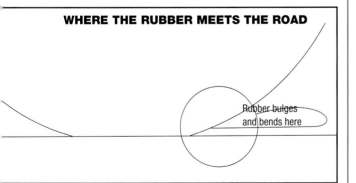

WHERE THE RUBBER MEETS THE ROAD

Rubber bulges and bends here

Footprint Seen from the Side. *The tread rubber bulges before and after it hits the footprint, passing through regions of fairly sharp curvature. The more footprint we design into the tire, the sharper this curvature becomes. This flexure of rubber generates heat, the archenemy of tires and traction.*

DUNLOP SPORTMAX II GP   10-'94

Cutaway Radial Tire. *Note the single radial ply (at 90 degrees to tire centerline), characteristic of all radial construction. This gives maximum sidewall flexibility, allowing the tire to lay down a long, large-area footprint. The tread region is specifically braced by one or two belt plies, sometimes called breakers. A single belt is usually wound onto the tire during manufacture, while racing radials often have two slightly bias belts for maximum stiffness. Trace the radial carcass ply as it wraps around the tire beads and then rises back part way up the sidewall. This is done to modify sidewall stiffness. Tires are full of invisible technology.* Dunlop Tires

TIRE SIZES

Because tires become bigger every year, many riders assume that *(a)* this is progress and *(b)* bigger must be better in every way. This leads to the temptation to overwhelm motorcycles with the biggest tires the owner can find. Little 250 racers from the 1960s—initially so nimble and quick-responding on their original narrow-section 2.75x18F/3.00x18R tires—become ponderous when their vintage-racing owners reequip them with the biggest tires that will physically fit into their fork legs or swingarms.

Look at a cross-section of a tire on a rim and you will see that, as a bigger tire is mounted on the same-sized rim, its sidewalls become more cantilevered, and therefore more flexible, which increases heat. Any tire is what it was designed to be only when mounted on the intended rim width. If you must put bigger tires on your bike, and they call for wider rims, use them. Otherwise, either be happy with tires that are right for the bike or trade up to a later model machine that already has the size tires you want.

In tires, everything is compromise, so you must consider the whole picture, not just a single variable, like size. The bigger the tire, the greater the rolling resistance and the lower the top speed. But a larger section tire may increase cornering grip. Balance against that the fact that a narrow, sharp tire profile handles quicker than a fatter, round-profile tire. On the other hand, braking can be more powerful and more stable on the round tire.

In the end, it comes down to somewhat arbitrary questions like: Would you rather have in-corner grip with slow, heavy turn-in and 2 miles per hour less top speed? Or

quick turn-in, less speed at the apex but a bit more on the straight? You might also ask yourself if fashion is influencing what you want. Custom bikes have the biggest rear tires of any motorcycle, but their corner performance is unimpressive.

History shows a never-ending cycle of tire and chassis development. As the late Dick O'Brien, for years head of Harley's race team, said back in 1969, "About the time we get the chassis handling really good, the damned tire people come up with more grip, the chassis starts to flex again, and we have to start over."

Although great big tires may look good on that 30-year-old Kawasaki Z, go carefully. At the time, those chassis had to be braced to make them even marginally stable with the grip of race-sized tires. Just levering on bigger tires is not enough of an update. If you want a vintage Superbike, build the whole bike—rims, tires, braced chassis, updated suspension.

RADIAL TIRES ON BIKES NOT ORIGINALLY FITTED WITH THEM

As with cars, the official line is no radials for bikes originally bias-equipped, and definitely no mix-and-matching. In actual practice, however, lots of people are having fine results either putting a radial on the front, or radials on both ends of such bikes—provided the rims used are not narrower than the call-out for the radial tire(s) in question.

Bias tires were normally cantilevered out over a rim significantly narrower than the tire; radials must not be. Particularly bad is putting a radial on a narrow rear wheel. As noted elsewhere, motorcycle stability gets most of its damping from the tire footprints. With radial construction, the footprints become larger and longer, tending to increase stability. Perhaps this is why those who are restoring and riding late 1970s Superbikes—which originally wobbled

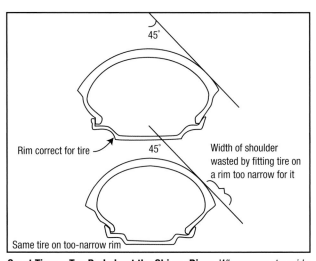

Great Tires—Too Bad about the Skinny Rims. *When you put a wide tire on a rim too narrow for it, its tread contour changes, being pulled in at the sides and wasting some of the tread shoulder area. Wide tires are just decoration unless they are on the correct-width rims.*

TIRES

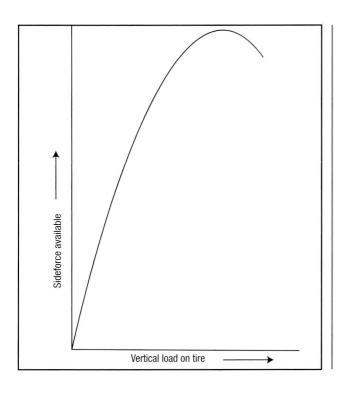

Sideforce available →

Vertical load on tire →

Overshooting the Flavor Peak. *If you close the throttle, your bike decelerates, throwing more weight onto its front tire. If you brake, it adds much more front tire load. Do these things in a turn and you can push your front tire up to the top of this curve—and over into the zone of falling grip, where ordinary mortals like us lose the front end and tip over.*

and weaved frighteningly on bias tires, even with braced chassis—are reporting good stability today with radial tires on the correct rim widths.

SOME GENERAL REMARKS ABOUT TIRE TRACTION

The classic lack-of-grip situations are these:

1. As you accelerate out of a turn, you notice yourself losing front grip. As you turn the bars more and more to compensate, the front end suddenly tucks. Only accelerating less hard seems to prevent this.

2. As you start your drive off a corner, your rear tire goes sideways instead of forward. Your bike is tending to spin out under throttle.

WET TO DRY

These photos from Michelin show the progression from a slick for dry conditions, through molded intermediate that can tolerate light rain, and all the way to full rain tires with complex tread drainage schemes. Full rains throw an impressive rooster tail of water when it's raining hard! *Michelin Tire*

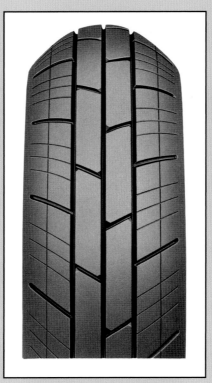
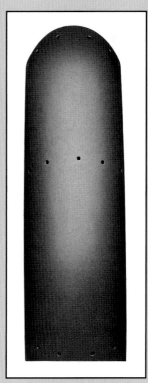

3. As you approach a turn, possibly with some front brake still on, and begin to flick the machine in, the front end goes away. You feel like a hero for saving it (or like an idiot for not doing so).

In the first two cases, the tire is failing to grip because there is too little load (weight) on it. Accelerating causes rearward weight transfer, reducing the available side grip at the front. Unable to grip, the front end drifts toward the outside. In an attempt to increase grip, the rider digs in the front end (turns it into the turn). This at first helps, but also consumes whatever reserve of traction the light front end may have. Finally, the tire gives up and the front end tucks.

Enterprising riders pull themselves forward, up the gas tank, to put more of their own weight on the front end as they accelerate. Watch top riders and you will clearly see them do this. It takes real upper body strength to be able to hold yourself forward in this way against strong acceleration, while still accurately controlling the bars. Lesser riders are content to just let the seatback push them. They make the bike steer by not accelerating hard enough to make the front end stop steering. And that is one reason they are lesser riders.

Because bikes have become so powerful in the last 25 years, their ability to make the front end too light to steer out of corners has constantly increased. Improvements in tire grip have only made this worse—look how far forward engines have moved in drag-racing classes. This has forced designers to steadily move both engine and rider forward. This is notably harder when the engine's cylinders are in V-formation, which pushes engine mass rearward. The second case (2) sometimes arises when this weight-to-the-front is taken to extremes, or an excessively long wheelbase is used. If for any reason the rear tire carries too little weight, when the rider tries to accelerate off a turn, the tire spins instead of driving forward because it has too little weight on it. The fix is to shorten the wheelbase (move the rear tire forward) or transfer some weight to the rear. The rider can do this by sliding back or chassis changes can be made.

In the third case (3), traction is lost because the front tire is carrying too much load. Here's how it works. Although rubber companies are as secretive as the National Security Agency, occasionally they let something slip. If you graph available grip versus vertical load, you'll get an upward-sloping straight line showing that each increase in vertical load provides a corresponding increase in available grip. This fact is used by Formula One cars to generate extra traction from the use of aerodynamic downforce.

However, this rising slope doesn't continue upward forever. At some high value of load, the tread becomes "stress saturated," which is a fancy way of saying that the rubber isn't strong enough to continue resisting increasing side force. Instead of continuing to rise on its straight line, the curve loses slope and hooks over—then actually starts downward. Further increases in load actually produce decreasing available side grip.

Riders losing their front end as they flicks over into a

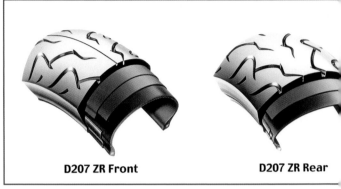

D207 ZR Front **D207 ZR Rear**

Differences in Radial Belts. *Here we see two under-tread belt constructions on D207 ZR Dunlop radial tires. The front tire (left) uses a pair of so-called cut belts, one with its ply angled slightly to the right, the other to the left, of the tire centerline. This kind of belt gives maximum tread-region bracing, peaking at about a 23-degree angle. The rear tire has a single zero-angle belt. Each construction type has its advantages. Cut-belt construction is used wherever maximum grip is important, but the greater tread-area flexibility of zero-angle construction can give a tire more warning—more useful to street riders than to racers. This is always a design issue in tires: absolute peak grip versus information about exactly where the peak is.* Dunlop Tire

turn have driven that tire up this traction-versus-load curve until it peaks and starts down the far side. That little front tire is trying to carry its normal load, plus the 40–50 percent extra required for cornering, plus whatever extra is thrown onto the front by either continued braking or simply being on a closed throttle (deceleration-induced forward weight transfer).

The result is that the front tire begins to slide. If you are Freddie Spencer, you instantly snap on some throttle, transferring just enough weight off the front tire to push it back up the friction curve toward the peak. The front tire recovers grip, and you proceed miraculously around the turn. As Dave Barry says so often in his column, "Don't try this at home." And most riders don't—when the front end starts to wash on corner entry, they conclude they've reached the limit.

TIRES AND STABILITY

The two tire footprints are your bike's major defense against buildup of either of its two natural forms of oscillation, wobble and weave. Wobble refers to the oscillation of the front wheel, typically at the very rapid rate of 8–10 cycles per second. Because this corresponds to the frequency of front tire rotation in the speed range 35–40 miles per hour, wobble is most likely there, especially when you remove your hands from the bars. At higher speeds, wobble is more and more strongly damped, and becomes less likely. Steering dampers are effective against wobble.

Weave refers to oscillation of the rear of the machine, typically at a rate of two to three cycles per second. Weave damping decreases as speed rises, so weave is usually associated with high speeds. Steering dampers are often ineffective against weave, or can even make it more likely.

Tire tread contour and carcass construction both affect stability, so bear this in mind any time your bike shows a tendency toward instability. A change in tires can be the cause—either because you have fitted new tires that your bike "doesn't like," or because the tires on the bike have worn to a bad contour. Some tire combinations just don't work on some bikes, and in some cases the motorcycle is clearly placarded by its maker for the use of particular tires only.

Because footprint area depends upon inflation pressure, a bike that is normally stable may show instability if its tires are inflated abnormally high (reduced footprint area).

TREAD RUBBER COMPOUNDS

Early tread compounds had to be hard, because tires were narrow, concentrating high load on every square inch of footprint. In the early 1960s, a big change occurred when Dunlop and others began to use so-called high-hysteresis rubber. In this case, hysteresis refers to the energy lost in a cycle of rubber deformation and elastic recovery. The energy difference would appear in the rubber as heat—effectively the result of internal friction acting during deformation and recovery. In a "snappy" rubber, energy out would be very close to energy in, giving nearly 100 percent elastic recovery. A good example is a rubber band. In a highly hysteretic

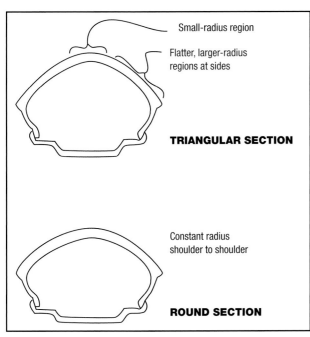

Small-radius region

Flatter, larger-radius regions at sides

TRIANGULAR SECTION

Constant radius shoulder to shoulder

ROUND SECTION

Tread Contour. *As you apply steering torque to the bars, the front tire generates side force in two ways: (1) by slip angle, as do car tires, and (2) by camber thrust, which is a function of the tire's tread profile, acting in combination with the machine's lean angle. Tires with a sharp triangular profile tend to steer more quickly than do those with a rounder profile, but looks can be deceiving.*

rubber, significantly less than 100 percent is recovered. Drive your thumbnail into the tread of a race tire and see how long it takes for the mark to disappear. This "deadness" of high-hysteresis rubber enhances grip—especially in the wet.

After the 1972 Daytona disaster, when 100-horsepower bikes demolished the best available race rubber, tire engineers realized that tires for such bikes had to be wider to spread the action over greater area. When this was done, softer rubber compounds could be used.

In early 1960s tests, high-hysteresis rubber tires slightly reduced top speeds of GP cars (because their internal friction ate some power), but their higher grip significantly reduced lap times.

In early days, people judged a tire by the number of plies used in its construction, for with cotton construction many layers were needed for adequate strength. But all those layers of rubber, flexing as a tire rolls, generate heat. It was not unknown for such a tire, run at racing speed, actually to catch on fire. Today, tires use much stronger ply fabrics, such that one or two plies provide plenty of strength. The beauty of this is that the resulting thin tire generates much less heat.

Tire tread wears faster the hotter it runs. As tire carcasses were made thinner, tires ran cooler, so they needed less tread rubber thickness. This, again, was good because the thinner the tread, the cooler it runs. Although you will see thick-treaded tires sold for high-mileage, low-speed applications like taxi service or in-city trucking, the faster the vehicle, the thinner its tires are. Tires for land speed record running at places like Bonneville may have as little as 1mm of tread rubber thickness.

The change from bias to radial construction produced another reduction in tire operating temperature. The result of all this work is that today's tires run so cool that very soft rubber compounds, formerly safe only for use in the rain, are now routinely used in dry tires. The result is increased grip.

Unfortunately, the softer the rubber, the faster it wears, so there is compromise between grip and life. If you want the ultimate in street grip, you have to give up any dreams of 20,000-mile tires. In pure racing tires, the rubber compounds are often immature, meaning that the chemistry of the curing process was not completed in the mold. Racing rubber operates in the dry at above boiling-water temperature (212 degrees Fahrenheit), hot enough to slowly drive the incomplete cure reaction forward. This gives an optimum combination of qualities, but the result is a tire that ages quickly in use. As it runs in race or practice, it may give 10 or more hard laps of use, followed by a steady and irreversible decline in properties.

For qualifying, the compromises are drawn differently, resulting in a tire with exceptional grip for two laps, followed by a steep decline in properties. These are the "gumballs" or "qualifiers" you often hear about in race reports, used just for one warm-up lap and one qualifying lap, and then thrown away. In these times of intense industrial espionage, "thrown away" means returned to the factory for secure disposal.

Colin Edwards has described the plight of trying to qualify on a "Q" tire whose life is less than one lap.

Compromises similar in concept but different in degree exist in street rubber. There are harder, longer wearing tires for the sport-tourers in our midst, and there are short-lived softies for those whose hearts pine for turn eight at Willow Springs.

WET OR DRY

The more a tire's tread is dissected by rain grooves, the more flexible it becomes, and the hotter it runs at speed. This fact was pursued to its logical extreme by Goodyear in 1974, when it introduced slick-treaded race tires for bikes. In the dry, nothing grips like a pure slick, because a slick's cool-running nature allows use of soft rubber compounds that would overheat on a grooved-tread tire.

Some old-timers were shocked by the coming of slicks, because their intuition told them that you need tread blocks with edges that "cut into the road" for traction. Of course, the reverse is true; it's the road that cuts into the tires, which is why the softer the rubber, the higher the grip. Slicks can give surprising grip in conditions of light rain and residual moisture.

What if it rains? A whole range of options has developed. A pure rain tire is intended for steady hard rain, with standing water everywhere. This tire type has a tread pattern consisting of deep crisscrossing grooves that leave the surface as an array of free-standing blocks. The deep grooves provide drainage adequate for maximum water removal. If full rain tires are used after the rain stops, the tires will quickly overheat and become useless, as these free-standing tread blocks flex extravagantly. Rain compounds are extremely soft and survive only as long as they are adequately water-cooled!

For a drying track with some standing water, and perhaps misting rain, a hand-cut slick or molded intermediate is the choice. In this case, the drainage grooves do not crisscross, but are just short wavy or straight lines of minimum depth. The intention is to provide some water drainage, but to leave the tread rubber still strongly self-braced by not being cut into flexible free-standing blocks that heat up.

I have seen many a race lost by riders who panicked all the way to full rains. I have seen quite a few races won on moist tracks by riders still on slicks or intermediates.

STREET CHOICES

Because the U.S. Department of Transportation (DOT) approval requires at least some water drainage, there are no streetable slicks. There are, however, some very close mimics—tires that are effectively "molded intermediates"—which are slicks in effect, with minimal, shallow drainage grooves. The grooves are oriented diagonally, leaving long strips of tread that are well-braced to handle the combined braking/accelerating/cornering loads applied to them. These are the tires for canyon-carving madmen who run essentially dry-only.

If your taste inclines more to taking the weather as it comes, so you need better drainage, you will choose tires that lie further along the line leading to full rains. Often you still see deep drainage grooves, but strengthened by thick tie-bars down in the grooves, which tie the islands of rubber together, reducing flex.

Some European tires are truly all-weather, approximating full rains in the depth and extent of their drainage grooves. If you've spent time in Northern Europe you'll know why—if they didn't ride in rain, they'd hardly ride at all.

WHAT'S RIGHT FOR YOU?

Mike Baldwin used to say, "Go see what the guys on the podium have on their bikes," and that remains the best advice. It's pretty unlikely that a Taiwanese manufacturer known for economy wheelbarrow tires will suddenly come up with a world-beating $25 motorcycle tire.

If you hang out at the club road races—it's nice there, except for the food—you will get to know what everyone likes in the different classes and on the various bikes. Or, if you don't go to the races, maybe you have a friend who does. Either will help you make a choice. If this seems like slavish copying, it is, but it's also way easier than buying a set of every tire on the market and testing them yourself. Start where the hot runners are, and use your own judgment. If someone is going measurably faster with 2 psi lower tire pressure than the people in the tire shirts say is best, go discuss it with them.

D 207 ZR Front   **D 207 ZR Rear**

Dunlop Sportbike Tires. *The chief visible characteristics of these tires are their size and the minimal nature of their tread drainage pattern. Both aspects trace back to designer Tony Mills' 1972–1974 development of new-technology race tires capable of handling 100-horsepower bikes at Daytona speeds. His tire was much wider than anything before it, which spread the load over a wider area, and it had the minimum tread pattern in the interest of reducing tread flex and associated heat generation.*

Honda's 1,000cc FWS. *This machine was created just to win Daytona. It was also an important progenitor of production Honda V-4s. To paraphrase Caesar's "veni, vidi, vici," they came, they had tire trouble, they were seen no more. Horsepower and tires are forever locked in a seesaw battle, and in this case, horsepower was too far ahead. Graeme Crosby won this Daytona on an assembled-from-parts OW31 (factory version of the TZ750 Yamaha), the ninth-in-a-row win for that venerable design. Lesson: Bring only proven technology to Daytona. Daytona eats new technology for breakfast.*

The issue here is possible tire overheating, which on high-speed courses can lead to tread chunking or separation.

The same thing holds in production drag-racing classes, where there can be some tire surprises. Paraphrasing Otto von Bismarck: The man who must learn everything from his own experience is a fool.

TIRE PRESSURES

Every tire and application has a recommended pressure. As noted previously, low tires are an invitation at least to hot running and accelerated tread wear, if not poor grip and outright tire failure. Therefore, own a good tire gauge and make a habit of frequent pressure checks. Any bad trends—such as a leaking sidewall or wheel rim—will quickly come to your attention.

In the old days, tire technicians at the races would suggest that you set a pressure to give a 6-psi track rise from cold pressure. The reason for this is that tread rubber gives best grip in a certain temperature range. Too cold or too hot and it will grip less well. You no longer hear about a 6-psi rise today, but riders will still use tire pressure to make minor adjustments in tire temperature. The lower the pressure, the hotter the tire runs.

Tire pressure goes up and down with temperature, and can even be affected by long stints in direct sun. For a street-only machine, this is less important, but it's useful to know anyway.

Another issue affected by tire pressure is wet running. Many people suppose—as I once did—that because you let air pressure out to increase grip in sand or loose going, you should also do so in wet weather. The reverse is true. The danger in wet running is that the tire will ride up on a film of water and lose grip. This is called aquaplaning, and it will put you down in a heartbeat. The bigger the footprint, the lower the speed at which aquaplaning begins, so reducing tire pressure in wet weather actually encourages this.

At high-speed circuits—particularly Daytona—tire makers' pressure recommendations are motivated as much by liability considerations as by operating temperature. You will see the comedy of riders leaving tech inspection, having their pressures non-optionally set high by factory technicians stationed there, then rolling out to their pit stations where their own crew resets the pressures to what they actually want. I am not suggesting that you ignore factory pressure specs, but I do expect you to develop and use judgment of your own.

There are variations in construction among radial tires. Race tires are usually provided with two belts, each at an angle close to 23 degrees to the centerline—the very angle that gives maximum carcass stiffness in a bias tire. Such a stiff tread region can give great grip. Yet for street applications, some makers argue that a less-stiff belt gives the rider valuable warning that the limit is near. This is provided by the circumferential or "zero-angle" belts used by another group of makers.

Because both basic types exist on the market, there is obviously a following for each. Some riders want maximum grip and don't mind dealing with a possibly more-sudden release when it comes. Others prefer the easier predictability of the zero-angle design. We are not talking ultimates here, just rider preferences. You decide what you are most comfortable with. Rider confidence is more valuable than any technical feature, no matter how racy its reputation. There are no style points awarded in motorcycle sport.

Tread profile is another issue. Tire makers are forever flying between two extremes in front-tire profile. The triangular, knifelike profile is attractive because it delivers maximum footprint when leaned over in a corner. It can also give instant steering response, but lacks a maximum footprint for braking. Such "sharp" tires can feel odd to some riders when the bike is not quite at the lean angle that gives maximum footprint. Rounder profile fronts may slow steering response, but give a consistent footprint as the machine leans over, as well as a large upright braking footprint. Likewise, some bikes may be stable on the round tire, yet less so with a sharper profile tire.

Tire design is a difficult thing because everything affects everything else. Therefore, design has to move ahead slowly as it searches for improved compromises among many, many variables.

CHAPTER 17
WHEELS

Wheels are half of the motorcycle, based on the idea that a bike is an engine, two wheels, and a place to sit. Wheel width must be right to give tires their correct tread contour, for best grip and handling. Information on correct rim widths is happily supplied by the tire manufacturers. Wheels, tires, and brakes constitute most of your machine's unsprung weight—the part of the bike that is not isolated from bumps by springs. Unsprung weight is an important handling variable, and the lighter it is, the better. Last but not often least, wheels are a major determinant of your machine's appearance.

In the late 1960s, all motorcycles had wire-spoked wheels, and the racy mod was to replace heavy chromed or painted steel rims with extruded aluminum rims. Cast, one-piece wheels could not come into existence until the hot part of the brake system—the drum in former times—ceased to

be part of the wheel structure. Drum brakes evolved until drums were so large that the spokes were little over 3 inches long, and brake heating in severe use was enough to make the spokes loose! Early disc brakes, such as the Pagehiln units seen on Triumph racers in 1971 or on early-1970s MV GP bikes, were used with spoked wheels. Peter Williams in England produced cast wheels for his own racing use, and other small, specialist makers like Elliot Morris and Dan Hannebrink in the United States soon appeared. Brake discs and calipers were at first borrowed from small racing cars. Honda offered production disc brakes on its CB750, and Kawasaki and Suzuki offered them on top models in 1972. Drums deservedly fell out of use almost instantly.

At first, the United States was the cast-wheel leader, with no less an institution than the legendary MV-Agusta using

Marchesini Cast Magnesium Wheel. *Cast or, in some cases, forged light-metal wheels like this are the dominant type in motorcycle roadracing. Racers seek light wheels not only because they reduce unsprung weight, but also 1 pound saved in a wheel rim or tire is worth 2 pounds anywhere else on the machine. A wheel has to be accelerated twice: once in straight-line fashion, and also in the second sense of rotating around its own center.* Slater Bros.

Dymag Carbon Fiber Reinforced Plastic (CFRP) Wheel. *Just as aircraft construction is moving on from metals into fiber-reinforced plastic, so are motorcycle components—including, finally, wheels. CFRP has much higher fatigue strength than metal, and also lacks metal's corrosion problems. These wheels are super light.* Andrew Wright/Superbike Racing Parts

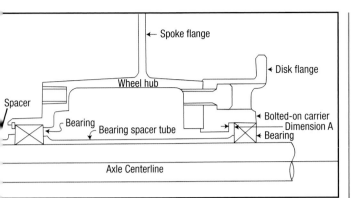

Wheel Bearing and Spacer Tube Fit. *In this cross-section of a wheel hub, the wheel is located laterally by its left-hand bearing, which is trapped against a shoulder by a snap ring. In order to avoid possible severe end-thrust to bearings when the axle nut is tightened, the right-hand bearing does not locate against a shoulder. End-thrust will be avoided as long as dimension A remains positive.*

Morris mag wheels on its racers. With the resurgence of GP racing in the later 1970s, Europe became, and today remains, the cast-wheel leader. Cast wheels have been made with all numbers of spokes from three upwards, and no advantage seems to go with any particular number.

There are now also forged magnesium and aluminum wheels. The forging process produces a more fatigue-resistant metal structure, safely permitting a bit less metal to do the job. The other development is the carbon wheel—the lightest of all.

MORE IS BETTER?

Because rim and tire widths have been growing for the past 30 years, many riders assume wider is always better, and find it better-looking, too. These folk try to cram big rubber into small spaces, trying to "update" their older bikes. If you feel this way, temper your feelings with some facts. Tires have been growing to match increasing horsepower and weight—true. But every width increase brings a weight increase and, when spinning, that weight acts as a heavier gyroscope, opposing more strongly your attempts to steer or flick your bike. To counter this increased resistance, wheel diameters have been reduced from time to time. Up at 23 inches in the 1930s, wheels came down to 19 and 20 inches around 1950, then to 19 and 18 in the 1960s. Road racers experimented with 16-inch wheels from time to time, but their lack of gyro stability made early 1980s bikes too twitchy for most riders. A compromise was struck at 17 inches, which lasted until 16.5-inch wheels were introduced, first in World Superbike, then in GP. Now 16 inches are the leading edge.

What's my point? It is that taking great hacks in major variables like tire and wheel size can easily make your bike into either a twitchy handful or a lumberwagon. Putting Sam Spade's fedora on Walter Mitty's head won't make him into a private eye. Bolting oversized wings onto a Piper Cub

will just slow it down. Many a light-handling early bike has been turned into a heavy steerer by well-meaning, vintage-racing owners, intent upon maximizing tire footprint area. Footprint area isn't the only tire performance variable! Let the stopwatch be your guide.

Currently, race bike design emphasizes the use of the lightest possible wheels, tires, and brake disc and carrier assemblies. Low wheel gyroscopic mass is a major ingredient in quick steering. A bike with large-diameter, heavy wheels and thick, heavy brake discs will snap into a corner noticeably slower than will the same machine with lighter weight rotating components. The more time it takes you to crank your bike over and back up again, the more track or road you waste that could have been used either for later braking or earlier acceleration.

Wheel and brake mass also affect acceleration, and they affect it twice; these parts not only move with the motorcycle, they also rotate. This means that 1 pound of mass removed from tire or rim is worth almost 2 pounds removed from any other part of the machine.

Control and stability are intertwined. When a machine is made more stable, it becomes more resistant to disturbance. It acts "as if it were on rails." The rider's attempts to steer also qualify as a disturbance, however, so as stability increases, control responsiveness generally decreases. Older machines, such as the classic bevel-drive Ducatis, have this "on rails" characteristic and must be committed to a corner line, from which they will be deflected only with difficulty. Locomotives actually are on rails and cannot be steered at all. Is that the desired ideal?

This makes it appear that motorcycles must be constantly losing stability, as their wheel sizes have been reduced over the years, but this is not so. As wheels have shrunk in diameter, tire and rim widths have increased, while rolling diameters have remained close to constant. Chassis stiffness increases have made it possible to combine adequate stability with quicker steering geometry, resulting in improved control response. Today's machines can change line in-corner with ease. Changing wheels and tires on 20-year-old bikes will not give them 1990s handling.

MAGNESIUM

Magnesium racing wheels are easily available if you don't mind the price. They (especially the forged variety) are the lightest metal wheels, they look great, but they are fragile and susceptible to corrosion. Mag wheel pioneer Elliot Morris asked a friend at Lockheed about aircraft use of mag wheels.

"Elliot," his friend replied, "We try not to use that awful metal at all any more. The engines we've got today will lift any damned thing, so all our wheels are aluminum now. With mag, it's got to be sealed in epoxy paint or it corrodes all to hell the minute it gets wet or even damp. To inspect it for cracks, which we have to do every year, the paint has to all come off. After the inspection, the surface has to be etched and primed all over again, then painted with that two-component nonsense. Too much trouble."

I know that some of you won't be able to resist running real mags on the street, but at least now you know some of the risks. Racing people have all seen bent, cracked, or broken mags. This metal, typically AZ81, has very little elongation before failure—typically 3 to 5 percent. That's not much. Racers accept the risks because, with the high levels of parts inspection in racing (mechanics give the bike a stare after every practice), failures can be made pretty unlikely. Street riders who want maintenance-free equipment will be happier with aluminum wheels—while longing for that mag look.

CARBON FIBER

Carbon fiber reinforced plastic (CFRP) wheels are here. Carbon fiber has better fatigue properties than metal and is potentially much stronger, which is why, after years of caution, the aircraft industry is finally committing to major carbon assemblies. The "black wheels" must be regarded as the coming technology.

WHEEL BEARINGS

All motorcycle wheels have their own bearings, with the important exception of Honda and Ducati rear wheels on single-sided swingarms—these slide onto a stub axle like a racecar wheel. Front wheels have two bearings, one pressed into either side of the wheel hub, with a spacer tube between them to prevent them from being jammed toward one another by the force of axle nut tightening. If the spacer is too short, the bearings' inner races will be forced toward each other, while their outer races are being held apart by the shoulders machined inside the wheel hub. The large forces involved will shortly cause the bearings to fail—possibly to seize. Check for this possibility by spinning the wheel before and after axle tightening. Any increase in wheel friction during axle tightening suggests that the bearings may be jammed. Some owners are maniacs on axle-nut tightening; don't be one of them, for this can compress the spacer tube enough to cause bearing jamming.

Weight-conscious owners sometimes replace their steel bearing spacer tubes with lighter aluminum ones. Unless this replacement is done carefully, it is an invitation to jammed wheel bearings. Aluminum is only one-third as stiff as steel, so an aluminum axle spacer will compress more than the steel one it replaces—possibly allowing the wheel bearings to become jammed.

CUSH DRIVES

Rear wheels on streetbikes are more complicated, for there are usually two bearings in the wheel itself, and one or more bearings in a separate sprocket carrier/cush-hub unit that engages the wheel. Cautions about the front wheel bearings and their spacer tube apply at the rear as well. An aftermarket or racing wheel will most likely be made in one piece, with the sprocket bolted directly to the wheel. This raises other concerns. Engines deliver power in a series of firm pushes, and to smooth these out, there is usually a cush hub consisting of springs or rubber elements in the clutch gear. This protects the gearbox from the worst of

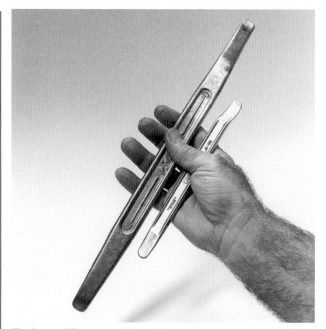

Tire Levers, Nice versus Nasty. *Few people change their own tires these days, but if you do, I recommend you not use a tire lever longer than your hand. The lever on the left is proven; I personally saw it break a mag wheel a few years ago. The one on the right is from my toolbox. If you learn how to change a tire, you won't need anything bigger than this small lever.* John Owens Studio

the engine's banging. At the other end of the driveline, there is a second cushion, built into the rear wheel, consisting of large rubber blocks trapped between vanes that are part of wheel and sprocket carrier. Quite often, these rubber cushions are eliminated in racing applications, but this can affect the durability of clutch and gearbox. Harley-Davidson tried (on the best advice) to run without a cush drive in its VR Superbike's first year, and it broke clutch hubs as a result. Sometimes doing without a cush drive works, sometimes it doesn't.

When you adopt racing technology in your modified motorcycle, you must also take up the necessary habits of constant vigilance and inspection. Stock production bikes are designed to be turnkey systems, just as are cars. When you make changes, that is no longer necessarily the case. Reliability and safety result from design *and* maintenance.

WHEELS AND BRAKE HEAT

Front wheels are pretty well insulated from brake heat because of the long thermal path from disc to hub. But rear wheels occasionally have discs bolted directly to their hubs, and this can cause problems. Some riders use the rear brake hard, and brake heat can do some funny things. I have seen it melt the grease out of wheel bearings, and one rider encountered a strange wheel vibration that happened only after several hot laps. It was traced to brake heat, expanding a three-spoke rear wheel from the hub outward, making it slightly triangular!

Sprocket Bolt Lockwiring. *This hub-only shot shows how lockwire is arranged to pull always in the tightening direction. Drilling for lockwire is tedious, but it provides visual proof that the bolts in question have been secured. Even so, high-stress bolts such as those on sprockets can stretch, so they should be checked for torque periodically. Why not use production tabwashers? They're great—if you have them in stock. But everyone involved in competition always has wire.* John Owens Studio

AIR TIGHTNESS

Always a concern with any wheel—new or used—is air tightness. Once tires are mounted, inflate them to the pressure you want and check them again next day. If there is pressure loss (and it's not caused by the weather having turned colder), check for leaks with a water trough or brush and soap solution. First check the obvious places—around the valve stem and between rim flanges and tire beads. Then check the rim itself. Normally, the inside of the rim will be sealed with epoxy paint, but this can be damaged by tire levers, or may be imperfectly applied.

Now that there are standards for wheel dimensions, it's less likely that you will come across an oversize or undersize wheel. Years ago, it was fairly common to find either *(a)* a wheel whose rim diameter was so big that it was hard or impossible to fully seat tire beads on it, or *(b)* a wheel with undersize rim diameter, on which a tire might slip in service.

If you mount your own tires, remember this rule: Never use more than 60 psi to seat the beads. If it takes more than this, something is wrong. Relubricate the beads with tire lube and try again. I have seen men injured by tire and rim explosions, caused by using excessive bead-seating pressure.

Conversely, sometimes you encounter a tire that has been on a rim so long that it's hard to break its beads. Before you get a "soft" hammer and start whanging away as our grandfathers did, remember that the rim Granddad was almost hitting was steel, not magnesium or aluminum. If you can't break the bead with steady pressure from your heel, take the wheel to a shop with a tire machine and have its pneumatic bead-breaker do the job without knocking a chunk out of your wheel.

I suggest you never use a tire iron that's much longer than your hand. Those long levers are made for car tires on heavy steel rims, and they will gouge or break cast wheels if used enthusiastically by inexperienced persons.

Tubeless tires are inflated through tire valves that are set into holes in the wheel rim. Insert such valves into the rim with care—this is a prime source of leaks.

Bear in mind that putting an inner tube into a tire intended for tubeless operation will make it run somewhat hotter; the principle is, the more rubber there is, the more heat it generates. This will reduce its safe speed rating—not a good idea.

WHEEL DAMAGE AND INSPECTION

People crash and whack their wheels. Rims get dented. People worry about cracks. At the same time, I hear constantly from street riders who want to buy used racing or street wheels, but wonder what condition they're in. There are firms that offer to straighten and/or weld damaged cast wheels, but I haven't tried them. If you want wheels inspected, it requires thorough cleaning, followed by complete removal of any paint. Then the wheel is sprayed with a penetrating dye and cleaned again. The dye lodges in any cracks (and in surface roughness or dirt, I might add). Then the wheel is inspected either by spraying it with an absorbent chalk-like dust, or with ultraviolet light (this requires a fluorescent penetrant dye). Used or repaired wheels don't particularly appeal to me, somehow. You decide.

WIRE WHEELS

Early sportbikes rolled on wire-spoked wheels, and today spoking and repairing such wheels is a specialist operation. There are sources for such work in the United States, supplying new rims and stainless spokes. Who knows? You may even decide to tackle this interesting discipline yourself. Back when cast wheels were just coming into use (1973–1980), many people assumed that cast must be better than wire spokes, but I never had a rider complain if we had to put a spoked wheel on a bike. Cast or pressed wheels eliminate spoke maintenance, but whether they are better in some provable sense is an open question. In some destruction tests I read through, one of the strongest wheels had wire spokes and a steel rim.

One manufacturer was being driven crazy in the 1990s by front chatter in production-based racing. Nothing worked—until it tried a wire-spoked wheel, which killed the chatter. The factory was not interested in the race team's proposal to make such a wheel an option on a "heritage model." Incidentally, the rapid adoption of much stiffer upside-down forks as stock on such bikes was, to a large extent, driven by the need to suppress chatter.

CHAPTER 18
BRAKES

A sports vehicle is all about acceleration, which comes in three flavors: acceleration, cornering, and braking. What use is a powerful engine if your opponent just outbrakes you at the next turn? Don't overlook braking just because it appears to be the least glamorous of the three forms of motorcycle acceleration. An improvement to performance in one area requires improvements in the other two.

A brake system must meet many criteria. It must generate enough brake torque to fully exploit tire traction; in racing, this means the ability to lift the rear wheel at will. It must be able to maintain brake torque during hard use—that is, it must resist fade. Fade is loss of friction with increasing temperature, caused by generation of gas in the brake pad, or by migration of resinous binder material to the pad surface. A brake system must also be linear in its action. When you squeeze harder, you should get a proportional increase in brake torque—not the awful feeling of shaking hands with a stone statue: you squeeze, but there is no further effect.

The big change in production bike brake technology has been the adoption of ceramic or carbon/metallic brake pads for heavy-duty use, replacing the tradition of organic pad materials that began long ago with patent formulations of leather, glue, and horsehair. The new materials work well in the wet, but result in fairly rapid disc wear and/or grooving. The result has been that Supersport racers use up discs and pads in quantity—the price of reliable, strong stopping power.

There are several levels of changes you may contemplate for brake systems.

1. Upgrade pad material and possibly hydraulic hoses. This leaves basic system parameters unchanged, but can deliver increased stopping power and a firmer lever. There are wide choices in both pad materials and hose kits. Some types of pads require break-in and, for this, manufacturers' recommendations should be followed.

2. If you are experienced in brake work, you can certainly change the pads and hoses yourself. If not (brake systems being as critical to safety as they are), you will want either to take the work to a specialist or have an experienced friend "walk you through" the process. The last thing you want, in your worst nightmare, is for one or more brake pads to fall

Stopping Power. *Brakes quickly and controllably convert the kinetic energy of machine and rider into heat. This heat makes discs and pads extremely hot, so materials are needed which retain consistent, predictable friction even when incandescent. The lightest material that can do this really well is carbon-carbon, a solid made of high-tensile carbon fiber fabric, impregnated with solid amorphous carbon. At temperatures that melt steel, carbon soldiers on happily.*
Brian J. Nelson

out as you ride. It happened to Eddie Lawson at Laguna, at high speed. He had the bike on the ground instantly, limiting his injury to foot damage. See that brake pads are secure.

3. Upgrade from stock carriers and discs. There's amazingly wide choice here. Be sure that carrier-to-wheel mounting bolts are of adequate quality, not stretched or otherwise damaged. Secure them with either bent tabwashers or locking wire. Race tuners suggest that you break in new discs with a gradually increasing rate of heat input—rather than just putting them straight into hard use. This prevents warpage that might otherwise occur.

4. Race-type brake system, including upgraded master cylinder and calipers, and possibly larger-diameter discs.

CALIPERS AND DISCS

When you brake hard from maximum speed to zero, essentially all your kinetic energy goes into heating the brake discs. This sudden energy shot raises their temperature sharply. The heavier and faster your bike is, the larger this energy shot is, and the higher your disc temperatures rise. Obviously, when you increase performance, you also increase this energy shot. This is one reason for brake upgrades.

Making brake discs heavier reduces their temperature rise in an energy shot. The same energy is spread over more mass, thus raising its temperature less. But heavier discs hurt performance in several ways; their inertia slows acceleration twice: once from straight-line motion, and once in rotation.

Solid-mounted brake disc from a TZ750 of 20 years ago, showing how discs were bolted solidly to their carriers. By 1978, we were having to slot these to keep them from coning. Every year, with ever-rising tire grip, brakes must work harder and get rid of more heat. At present, brake discs get so hot, even in production racing, that if they were solid-mounted like this, they would quickly cone or crack. John Owens Studio

Extra gyro mass slows steering response and may affect stability adversely. Designers therefore try to minimize disc mass, but when disc mass is too small, the discs run too hot in hard use (Honda did this in 500 GP in 1988—at Laguna, their discs were black and pads were gone at the end). As a result, discs may warp or crack, and their high temperature may cause fading of the pads' grip.

Stock brakes are so good these days that it's hard to imagine needing anything better on the street. But I sympathize with anyone who is repelled by the clunky appearance of some stock components. There is a classic simplicity about racing calipers and full-floating iron discs on alloy carriers.

On the other hand, in production racing, it's common for a Supersports machine to require a fresh set of front pads *and discs* for every national event. That indicates that stock parts are made of cost-cutting materials that don't remain dimensionally stable during hard use. Hence there is now a very active brake-parts aftermarket, making upgraded parts.

Any time new calipers are fitted to a machine, you must check to be sure the disc runs centered and parallel in the caliper's slot. Aftermarket caliper brackets may be made on "infallible" CNC machines now, but that doesn't stop the programmer from entering a wrong digit, or the stager from missing a metal chip in the fixture. Use good bolts and see that they are secure. Brakes are serious business. Squeeze the lever a few times, then test for free wheel rotation and good pad retraction.

A BIT OF HISTORY

Years ago, thick, heavy discs were riveted or bolted rigidly to aluminum carriers that were, in turn, bolted to the wheel hubs. Rigid-mounted discs are obsolete now, but when they are used, total indicated disc runout, measured in the middle of the pad track with a dial gauge, should not exceed 0.004 inch or you will feel pulsation in the brake lever.

All of the early calipers had either a single piston, or two pistons facing each other. This simple design was initially all that was needed, simply because tires didn't yet exist that could handle more brake torque. Slick tires arrived in 1974, and riders could then begin to brake harder and harder. Street tire grip has improved in step with race tires. A few coated aluminum front discs were tried in the mid-1970s, but the rapid increase in braking severity soon pushed these to temperatures that had the aluminum oozing out at the edges (Oreo cookie effect).

The big, clunky 7mm-thick stock discs (at a massive 7 pounds each) were first lightened by drilling (this reduced friction surface area, but street riders loved its rad look anyway), and then by Blanchard-grinding to reduced thickness. I believe the first set of 5.5mm discs I saw were on a Honda four-stroke racer at the 1972 Tokyo show.

BRAKE DISC CONING

Better tires and harder braking introduced the problem of disc coning. Coning occurs as follows: when braking, the disc's outer edge is heated more rapidly than its inner edge, because its velocity through the pads is higher (the circumference of the disc at the OD is greater than at the disc ID). The hotter, more rapidly expanding outer parts of the disc pull the cooler, less-expanded inner parts of the disc outward with them, stretching the metal of the inner region permanently. When the disc cools after use, this stretched inner part is too big, but the outer part is still contracting, so the disc deforms into a slight cone shape. When coning occurs, it first pushes the brake pads back farther than normal, giving you a bad scare at the next corner when the lever comes to the bar on the first pull. As it gets worse, the discs can scrape on the calipers.

You can detect coning by laying a straightedge across the disc face. Any coning will be obvious, as the straightedge will not lie flat if coning is present.

Coning is prevented in a variety of ways. "Floating" the disc—mounting it so it is free to expand—is a first measure. Be aware that some production floaters are only simulated. In a real floater setup, you can always feel some free movement between disc and carrier.

ORIGIN OF MULTIPISTON CALIPERS

As riders braked harder to match the constant improvement of tire grip, disc deformation began again. This time, calipers were redesigned. A big one- or two-piston caliper needed pistons that were 40–50mm in diameter to get enough piston area to develop the necessary pressure behind the pads. This meant wide pads and a wide pad track on the disc. The result was that the disc OD was much bigger than its ID, and this produced a corresponding difference in OD and ID heating rates, thus deforming the discs as described previously. For example, on a 320mm disc used with 50mm round pads, the OD of the pad track is 45 percent greater in circumference than its ID. A 45 percent difference in sliding velocity is a lot.

This was moderated by Brembo's four-piston caliper of about 1982. It used a narrow rectangular pad, about twice as long as it was wide. The 2:1 aspect ratio of this pad allowed use of discs with narrower pad tracks, so OD and ID heating rates were no longer so different and disc distortion became less of a problem. Later, entering the 1990s, the Swedish ISR company and others moved onward to six-piston calipers, pad aspect ratio became more extreme, and discs and their pad tracks became even narrower.

In some multipiston designs, instead of there being a single long pad, there is one small pad per caliper piston. There is a reason for this. Each brake pad is bonded to a backing plate (usually steel) and, traditionally, these backing plates have been stamped from sheet. But as braking has become more vigorous, heating of these stamped backing plates has caused them to warp, just as stamped brake discs do (stamping puts a lot of stress into the metal, and heating allows this stress to bend the part). One answer is to machine or water-jet the backing plates rather than stamp them (expensive). Another is to provide one little pad for each piston, thus limiting the

This production floating brake disc is on a factory race bike. After emerging racing technology defines a new look, production engineers have to figure out how to incorporate it into the product line. Brian J. Nelson

area of backing plate over which warpage can occur. Some recent pad designs are made without metal backing plates.

This warpage is a classic cause of low brake lever in races. At the start, the pads are new and their backing plates nice and flat. As the race progresses, heat reaches the backing plates, which warp. When you squeeze the hand lever, this warpage must first be pressed flat, and this uses up lever travel. When you release the lever, the backing plates arch up again, pushing fluid back to the master cylinder. If this gets bad enough, the lever will come to the bar. Yet when new pads are fitted, the problem magically disappears.

A walk around Daytona's garage area reveals pad tracks anywhere from 22 to 28mm wide—a big change from the original 50mm width of 1972. Don't assume that more caliper pistons must be better—over many years Brembo's four-piston caliper has continued to evolve and continues to serve on a great many top race bikes today.

DISC MATERIALS

The early Japanese production-bike brake discs were made from low-cost magnetic grades of stainless steel for appearance reasons (let's call it "rust resistant," because it wasn't rustproof—a moist pad would leave a circle of corrosion on the disc if left long enough). Race car discs were made of cast iron or materials euphemistically called semisteel. Pad grip was better on iron than on stainless, but iron discs were more vulnerable to cracking. Some iron materials developed "hard spots" in vigorous use, which could become actual bumps on the disc surface, making the brakes judder when applied. Owners of Honda's RS500 two-stroke triple race bike had to sit for long hours, sanding away hard spots that appeared like measles on their narrow, hard-worked front discs.

GETTING HOTTER

As the mentioned developments have occurred, discs have become steadily narrower radially, while staying in the range of 4.5–5.5mm thick. To save weight, the extra material involved in connecting the disc to its carrier has been minimized. The lighter the disc, the hotter it gets in operation. The result was the abandonment of metal discs in GP racing and adoption of ultra-light discs made of the aerospace material, carbon-carbon.

Carbon-carbon is simply amorphous (noncrystalline) carbon, reinforced with carbon fibers. To make a carbon-carbon missile nose-cone or rocket motor throat, a "preform" of carbon fibers is given the desired shape, then soaked with some carbon-rich substance, like tar or plastic. It is then heated in a special oxygen-free furnace for an extended period to drive off all but the carbon. This process is repeated until the desired degree of density is achieved. Carbon is perfectly happy and very strong at temperatures that would leave an iron disc as a glowing puddle. Its weakness is that it doesn't display much friction until it gets fairly hot. Early carbon discs were tricky. Riders had to drag the brake during a warm-up lap, being careful that the rising friction didn't take them unawares. Pads were likewise carbon-carbon.

To keep disc temperature up, covers were sometimes fitted. Today, carbon brakes are used only in GP racing,

having been banned in other kinds of bike racing, supposedly because of high cost. Of course, the carbon people hasten to point out that 10 or 12 sets of iron discs and pads per season aren't exactly a savings, either.

A new lightweight disc material is now entering use: carbon-ceramic matrix. Just like the carbon-carbon discs, the strength of this gray, rock-like material comes from embedded carbon fabric, but the matrix that fills it is the extremely hard, ceramic silicon carbide, deposited there by the decomposition of a special polymer. The extreme hardness of such discs has resulted in their adoption as options on certain premium automobiles. This could be the development that brings ultra-light brakes to production motorcycles.

PAD MATERIALS

The first disc brakes used organic pads—a matrix of resinous material, given mechanical strength by embedded asbestos fibers (now replaced by Kevlar), with perhaps a glint of metal powder or wire to improve heat conductivity. The effect of this stuff was rather like very hard rubber. The smell of hard-worked organic pads, like that of burning pot handles, is caused by the breakdown (pyrolysis—I love the word) of the resin.

Such pads have limited grip in the wet. They will also fade if made hot enough, so ceramic (stone-like, and therefore very heat-resisting) and sintered metal pads were developed. These were harder on discs but gripped well—even in rain. Metallic pads may conduct more heat to caliper pistons; in some cases, special insulating design is required to prevent this, allowing air to circulate behind the pads and into caliper pistons. Pads for the new carbon-ceramic-matrix discs contain brass wire that melts to form a layer on the disc. Friction is said to take place within a mutual layer of hot, viscous metal in service.

Don't upgrade rear brake pads with others of higher friction without considering brake sensitivity. Many bikes already have overly sensitive rear brakes, and higher friction pads would only make this worse. Feet are more powerful than hands!

The friction coefficient, or mu, of a pad material is not a constant, but may change with such variables as temperature, humidity, age, or the presence of water. Everyone has experienced the fierceness of organic friction material in humid conditions, and everyone has also felt momentary panic as organic pads fail to bite in rain. Fewer have been exposed to the steep mu-versus-temperature curve of the touchier carbon-carbon compounds; you pull the brake hard but the cold material has little friction. Then, just as you feel the grip coming and try to release the lever, it's too late, you're already down. This situation has since been improved by orienting the carbon fibers in carbon-carbon pads and discs. Heat travels fastest along the fiber direction, so materials with the fibers perpendicular to the friction surface will warm up slowly (heat is rapidly conducted into the interior), while those with fibers more parallel with the surfaces will warm up faster (heat stays near the surface).

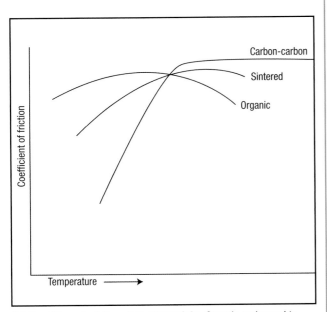

Friction Characteristics of Pad Materials. *Organic pads used to be the only choice, but as you see, their friction rises moderately as they heat up, then falls or fades after a certain temperature. Sintered pads fade less, but they have a steeper early rise of friction versus temperature, making them possibly less suitable for street use. Carbon-carbon pads on carbon-carbon discs give wonderful friction out to frightful temperatures—but their low-temperature behavior can be tricky. The steep rise of friction as the pads and discs warm up from cold can lock a wheel. This stuff is for racing only—or for stopping airliners.*

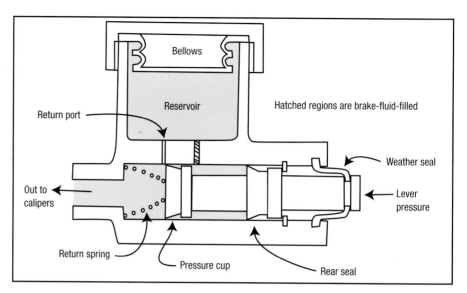

Cutaway Brake Master Cylinder *One piston supplies pressure to the calipers, while a second piston behind it prevents leakage from the return port after the front piston moves past it. It is very important that the master cylinder's bore surface be smooth—both fluid and air can leak along corrosion tracks. Brake fluid takes up water from the atmosphere, leading to corrosion in master cylinders not in use.*

Labels in figure: Bellows; Reservoir; Return port; Hatched regions are brake-fluid-filled; Weather seal; Out to calipers; Lever pressure; Return spring; Pressure cup; Rear seal

Some organic pads require a specific break-in procedure, described in the maker's literature. Failure to carry this out can result in the pads' becoming glazed by resin rising to their surface.

MASTER CYLINDER FUNDAMENTALS

A master cylinder is a small piston pump with a fluid reservoir attached to it (fancy race-type master cylinders sometimes have remote reservoirs). When you pull the lever, fluid is forced through the lines to the caliper pistons, pushing them against the discs. When you release the lever, the springiness in the caliper piston seals pulls the pistons away from the discs slightly, and pushes fluid back to the master cylinder, ready for the next brake application. And what if the fluid in the calipers gets hot and expands? (Typically, organic fluids like this expand at 1cc per liter, per degree Centigrade.) Expanding fluid, unable to return to the reservoir, unable to push the master cylinder piston back beyond its stop, would apply the brakes, causing a lockup. To prevent that disagreeable outcome, there is a tiny hole drilled between reservoir and master cylinder bore, just ahead of the edge of the master cylinder piston cup in the brakes-off position. Expanding fluid passes through this hole and returns to the reservoir above. Likewise, extra fluid needed to compensate for pad wear is drawn into the system through this same hole at each brake return.

When you apply the brake, the first thing that happens is that the master cylinder's piston cup slides across this little hole, closing it off so that system pressure can be generated by your grip on the lever.

Aha, but now what happens to the fluid in the reservoir? Doesn't it leak into the space behind the master cylinder piston cup when the brakes are on? No it doesn't, because on the master cylinder piston shaft there is a second cup whose purpose is to prevent precisely this: even at full master cylinder stroke, this second cup is still behind the little hole, preventing leakage.

OK, another question: What if the fluid between the two master cylinder piston cups expands, or dries up? Answer: it can't, because there is a second, larger hole into the reservoir, located between the two cups. Its purpose is to keep the space between cups full at all times, and to allow any expansion or contraction of the fluid to occur easily.

Clearly, it's important that the inner surface of the master cylinder bore be smooth and defect-free. Otherwise, fluid may leak past the piston. Never, therefore, use sharp objects to try to extract master cylinder parts. Another point: Some fancy master cylinders are actually made of nasty magnesium, whose chemical activity makes it highly subject to corrosion with water. Don't attempt to reuse an old mag master cylinder without examining its bore in strong light. I spent a long evening once, trying to bleed out a brake system with one of these master cylinders. Upon inspection, I could clearly see the "hen tracks" of corrosion all over the inside of its bore. The same can happen, although more slowly, in aluminum parts left for years with water-logged old fluid in them.

Moisture absorbed into the fluid can also corrode master cylinder and caliper bores, or rust any iron-based parts in the system. This can lead to leakage or to seized pistons. This is why, for best performance, brake fluid should be replaced at intervals.

Rebuild kits are usually available for both master cylinders and calipers, so that any suspect parts can be replaced.

BRAKE FLUIDS

One brake fluid seems to follow another, like versions of popular software packages. The early fluids, DOT 3 and 4, are polyglycol-based and have fairly high boiling points when dry. Unfortunately, the polyglycols, like the alcohols to which they are related, are hygroscopic—that is, they take up water from any source. You will feel the moisture avidity of brake fluid on your skin if you touch it; it dries out skin powerfully. Protect your eyes.

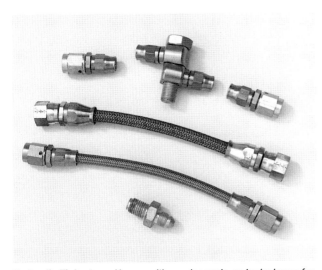

Hydraulic Tinkertoys. *You can either order made-up brake hoses for your specific make and model, or you can order bulk hose, fittings, and adapters like these and make up your own custom lines. These are Earl's Performance Products pieces.* John Owens Studio

Boiling point is important because, if calipers get hot enough, the fluid in them can boil. The resulting gas expands, pushing fluid back to the master cylinder. The rider gets a nasty surprise at the next corner, when he finds springy gas in his brake lines—and no brakes. When glycol-based fluids absorb water, their boiling point falls. This sounds scary, but remember that a bike's brakes are up front, exposed to full slipstream air—not buried in some wide race car wheel, surrounded by hot metal.

When DOT 5 fluid came along, we all read the can. "Silicone," it said. "Non-hygroscopic. Super-high boiling point." This is better, we thought. Gotta have it. Not only that, but DOT 3 and 4 fluids eat paint, making every bleeding operation into a vain attempt to protect the front fender. We took the new fluid home and filled our brake systems with it. Alas, now we had lever-return problems. Silicones, any textbook will tell you, are not very good lubricants. Wistfully, we drained the hi-tech stuff back out and replaced it with fresh DOT 4, resolving to change it often enough to avoid boiling-point degradation. The bottom line is that motorcycle brakes are not set-it-and-forget-it systems, even though most riders treat them that way. Brake systems should be serviced at least yearly, with a cleanout and fluid replacement. Otherwise your punishment could be corrosion and crud growing in your system from water absorption. Moisture not only reduces fluid boiling point, it forms gooey crud over time that can block master cylinder return ports, and it can cause rusting and/or seizure of pistons in their master cylinder or caliper bores.

Some master cylinders provide a lever height adjustment, much appreciated by persons with smaller hands. Take care that nothing prevents the master cylinder piston from returning fully to its stop when you release the lever. This would cover the return port, creating the possibility that fluid expansion in a hot caliper could apply the brakes unexpectedly.

Limit the exposure of brake fluid to air, from which it can absorb moisture. Don't leave the cap off a master cylinder or can of fluid while you do something else. Don't store brake system parts with fluid in them unless they are tightly capped and plugged. When replacing the rubber bellows atop the master cylinder reservoir, try not to trap air under it, against the fluid surface. Some fluid will be pushed out of the reservoir in the process, but you can catch it with strategically placed rags before it can eat up your paint.

Never expose any brake-system rubber parts to anything but brake fluid or isopropyl alcohol (rubbing alcohol, available at all drugstores). Solvents, gasoline, kerosene, parts-washer fluid—all of these are absorbed into this type of rubber, causing it to swell grotesquely. A rider I knew added some kerosene-based Teflon anti-friction additive to his TZ750's brake system. In the next practice, his brakes dragged so hard that the bike slowed down and stopped on the track. It had to go back to the pit on the truck. Every rubber part had to be replaced.

THE BOTTOM LINE ON HYDRAULIC LEVERAGE

Brakes are hydraulic because hydraulics give a smooth, low-friction means of multiplying the force of your hand and applying it to press the brake pads against the discs. I want to explain how a force at your hand translates ultimately to a rate of deceleration of your bike, and how you can use this understanding to choose components.

At one end of the spectrum would lie bikes known for their heavy lever effort—Harley-Davidsons, for example. At the other would be racing brake setups that produce maximum deceleration for relatively little lever pressure.

Be careful in any changes you plan. If you are used to heavy lever pressure, don't change suddenly to a system with much lighter pressure needs. You may, in an emergency, pull the lever too hard, causing a fall. Time and again, I have seen racers go slower after "upgrading" their brakes from one disc to two, or from firm lever to light. New brakes take some getting used to.

CALIPERS

Almost all production caliper bodies are cast. Caliper pistons are generally of steel, hard chrome plated for wear—and weather—resistance. A few are now being made of titanium—only 60 percent of the weight of steel. The caliper piston seals are located in the caliper body, not in the piston, and are square in section. Caliper pistons are inserted hollow-side out, as this places maximum distance between the hot pad and the fluid. On street calipers, there is often a flexible weather boot as well, retained in grooves on both piston and caliper. Race calipers lack this feature. At the highest point in the caliper's fluid cavity is a bleed screw to allow air to be bled from the system when required.

Some calipers have only a single piston, on one side of the disc, with some mechanical means of equalizing pressure on both sides of the disc during braking. Early Honda calipers swung on a hinge; others slid sideways on a pair of bolts. Calipers with pistons on both sides of the disc have internal or external fluid balance lines to equalize pressure on the two disc faces.

Caliper pistons are lubricated during assembly, either with brake fluid itself or with a special brake system grease.

HYDRAULIC LINES

The main thing to know about hydraulic hoses is that hose stress depends on hose ID; the smaller the hose, the lower the stress and the less springy the system will feel on the lever. Stock hose is reinforced rubber, but in the early 1970s enthusiasts quickly adopted aircraft-type braided-stainless-jacketed plastic hose. We all learned how to cut and fit this stuff back then, but today hose kits are made up for just about any bike you can think of, so it's no longer necessary. Other popular hose types are jacketed with Kevlar or carbon fiber instead of stainless braid, so they are lighter. Guzzi's brilliant engineer Giulio Carcano, who refused to have gel-coat on his bike's fairings because it added weight, would surely choose the Kevlar! Riders say they get a firmer lever with aftermarket hose, but I suspect they like that shiny, high-tech-looking stainless braid just as much.

Hose connections are of two types. Threaded connections seal by forcing conical terminations together metal-to-metal, so no seal is required. The other uses a banjo bolt and requires soft, deformable metal washers (copper or aluminum) between each pair of surfaces. For example, a single banjo bolt holding two brake lines to a front master cylinder would require three such metal seal washers. Keep some on hand so you won't have to gamble on trying to reuse them.

Check to be sure that hoses cannot contact tires or chain, even at full suspension compression. If there is hard line anywhere in the system, it must be supported to prevent vibration from breaking it. Vibratory fatigue failure of hydraulic lines brought down one of the F14 prototypes.

FIGURING HYDRAULIC SYSTEM LEVERAGE (OPTIONAL)

A brake lever is actually two levers in one part. The length of one is from the pivot bolt to the middle of your four fingers on the lever—maybe 3 1/2 inches. The other is from the pivot bolt to the point of contact on the master cylinder piston. The ratio of these two lever lengths is about 3:1, so if you pull the lever with 60 pounds of force, you are applying 3 x 60 = 180 pounds of force to push the master cylinder piston inward.

That piston will have some diameter—often stated in raised letters somewhere on the master cylinder—and a typical number is 16mm, or about 0.63 inch. There are cylinders available from 12mm all the way to beyond 20mm. To calculate hydraulic line pressure produced, we need to know over how much area our 180 pounds of

applied piston force (just as an example) are acting. Area of a circle is pi times diameter squared divided by four, or in this case, 3.14 x (0.63 x 0.63)/4 = 0.312. Here we have about 180 pounds force, acting on roughly 1/3 square inch, so we divide the area into the force to get the pressure in psi. This is 180/0.312 = 577 psi.

Now we need to convert psi into total force acting against brake pads. In order to do this, we need to add up the caliper's piston area. Now some explanation is needed. To get the pressure on the pads, we need only add up the total piston area on one side of each caliper. Each caliper has a balance line in it, so that equal pressure is exerted on both faces of the disc—otherwise the disc would bend. Suppose we have a four-piston caliper with 32mm pistons. The pressure on each pad will be line pressure (577 psi in our example), multiplied times the total piston area on one side of the caliper. The area of a 32mm (1.26 inch) circle is about 1.25 square inches, so the area of two pistons is twice this, or 2.5 square inches. When we multiply this times line pressure, 577 psi, we get 2.5 x 577 = 1,443 pounds. This is the pressure on one pad.

FRICTION COEFFICIENT (MU)

The friction coefficient of the pad material is the friction force we get for each pound of pressure we apply to the pad. A typical older pad material has a mu (pronounced "mew") of 0.3, so this means that for every pound of caliper piston force we apply to that pad, we will get 0.3 pound of frictional force on the disc. Bear in mind that some pads are intended for use only on certain disc materials, and their mu may differ on other materials, or there may be other effects such as scoring, etc.

Back to our example. We apply 1,443 pounds of caliper piston force to this 0.3 mu pad, to get 1,443 x 0.3 = 433 pounds of friction at the disc. Now we have to convert this to brake torque, and to do this, we have to know how far out from the disc's center this force of 430 pounds is acting. Force, multiplied by this distance, will give us torque. We can approximate this by measuring out from the disc center to the middle of the pad track. Let's say we measure this distance on our 300mm disc and find it is 5.2 inches. Now we can figure the brake torque from one pad, in in-lb. It is 5.2 inches, times 430 pounds, or 2,236 in-lb. Most of us are more accustomed to ft-lb as a measure of torque, so to get this, we divide by the number of inches in a foot to get 186 ft-lb of torque from each pad.

There are pads on both sides of the disc, so we have to double this to get the total brake torque: 186 x 2 = 372 ft-lb.

Motorcycle tires are approximately 2 feet in diameter, so this torque of 372 ft-lb, acting on a radius of 1 foot, creates a stopping force (assuming the tire isn't sliding on oil or snow) of 372 pounds.

We know that acceleration or deceleration is driving force, divided by weight. In this case, the force is that 372 pounds of brake force, and the weight is the total weight of

This EBC floating disc and carrier assembly is an example of the wide aftermarket for such items. Aftermarket discs are often both better and cheaper than stock parts. EBC Brakes

Here you see how EBC mounts its floating discs to the carriers. Short ferrules are retained by washer and circlip. EBC Brakes

bike, fuel, and rider. Let's say that total is 600 pounds, so now our deceleration rate is 372/600 = 0.62 G. This is a healthy rate of deceleration—not as high as the 1.1–1.4 G an expert rider might reach in a maximum-effort stop, but a lot of braking all the same.

Now we can calculate deceleration as a function of hand pressure. This makes certain assumptions, such as our hand lever and hydraulics are all 100 percent efficient—no friction loss—and the mu of our friction material is constant regardless of temperature. None of this is strictly true (Mother Nature serves no free lunch), but it's close enough to be useful. If 60 pounds of hand force produce 0.62 G of deceleration, then it will take 60/0.62 = 97 pounds of hand pressure to produce 1 G of deceleration.

Now we can see how things work. A bigger master cylinder piston spreads the same hand pressure over a bigger piston. Result: lower line pressure and lower deceleration. Conversely, a smaller master cylinder piston *increases* line pressure and deceleration. There are pretty solid limits to how small you can go with master cylinder size on a given setup, and we'll get into that in a moment.

CONVERTING SINGLE DISC TO TWIN

Now imagine that you convert the single front disc of our example above, to twin discs. If you leave master cylinder piston size as it is, you will be applying the original line pressure to twice as many pistons and pads, so your brake torque will double. You won't like this because your brake will become terribly touchy. Instead of 97 pounds per G, it will now be only 48.5 pounds per G. When you instinctively grab the lever hard in an emergency, your front wheel will lock and you will tip over. I've seen it often; a rider buys more brake, and then goes slower because the difference scares the rider!

If your system requires *too much* lever pressure, you have options. You can decrease master cylinder diameter (within limits), increase total caliper piston area, or change to a friction pad with a higher mu. Don't go nuts with this; no one is happy with a 50 percent increase in braking power because it's too easy to overbrake and lock up. Changing from a 16mm to a 14mm master cylinder seems like a small change, but it increases pad pressure by 30 percent (piston area is proportional to diameter squared, so the area ratio will be 16/14 squared). Changing from a 0.4 mu pad to a 0.5 mu increases braking force 25 percent (0.5/0.4 = 1.25).

Any time you increase braking force, you have the potential to put heat into discs and pads faster, and this may have effects that will have to be dealt with—such as disc warping and pad flaking or fading. Everything is painfully interrelated!

I suggest that you work through this computation for your present setup, then again for the components with which you plan to replace it. The pounds-per-G figure should not be too much smaller for the upgraded system, or you will find it feels too grabby.

SYSTEM FLEXIBILITY

When you apply the brakes, some part of the lever's stroke is used to cover the return hole, and more is used up in advancing the pads to the disc(s). This is normally small but significant. The next part of the stroke is what raises the pressure in the system enough to deliver the desired brake torque or rate of deceleration. In this part of the stroke, you are really "inflating" the system, loading up all of its springy parts. The brake lever bends a bit, the fluid lines expand somewhat, and the calipers spring open a bit, too, because rugged as they look, they are not infinitely stiff. If the brake system has not been properly bled (purged of air by any of several possible processes), there may be another source of springiness: air in the system. Each of these sources of springiness causes the brake lever to come in closer to the bar during hard braking—possibly enough to either erode the rider's confidence in the system, or result in impaired braking.

Many riders feel that stock brake lines are too springy, giving a lever "feel" that is overly spongy. For such persons there are the stainless-braid lines referred to previously.

As hydraulic leverage ratios have climbed in response to riders' demands for ever-faster deceleration, a systematic attempt has been made to take springiness out of the system.

Since cast calipers are somewhat less stiff than those machined from solid, racing calipers are usually machined. Likewise, for critical applications, calipers machined in one piece are preferred to those bolted together from two halves. Currently the high-end Brembo caliper is made from one piece of wrought material, and the piston bores are machined by a special boring head that fits into the pad/disc gap—there are no bore plugs. A further step toward rigidity is the use of metal matrix composite (MMC) material for calipers. MMCs are rendered more rigid by reinforcement with very stiff ceramic, or other fibers, in a matrix of aluminum. Eventually, F1 cars were equipped with calipers made from beryllium (Be), a metal with a very high stiffness and extremely low weight. Beryllium has long been used for critical applications in aerospace. You guessed it; it's expensive. As an added bonus, the dust that results from machining it is poisonous, too. As part of the "NASCARization" of F1, advanced materials such as beryllium have been banned. Will MotoGP bikes, too, be transformed into standardized bowling balls in the interest of close racin'? We wait and see.

A LIMIT ON HYDRAULIC LEVERAGE RATIO

Lack of system stiffness sets a limit to how high a hydraulic leverage ratio you can use. Here is how it happens.

Because of friction, the caliper pistons can't slide perfectly smoothly through their seals as brakes are applied and released. Instead, the pistons mostly stick to the seals and deform them very slightly as they advance toward the disc. When the brake line pressure is released, the deformation in the piston seals acts as a return spring, pulling the caliper piston back to its original position. So long as the pads don't wear, this process can be repeated forever, always resulting in a nice, high lever.

But pads do wear. As the pad wears, the piston seal still sticks to the piston up to a point, always trying to pull it back to its original position when brakes are released. Therefore, as the pad wears, it takes more and more lever

Old-Style Wide Pad Track Brake. *This brake, used on a Honda air-cooled F1 bike of the early 1980s, employs a giant two-piston caliper, clamping wide pads onto a hefty cast-iron disc. Result: a big difference in heating rate between the outside diameter of the pad track and the inside diameter, tending to produce disc distortion or cracking. The gadget the caliper is attached to is Honda's torque-reactive anti-dive, which employs brake torque to click in a firmer fork compression damping.* John Owens Studio

stroke to advance the pad surface to the disc. This causes the lever to come in closer to the bar the more the pad wears. When the pad wear reaches some threshold level, the seal's deformation can no longer accommodate the whole movement necessary to bring the pad to the disc and back again, so the pistons finally slip slightly through their seals, taking up a new position a bit closer to the disc. Now the lever height is restored because once again, it takes minimum fluid pumping and lever stroke to get pads to disc. This cycle of wear, falling lever height, slippage of the caliper pistons through their seals to new positions, and restoration of lever height, is repeated as the pads wear. If the master cylinder is big enough in diameter, the rider hardly notices the slight rise and fall of lever position.

But if the machine has an abnormally small master cylinder piston size, chosen to produce an unusually high hydraulic ratio, the normal fall of the lever as the pads wear can bring the lever too close to the bar—maybe close enough to prevent full application of the brakes. This is what sets a limit to how small a master cylinder piston you can use.

BLEEDING BRAKES WITHOUT GOING CRAZY

Brake bleeding is the process of eliminating air or gas from a brake system, leaving nothing between master cylinder piston and caliper pistons but fluid. This ensures solid, direct action.

Do follow the bleeding directions supplied with your bike or aftermarket equipment, but remember that there is always another way. After spending hours trying without success to bleed a brake system, we have all wished we could assemble the parts on the bottom of a swimming pool full of brake fluid. Some supplementary techniques that can help are these:

1. Back-bleed using a pressure bleeder, pushing fluid in at the bottom, through a caliper bleed screw, up through the lines and into the master cylinder (its lever must be fully released or the return port will be blocked, preventing fluid from reaching the reservoir). Keep an eye on the reservoir because it can overflow as you back-bleed.

2. Remove the whole system from the bike and hang it up, calipers at the top. Now air bubbles, dislodged from where they like to hide inside of banjo bolts and anywhere that there are sharp corners in the system, will rise to the top and you can bleed them from the calipers. Secure a piece of metal stock between the pads to prevent the pistons from being pushed out.

3. Tapping on system parts with the plastic handle of a screwdriver can help dislodge air bubbles within. Similarly, some people employ rapid, fluttery motions of the brake lever to use brake fluid motion to scour loose bubbles. Easing off on the banjo bolt holding fluid lines to the master cylinder can allow bubbles trapped there to be pushed out. Hold some pressure on the lever as you do this to avoid drawing air into the system. Retighten firmly once clear fluid comes from the joint.

Always be sure, when bleeding from the master cylinder, to keep the reservoir full. There's nothing more annoying than to get the system nearly bled, only to suck in air from an empty reservoir.

Protect your eyes—brake fluid can damage them.

TESTING YOUR WORK

Test a finished and refilled system for leaks by holding the brake on firmly while inspecting connections for any leakage. Some systems employ deformable copper or soft aluminum seal washers. It's a good idea to start with fresh ones. Be careful when fitting new lines to be sure threads on new banjo bolts are the same as the originals.

When you fit new pads, always think of how Eddie Lawson must have felt at Laguna in 1990, when the pads fell out of one of his calipers just as he was approaching turn one. Make doubly sure you have done this job right, and that all safeties are in place. If the system uses cotter pins or other metal items that must be bent to keep them in place, don't re-use old parts that have been bent back and forth before.

Total brake failure is nothing you'd want. It is to prevent accidents like this that the AMA has tried to get brake manufacturers to make split systems, with two pistons in one front master cylinder, one for each disc on the front wheel.

CHAPTER 19
OILS

Every week, some new oil or additive comes on the market, tempting us with claims so extraordinary that it seems we must be destroying our engines by using anything less. The facts about oil are extraordinary enough without this kind of hype. A little basic understanding goes a long way to protect us from commercial nonsense, as well as to make what goes on in engines a little more interesting.

Oil does more than one job in an engine. Its first job is to lubricate—that is, to separate moving surfaces that would otherwise destroy each other in contact friction. Its second job is to carry away heat, not only from bearings themselves, but also from every hot engine surface the oil touches. Oil as coolant is especially important in air-cooled engines and was once used as primary coolant in an important series of air/oil-cooled engines from Suzuki. A third job of oil is to wash the engine's insides. It carries wear particles to a filter. Carbon, acids, and sludge become suspended in the oil, thanks to additives, and are removed at scheduled oil changes.

Oil's most important property is viscosity—its internal friction. If oil were perfectly frictionless, it would instantly squirt out from between moving parts, leaving nothing to separate and protect them. Unfortunately, viscosity also produces mechanical friction in bearings. About 15 percent of the power of a street-operated vehicle engine is consumed by such friction. This is a compromise; oil viscosity must be high enough to protect parts, yet not so high as to produce excessive friction loss.

Two sets of markings on an oil can or bottle reveal basic facts. The viscosity appears in two numbers, such as 20W-50. What this means is that the oil behaves as SAE 20 viscosity at 0 degrees Fahrenheit—hence the W, which stands for "winter"—and as an SAE 50 viscosity at 210 degrees Fahrenheit. The fact that two numbers are given indicates that this is a multi-viscosity oil.

All oils lose viscosity as they heat up. The rate at which they do so—the slope of the curve relating temperature and viscosity—is called the oil's viscosity index (VI). Through a little chemical trickery, additives can tilt an oil's VI in our favor, resulting in less viscosity loss as the oil heats up. This is good for two big reasons: (1) we need oil to be as thin as possible when cold to enable engines to be started in cold weather, and (2) we need the oil to retain adequate viscosity to support the load it's carrying in a warmed-up engine, even in very hot areas, such as between the top piston-ring and cylinder wall.

Oils bearing a single viscosity number, such as 30, are single-viscosity oils. These were made for special applications such as lawnmower engines, whose primitive cooling systems allowed the oil to become hot enough to damage the usual additives. Improved oils have changed this.

Oil actually has an easier time in high-performance engines, with their large bearing loads and speeds, than it does in 3,600-rpm lawn-care devices. This is because of one single factor—temperature. Keep bulk oil temperatures down to reasonable levels—the makers would like 180 degrees Fahrenheit as a maximum—and today's marvelous

NUMBER 1-800-274-5263
MEETS OR EXCEEDS
API SERVICE SJ/SH
And All Preceding API Gasoline Categories, ILSAC GF1, GF2 and Requirements of API Certified Engine Oil

API SERVICE SJ
SAE 10W-30
ENERGY CONSERVING

Part No. 75-130
DON'T POLLUTE. CONSERVE RESOURCES.
RETURN USED OIL TO COLLECTION CENTERS.
Manufactured for NAPA

An Oil Data Panel. *The information you want is the viscosity grade (for example, 10W-40) and the API category (for example, SM). Viscosity grade matches an oil to your engine's internal temperature environment; some engines are more severe than others. Typically, air-cooled engines run hotter than water-cooled ones, so they tend to need higher-viscosity oils. The API category designates that the oil's additive package meets particular standards with respect to anti-wear, pour-point temperature, antioxidant ability, and so on. Don't assume that the most recent API category is better for your engine than the older oil specified in your manual.*

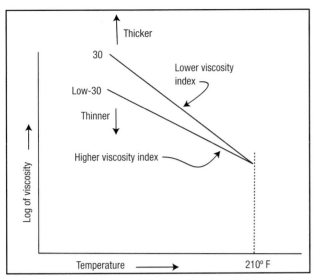

What Viscosity Index Means. *All oils lose viscosity as their temperature rises. Viscosity index (VI) is a measure of how fast an oil loses viscosity. These two plots show how two different oils—each with the same viscosity at 210 degrees Fahrenheit—have differing viscosities at lower temperatures. The oil with the higher VI is thinner at lower temperatures than the oil with the lower VI. This is useful because such an oil can be thin enough for easy cold-starting at low temperature, yet retain adequate viscosity to carry loads at engine operating temperature.*

oil additives can do their job of protecting your engine. And that's just why modern sportbike engines have capable liquid-cooling systems. Old-timers imagine they are doing their engines a favor by running straight-viscosity oils ("It's all oil, y'see, none o' them additives"), whereas in fact they are thereby denying their engines the benefits of anti-wear, anti-corrosion, anti-foam, and other additives.

Currently, even operators of heavy-duty diesel engines have accepted the superiority of high-quality multi-vis oils. With such oils, as temperature rises above 210 degrees Fahrenheit, the high-temperature viscosity of the oil continues to rise above the curve of a single-viscosity oil of the same 210-degree viscosity number. This, they find, provides increased protection in hot areas, such as the top piston-ring groove.

There is a second code on the oil can, and this is the API (American Petroleum Institute) oil service category. Each time the engine manufacturers need help in keeping their piston-rings from sticking or their cams and tappets from gouging each other, the oil companies hurry to come up with answers. Once they do this, the results become a new, higher standard for oil capability.

Oils for spark-ignition engines carry API codes such as SJ, SI, and so on. The "S" designates the oil as for spark-ignition engines. The second letter is an arbitrary designation that you can look up on an API document, telling what standard tests such an oil must pass. Early standards, such as SA or SB, date back to the 1950s and describe oils with very rudimentary additives, or no additives at all.

With every new vehicle, you will get an owners' manual in which the required oil is identified, with its API code. Pay attention, and do not use oils with a lower API letter than called for in the owners' book. There can also be reasons not to use a higher code, but we'll come to that presently.

WHAT'S IN OIL?

Oil is not just oil, although long-chain oil molecules perform the major job of separating moving parts through the action of viscosity. Oil also contains a package of additives that perform a variety of useful functions.

Viscosity Index Improvers (1)

Almost all types of oils lose viscosity as temperature rises. Because of this, an oil viscous enough to lubricate an engine reliably at 210 degrees Fahrenheit will probably become too viscous at 0 degrees for the starter to turn it. A VI improver is an additive that makes the oil less stiff when cold, less watery when hot.

Conceptually, VI improvers work like this. Start with a single-viscosity light oil, thin enough to flow easily at the lowest desired cold-starting temperature. Now mix into it very long chain molecules whose shape changes with temperature. At low temperatures, they roll up into compact balls that make little contribution to viscosity, so the oil remains fluid. As the oil warms up, however, these balls uncoil progressively into masses of long, lashing chains that work to counteract viscosity loss—rather like dumping limp spaghetti into flowing water. The oil as a whole still loses viscosity as it warms up, but it loses less as a result of containing the spaghetti-like VI-improving additive.

Thus, an oil marked 10W-30 is a multi-viscosity oil that displays an SAE 10 viscosity at 0 degrees, but acts like an SAE 30 viscosity oil at 210 degrees. Although this makes it sound as though the oil's viscosity has increased as it has warmed up, remember that a 30 oil at 100 degrees has less viscosity than a 10 oil at 0. Its viscosity did not increase; it just lost less viscosity than would a single-grade oil at that temperature.

VI improvers are available in various chemical forms such as olefins, polystyrenes, and polymethacrylates. These molecules, being long chains, are fragile to a degree and are slowly chewed up in the engine by passing through high shear conditions—gear meshes or under cam lobes. Because of this steady loss of VI improver, a multi-viscosity oil slowly loses its high-temperature viscosity. That is, a 10W-30 oil slowly changes into a 10W-20 oil if it stays in the engine long enough. This is called "falling out of grade."

Friction Modifiers, Anti-Wear Additives (2)

Because there is not always a full film of oil between moving parts (during startup, or between cam lobe and follower at idle speed, etc.), oil must contain additives to help protect parts that do come into contact with each other. A large gray area exists between full-film hydrodynamic lubrication—explained in Chapter 3—and destructive metal-to-metal contact.

OILS

Friction modifiers are oil-like molecules that have the property of adsorbing onto surfaces to form a solid layer. These are sometimes referred to as "oiliness additives," and one class is the fatty acids.

Anti-wear additives are chemical compounds that, at high local temperature, form salts or soaps in a surface reaction with metals. The resulting molecular layer has a low coefficient of friction, and may be sacrificed locally by heavy, unlubricated pressure. A new lubricating layer forms—it "heals"—once the pressure is removed and fresh oil reaches the site.

A common anti-wear additive is zinc dialkyl dithio phosphate (ZDDP). It, too, is consumed over time as the engine runs, forming a coating, being sheared away, then being carried as particles to the oil filter. Thus, over time, any oil will suffer a loss in its anti-wear protection.

Antioxidants (3)
Even if the oil's so-called bulk temperature—measured in the oil tank or sump—is low, engine oil is exposed to very high local temperatures in places like the top piston-ring groove or on the exposed cylinder walls during combustion. When hot oil is exposed to the oxygen in the air, its molecules may cross-link to form thick gums or sludge. In extreme cases, the entire oil quantity can be transformed into a Jell-O-like material.

Antioxidants work to prevent this reaction by interfering with the chemistry of oxidation. Antioxidants enable oils to survive longer at higher temperatures than they would otherwise.

Dispersants (4)
Lots of old-timers are critical of detergent oils, saying, "Just give me an oil that's all oil." Detergents got a bad name when they first appeared because they worked. When detergent oil was used in a sludge-encrusted old engine, the detergent set free a flood of sludge that could block oil pump screens or plug filters. When additive-containing oils are used right from the start, engines stay clean and form less sludge in the first place.

Today these additives are called dispersants, and higher piston-ring operating temperatures have made them a necessity. Without dispersants in the oil, piston-rings become stuck in their grooves. With dispersant action, they remain free and continue to seal. Engine manufacturers' lubricant recommendations are the result of testing that we, the consumers, are not equipped to second-guess. Don't.

Anti-Rust/Corrosion Additives (5)
Because moisture and acids are generated in engines, there is potential for rusting. These additives "marry" any exposed steel surfaces, forming a coating that prevents rusting by displacing water.

Anti-Foam Agents (6)
Air is the enemy of pressure-fed bearings. If the oil pump picks up air or foam, that springy gas moves along the oil gallery until it reaches a bearing. There, the gas expands in a kind of "sneeze" that can blast all the oil out of the bearing, causing it to fail. Anti-foam agents cause bubbles to collapse by reducing surface tension.

Pour-Point Depressants (7)
Get oils cold enough and their heavier components can "wax out," forming a network of solids that retard or prevent flow. Pour-point depressants (PPD) surround incipient wax particles, preventing them from clustering together.

THE FOUR REGIMES OF LUBRICATION
There are four basic regimes of lubrication.

Full Film or Hydrodynamic (1)
In this regime, one surface "flies" over another, supported completely on a wedge-shaped film of lubricant, just as an airplane in the final stages of landing is supported by air trapped between the ground and the inclined lower surface of the wing. This support depends on motion rapid enough to sweep oil between the surfaces faster than the pressure between them can squeeze it out.

It is the oil's internal friction, or viscosity, combined with the speed of relative motion between the surfaces, that prevents the oil from being instantly squeezed out from between. Full film is the normal condition in main and rod bearings, and between piston or piston rings and their cylinder wall in mid-stroke. Full-film lubrication produces remarkably little friction, with friction coefficients in the 0.001 range—this means that a 1,000-pound load would generate only 0.001 times as much friction, or 1 pound.

It's interesting to note that, at maximum speed and load, a roller bearing crank and a plain-bearing crank have about the same friction. Don't sneer at plain bearings; they are compact and light, while rolling bearings are heavier and bulkier. A plain-bearing crank can be a strong, light, one-piece forging, while a roller crank must be built up out of many pieces. The area in which rolling bearings excel is in starting friction.

Boundary (2)
Boundary lubrication occurs as two surfaces, protected only by solid lubricant films, slide over each other with no other form of lubrication. The solid films, designed to be weaker than the metal under them, are sacrificed in operation. Once oil supply resumes, any damage to such surface coatings is repaired by additives in the oil.

Coefficient of friction in boundary lubrication can be surprisingly low, which prevents the rapid heat generation that leads quickly to failure. Typically, coefficient of friction for boundary lubrication is of the order of 0.1. A 1,000-pound load generates 100 pounds of friction.

Mixed (3)
Mixed lubrication is the transition zone from full-film to boundary lubrication. A partial oil film supports part of the

load, and the rest is carried by actual contact between solid lubricating films formed on the parts by oil additives.

Mixed lubrication occurs every time you start your engine, because oil has mostly drained away from bearings and cylinder walls, and because parts are moving too slowly to generate a full film. It also occurs in normal running, as piston rings slow and stop near top and bottom center, and sink through their oil film—coming into partial contact with the cylinder wall. Cam lobes and tappets also depend on mixed lubrication at idle rpm.

Unlubricated Metal-to-Metal Contact (4)

This occurs when oil supply has ceased and any boundary lubricant has been scrubbed off. Coefficient of friction is high, so heat is generated rapidly, leading to melting and seizing of the two surfaces. Seized pistons smear their own aluminum up and down the cylinder walls, and crank or rod bearings "spin," meaning they seize to the journal so tightly that the bearing inserts rotate in their housings.

During break-in, limited metal-to-metal contact occurs, as follows. As-manufactured surfaces carry taller asperities (peaks and valleys) than broken-in surfaces, but oil plus additives can keep even these rough surfaces from making contact and wearing each other into smoother finishes. Therefore heavy

pressure must be used to drive the surfaces close enough so the asperity peaks do touch and, in a relatively benign way, weld, tear, and grind each other down to a lower, smoother finished profile. Once this is done, oil plus additives on these finer surfaces can carry greatly increased loads without contact. Break-in is the final manufacturing operation.

In this era, emissions requirements exert pressure upon design. For a time in the 1980s and early 1990s, heavy anti-wear and friction modifier loadings made break-in difficult, or interfered with things like starter clutches. Now that ZDDP is known to poison exhaust catalysts, its use in motor oils has been reduced, making the latest auto oil formulations unable to lubricate some engines not designed for them (rebuilders of older car and bike engines consistently report problems with such oils). This is what lies behind claims that recent automotive oils are non-optimal for motorcycle engines. You have options here. By staying with the oil specified in your owners' manual, you keep your warranty in place. You may also choose to use motorcycle-specific oils, or high-performance oils marketed for "off-road" (i.e., racing) applications. Pay particular attention to the API Service Category called out in your manual—the pair of letters such as SI, SJ, etc.

How Oil Lubricates Bearings

Oil supports a moving load by forming a wedge under it. Fresh oil enters the wedge at its larger, low-pressure end and is swept by relative motion steadily toward the high-pressure thin end of the wedge, while its viscosity makes it resist being immediately squeezed out of this narrow space. The load carried by a plain bearing may be many thousands of pounds per square inch of projected area, so it's clear that oil pump pressure (typically 60 psi) is not what's supporting the load. The load-carrying pressure in a bearing is generated by relative motion and viscosity alone.

A piston, for example, tilts slightly in the bore to form such an oil wedge between its own skirt and the cylinder wall. A crankshaft journal is pushed off-center in its bearings by the load it carries. This creates a crescent-shaped wedge inside the bearing. Oil from the pump enters the thick, low-pressure, unloaded side of the bearing clearance and is swept around by the rotation of the crank journal, "pumping" it into the thin, heavily loaded zone as fast as it is squeezed out at the bearing's edges. In this case, the thick end of the wedge may be 0.0018 inch thick, while the thinnest part may be only 50 millionths (0.000050) of an inch thick.

The thicker and more viscous the oil, the greater the friction loss, so new engines are being designed to use thinner oils for their slightly improved fuel economy. The thinner the oil, the thinner the load-bearing film that is generated. If the oil film becomes thin enough, the highest peaks on the profiles of journal and bearing surfaces will touch each other across the film, accelerating wear. To prevent this, parts are now being finished to ever-finer surfaces.

You can understand from this why it's essential to avoid introducing any dirt during engine assembly, and important

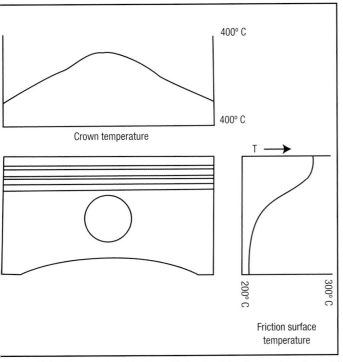

Piston Temperature Profiles. *Obviously, piston temperature rises and falls according to how much power an engine is making, but these curves give some idea of temperature distribution on a piston in a running engine. Peak crown temperature is at the center, while peak wearing-surface temperature is at the top, decreasing rapidly across the piston-ring pack, to a lower figure along the lower skirt.*

to protect bearing surfaces from contact with anything that might nick or scratch them. The oil film, only 0.000050 inch thick at maximum load, is the wall that separates your engine from sudden failure!

Do not switch an older engine to one of the new, lighter viscosity, high-efficiency oils, thinking you will improve power by doing so. The potential gains are small (only 1 percent or so) and the danger of oil film failure at high load is increased.

As noted previously, all oils naturally lose viscosity as they get hotter. Therefore, the hotter your engine runs, the thinner its internal oil films become, and the closer it comes to failure. This is why liquid-cooled engines can use light oils such as 5W-20, but air-cooled types typically run oils as heavy as 50. At their respective operating temperatures, the viscosity of these different oils is quite similar.

An oil radiator may be necessary, especially on air-cooled engines, to hold oil temperature to reasonable values. But don't add a cooler unless you know you need one. Measure oil temperature in operation with a gauge or, after shutdown, with a high-temp thermometer inserted through the dipstick hole or filler.

SYNTHETICS

Synthetic oils are those made from neither petroleum base nor vegetable stocks. Instead of the wide range of molecular structures present in petroleum-derived oils, a synthetic has only one or a few chosen structures present. This enables a synthetic potentially to display higher load-carrying ability, because a greater percentage of it is of the desired structure type. This can also give a synthetic greater oxidation and temperature resistance.

Think of petroleum oil as an army made up of a normal population—some soldiers are tall, some short, some stronger, some less so. Think of a synthetic or a synthesized petroleum oil as an army of identical clones, all 6 feet tall, all strong and healthy. Otherwise, synthetics are no miracle—just more uniform molecules, their structure chosen for its good lubricating properties and oxidation resistance. The molecular uniformity of highly refined petroleum oils approaches that of synthetics.

There are several principal species of synthetics. A first one is synthesized petroleum oils. Just as an oil refinery can synthesize particular, desired fuel molecules such as isooctane, so can it produce desirable, single-species lubricant molecules. A second class is the diesters, derived originally from second-generation gas-turbine oils. This class of oils displays high oxidation resistance and adequate lubrication. A third class is the polyol esters, which derive from third-generation gas-turbine oils, displaying yet higher oxidation resistance and temperature tolerance. Yet another category is the polyglycols.

No doubt there are even more stable fluoropolymers out there in some laboratory, originally developed for lubricating atomic bombs, which are just waiting for some clever marketeer to charge us $100 a quart. There will be buyers, you can be sure.

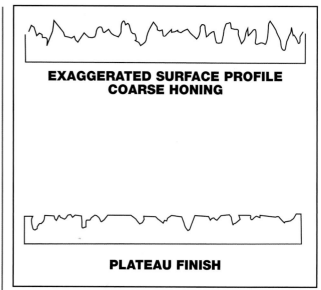

EXAGGERATED SURFACE PROFILE COARSE HONING

PLATEAU FINISH

Coarse-Honed Cylinder Wall Finish versus Plateau Finish. *The upper figure shows an exaggerated surface profile of a coarse-honed cylinder wall. The lower figure shows the so-called plateau finish, which results from fine-honing or plateau-brushing the above profile, shaving off the tallest of its asperities. This results in a surface made up of smooth plateaus, separated by the deeper incisions left by the coarse hone. This interrupted surface is more resistant to seizure, because a seizure beginning on one plateau cannot plow material onto the next one. Instead, it is "pushed into the ditch," and normal lubrication has a chance of re-establishing itself on the next plateau.*

Wonderful and exotic though these substances sound, all are simply oil molecules, and they lubricate as a result of their viscosity just like any other oil. Their special properties lie in other areas, such as oxidative stability, polarity (ability to bond to metal surfaces), and so forth. It's perfectly possible for an oil manufacturer, by skillful use of additives, to make a mineral-based oil that performs better in a given application than another maker's synthetic with a worse additive package. There are no simple rules.

The fact that motorcycle manufacturers do not require owners to use synthetic oils indicates that satisfactory operation can perfectly well occur with petroleum oils of appropriate grades. However, many owners feel strongly that synthetic oils must be better, and so they use them. Little by little, manufacturers are becoming more willing to specify only synthetic oils for their most severe engines, but this does not mean that synthetics must be better in all cases. This subject becomes so heated that it begins to seem more like politics or religion than engineering. I certainly don't wish to argue with you. Find oil that satisfies the callout in your owners' manual, and pay as much or as little for it as you like!

In time, engines will "grow into" synthetic oils, in the sense that some applications may become so demanding that only properly formulated synthetic oils will handle the conditions. This may already be the case in racing, where synthetics are widely used. However, beware of claims based upon oil use in racing. Neither you nor I have any way of knowing for sure what is in the winner's oil system.

BREAK-IN WITH SYNTHETICS

Any tuner in Superbike racing will tell you that you must break in a new engine on mineral oil if you plan to run it on racing synthetic. The strong anti-wear additives in synthetic racing oils seem to act to prevent or considerably delay break-in, resulting in an engine whose blow-by volume remains high for a long time, with poor oil control and some power loss.

The makers of synthetic oils do not publicly agree, stating that break-in with their products can be perfectly satisfactory. The Superbike tuners reply to this by saying, "Maybe, but it takes so long we've never been able to see it."

Thirty years ago, piston rings were less well-finished, and the cylinder wall had to be used as a file to shave them into intimate contact. This was the function of the old, relatively coarse, 60-degree crosshatch honing pattern used as a cylinder-wall finish. This degree of roughness was essential to remove the necessary metal from the rings to make them seal.

Today, the standard wall finish is what is called a plateau finish. The cylinder is first coarse-honed, then finished with either a much finer hone or a plateau brush. This leaves the cylinder wall as a series of smooth-surfaced islands, surrounded by the deeper incisions left by the coarse hone. The incisions limit how far any scuffing—smearing of metal—can go, and they also serve to retain oil.

After honing, an iron cylinder or cylinder liner should be scrubbed hard with soap and hot water, to remove abrasive grains and metallic wear particles. Others recommend rubbing cylinder walls with cloths dipped in motor oil. The cylinder is clean enough only after it ceases to discolor a clean paper towel rubbed hard against it. Chrome or Nikasil bores can only be honed with special equipment.

Even with such accurately manufactured parts, bike engines still require break-in to finally seat their piston rings.

Asked about break-in of race engines, Wiseco Piston Company's Tom Kipp Sr. said, "After about 20 hard pulls on the dyno, the blowby volume has dropped by half and that seems to be it." A "pull" on the dyno is one cycle of acceleration under full throttle, usually taking 10–15 seconds, from the bottom of the powerband to the top.

Sensible instructions for breaking-in on the street call for something surprisingly similar: frequent applications of full throttle acceleration, but without holding high rpm or load for long periods. Between throttle applications, the engine's oil system can carry away wear particles to the filter, and excess heat developed in areas of contact has time to diffuse, ready for another go.

Engines today are so well-manufactured, with such good surface finishes, that it takes real power to push the smooth parts through the separating oil-and-additive film, into the partial contact that is necessary to achieving a final, high-quality fit. Cruising around mile after mile on 10 percent throttle won't do the job. It takes real load.

You may have heard old-timers say, "Break it in fast, and it'll be fast. Break it in slow and it'll always be slow." There is enough truth in this to make it memorable.

OIL CHANGE FREQUENCY

The lube-oil business is driven by its major customers, and the auto manufacturers want their products to become turn-key, zero-maintenance systems with no points or timing to adjust, no spark plugs to change, and no oil drain intervals. While they work up to this ideal, they have to be satisfied with extended drain intervals. When I was a little boy, oil was changed every 1,000 miles. Later it was 3,000, then 6,000, and now oil monitors on late-model cars allow over 10,000 miles in conservative driving. Naturally, bike makers are carried along by the wind of all this progress.

The first thing to consider is the oil drain recommendation in your owners' manual. If you don't trust that, send a sample of your oil, drained at that interval, to an oil analysis lab and act on whatever result comes back with their bill. There's certainly no harm in changing oil more often than recommended.

OTHER LUBRICANTS

Some older engines have separate engine and gearbox oils, which in my opinion is a desirable situation. In such a case, you have to choose a gear oil. The first choice is the manufacturer's recommendation, but you might, like the previously described, more-frequent oil changer, want something fancier. All right, your next question will be: will this oil interfere with wet-clutch operation? Gears love real gear oils such as GL-5 rated 90 rear-end fluid, but a wet clutch may not.

The desirable feature of real gear oils is that they contain EP additives that allow gear teeth to survive heavy contact pressure without scuffing. Some lighter fluids, such as Mopar limited-slip rear-end lube, are compatible with wet clutches, and there are bike gear oils claimed to be compatible with wet clutches. Gear oils that bear the code GL-5 are the real thing. Their stinky smell results from the chlorine EP compounds they contain.

How do the gearboxes and primary gears survive in engines that lube both engine and gearbox with the same oil? They are designed with lower tooth loadings or better materials to survive operation on ordinary engine oils. More recent engine oils also contain competent anti-wear additives that give some gear-tooth protection.

A number of greases compete for your lubrication dollar. Wheel-bearing grease is compounded to stay where it's put and not get melted and centrifuged away from the parts it's intended to lubricate. Grease with molybdenum disulfide added is good for torquing critical bolts. White greases are not usually such hot lubricants, but they look better on your clothes, so people like to use them on things they might accidentally touch—handlebar levers, etc. Makers of high-performance connecting rods supply special EP grease for the important operation of torquing the cap bolts. Use only such grease for this application.

OILS

Little cable-oiling kits are available to lube cables from a pressure can. Alternatively, there is Dri-Slide, which is slippery graphite in a volatile liquid, put up in a little can with a really useful dispenser needle that will put the stuff exactly where you want it.

Everyone uses O-ring chains nowadays. At each chain joint, tiny O-rings seal in factory-installed chain grease so it stays there for a good long time. Keep the chain free of dirt (Mother Nature's grinding compound) and it lasts many thousands of miles. Some people, feeling the stiffness of such chains when cold, prefer to use non-O-ring chain for the possible reduction in friction.

If you feel you have to do this, I'd suggest a lube other than the mouthwash usually sold for bike chains, which quickly flies off. Instead, I've liked the gooey brown "chain and mast lube" sold in industrial bearings and drives outlets, especially if it has some molybdenum disulfide (moly) content. It's sticky because it has polymers in it, intended to make it stick to the chain, not fly off. Unfortunately, if you get any on your clothes, they, too, are lubed for life.

WHAT SHOULD I DO?

The volume of Internet postings on the subject of oils reveals that riders very much want to "do something" for their engines. They want passionately to believe that some correct course of action will make everything last longer and give more power. They want a "daddy" to assure them that their brand or additive is doing just that. Unfortunately, only expensive, instrumented back-to-back testing can answer their questions. Short of that, here are some reasonable guidelines about oil.

First of all, use the SAE viscosity and API category called out in your owners' manual. The manufacturer has provided these specifications based upon testing, not on the advice of a friend who works in a bike shop.

If you want to use synthetic or synthesized petroleum oils, by all means do so, but break in on mineral oil first, preferably with one of the special break-in oils now offered by manufacturers. When break-in is complete, drain the oil and remove and replace the filter. Refill with synthetic oil of the SAE viscosity and API category stated in your owners' manual.

Recent API oil standards, such as SM, are increasingly aimed at reducing fuel consumption in new automobiles. Such oils are termed "energy-conserving" oils, and they contain additives designed to reduce friction at moderate speeds. There have been some reports of such oils interfering with wet-clutch operation, so unless your owners' manual calls for such oil, it is best avoided for the time being.

There has been a lot of talk lately about super-low-viscosity oils adding horsepower in racing applications. Some owners seem to believe that such oils are liquid horsepower. The use of low-viscosity oil in racing is made possible by two special facts:

1. A typical race engine is completely overhauled at least every 1,000 miles, and probably more often, as failure in 500–1,000 miles in a race engine is considered acceptable life.

Miscellaneous Lubricants. *Everyone who performs any bike work at all accumulates a collection of special-purpose lubes. Wheel-bearing grease, cable lube, assembly lubes for cams and for threaded joints, fork and damper oil—the list is endless. Here are a few of mine.* John Owens Studio

2. Manufacturers have experimented with ultra-fine-finishes on crank journals and other wearing parts; this allows engines with such finishes to tolerate the thinner oil films that result from use of low-viscosity oils.

Street riders want more than the few hundred miles that race teams expect from their engines. Production engines are not manufactured with fine experimental surface finishes. Therefore, owners should not be surprised if using low-viscosity "liquid-horsepower" oils results in a bad surprise and a large bill.

Does it make sense to fill a perfectly good engine's sump with some "maybe" or "what-if" oil, based only on the owner's personal conviction—or that of his buddy at the bike shop—that it might reduce friction 3 percent? Remember that typically 15 percent of an engine's power is consumed as friction, and 3 percent of 15 percent is less than 1/2 percent. Is power so hard to get that people are willing to risk everything for maybe 1/2 percent? It doesn't make sense. You can get a lot more power than that just by correcting the average bike's cam-timing error, or from race-style valve seat work—and those don't thin the engine's oil films.

The more worn an engine is, the more it is placed at risk by low-viscosity oils. Many classic sportbikes from the 1970s have rolling-element main and rod bearings, which require some minimum viscosity for their operation. Read your manual. Respect the knowledge of those who designed and manufactured your bike. If, for reasons that are non-testable and cannot be discussed, you must run economy car low-viscosity oils, wait until a sportbike is produced that uses them, and buy it. If you want more power from your existing bike, modify the engine in proven ways.

Oil advertisements based upon racing success should be disregarded. All oil manufacturers employ engineers capable of compounding special oils to solve special problems—and that is what they do just for contracted race teams when necessary. There is no way for us civilians to know that the oil in the racer's oil system is or is not the same as we can buy.

CHAPTER 20
FUELS

Your bike runs on gasoline, but what is gasoline? How does it affect the way your bike runs? Are some fuels better than others? Are some fuels harmful? What are lead, MTBE, reformulated fuels, octane number? I'll try to cover the most important fuel-related subjects in this section—in enough detail to be useful.

There are five basic areas of interest in fuels, and only two of them affect the pure street rider. Those areas are (1) the meaning of lead-free fuels, and (2) the effects of the new reformulated gasolines now being mandated in some states.

LEAD

Lead, compounded as the organometallic, tetraethyl lead, was the wonder compound that in the late 1920s made it possible to boost fuel octane greatly—from the 50s straight up to 78 octane—with additions of only 1 or 2 grams per gallon. Higher octane ratings permitted rapid increases in compression ratio, leading to more economical engines in the 1930s through the 1960s.

The coming of catalytic converters in the 1970s required the banning of lead in motor gasolines, as it poisoned the catalyst, making it useless. All motor gasoline in the United States is now unleaded by law, and obtaining adequate fuel octane rating without lead has required new fuel formulations. In general, the response of engine makers to lower fuel octane has been to reduce compression ratio, although this trend is now being reversed through better cylinder head design.

In engines operated at steady high power (aviation, marine), lead also acted as an exhaust valve anti-seize, preventing plucking of material between hot exhaust valves and seats. There has been concern that engines designed for leaded fuels would therefore suffer seat and valve erosion if operated on lead-free fuels.

Exhaust-valve deterioration has turned out to be pretty much a non-issue, as street-driven vehicles operate on very low average duty and seldom get their valves hot enough to erode. Later-model engines have hard-faced valves and hard seats to protect them from potential damage. In engines with mechanical tappets, any unexplained loss of valve clearance is the signal that seat erosion is occurring. Those who lie awake at night worrying about valve erosion and loss of valve clearance can always have hardened seats installed in their engines!

REFORMULATED GASOLINES

These have caused legitimate concern. After the first fuel crisis in 1973–1974, alcohol was sometimes added to gasolines to persuade the public that something was being done about dependence on foreign oil. Alcohols were incompatible with some plastic and rubber fuel system parts, causing leaks. Alcohol absorbs water from the air, leading to occasional "water bottoms" in fuel tanks.

When lead was removed from fuel, octane number had to be boosted in other ways. One was to increase the use of so-called aromatic compounds (toluene, etc.) in fuel, from 15–20 percent up to 40 percent or more. This caused more problems with plastic and rubber parts (like the sinking of plastic carburetor floats, causing very rich idle running and stalling).

In an effort to lean out combustion in older, non-computer-controlled autos, large amounts (as much as 15 percent) of methyl tertiary butyl ether (MTBE) were added to fuels, giving them a characteristic sharp, unfamiliar odor. Then MTBE turned up in water supplies in California and elsewhere, causing a minor scandal. Its use is now banned and we are back to ethanol as planet saver. Like MTBE before it, alcohols are chemically combined with some oxygen, which reduces their energy content per gallon to about two-thirds that of gasoline. Use of such fuels in engines whose fuel systems are open-loop (that is, do not self-correct by use of oxygen sensor data) will make them run slightly leaner than normal.

RACING GASOLINE

For the occasional user of racing gasolines, there are three other areas of concern: octane number, specific gravity, and volatility.

Octane Number

This is the measure of how well a fuel can resist detonation, a destructive form of abnormal combustion. It is not a measure of the fuel's energy. When you raise an engine's compression ratio, you may also be raising its fuel-octane requirement. Many street-legal vehicles will run just fine on regular (87 [r + m]/2 octane and some need premium (92 [r + m]/2) to avoid detonation, but modified engines with higher compression may need something better yet. That something is provided by racing gasolines.

Specific Gravity

Specific gravity is the density of the fuel, as compared with that of water. One gallon of fuel with a 0.700 specific gravity weighs only 7/10 as much as 1 gallon of water. When you switch from one fuel to another of different specific gravity, this number affects your engine's mixture strength. Occasionally, the

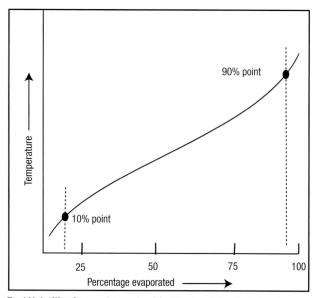

Fuel Volatility Curve. *A sample of fuel is placed in a test chamber connected to a condenser and is then slowly heated. At each temperature, a certain percentage of the sample will have evaporated, passed over to the condenser, and been condensed into a collecting vessel. Because gasolines are mixtures of many compounds, each with its own volatility, the result of such a test is usually a smooth curve such as this one.*

difference can be great enough to affect jetting. The higher the specific gravity, the richer the fuel will run in an engine. Specific gravity is measured by placing a weighted float into a fuel sample, and noting the how deeply it sinks into the liquid.

Volatility

Volatility is the measure of how easily a fuel evaporates to form an air/fuel mixture. It is possible for a fuel to be blended to have high octane and low volatility, however, and such a fuel may work poorly in engines run at low coolant temperature or at high rpm.

GENERAL INFORMATION

Motor gasoline—the stuff you get at the pump—is a complex mixture of more than 100 different molecular species, mainly hydrocarbons, which are compounds of hydrogen and carbon. Think of molecules of hydrogen and carbon, and the bonds they can form, as a subminiature erector set, from which a huge variety of structures can be made. Some take the form of straight chains of carbons, flanked by hydrogens. Others are branched chains. Still others are rings.

Heat is simply increased molecular activity, and a hot gas is like a storm of tiny billiard balls, whizzing and colliding in all directions. In combustion, such collisions break up hydrocarbon molecules, and their fragments begin to combine with oxygen from the air, a reaction that releases yet more heat as the combining atoms rush violently together. In complete combustion, every carbon atom reacts with two oxygen atoms to form carbon dioxide, and every pair of hydrogen atoms reacts with a single oxygen atom to form water.

In the early days, gasoline was simply that fraction of crude oil that boiled away in a certain temperature range. This is "straight-run" gasoline. After 1912, as more gasoline was needed, ways were found to break down or "crack" higher-boiling-point, heavier fractions into lighter compounds in the gasoline boiling range. Today, custom-made catalysts and chemical synthesis are employed to create specific compounds for blending into gasoline, to achieve specific performance goals.

To power a spark-ignition gasoline engine, a fuel must be volatile enough to evaporate quickly to form a combustible mixture. This requirement eliminates higher-boiling-point fuels, such as kerosene or fuel oil, from consideration. To make engines cold-start in winter, extremely volatile compounds—gases at room temperature such as propane or pentane—are dissolved in gasoline. The audible "Pshh!" you hear when you uncap a fuel tank or drum is the escape of such volatile gases. Winter gasolines are blended with higher percentages of volatiles to make starting easier.

If a gasoline is too volatile it may vapor lock—boil in fuel lines, pumps, carburetors, or injectors. Summer gasolines are therefore made less volatile to avoid this problem. Aviation gasolines must not evaporate rapidly at high altitudes, so they are blended to achieve low volatility.

THE VOLATILITY CURVE: SEEING A GASOLINE'S "SHAPE"

This brings us to one of the useful ways of characterizing gasolines: the volatility curve. We place a sample of fuel in a heating chamber that is connected to a condenser. As we raise the temperature of the sample, at first the most volatile materials evaporate and pass over into the condenser. These early boiling fractions are called the fuel's "front end," because they boil off first.

We begin to make a graph, relating the sample's temperature to the percentage of the sample that has come over. When 10 percent of the sample has come over, we note the temperature. This is called the "10 percent point" and is a good measure of the fuel's cold-starting qualities. The lower the temperature at the 10 percent point, the better this fuel will cold-start, but the worse its problems with vapor lock will be.

As the sample gets hotter, heavier fractions boil off until, at some high temperature, 90 percent of the sample has come over. This temperature is called the "90 percent point." This number gives some idea of how volatile the fuel is as a whole. Much motor gasoline has a fairly high 90 percent point, and therefore needs a hot engine to evaporate thoroughly. Beyond a certain point, gasoline can be made so lacking in volatility that mileage begins to suffer; the unevaporated part of the fuel passes right through the engine, either unburned or only partially burned.

Why bother about volatility? For exclusively street-driven vehicles, it's not an issue, but once you begin to dabble in racing, it can become one. In drag racing, for example, there is an incentive to run engines cold; they may make more power when cold because the intake air expands less, allowing more to fit into the cylinders.

Motor gasolines of modest volatility may not evaporate entirely in cold engines, especially run at higher rpm, simply because there's less time for evaporation to take place. Consequently, a more volatile racing fuel may work better. Motor gasolines may work fine at steady throttle, but cause stumbling when the throttle is suddenly opened. Again, lack of volatility can make the fuel slower to respond.

If you do choose to run racing gasoline at some point, don't focus exclusively on octane number. The very highest octane fuels are those intended for turbocharged/supercharged drag engines. In both these engine types, lots of heat gets added to the intake charge by blower compression, and this evaporates just about anything the fuel blender cares to put in. Therefore, the fuel blender can and does use fuel components of high knock resistance but middling volatility. The result, in a cooler running or high-rpm engine, can be poor throttle response or leanness caused by incomplete evaporation. Such fuels are said to have a "hole in the volatility curve." The lack of performance takes the form either of poor throttle response or a mysterious missing few hundred revs on top.

Any fuel blender will give you a fuel data sheet. Look not only at the octane number, but also at the 90 percent point. You may get better results with a fuel with a lower 90 percent point than one with a higher octane yet higher 90 percent point.

OCTANE

Octane number is a measure of a fuel's resistance to detonation. It is not a measure of the power of the fuel or of its burning speed. A gallon of normal heptane (octane number 0) and a gallon of isooctane (octane number 100) contain identical amounts of potential heat energy. Benzene, a somewhat carcinogenic ring compound, has excellent octane number, but burns 15 percent faster than most compounds of lower octane number.

The value of higher octane fuels in unsupercharged engines lies in the higher compression ratio they will tolerate without detonation. Simply replacing a lower octane fuel with a higher one does nothing for power. Essentially, the octane number measures the temperature stability of the fuel molecule. To obtain the value of a higher octane number, the compression ratio must be raised.

Many racers, however, use racing gasoline simply for its consistency, rather than for its knock resistance. Pump fuels

contain, as industry people like to say, whatever was in the barge that got to the terminal first.

DETONATION

In the intake port and combustion chamber, the fuel and air are heated by the hot metal of the engine. As the piston rises, the charge is further heated by compression. In this high-temperature environment, the fuel molecules are bombarded by other molecules in a colliding billiards free-for-all. As the temperature rises, the average velocity of the molecules rises, until the very fastest of them carry enough energy to begin knocking weakly bonded hydrogens off the least-durable hydrocarbon structures.

Once combustion begins, much more rapid heating and compression occur in the part of the charge still unburned, out near the edges of the combustion chamber. The battering from other molecules now breaks up even durable hydrocarbons. Partial reactions with oxygen create highly reactive fragments that accelerate this breakdown.

If this process of heating goes on long enough, and the fuel molecules are vulnerable enough, a critical percentage of reactive fragments may be reached. At this point, combustion can begin by itself in the remnants of still-unburned charge out at the edges of the combustion chamber. This is called auto-ignition. With the fuel and oxygen in this hair-trigger state, combustion no longer proceeds smoothly at its normal 50–150 feet per second, because the altered chemistry of the mixture now makes it an explosive. Combustion occurs at the local speed of sound—several thousand feet per second in this hot gas—generating a shock front.

The violent result is called detonation. You hear it as a high-pitched tinkle if you hear it at all—in small cylinders it may be too high-pitched to hear—but detonation is far from harmless. Shockwaves hammer the pistons and may damage crank bearings. During even light detonation, the insulating boundary layer of stagnant gas normally clinging to all interior metal surfaces is blasted away. This creates a rapid increase in heat transfer from the hot combustion gas into the cylinder head, cylinder walls, and piston.

Light detonation leaves hot parts, particularly the piston edges, looking as if they had been lightly sand-blasted. The classic signs of severe detonation are piston and head erosion,

Piston Destroyed by Detonation. *Fuel is a lot like popcorn, the longer you keep it hot, and the hotter you keep it, the more likely it is to pop. Too much compression, too early a spark, too much engine temperature, too low a fuel octane number—any of these can lead to detonation. Every veteran engine builder or racer has a collection of these—with stories to match. Start your own collection real soon! John Owens Studio*

Piston Destroyed by Preignition. *The hole in the center is the giveaway. Although this is a two-stroke piston, the idea is the same: too hot a spark plug heat range can turn your plug's electrodes into glow plugs—sources of premature ignition. Preignition concentrates the heat in the center of the piston, blowing a hole in it in very few revolutions. Collect 'em! Trade 'em with your friends! John Owens Studio*

even to the point of blasting away the piston metal enough to expose the piston rings.

Anything that heats the air/fuel charge and/or holds it longer at high temperature makes detonation more likely. Thus higher compression ratio, earlier spark timing, higher engine or intake temperature, or abnormally low rpm and heavy throttle, tend to promote detonation. Turbochargers and superchargers, with their high-pressure heated intake charges, also create ideal conditions for detonation. Another prime cause is a fuel octane number too low for the application.

Detonation is made less likely by anything that reduces the temperature of the air/fuel charge, or anything that speeds up the combustion process—completing it before conditions for deto can mature. Lower compression, rich mixture, retarded ignition timing, lower engine or intake air temperature, and rapid combustion either through higher rpm or increased in-cylinder turbulence, all tend to suppress detonation.

Most motorcycle engines have smaller cylinders than car engines have, and this speeds combustion by shortening flame travel. This is one reason why so many bike engines can run compression ratios of 12:1 without knock, while many auto engines are limited to the 8–9:1 range.

PREIGNITION IS NOT DETONATION

Detonation differs from preignition, but one can lead to the other. Preignition is the beginning of combustion before the ignition spark—caused either by some abnormally hot object in the combustion chamber, or by residual chemistry from a previous cycle. The most common cause is either *(a)* use of spark plug of heat range too hot for the application, or *(b)* glowing carbon deposits.

Preignition destroys an engine very quickly because it usually takes place somewhere around BDC on the intake stroke. Compressing burning gas through a full stroke overheats the piston very fast—it just takes a few cycles to push in the center of the piston. Why the center? Because that is the part of the piston that heats up fastest. The simple way to distinguish preignition from detonation is that preignition punches through the center of the piston, while detonation nibbles at the piston's outer edges.

CARE OF GASOLINE

When you use racing gasoline, there is the problem of storage and handling. Never permit yourself to become complacent about gasoline. Its volatility makes explosion and fire hazard extreme. I traveled for years in vans full of drums or jerrycans full of gas and never had an accident, but I have known people who crawled from their wrecked vans, their clothes soaked in fuel, lucky to be alive.

Many a racer has found that the last third or quarter of a drum of race gas just doesn't run right, and there's a simple reason for this. Every time the owner has opened the drum, that "Pshh!" of escaping vapor signaled the gasoline's front-end—the volatile part so necessary for rapid vapor formation—escaping. After the drum has been opened enough times, what remains is significantly less volatile, enough so to produce weird jetting (having to go richer to make up for the part that's not evaporating

quickly enough) and sluggish throttle response. It's just like what happens when you buy soda water in quart bottles; after you've taken two or three glasses of soda, the rest is flat.

The best way to avoid this problem is to buy the fuel in quantities small enough to be used up quickly. Buy in a drum only if you can use that much fuel in a short time. If you must buy gas in a drum, put a tap in the drum and set it on its side, submerging the tap so no vapor can escape. Never stand a fuel drum in the sun; the warmth drives off volatiles faster than ever. Store fuel in a cool place, far from human habitation.

If you have ever tried to start an engine that has been in storage for a long time, you may have encountered fuel volatility loss. During storage, the volatile part of the fuel floats away, leaving behind only the heavy stuff. The engine coughs but won't start, or if it starts, it won't accept throttle because the heavy fuel can't evaporate fast enough to "follow the throttle." Once the tank is refilled with fresh stuff, these problems disappear (I almost wrote "evaporate"). Town junkyards are full of perfectly good power mowers that need only a tank of fresh fuel and a spark plug to start and run normally.

Never store leaded fuel in transparent or translucent containers. A reaction with light causes the lead compounds to precipitate out of the fuel and fall to the bottom of the container. The fuel gradually loses its octane rating and becomes, for racing purposes at least, quite useless.

PRIVATE BLENDS

You may have heard that blending leaded race gas with unleaded premium results in something with higher octane than either by itself. This sounds pretty strange but it can actually work. The reason is that the effects of tetraethyl lead are nonlinear; the first gram of lead in a gallon of gas has a very strong effect, the second gram much less, and the third, fourth, etc., grams hardly any. Therefore, a gallon of race gas carrying the surgeon general's "recommended" maximum of 4.3 grams of lead, mixed with a gallon of unleaded pump premium, boosts the octane of the unleaded a lot more than it lowers that of the race gas.

If you need race gas octane but can't afford the price, this is one way to stop that knock—provided you have a safe place to keep fuel, where any mishap has no chance of burning up people or their houses or shops.

FUEL AND BIKE STORAGE

If you stop running your bike in the fall, the temptation is to move on to the next activity and let the bike take care of itself. Sometimes this is OK, but often enough, come springtime, the bike won't start, or it won't idle.

Springtime problems can usually be avoided by running the bike out of fuel before storage. Back in the days of carburetors, the fuel in float bowls would evaporate, leaving behind residue that loved to block up idle jets so engines couldn't be made to idle.

Remember, gasoline in long storage loses its volatile front end—the light gases that make cold-starting easy. Don't be surprised if your stored bike doesn't run, or doesn't start well until you replace the stale fuel in it with fresh fuel.

FUELS

CHAPTER 21
WEIGHT REDUCTION

Acceleration equals the thrust, divided by the weight—it's as simple as that. So far, we've talked about increasing the thrust as a means of boosting acceleration—but there's another way. On a 100-horsepower, 380-pound sportbike, with rider and fuel, every 6 pounds of excess weight you dump is equal in effect to 1 more horsepower. Think about it.

How much of your bike is ugly fat? Older stock exhaust systems weighed as much as 45 pounds! Durability was assured by thick, rust-resisting tubes and muffler, crossover pipe(s), resonators, and brackets. Compare that with an aftermarket steel system at one-half to one-third the weight. Compare it with a 7-pound racing titanium system. Even if an aftermarket exhaust system has no other effect, saving 10–15 pounds is equivalent to a 2-horsepower boost. Replacing a 40-pound system with an ultra-light 7-pound item is equivalent to a more than 5-horsepower boost—just from the weight saving.

Now pull off all of your bike's heavy, thick, ABS plastic bodywork and weigh it. With phone in one hand and the *Cycle News* classifieds in the other, call any of several makers of lighter-weight aftermarket bodywork. Ask the weight of their equivalent parts. Do the same with the seat. Take the difference between stock weight and weight with aftermarket parts, and divide that by 6 (see the first paragraph of this chapter). The number you get is the equivalent horsepower gain that this weight saving earns you. Manufacturers are doing this same job on new models—looking for ways to unlock free power by dropping weight.

You can go nuts this way, so be careful. But the catalogs are filled with neat little lighter-weight brackets, carbon-fiber bodywork, seats, and other gadgets that will save you weight. Lightening your bike brings a sure performance gain, the modifications are easy to make, and you can feel the difference in your bike's handling.

It gets even better. Some parts of your bike make a double contribution to inertia during acceleration—the parts that rotate. The engine must not only shove these parts down the road, but it must also spin them up at the same time. Tires, wheels, and brakes are big items on this list, and the bigger the diameter of the spinning object, the more it holds you back.

Think of it this way. When you accelerate down the drag strip, at the far end your wheels are spinning at close to 2,000 rpm. The power to spin those 35-pound lumps up to that speed came from your engine. That power was subtracted from the power available to accelerate your bike as a whole.

This is the reason for the existence of lightweight cast, forged, or carbon racing wheels and, in the previous era, the availability of light aluminum rims to replace stock steel ones.

Many bias-ply sportbike tires of the previous era weighed over 10 pounds apiece, with an extra 3 pounds or so for an inner tube. Every pound saved out at tire diameter is equal to 2 pounds saved in non-rotating parts. Radial-ply tires tend to weigh only 70 percent of what bias tire do—and they don't use tubes, either.

Stock wheels can be very heavy. The gain from lighter wheels isn't as large as that from lighter tires, because the tire's diameter is larger, and much of the wheel's weight is in its hub, at a much smaller diameter. But lighter wheels do count, as do lighter brake rotors and carriers. Look at late-model sportbikes or at race bikes; the brake rotors are radially very narrow. Where stock discs on older bikes may measure 50–60mm wide across the pad track, and 7mm in thickness, those on race bikes are down to 23–30mm, with recent street parts following close behind. Thickness is 5.0mm or less. The first production brake discs weighed as much as 7 1/2 pounds apiece, making 1972 vintage disc brake front wheels weigh over 50 pounds! For contrast, consider that a super-light wheel with a single big disc now weighs more like 15 to 20 pounds. There's work to be done.

On the performance bikes of the 1970s, tuners wasted no time in having those 7.5mm-thick discs Blanchard-ground down to just over 5mm—a weight-saving of over 25 percent. Bear in mind that disc mass and disc maximum temperature are related. As you make the discs lighter, they rise to a higher temperature during a stop from a given speed.

Weight loss can be best accomplished by the factory. Note how compact is the design is of Ben Spies' factory race bike. Brian J. Nelson

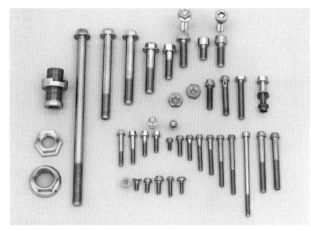

The Gleam of Titanium. *This fastener smorgasbord is from Mansson and allows you to subtract 40 percent of the total weight of steel fasteners replaced. An amazing variety of fasteners are available in the light metal.* Mansson Technologies

Let's Get Specific. *Here are axles, swingarm pivot shaft, steering stem, and engine locator set for Kawasaki ZX7. Good enough to eat.* Mansson Technologies

HOLEY BRAKE DISCS

There was a tremendous fad for holes in brake discs back in the early 1970s—and the practice is occasionally seen today. It began when Yvon DuHamel's mechanic, Steve Whitelock, saw holes in Indy car discs over at Dan Gurney's nearby race shop and decided to try them on the Kawasaki H2R's seriously overweight front discs. The latest brake craze is to use "wave rotors," which are brake discs that are no longer round but wavy, and which have all sorts of slots and holes through them, all claimed to improve disc cooling.

CHAIN AND SPROCKETS

Another concentration of excess weight on sportbikes is in the chain and sprockets. Giant 630 O-ring chains are used to make chain maintenance a thing of the past (bravo, in my book). Keen observers, however, will notice that road race

bikes use much lighter, smaller 520 chain, with its thinner sprockets (and these chains are changed often). There is a strong aesthetic element here, too, because the nicely machined, race-oriented sprockets are much more satisfying to look at than the usual clunky, thick, stamped stock items. There are several pounds to be saved here—but at a price of more rapid chain and sprocket wear; the smaller parts concentrate load on smaller pins, bushings, and sprocket teeth. And, although sprockets are smaller even than brake discs, they do spin as does the chain, so a pound saved here is worth a bit more than a pound saved on non-rotating parts. When I asked Erik Buell why he had put a rubber tooth belt on his new 1125R sportbike, he replied, "The belt weighs just over a pound, but a chain is four to five pounds."

FOOTPEGS, BRACKETS, AND BARS

Rich resources for weight savings lie on this miscellaneous list. Next winter, when the snow is banked up to your windows and the wind outside sounds like Daytona practice, curl up with the catalogs and make a detailed weight-saving plan.

On all but the highest-zoot streetbikes, footpegs and controls are, to put it kindly, utilitarian. Countless CNC machine shops are selling surplus production time to outfits with attractive footpeg and foot-control designs, and the back pages of the newsprint sportbike magazines bulge with their ads for them. An engineer at Ducati pointed out to me that some riders are bothered by flexing footpegs, mentally confusing it with the sensations of early traction loss. Do you carry a passenger, or do you just wish you would? (They're extremely heavy—I have no idea why any sportbike owner would want one.) If not, remove all those heavy passenger amenities like pegs, grab-rails, and seat extensions. Away with ugly, heavy steel exhaust-pipe brackets, too. You will also find offerings of light-metal or even carbon-fiber brackets and struts for fairing and tach mounting, etc. There are now several sources for aluminum clip-on handlebars, some of which are hinged, so they can be changed without removing the top fork crown.

Some riders research the battery scene to see if there's a lighter battery that will still reliably start the bike. Soon tiny lithium-ion batteries may make heavy lead-acid cells as obsolete as spears. It's common on Supersports-modified machines to eliminate the entire stock instrument cluster, with its tangle of wires, brackets, and housings, and run an aftermarket dashboard in its place.

Older bikes may have both a centerstand and a sidestand. Do you need both? Detail items, but capable of large reductions in some cases, are cranks and cylinder liners. Some Kawasaki Z1 variants had cranks that weighed 32 pounds, but others were almost 10 pounds lighter. Today, many racers are replacing iron cylinder liners with hard-coated aluminum liners at one-third of the weight; the OEMs have been doing this for a while. Iron is for making stoves. Check the foam rubber in your seat; that stuff can add up, and there are some much lighter materials out there. Do you have a steering damper on your bike? The

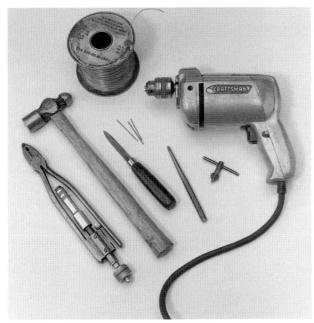

Tools for Lockwiring. *Yeah, laugh if you like—my stuff's old and so am I. Center punch and hammer make a dimple to hold the drill point. A supply of 1/16-inch drill bits prevents frequent trips to the hardware store when you break one or two. The three-cornered machinist's knife removes the sharp edges from the holes you drill, keeping them from chafing the wire. The commonly used wire is 0.032-inch stainless, but this is nickel-copper wire I received from a benefactor at the airbase.* John Owens Studio

frame clamps for some of these units look like wheelbarrow parts—big, clunky steel pieces. The lighter aluminum variety cost more, but so does the high-priced spread.

FASTENERS

Bikes are held together with fasteners—bolts, nuts, studs, washers—and the aftermarket is full of special-purpose and lightweight replacements for stock components. As I see it, there are three basic categories here:

1. High-strength upgrades to improve security: this would include such things as high-strength cylinder studs to be used with big-bore kits, special connecting-rod bolts, and higher grade general fasteners.

2. Lighter-weight fasteners: in this category are the titanium and even aluminum bolts and screws so glamorously seen on factory race bikes.

3. Vanity applications: this includes the use of fasteners as customizing items, as distinct from their use for other purposes.

Production bikes must be sold at a competitive price, and this stops the maker from using fancy, expensive materials. But no one wants to lose the investment in a racing or modified engine because of a con-rod bolt breakage. No one wants to blow head gaskets because stock cylinder studs don't provide enough head-clamping force to seal a big-bore (more

area pushing the head upward), high-compression (higher peak combustion pressure) modified engine. Therefore, when there is an option of better con-rod bolts or larger or higher-spec cylinder studs, don't economize. Get the good bolts and studs and keep your engine together.

Sometimes the better bolts are part of a general upgrade—for example, Carrillo rods include good bolts—and sometimes they are an option for use with stock rods. Either way, remember that internal forces are increased in modified engines, and it takes increased parts strength to contain them.

When you have a fastener catalog in your hands, it's tempting to order Grade 8, 10, or 12 replacements for what is on your engine. This is usually overkill, because things like case screws are sized to provide adequate holding torque with the stock material. Upgrading to a fastener with twice the tensile strength isn't really useful if you aren't going to use that double strength by torquing the fasteners tighter. And that, in turn, often just crushes the metal under the bolt heads and makes a mess. If you decide to drill any of these Superman fasteners for lockwire, you'll discover that they are also twice as hard to drill. The sensible thing is to replace Phillips head screws (if any) with longer-lasting Allen socket-head equivalents, in a material of reasonable strength, like Grade 8.

The place for super-strength fasteners is where there is real stress: in cylinder studs and con-rod bolts. Elsewhere, all you need is adequate strength.

Years ago, weight-conscious riders on a budget used to spend hours drilling out the shanks of steel bolts, based upon the obvious truth that the bolt is no stronger than the root diameter of the thread. The idea was to maintain a constant cross-section along the bolt's length. To me this seems like a painstaking lot of nonsense, because the role of rider skill is so much more important than a few ounces of weight. Still, if you enjoy standing at the lathe, peeling bits of weight out of your scooter, don't let me stand in your way.

Production bikes are designed for rapid assembly, with later disassembly as a more remote possibility. This means self-centering Phillips screws, the kind that get ruined when the screwdriver tip slips as you're trying to remove them. Better to buy one of those hammer-drivers, which use internal ramps to simultaneously apply great torque and axial pressure to the screw. This usually breaks loose even the tightest ones with never a slip. If you plan to service your engine frequently (as in racing), you may wish to replace the hated Phillips screws with Allen socket-heads instead. Their six-sided sockets never slip and they can be reused again and again. They also (to me at least) have a workmanlike look.

There is one exception here, and that is flat-head screws. Because of the conical underside of flatheads, only a small socket can be provided, and this greatly reduces the torque you can apply to these fasteners. I therefore recommend (from bitter experience, I should confess) that you not replace Phillips flatheads with socket heads, especially if they are to be secured with thread-locking compound. You'll be able to unscrew the

Phillips flatheads with a hammer-driver, but you may just round off your Allen driver and end up drilling the fasteners out.

Another item on production bikes is split washers, used to keep things like case bolts from loosening. I hate what the sharp edges of these washers do to cases and bolts/nuts when you un-torque the fasteners; they gouge up great, sharp slivers of metal. On race engines that will be frequently serviced, I therefore like to replace these horrors with plain flat-washers.

ABOUT TITANIUM

I like to say that when racers and modifiers run out of ideas on how to go faster, they turn to lightness as the answer. While it's true that a lighter bike handles better and accelerates faster, how much lighter would your bike be if you could throw away all its fasteners? Five pounds? Replacing all your steel fasteners with titanium will save only 40 percent of that (2 pounds), so the weight saving is small. On the other hand, titanium does look wonderful on a bike, with its special gleam that whispers, "Exotic materials in use here." If you love the stuff, go wild, but know what you're doing.

First of all, although heat-treated alloy titanium can develop strength equal to that of decent high-strength steels, the material is only about half as rigid as steel. This means that, while it can carry the load without breaking, it deforms more in doing so than an equal amount of steel does. All materials have a tensile "spring constant," which is called Young's modulus. That of steel is roughly 30 million, while that of titanium is 15–17 million. As an example, replacing an existing steel axle, swingarm pivot bolt, or steering shaft with a titanium one may result in detectable flexure during hard riding. This is why race bikes with titanium axles are designed with large-diameter tube axles, whose shape contributes the extra rigidity that is lost by using titanium (the bending strength of a tube increases very rapidly with its diameter). The titanium axles on the Britten motorcycle and on GP and MotoGP bikes are made in this way. If your front wheel is able to twist laterally, more than usual between the fork legs, it may have the effect of knocking the brake pads back into the calipers, so that next time you go for the brakes, the lever comes to the bar on the first try. The brakes pump back up on the second pull, but that first pull can be breathtaking. Any time you have this symptom (not likely anywhere but in racing), think about the possibility of front wheel lateral twist and what might be causing it.

Titanium has some special qualities that must be respected when using it. The material should not be made hot while in contact with any cadmium-plated item such as a washer. Titanium is heat-resistant enough to be used in exhaust valves, but the metal has an avid appetite for anything it can absorb. Cadmium is a no-no because it makes titanium brittle. No titanium exhaust pipe should ever be heat-wrapped, because the material will oxidize to a flaky, yellow mineral form if overheated. Titanium welds readily to other materials by accident. Titanium pipes weld to their manifold adapters from heat and vibration, uncoated titanium valve stems seize in their guides, and close-fitting titanium axles, bolts, etc., can easily become tight or seize in their bores if not coated with some antifriction surface.

If you buy titanium fasteners or other heavily loaded parts, be sure that they are made from one of the higher strength titanium alloys, such as the common aircraft grade 6Al-4V. The chemical and marine industries also use titanium, but in low-strength, chemical-resistant alloys that should not be used for critical loaded parts. It's not a good idea to have your machine shop buddy make you up titanium parts unless you can be sure what the material is.

Because of its gas-absorptive tendencies, titanium should never be welded except by a specialist in titanium welding, in a glove box filled with inert gas.

WHEN YOU RUIN THE THREADS

No matter how careful you are, the day comes when the threads pull out as you tighten a fastener. Now you will need to use one of the several kinds of thread-repair inserts on the market. The original is the Heli-Coil, which is a thread-shaped, springy spiral of diamond-section stainless wire, fed into a cut-oversize thread with a special tool. Other systems employ solid inserts with one thread on the OD and another (the original size) on the ID. Inserts can sometimes come loose and unscrew with the bolt.

You can buy kits for this from fastener houses or from auto-parts outlets, or you can take your work to any bike or auto shop that has the equipment. What you'll find in a Heli-Coil kit is:

1. An oversize tap that you will thread into the damaged threaded hole; it cuts at the original thread pitch, but to a larger diameter.

2. A small supply of the bright, spring-like Heli-Coils that will form the new threads when fed into the oversized threads cut in (1).

Ready to Drill. *I'm holding the drill with a precautionary thumb against the vise, to keep the drill from breaking through too fast on the far side (breaks 'em every time!). That thumb also steadies the drill, keeping it from flexing the bit and breaking it that way. Naturally, the vise has to be attached to the bench, but I couldn't do that in the photo studio.* John Owens Studio

3. An installation tool onto which you will thread the Heli-Coil, and which will drive it into the freshly tapped hole; the tool can then be backed out without taking the new threads with it.

Chips are produced in cutting the new thread, so some disassembly may be required to perform this work safely without getting metal chips into your engine. Or, you can trust to the time-honored system of greasing the tap to hold the chips—most of them, anyway. A thread repaired in this way is stronger than the original, because the hard insert or coil engages a bigger thread in the surrounding metal than what was originally engaged by the bolt.

DRILLING FOR LOCKWIRE

This is an acquired skill, and not everyone will have equal luck with it. Some people break a drill with every hole or two, while others may get 10 or 20 holes to a drill. You will need a bench vise, small hammer, center punch, high-speed drill motor (2,500 rpm is good, slower is tedious), and a good supply of 1/16-inch twist drills—all hardware store items. The following is a method that I have used for years, can be applied in the field without much special equipment, and, done right, will break few drills. Here it goes.

If you are drilling socket-head cap screws, hold the fastener in the vise so that a pair of the internal flats is parallel with the vise jaws. Using a small hammer and a sharp center punch, make a dimple in the OD of the socket head. Dab a finger of grease on the vise nearby. With a 1/16-inch bit and a high-speed drill motor, place the point of the drill in the punch mark. Hold the drill in such a way that a couple of fingers of one hand act to hold the drill back. What breaks most bits is when the hole breaks out on the far side. Begin drilling and bear down firmly but not maniacally. Chips should come out steadily. If they do not, take another drill, check that the drill is turning clockwise, or bear down harder. If chips don't come, you're not drilling! Stop every few seconds, pull the drill out of the hole, and dip it into the dab of grease to cool and lube it. Make sure to keep those "safety fingers" braced to prevent the drill from wobbling or moving suddenly.

When the drill point is about to break out into the socket, you'll hear the drill motor rev a bit higher. That is your signal to ease up and begin to drill in little pecks—push the drill, then ease up, and so on. When you feel resistance lighten, go very easy because otherwise, the bit gets such a big bite as the center of the hole breaks through that it can't stand the torque and breaks off.

DRILLING HEX-HEAD FASTENERS

This is the one that makes strong men weep (strong women are more philosophical), so prepare to allow yourself to fail before you succeed. Set the hex head in the vise jaws, with the shank of the fastener parallel to the jaws and high enough to give access for the drill. Don't chuck the drill bit too short for the same reason. With punch and hammer, make a punch mark about 1/8 inch from the apex, in the middle of the face. With the drill, begin by drilling straight in, perpendicular to the surface. When you have made a hole 1/16 inch deep, stop and pull the drill point out. Now come at the hole at an angle, and gently reseat the drill into the metal. There is a little fussiness as it drills at an angle, so you should go easily. Stop, pull the drill, and begin again at yet a steeper angle. In three or four steps, you can get to the final angle, and be able to drill at that angle until the drill begins to break out on the far side. This breakout is even trickier than the one with socket heads, because it is taking place at an angle. This side-loads the drill, and it will fatigue and break quickly if you push hard. Drill with light pressure until you see the dimple that tells you the point is right at the surface, ready to break through. Now go into your peck-drilling routine, being careful and gentle until the point gets through this critical phase. Don't be in a hurry because that always breaks drills.

If the bit doesn't cut, no shavings will come out. This means it's dull. Replace it and begin again. You'll break more bits at first, but in time you'll get several fasteners from each bit.

Once you have drilled a fastener, usually in two places 180 degrees apart, you should deburr the holes using a machinist's three-cornered knife, to prevent them from cutting the wire in service.

There are patent lockwire-drilling jigs that you can buy, and they may work better than the one I tried.

LOSING YOUR MIND

From time to time there is a fad for putting lightening holes in everything. Everything gets drilled until it is ready to break. The world doesn't need this, because now we know that rigidity is almost always more valuable than 1 or 2 ounces of weight saving. I must confess, however, that I have made some pretty light parts from inappropriate metals. Fortunately, no one was ever injured with any of this nonsense. Even factories get carried away; in the mid-1970s Suzuki was desperate to lighten its F750 bikes and made up crazy stuff like aluminum shifter drums. None of it worked and it all had to be taken off again. I guess my point here is that lightness-seeking can become a sickness like anorexia or flow bench compulsion. Don't let it happen to you!

Lightness is great, and it can be entertaining up to a point. But in the end, someone's got to ride the bike.

Heaven and Hell. *On the left is an Allen socket screw, whose internal hex head seldom fails to drive the fastener in a trouble-free manner. On the right is a Phillips screw, damaged when the screwdriver slipped, as it so often does with this screw type. When Phillips screws are tight, it takes an impact driver to remove them without damage.* John Owens Studio

CHAPTER 22
UPGRADING YOURSELF

We stood behind the Loudon pit wall with rapidly beating hearts, watching our man lead the national, with the famous names all behind him. He had the skill, and he had the power. We were a mile high. Then the comedown. Inexorably, the watch showed he was fractionally slowing, and we could see the others catching up. At the finish, he was third—a fine result, but nothing to compare with that glorious taste of first. What had happened? He had, in the borrowed language of motocross, "wheezed out." He had the skill and the power—but not quite the endurance. Richard Schlachter went on to achieve the necessary stamina—and become national road race champion—but it was a hard lesson. The mind, the body, and the equipment must all be capable of equal performance.

When you begin riding motorcycles, the machine seems like a tool for multiplying yourself. With it, you can hurl yourself forward, around corners, over hill crests. You can brake and accelerate. It is a grand feeling. As you learn more and mature in your appreciation for this device, you begin to realize that the machine is not doing this; you are doing it. In any sports or racing situation, the rider counts much more strongly than the machine—that's why good riders on chuffing 650 BMW singles can run mountain-road rings around so-so riders on a top-performing 750 or 1,100 sportbike. What is really happening is that the 650 riders are braking deep, getting the power on as soon as traction allows, and are thinking far ahead of the action. Other riders are yanking the throttle and brake and scaring themselves. They're slow because they lack the skill to use their bike's capabilities.

Not surprising. After all, does purchase of an airplane make the new owner into a pilot? Operation of a motorcycle is a high-level skill that takes time to learn—and some method. Anyone with even a rudimentary sense of balance can yank the throttle and brake, make noise, and double the speed limit on a motorcycle. This is not skill. It is making an ass of oneself.

There is more than one way to acquire the skills that go with a modern sportbike. Young maniacs, completely devoted to riding, go out in every spare moment and tear around their favorite roads, building up hours, concentrating, learning, falling down, getting up, and trying again. This works for some people—it worked for Mike Baldwin, for example.

The more you know, the safer you become. This is the master, Lawson, on the 1025 Kawasaki superbike. He went on to win four 500cc Grand Prix World Championships. John Owens Studio

Alternatively, there are riding/racing schools that provide some valuable information for "free" (not free in terms of dollars, but in terms of hard falls) and give you the opportunity to try going fast under controlled conditions (for example, there is an ambulance and medical team present, there are corner workers, etc.).

In any case, it's best to approach the matter seriously and devote plenty of time to it. As with flying, it's better to give motorcycling your full attention.

Many riders are offended by the word "safety." It suggests people who want everything in life to be made as safe as sitting on the living room sofa. It suggests the hated "safety-crats," the no-fun busybodies who want to put airbags on bikes (where?) and limit highway speeds to idle. There is so much negative charge on this word that I am going to suggest another: security.

When nations feel endangered, they create "security forces," not "safety services." Grand Prix and World Superbike motorcycle racers have a 99.99 percent certainty of making it around the next turn, according to a computation I made from statistics a few years ago. They know that they can't win unless they get around **all** the turns, every lap of the race. That makes them interested in security—tire grip, vehicle mechanical condition, and techniques for overcoming all hazards. They are trying to achieve something with their skill—not to throw dice with the Devil. Is that wishy-washy?

I have met racers who claimed they had come to get the danger. That may be so, for they certainly didn't "get on the box." Danger is easy to find. Skill is hard to achieve. Security is simply a measure of how big a mistake you have to make to hurt yourself. Security is your margin of error. The more skillful you are, and the better your equipment is, the larger your margin becomes, and the more secure you are. I stood in the infield at Valencia, watching Valentino Rossi lead the Spanish MotoGP. He looked fast but very secure, for there was no spinning, sliding, or wobbling. The farther downfield I looked, the worse the machines were behaving, and the harder

When you're a novice, everything seems to happen at once. As you accumulate experience, sense emerges from chaos and you may emerge from the pack. These happen to be expert riders, but their crowded, crisscrossing trajectories exemplify the confusion of those first novice rides. Brian J. Nelson

their riders were having to work to hold their positions. This is the normal situation in motorcycle racing.

What you do with the margin is your business; racers have to run it down pretty small sometimes, but they do this reluctantly. The proof is in the lap times; when a rider is pushing, intentionally shaving the margin of error, lap times become faster, but less consistent. The inconsistency results from errors having to be corrected. The harder the rider pushes, the larger these errors become—until one of them puts the rider out. That takes fine judgment and intense concentration that can't be maintained indefinitely. The higher the speed, the greater the cost, physically and in concentration. If the rider gets away to a 10-second lead, he or she will, if possible, settle on a slightly slower pace that increases security—and the rider's lap times will again become very consistent. The rider is now operating at a speed at which errors are much less frequent. The rider is secure.

Several times I have watched two riders race from Daytona's second gas stop to the finish. According to the "dicing with death/big balls/hot blood" theory of racing, they should have been pushing and shoving, sliding, and trading paint as each man fought for testosterone supremacy. But nothing of the kind took place. Each rider knew his job was to come away from Daytona with maximum points. Carving each other up for 18 laps is a stupid risk of falling and taking home zero points. Therefore they rode smoothly and quickly, knowing that the action would all take place in the last two laps. At that time, each rider would spring his plan to exit the Chicane in the winning position—second—so he could draft past the other to win at the line. The rest was just cruising.

Another way to think of security is as the software that keeps you alive. Watch any woodland animal and see its constant vigilance; it's trying to stay alive, avoid the cat and the fox, eat, and go about its business. If animals relax this vigilance, they are shortly seized and eaten by a predator. Read the book *Chickenhawk*. Author Robert Mason was an assault helicopter pilot in Vietnam who survived 1,200 missions. He was lucky, but he was also studious; he remembered and used every single useful, security-enhancing trick he encountered—like never approaching a "hot" landing zone the same way twice. He was bold when there was no other way to get men out of tight spots, but he knew that in the long run, survival required that he stack the deck in his own favor in every possible way.

Motorcycle safety (there's that word again) courses teach proven techniques that stack the deck in this same way. Set aside black-leather-and-dark-glasses macho long enough to see the truth; you look a lot cooler on two wheels than crumpled on the pavement, surrounded by cops, EMTs, and flashing lights. A veteran carrier pilot flies the approach by the book and tries to pick up the third wire—not the first. His intelligent, informed conservatism centers him among many dangers, in the sweet spot that gives him the best chance of surviving to fly another day.

The choice is between motorcycle safety courses and riding/racing schools. In the first case, the emphasis is more overtly on survival through good judgment on the street and highway, while in the second, students seek to expand their ability to use their machine's full performance envelope. Either of these kinds of formal training can give you in-depth defense knowledge, enable you to find the sweet spot in any riding situation. Both are available in most parts of the country and are eager to hear from you.

Another valuable kind of training, for which a riding school is an entry requirement, is actual motorcycle roadracing. Your first novice practice will sweep away all the cobwebs of illusion about your own skills, and make it clear how much there is to learn. The rush you get from twisting the throttle makes you feel like a god, but the fear that comes from a misjudged corner entry soon sets matters straight. Those who reach expert status or a national license are part of a skilled elite group who know that you go faster only when you learn something new—never by "trying harder" (the constipation theory of improving lap time). Motorcycle racing is an intelligence test, and it can make you into a more assured, more secure street rider. Lots of street riders have the dangerous idea that they must display racy derring-do on the public roads, blowing off old ladies and families in minivans. To a racer, this is trivial nonsense. Racers ask themselves, "Whom did I beat?"

Of particular value is endurance racing, in which you accumulate hours much faster than in sprint racing. This compels you to learn how to go fast while conserving your energy and find ways to manage your concentration without tiring quickly.

Too often, those preparing to enter a riding school or other program imagine that they must have impressive, horsepower-laden machines. The reverse is true; what you need is a pushbutton streetbike, something that will run reliably and mind its own business—not intrude upon your concentration as you try to do something you've never done before.

Even if no formal schools are available to you, you have an analytical, critical brain. Listen to its little voices, the ones that whisper things like, "That was a stupid move—you should've known that idiot didn't even see you." Racers, like other athletes, regularly play back action in their heads when they can. There is no reason why serious street riders can't do the same. Mentally play back tight situations frame by frame, and analyze them to see what you could have done better or differently, what you should do next time. One of the first things beginning riders learn is to forget about right-of-way, and concentrate on seeing. In 1971 a friend complained from his hospital bed, "But I had the right of way!" and his brother replied, "Yes, but the other fellow was driving an oil truck."

Another level of self-upgrading is physical. Are you healthy? Do you have any physical problems such as poor vision or balance? Do you have any habits that might impact riding skills, such as the all-too-human temptation to intoxicants of one sort or another? Are you on any medication that affects concentration or balance?

Penguin Racing School in Session. *Many racing schools, such as this one that operates at Loudon, New Hampshire, provide beginning instruction as a basis for a novice license, more advanced instruction, and opportunity for serious street riders to see what the track looks like from behind the windscreen. Many schools feature special advanced sessions given by top riders.* Penguin Roadracing School

My great-grandfather Fred was an Indiana farmer, and he said, "Never get down on the binder side." This referred to getting down from a horse-drawn harvesting machine, and meant that no matter how calm your horses, no matter how nimble and alert you are, there is always the chance that the team will spook and the cutter-bar will hit your ankles. If you're never in front of it, it can never happen. He farmed until he was 92. Likewise, if you refuse to operate a motorcycle while in any impaired mental state, you can cross off a whole class of potential accidents from your list. This makes sense. Never get down on the binder side. And live to be 92.

Correct your vision to the best it can be, and wear your corrective lenses when you ride. It's no accident that the finest competition riders have superior eyesight; this gives them more time in which to plan action.

Without exception, top racers maintain high physical condition. There is a difference between strength and endurance. Yvon DuHamel was small and tough as a racer. He could stay on his bucking, weaving Kawasaki H2R throughout a long race and still be ready to go to the party. His son Miguel has displayed the same stamina throughout his long career. Others, possibly stronger in terms of body strength, were physically and mentally drained at the end of an event. The same applies in sports riding. If you find you are all done after only a few minutes of high-concentration riding, get busy and build yourself up, using endurance exercises, preferably under expert direction at a gym. Tell the fitness director what your goals are, and perform the boring but necessary recommended regimen until you have the endurance to ride the way you want to, without wheezing out. As the eighteenth-century Russian general Alexander Suvorov said, "Train hard, fight easy."

It is also common for top riders to coordinate their conditioning plan with sensible diet, and many employ personal trainers. Even if you are not planning to race or even to ride in a highly sporting manner, you are operating a demanding vehicle, and the better your physical condition, the greater your security.

Hot weather can cause accidents all by itself. As your body loses moisture through breathing and sweating, blood electrolyte levels are disturbed, causing prompt loss of mental functions. Judgment, balance, and reflexes deteriorate. Numerous times in hot, humid weather, I have seen racers pull unexpectedly into pit lane, get off their machines, and then collapse from heat prostration. Police see the same with road riders.

The rule is that in hot weather, you must drink fluids until you actually need to pee. You may not even feel thirsty, but dehydration proceeds all the same. When it's hot, drink. And that means water, soda water, or sports drinks compounded for quick fluids-replacement—not sweet sodas, juices, or alcohol, all of which are diuretics—they consume more water in elimination than they supply, so although they make you feel less thirsty, they produce a net water loss from the body. If you feel nauseated, light-headed, or just plain weird as you ride in hot weather, head for water.

Probably the best way to begin riding is to combine a rider course with large amounts of highway/street riding. The best pilots are people who begin young and devote major energy to building up their hours quickly—not those who fly an hour or two every now and then. Motorcycling is an intense activity, and the longer you ride, the better you get and the more secure you are. Sometimes you will hear the argument that, "Sooner or later, the law of averages is gonna get you, and you'll have a bad accident." This foolishly assumes that having an accident is a random, statistical process, like the probability of a bomber's being hit by flak. Motorcycling has a statistical component—anything can happen to anyone—but this is far outweighed by the large skill-based component. This is why the first six months of motorcycle operation are crucial, as the rider strives to gain the skills and experience that steadily increase security. If accidents were caused by the "law of averages," then the safest way to fly would be with beginner pilots. This is obviously not true, because experienced operators have the best safety records, and exactly the same is true of motorcycling.

Always remember, however, that while car drivers' security depend to a great extent on hardware—the mass of metal around them, and the visibility of their large vehicles—motorcyclists must compensate with better software. Skilled, secure motorcyclists are alert like wild animals or combat pilots, identifying threats and coping at a high level. Everyone who learns to ride a motorcycle finds that it makes him or her a better auto driver!

Your comfort on the machine influences your ability to handle emergencies and your staying power in the saddle. Some seats, some bar heights or angles, or some foot controls cause cramping, restriction of blood flow, or just plain soreness. Poor adjustment of controls can result in your reaching for them where they ought to be in an emergency. If they are somewhere else, you'll fumble and your response will be delayed. This is serious business. Chapter 2 describes how to make your machine fit you.

Boredom is the great enemy of concentration. Efficiency of anti-submarine aircraft crews in World War II fell to only 30 percent during long, droning patrols of 10–14 hours over the featureless sea. But when competitive exercises were instituted, and aircraft were equipped with rest facilities and real kitchens, performance improved a lot. In factories, managers have learned that a 10-minute break every hour or two greatly boosts quality and production. If you must ride for many hours, give yourself something to look forward to from time to time. Stop, have a bite to eat, take a walk, make a call. Then ride on, refreshed, protected again from white-line hypnosis.

These considerations can even affect your choice of machine. The most extreme sportbikes impose a riding position that doesn't wear well if you are going far. Their quick steering response is enjoyable as you carve the backroads, but it also responds to every imperfection in the road. This can be tiring because it asks for your attention, but on a longer ride, you may not have it to give. This is why there exists a range of sportbike qualities. For those who demand ultimate sporting response for intense but shorter rides, the extreme bikes like the Suzuki GSX-Rs are a likely choice. For the rider who rides farther and longer, there are moderated sportbikes. Be realistic about how you will use your machine, and choose accordingly.

Are you in or are you out? That is racing's big question. This novice's race didn't end well and everyone else has gone home. Not every day at the races is a good day, but there's only one worthwhile way to be in, and that's entirely—100 percent. Naturally, that sometimes means thinking it all through before beginning again. We get tired and we get discouraged. Then we sleep. Tomorrow, our enthusiasm is back, good as new. John Owens Studio

Bearings, Bearing Clearances: Racing or heavy-duty plain bearings, if available for your engine, exist to increase the fatigue strength of the bearing. Plain bearings consist of thin, semicircular shells of steel, on the inner surfaces of which is plated a soft bearing material. This soft, low-melting-point material does not abrade the crank journal should the two happen to touch, and is soft enough that any grit that gets in between will hammer down into the soft metal until it becomes harmless (embedability). Unfortunately, the soft metal has low fatigue strength, which is why only a thin layer is used. For heavier loads, a matrix of harder copper and lead may be substituted, and there are also various aluminum-bearing alloys.

Big Bore Kit: More displacement brings more torque at all speeds, but the engine's increased need for air may cause it to run out of breath at somewhat lower revs than before (bigger cylinders sucking through same-sized valves and ports). You can remedy this with mild porting or higher lift (not longer duration) camshafts. Are the bigger pistons heavier? If they are, your safe redline may have to be lower than before to save your con rods from overstress.

Big Valves: Lots of older engines received bigger valves on their way to road or drag-racing use. Not all engines can accommodate bigger valves because they bring the intakes and exhausts closer to each other during overlap (mainly a problem of two-valve engines, where the angle between valves is larger). There may also be a need to increase the size of the valve cut-outs in the pistons. Big valves don't always have to go with bigger ports, because they can be useful in restoring a correct relationship between valve head diameter and port throat diameter; too big of a throat hurts low and mid-lift flow.

Cam Chain: In some cases, special high-reliability or heavy-duty cam chains are offered to reduce the chance of a disastrous failure. For some Superbike basis models, gear-drive kits are offered as replacement for the stock chain camdrive (latest Kaw, Suz 750s). The gear drives are said to reduce the horsepower loss over a long race, otherwise resulting from gradual loss of timing accuracy through chain "stretch" (which really means wear). As with other Superbike kit items, if you have to ask the price, you probably can't afford it.

Cam Degreeing: In one set of tests I did at *Cycle* magazine, we were able to raise the peak power of a GSX-R 1100 by 3 horsepower, by degreeing the cams and then dyno-testing each change. You can do the same.

Camshafts: The cam profiles open and close the valves. Lift is how far a valve has been lifted, while timing determines how long it is open. People who enjoy this sort of thing make a graph of valve lift versus crank angle, called a lift curve. The point at which the valve is fully open (the center of the profile in symmetric cams) is called the lobe center angle, measured from crankshaft TDC. The horizontal axis represents time that the valve is open, and the vertical axis gives us the flow area exposed under the valve. Therefore the area under this lift curve is called "time-area," a measure of your engine's total opportunity to flow air. As I'm sure you can see, there are different ways to get a given time-area; you could use a moderate lift with a long duration, or you could use a high lift for a shorter duration—or any combination between. Each has its uses.

Carburetors: The CV carbs fitted to sportbikes in the 1990s were huge—bigger than the race carbs that would have been used 10 years before. Today's fuel injection throttle bodies make them all look small. The only reason to switch to bigger carbs is if they are part of a comprehensive modification that greatly increases the engine's air needs, and/or because the rider actually needs the (potentially) quicker response of well-tuned slide carburetors. Carburetion remains a special priesthood—don't mess with it unless you are now a competent carburetion technician, or are willing to become one. The carburetion you get is the carburetion you create.

Close-Ratio Gearbox: This is a specialty item, but it can be very useful to the racer or other limit-seeker. If you narrow your powerband enough, you must also narrow the spread between transmission ratios. With a stock gearbox, upshifting from first to second may cause a 30–35 percent rev drop, but a modified engine may be too weak at such low revs to pull well. With a close-ratio set, the first-second shift produces a smaller rev drop of maybe 25 percent, thereby staying within the engine's powerband.

The downside of closer ratios is, of course, that first gear becomes taller than is really usable on the street.

Clutch Options: Some stock clutches need help, and the aftermarket is ready with alternative friction and steel plates, stronger clutch springs, roller throwout bearings, and even special thinner plates that make it possible to stack one extra plate in your clutch.

How will you know? Clutches slip most in top gear, at peak torque. The engine note will rise faster than it should, and fall if you roll off a bit.

Now such a necessity in racing that it's beginning to be featured on production bikes is the slipper, or back-torque-limiting clutch. Big four-stroke engines produce so much engine-braking that on closed throttle they can drag or hop the rear tire, or cause rear breakaway during corner entry. The slipper prevents this by placing a ramped coupler in the drive. When the engine drives the rear wheel, the drive is solid. When the tire drives the engine, the ramps exert an axial force used to reduce spring pressure on the clutch stack, allowing slippage.

Clutch slip generates heat, so the coming of slipper clutches has required more robust construction to deal with the extra heat they make.

Compression: Usually, if compression is raised, it is done with new pistons with higher domes, but it can also be achieved by decking the cylinder or removing material from the underside of the cylinder head. The great thing about compression is that it boosts torque at all rpm, and is especially useful in improving acceleration at speeds below the pipe threshold—the rpm level at which the pipe begins to work strongly. Drag racers use high compression ratios because they need big torque to get their bikes moving off the line. Road racers may use extra compression on shorter courses, where engine speed is pulled down below the pipe band in lower gears (which are farther apart).

Crank and Con-Rod Options: These parts become necessary only when rpm levels are raised and stock parts might fail, and are further complicated by new Superbike rules calling for stock materials. Racing steel and titanium rods are available from the aftermarket, and there are some sources for cranks if better than stock is required.

Crack Checking: When you examine the fracture surface of a broken part, you can usually see that a crack existed for some time before the actual failure. A variety of techniques exist for detection of such cracks in critical components—before the failure occurs.

The low end on this scale is the dye penetrant kits sold in welding shops. Degrease and dry the part to be checked, then spray with penetrating dye, which is drawn into any cracks. Clean the part by wiping with solvent provided. Then spray on chalk-like developer. Cracks show up as lines of dye, wicking up into the developer. Dye penetrant works with all metals.

Magnaflux makes use of the fact that there is a magnetic discontinuity at a crack in a ferrous metal part. The cleaned part is magnetized and placed in a bath of magnetic particles. Any crack is outlined in particles. Magnaflux is useful only on steel or iron-based items.

Use these methods if you are having chronic failures with particular parts, such as cranks (crankpin fillets are fruitful candidate areas for cracking), con rods, or gears. Or, use it just to be sure.

Crankshaft Work: There are several sources for crank rework, and the popular operations are balancing, lightening, knife-edging, and polishing. Balancing may be useful especially when you build an engine with reciprocating parts of non-stock weight. Some builders like to balance just to improve on the job done at the factory. They equalize piston weights, and con-rod big-end and small-end weights.

The idea of a lighter crank is to reduce the amount of power that goes into accelerating the crank as the bike itself accelerates. Material is machined from the sides of the webs, leaving the balance as before. The power difference will be small, but two bikes differing only in crank mass will have slightly different acceleration rates, favoring the one with the lighter crank.

Knife-edging comes to us from NASCAR racing, and is aimed at making it easier for crank counterweights to "cut" through the fog of air and oil in the crankcase. Small gains of less than 1 percent are reported, especially for full counterweight streamlining, which tapers the trailing edges of the counterweights as well as their leading edges. Polishing is aimed at reducing the residence time of oil that happens to hit crank surfaces, notionally making it easier for said oil to slide off the crank, taking a minimum of energy with it.

These operations are expensive in relation to their results and would be low on the mod list unless the aim is (a) to spend a lot of money, or (b) to perform every imaginable mod (same difference).

An item in a separate category is the roller cranks used in early Kawasaki and Suzuki air-cooled fours. There is a lively business in rebuilding, upgrading, and welding these pressed-together cranks, mainly for drag racing. Look in the drag mags, or call veteran builders like Fast by Gast or Falicon.

Elixirs, Coatings, Refrigeration: The world is full of temptation. Why bother with the work of installing cams and other messy moving parts, when a simple oil change can make you a winner? Or can it? Should I have my pistons Teflon-coated? What about having my engine frozen in liquefied gases? All these techniques may have their place, but they do not replace proven, hardware-based power-boosting techniques. For every story, there is a counter-story. My favorite comes from an engine-builder who, when asked if he recommended Teflon coatings, replied, "Yes, if you've had trouble with eggs sticking to your pistons."

Engine Side Covers/Protectors: Some racing classes require these, which are extra-thick right and left engine covers that can withstand light to medium crashes without cracking or wearing through, and dumping oil on the track. These are nice-looking parts, cast or CNC-milled from solid, and if you accept the possibility of falling down while enjoying your motorcycle, you may want these.

Exhaust Pipe: Pipes are popular because it's an easy mod that makes your bike look different and sound different. An aftermarket pipe is also much lighter than stock.

Sadly, not all pipes work. Any fab shop can bend tubes, but getting real power requires expensive dyno development. Stock systems are very good today—hard to beat in all respects except weight. They are heavy because effective silencing requires bulky chambers made of material thick enough to last more than one riding season.

Four-into-ones are easiest to make and have the fewest parts. Their boost is generally limited to the top 2,500–3,000 revs of the band, with flat spots and fussiness tending to appear below that—especially if your cams are not stock or are degreed with significant overlap. It's easy to be fooled by the way a bike feels. A pipe is said to "hit hard" if its power comes on suddenly, but this feeling can just as easily come from a pipe climbing out of a deep hole at one rpm and hitting peak torque a few hundred revs higher. A stock 4-2-1 pipe may make just as much or more power, yet feel unexciting because its torque isn't rising steeply out of a hole that shouldn't be there in the first place!

The 4-2-1 pipe is the design used in almost all stock and racing pipes, the reason being that the last place you want a torque "hit" is in the middle of acceleration off a corner.

Ignition and Fuel Mapping: As noted elsewhere, many people imagine that "stronger" ignition can make more power, but that's true only if the stock ignition is bad or weak. The real gains to be made in ignition today have more to do with matching the ignition advance curve to a modified engine's real needs.

Mapped ignitions are capable of delivering any desired timing curve. The map is made originally by running an engine on the dyno, and searching at each rpm level and throttle angle for the minimum ignition timing that gives best torque (MBT). These data points are electronically stored in the engine's computer. As the engine runs and conditions change, the computer notes the current rpm and throttle angle, looks up the corresponding ignition lead in the map, then fires the plug at that point. It repeats this read data/look up/fire sequence many times a second. Information controlling fuel injection is stored and handled in the same way.

The trouble starts when you modify your engine in certain ways. The original maps are right for the stock pipe, cams, intake length, and so on. Now, however, you may have moved the torque peaks and created flat spots, and may also want a higher rev limit. Your system is now mapped incorrectly for the modified engine. Ideally, you would go back to an instrumented dyno that allows continuous engine running and create new maps, then load them into your existing computer. In some cases this is possible—there are ways to address some engine computers from a laptop or with a special handheld unit.

The easier road to success is via devices like the Dynojet Power Commander III, which "fox" your engine's stock ECU into delivering altered ignition and fuel curves. Beyond this are complete racing ECUs from companies such as Marelli.

Jet Kit: To meet emissions standards, carbureted bikes were jetted to run on the lean side. Manufacturing error plus differences in machines result in cases of weak acceleration, poor throttle response, slow warmup, and so on. The basic, stock-bike jet kit was made to correct these problems. It consisted of several things, such as different, richer needles; tiny, thin washers with which to raise your stock needles to a richer position; and possibly tools and directions for resizing the air orifices that control rate of slide lift during acceleration. When the machine is accelerating and the throttle slide is lifting, its lift rate also strongly influences mixture. If the slide lifts too fast, the mixture becomes lean, and vice versa. For sports use, we would like both correct—responsive carburetion and rapid response.

Because aftermarket exhaust pipes changed the "signal" (the suction pulse) that the carburetors received from the pipe during overlap, a pipe often required corrected carburetion. Pipes were often sold with a matching jet kit for this reason.

A jet kit is installed by pulling the tank to get access to the carb tops. Then you remove the cap atop each carb, being careful not to cut or puncture the thin rubber vacuum diaphragm that lifts the slide. Pull the slides and exchange or shim the needles as directed.

Oil Cooler: Yes, race bikes have oil coolers. That is because they are running at a high duty cycle that pushes a lot of heat into the oil. Oil makers like their product to run at or below 180 degrees Fahrenheit, but overcooling oil just increases friction by raising its viscosity. Use a cooler if your oil temperature is too high. Do not accept inferior plumbing of the "heater hose and worm-drive hose clamp" variety, which is prohibited in racing because of the crashes it has caused when the hoses have popped and the clamps have loosened.

Particularly nice are the oil-to-water heat exchangers used on some recent bikes. These bring oil temp up faster by thermally tying it to cooling-water temperature.

Pistons: Most of the friction in an engine comes from pistons and rings. Stock parts are designed to last—to seal durably, run quietly.

The aftermarket offers a variety of piston options. In years past, builders changed pistons mainly to increase displacement or to raise compression. These can still be useful goals, providing the resulting engine can run knock-free on the fuel available. Sportbike compression is in the range of 11:1 or 12:1, while Superbike racers are near 14:1, and pure drag race engines (no street operation) may have compression above 16:1. There's no harm in being a skeptic where compression ratio is concerned. I learned to measure it for myself and so can you. (See discussion of compression ratio in Chapter 3.)

Be sure valve cutout size is adequate for the valves you have, and that there is adequate valve-to-piston clearance during overlap. Another crucial clearance is that between piston and matching squish areas of the head. This may be as tight as 0.025 inch in some production 750 fours, and this is a reasonable lower limit.

There is another trend in piston design: friction reduction. Therefore, some race pistons have only two rings—a single gas ring and an oil ring. This cuts friction but gives a shorter-lived seal. Such racy pistons will have very short skirts of minimum area, and will use stubby wristpins to reduce weight.

Because of the demands of rising power and rpm, most stock pistons are now forged, as most aftermarket pistons are. Forging squeezes a slug of hot metal into shape between matched male/female dies. This results in a tougher, more fatigue-resistant metal structure.

Porting: Ask any Superbike tuner and you'll get the same answer: Ports are so good today that it's hard to improve them. Supersport-class

racers look over as many cylinder heads as they can get their hands on, evaluating them on a flow bench if possible, or at least seeking those most free of casting crud, and with good alignment of the valve seat rings to the ports. This is one reason factory Supersport bikes are fast; the factory sees all the heads (to say nothing of controlling the production process).

The first and most important level in porting is careful valve seat preparation—converting a stock three-angle valve job to a smooth, modern blended shape. This has to be done by a professional who knows the head in question. Tiny changes can result in large flow differences, because this is the prime "choke point" in your engine's airflow path. Supersport rules permit modification to the seat ring, but to nothing else. Some intake valves show a useful low-lift flow increase from a 30-degree back cut, just inside of the 45-degree seat, and there are other tricks you'll have to learn from specialists or on your own.

Lots of outfits prepare cylinder heads for drag racing and get impressive power, but unless you plan to use your bike this way, you will probably find this type of power useless on the street.

The trend of cylinder head design is to get more flow per square inch of port area, not to increase that area. A well-developed racing engine at peak torque fills its cylinders to 125 percent of atmospheric pressure. The only way it is able to do this is to convert intake piston motion into very high speed intake flow that acts as an "inertia pump" after BDC, to supercharge the cylinder. Making ports bigger reduces this essential flow velocity and its supercharge effect. Yes, big ports give big airflow *numbers on the flow bench*. The flow bench is a steady-state abstraction that is unable to model the pulsed flow of a real engine. It is the pulsed nature of the real flow that makes inertia supercharge possible. This is why smaller ports are the trend—they make inertia effects stronger.

When moving air is brought to a stop, its velocity energy is converted into pressure energy. Air decelerating to 0 from 250 feet per second generates a pressure 3 1/2 percent above atmosphere, but air decelerating from 500 feet per second generates almost 15 percent extra. This is how higher intake velocity translates to extra power. The piston gets the intake flow rushing toward the cylinder at high velocity, then that speed is used to cram air in after BDC until all the velocity energy has been converted to pressure in that cylinder.

Another benefit of high intake velocity is turbulence. The more energy the intake flow carries into the cylinder, the more vigorously the air/fuel mixture will be stirred and the faster the combustion flame will burn through it. Lack of intake velocity at middle rpm is a classic cause of weak acceleration, and is why

some four-valve automobile engines now carry systems that close off half the intake ports at lower revs.

Sometimes it's as simple as making existing ports smaller. Drag racers have used GSX-R750 heads on 1100 engines, and Yoshimura is rumored to have tested its old 750 Superbikes with a 600 head. Big midrange results from replacing a 1200 Harley Sportster head pair with 883 heads. Usually, the smaller ports require careful streamlining to make them deliver both velocity *and* adequate airflow.

The current technique in Superbike is to fill stock ports with epoxy and let CNC porting execute copies of an improved port shape that has been developed on a flow bench.

Radiators—Big or Extra?: What do you do if your modified bike overheats? Don't despair at the huge price of Superbike kit rads. First be sure your water pump impeller isn't slipping on its shaft. A little "porting" of the entry into the water pump will often pull engine temp down several degrees. At high flow, the suction side of the pump can cavitate the flow across sharp edges or turns, reducing water flow. Make sure air can get *out* from behind the rad, and that obvious flow paths aren't blocked by things like coils and brackets. Check the front surface of your rad; are the fins hammered shut by pebbles thrown off the front tire? Get a radiator comb at the auto-parts shop and open those fins back up. Blow out accumulated insect corpses with air pressure, from the back of the rad. Consider a bigger rad from another make or model; a good aluminum welder can relocate the plumbing where you need it. As a last resort, there are radiator shops that advertise in the magazine *Circle Track* that will make you anything you want, in aluminum, for less than one-tenth the price of the usual kit rad.

It has been customary to run the lowest coolant temperature possible (65 degrees Centigrade/150 degrees Fahrenheit was common) in order to limit expansion of intake air. In MotoGP, higher coolant temperature is being used by some in order to use a smaller, lower-drag radiator.

Shot-Peening: This is a well-proven way to increase the fatigue life of heavily loaded parts. Crack-prone areas of cranks, con rods, and even gears can be treated by shot-peening. In order to crack, a material must be in tension. Peening hammers the surface into compression. Since most cracks are initiated at or very near a part's surface, peening increases durability.

Before about 1943, critical aircraft engine parts were highly polished to eliminate surface defects, but since then, controlled shot-peening has been used to prevent or delay cracking from surface defect. Seek this service from a shop with racing experience.

Slip-On: This is a fancy name for a new muffler. Instead of the heavy stock canister, with its stock appearance, you slide on and clamp in place a spiffy, lighter-weight new unit. Now you may find your engine strikes a louder note, but it will be hard to discover whether your accelerated heart rate comes from more performance, more noise, or the thrill of making your own mod. Only the dyno and the timing lights at the strip know for sure.

In defense of the slip-on, I suggest that if you want to rework your bike but don't want to flop in at the deep end of the pool, this is a place to start. Expect weight savings and different appearance as the real benefits.

Stud Kit: Stock cylinder studs are sometimes stretched or pulled up by the roots when a big-bore kit and/or high-compression pistons are installed. A stud kit provides the extra clamp load required to prevent this.

Sump, Deep: Some earlier sportbikes had shallow oil sump plates in which oil could slosh away from the pump pickup, leading to oil starvation and possibly spun rod bearings. A deeper sump may correct this tendency, while holding some extra oil. Check for exhaust pipe clearance. Sumps on late-model sports engines are very deep, located to one side to make room for the pipe.

Valve Springs: The obvious reason for special valve springs is to provide the extra pressure to make the valves follow a more vigorous cam contour at high revs, but there are other reasons, too. The wire used is drawn from high-purity steel, containing fewer-than-normal nucleation sites for cracking. It is crack-checked with Magnaflux and shot-peened to place its surface in compression (tension is required to propagate cracks). Various means are used to prevent traveling waves (spring surge) from fatiguing the springs to death or provoking early valve float. Nested pairs of springs may be dimensioned to rub against each other, providing friction damping. Coiled flat wire dampers may be placed inside the springs. Or the spring's natural frequency can be raised very high by reducing the number of coils, to something like three and a half instead of the more usual five or more. The latest high-performance springs may be tapered ("beehive" design), which helps to prevent surge, or they may be wound of oval wire to get greater stiffness-to-weight from each coil.

Springs have to be installed at the specified height to produce the desired seat pressure while not overstressing the wire. This is accomplished with measurement and shims. Springs don't last forever; in racing they are changed regularly (in MotoGP that has often meant every day) to avoid fatigue failure and/or loss of pressure.

The limit to increased valve spring pressure is reached when seat pressure rises so high that exhaust stems begin to stretch—one more reason to measure and think about valve clearances.

Windage Trays, Oil Scrapers: These devices were more important in earlier designs, whose crankshafts were not so far above the oil level in the sump. The idea was to prevent the crank from picking up and whirling masses of oil. Any momentum transfer from crank to oil is a power loss and a source of unwanted oil temperature rise. One horsepower put into the oil in this way is the equivalent of 746 watts of heating effect.

Particularly on engines with large, full-circle flywheel pairs rotating inside a close-fitting crankcase, there can be a problem with what is called "wet-sumping." This is a situation in which the crank picks up oil and whirls it into the small clearance between flywheels and case, causing huge viscous friction loss and heat. To prevent this, scrapers are located very close to the crank, to "peel off" any adhering oil.

APPENDIX B PERFORMANCE MATH

SEPARATING NONSENSE FROM HORSEPOWER

You know how to work a calculator, right? Working through a few numbers can tell you a lot about what an engine is doing, or where it stands on various scales of excellence. This knowledge is worth a bit of concentration.

The basic variables that determine engine power are these:

Displacement

This is the volume swept out by the pistons in one stroke. It is a measure of how much air/fuel mixture the engine can potentially inhale. Displacement is area of one cylinder, multiplied by stroke, times number of cylinders. Find bore area by squaring the bore, dividing this by four, and multiplying by pi (3.1416).

Averaged Effective Combustion Pressure, or BMEP

This is the pressure which, if it acted over the whole power stroke, would produce the same horsepower as results from the actual, varying combustion pressure. This pressure, called BMEP, is the result of cylinder-filling and combustion efficiency, minus friction, and it allows useful comparisons to be made from engine to engine.

Cylinder-filling efficiency is usually called volumetric efficiency (VE) and is just the ratio of charge volume to cylinder volume.

Having 100 percent VE means the cylinder is completely filled, while having 85 percent VE means the cylinder is 85 percent full of fresh charge, and 15 percent full of something else (like intake vacuum or exhaust gas).

Combustion efficiency is the ratio of the heat the fuel would give if completely burned, to the heat release that actually occurs in our engine. The two are different because mixture can be incorrect, evaporation may be incomplete, there can be quenching near metal surfaces in the chamber (flame goes out if too cool), and some charge is always jammed into places like piston-ring grooves, where it doesn't burn at all or burns too late to contribute to power.

BMEP and torque are based on the same thing, so BMEP and torque curves have the same shape for a given engine. To convert torque into horsepower, use this:

$$HP = (Torque \times RPM)/5{,}252$$

RPM

This simply tells us how often an engine can perform its power-producing cycle.

Horsepower is the above three numbers, multiplied together, then divided by a constant that makes the answer come out in the right units. As follows:

$$HP = (Displacement \times BMEP \times RPM)/793{,}000$$

Enter displacement in cubic inches, BMEP in pounds per square inch, and RPM in revolutions per minute, and the answer comes out in horsepower. For two-stroke engines, BMEP must be multiplied times 2 because a two-stroke cylinder fires twice as often as does a four-stroke.

BMEP is highest at the torque peak. The highest figure I have seen for a non-supercharged engine is about 230 psi, for a late version of the late Keith Duckworth's venerable DFV F1 car engine. The old Norton Manx singles may have reached 200 or thereabouts, while late-model streetbikes get very close to 190 psi. In general, engines that turn extreme rpm have lower BMEPs because *(a)* their combustion is not so good, and *(b)* they suffer especially large friction loss.

How the Variables Work

The simplicity of the horsepower formula makes it appear that, for instance, if we double any of the variables, we'll get double the horsepower. That's true, but pushing the variables isn't that easy.

Displacement

If we increase displacement, as with a big-bore kit or stroked crankshaft, we *will* get more power, but not in strict proportion to the increase. This is because bigger bore pistons try to pull more air through intake systems and valves sized for the *original* displacement. They are now a bit small for our big-bore engine, so the engine won't fill its cylinders as completely as before. The result will be more power, but at somewhat lower rpm, and in less than strict proportion to the displacement increase.

BMEP

This is the result of everything that goes into filling the cylinders and burning their contents. This includes airflow, exhaust function, compression ratio, combustion efficiency, heat loss, and so on. Normally tuners work to raise BMEP by improving intake and exhaust airflow, raising compression as high as knock will allow, and providing a smooth-surfaced, compact combustion space that burns quickly. Another point is to minimize the volume of charge hidden from the flame in squish and in piston ring crevice spaces.

RPM

Pushing this one can be expensive because, as we rev an engine up, reciprocating parts stress rises not in simple proportion to rpm, but as its square. This means that if we raise rpm 10 percent, we raise parts stress by 1.1 x 1.1 = 1.21 times, or 21 percent. Raise the revs 20 percent and the parts "see" 1.2 x 1.2 = 1.44 times more stress. This extra hammering may be tolerated for a few seconds at a time, as in drag racing, but to make engines last and turn high revs calls for good quality stuff.

This is why late-model streetbikes are now so often built with forged pistons, shot-peened or nitrogen-hardened con rods, and alloy-steel crankshafts. The aftermarket offer premium steel and titanium rods—with the best-quality con-rod cap bolts. Valve gear is especially rpm-sensitive because, at some rpm level, the valve spring pressure will no longer be enough to make the valves follow the cam contour, and they will float or bounce. It

doesn't take much of this rough treatment to break or bend something.

Some street and track riders, aware that higher revs *can* lead to higher power, simply upshift their engines above redline, hoping this by itself will magically improve performance. But the sizes and timings of valves are what determine your power curve—not how long you hold each gear. Forcing an engine to rev on into its "red-zone" of falling power not only wears it out sooner, and possibly floats the valves, but it also slows you down. Even where a rev limiter is present, there is some overrev capability, but power is falling in this zone. Usually, 1,000 revs above peak power, power has fallen by at least half, if not more. These are "empty revs" producing noise and little else.

Another way to put it is that the engine's air-pumping ability doesn't go on increasing forever as rpm rises. At some point, the rising gas friction in the ports stops any further increase, so power peaks and then falls again.

Another ill effect of higher revs is increased mechanical friction. The inertia forces generated at high revs cause parts to flex and bearings to deform, generating extra friction and decreased mechanical efficiency. Even when valve and port sizes are increased to work at higher revs, it can happen that the power gained is mostly eaten up by rising friction loss. Higher revs look tempting but can disappoint even the experts. Designers try to cut friction by making pistons and rods lighter and smaller, downsizing bearing diameters, and finding safe ways to use thinner oils, but it's a tricky business. Nevertheless, in a fully coordinated, developed design, high revs can make high power. Today's 2.4-liter Formula One GP car engines turn 20,000–21,000 revs. Ducati's 800cc V-4 MotoGP engine is making maybe 220 horsepower at close to 20,000 rpm.

MAKE SENSE OF RPM

The higher an engine revs, the faster its pistons move and accelerate. The strength of materials and the action of piston rings put limits on piston speed, and from this, you can get an idea of what is reasonable to expect at various rpm. Piston speed, in feet per minute, is just the distance the piston moves in one minute at the given rpm. In one turn of the crank, the piston performs its stroke twice.

It used to be that engineers regarded 4,000 piston feet per minute as "the limit" for race engine piston speed, but times change. Today, 4,500 feet per minute is a respectably high piston speed, but is not a limit because a variety of engines regularly run to 5,000 piston feet or more. In Europe, they figure piston speed in meters per second, so 4,500 feet per minute = 22.8 meters per second. The 27 meters per second that the Europeans speak of as an upper limit translates to about 5,300 piston feet per minute. Better materials and design allow constant small increases in

permissible piston speed. Unreliability is always the penalty for extremes. Piston speed is not what breaks engines, thereby setting rpm "limits." It is piston acceleration that does that. Push piston acceleration too high, and pistons crack and rod bearing inserts streak and seize. Too much piston acceleration can also unstick piston rings from the bottom of their grooves, destroying their seal. Constant detail redesign pushes the limits in each of these areas.

FIGURING COMPRESSION RATIO

Compression ratio can be made as complicated as an income-tax form, but the idea is simple. It is the ratio of the volume above the piston at BDC, divided by the volume above the piston at TDC.

We can find the volume above the piston at TDC by measuring the oil it takes to fill it. The volume above the piston at BDC is that volume again, plus the volume swept out by the piston on its way from TDC to BDC—that is, the displacement of one cylinder. Thus, if we are doing the CR for a 1,000cc four, the displacement of one cylinder (at standard bore) will be 1,000/4 = 250cc. If, for example, the clearance volume above the piston at TDC measures out to 22.7cc, then compression ratio will be:

$$CR = (250 + 22.7)/22.7 = 12$$

Or, to review in words:

CR= Clearance Volume + Cylinder Displacement

CLEARANCE VOLUME

Now to find the clearance volume. First, pull the tank so you can get at the spark plugs. Remove them and the ignition cover, so you can put a wrench on the end of the crank to turn it easily. Bring one piston to TDC after the compression stroke (so all valves in that cylinder are closed). Next, raise and support the front of the engine or machine, so the spark plug hole is vertical (assuming we are doing an inline four; for other engine types it's pretty obvious what the appropriate arrangements are). This way the measuring oil we are putting in won't dribble from an angled plug hole. Fill the syringe with light oil that you don't mind having in your cylinders, and set the piston at the full line, making sure there is no air trapped in the syringe. Squirt oil into the plug hole, rocking the machine from side to side to knock loose trapped air. Go ahead and fill the thing right up to the top of the plug hole, so that the surface of the oil looks flat. Shake the bike some more to see if more trapped air comes up. Add oil as needed. Rock the crankshaft back and forth slightly to be sure you really are at TDC—you will see instantly from the motion of the oil in the plug hole. Add oil as needed again.

Now note how much oil has been pushed out of the syringe by reading the new piston position. Write this number down.

You're not quite there yet, because now we have to subtract the volume of the spark plug hole. For long-reach plugs, as used on modern sportbikes, the volumes are as follows:

14mm = 2.2cc

12mm = 1.7cc

10mm = 1.2cc

Thus, if your measurement is 18.6cc, and you have 10mm plugs, subtracting 1.2cc from 18.6cc leaves a clearance volume of 17.4cc.

If your engine has oversize pistons in it, you will have to calculate the displacement of the cylinder accordingly. If your engine is 0.5mm oversize, add that to the stock bore and then calculate the displacement in the usual way. Displacement equals bore area, multiplied by stroke. Bore area is diameter squared, divided by four, then multiplied times pi (3.1416). Example:

Stock bore 70mm, stroke 48.6mm, 0.5mm oversize

Stock bore plus oversize: 70 + 0.5 = 70.5mm

Oversize bore area: (70.5 x 70.5 x 3.1416)/4 = 3,903

Oversize displacement is bore area times stroke: 3,903 x 48.6 = 189,685

What is this gross result? The displacement of a ship engine? No, we've just used millimeters to do this calculation, but we want the answer in cubic centimeters. Since there are 1,000 cubic millimeters in a cubic centimeter, we divide the huge result by 1,000 and get 189.7cc as our oversize cylinder displacement.

If our clearance volume measured 17cc in this example too, we'd have a compression ratio of:

(17 + 189.7)/17 = 12.2

This is marginally higher than in the first example, because of the slightly increased displacement. Supposedly piston makers take care of all this when they make oversized pistons, but it's never a bad idea to check. Too bad it's such a messy process—now there's oil all over the calculator and the notebook, to say nothing of the oil-filled engine cylinder. If you suspect your result, check another cylinder.

This test is, naturally, easier to make on the bench. Be sure to remove the oil after this test. Turning the engine with oil in one or more chambers and spark plugs in place can bend a con rod.

COMPUTER SOFTWARE

If you are comfortable with computers, you may enjoy exploring some of the predictive engine software now on the market, such as Dynomation's Advanced Engine Simulation software package.

MEAN INTAKE VELOCITY

This is another of those figures of merit that allow you to compare engines, in this case with respect to intake velocity. You often hear V-8 tuners talk about intake port volume; since these engines all have about the same intake length, they are really talking about average intake port cross-sectional area. This is important because, with the piston stopped at BDC after the intake stroke, the only thing that can keep intake flow continuing into your cylinder is its own velocity. If intake velocity is low, the piston rising on compression will soon stop the flow and cylinder filling will be terminated. But if somehow the intake port is small enough to keep velocity high, and yet streamlined enough to keep friction loss low, intake flow can continue much longer after BDC. For this reason, it's sometimes interesting to compare mean intake velocities at peak torque. Begin with piston speed, then multiply it by the ratio of piston area to port area. This will give you average, or mean, intake velocity.

For example, suppose that a given engine has a 72mm bore and a 31mm inside diameter (ID) intake port. To get the area ratio, we would divide 72 by 31, and then square the result: 72/31 = 2.32, and 2.32 squared is 5.38. Now, if piston speed at peak torque is 3,300 feet per minute, that is 3,300/60 = 55 feet per second, and that multiplied by the area ratio of 5.38 is 296 feet per second. It's interesting to collect this kind of data for a variety of engines—something to do when you're home recuperating from your latest elbow and knee pepperonis. As I keep saying *ad nauseam* in other parts of this book, the trend is toward higher mean intake velocities, and the desired result is increased ability to flow mixture after BDC. The trick, of course, is to combine higher velocity with lower flow resistance—not a trivial combination.

German aircraft engines of World War I, turning at 1,200–1,400 rpm, were designed to a mean intake velocity of 250 feet per second, while at the other extreme, F1 engines today are allegedly working to 400 feet per second or more. If this area interests you, see Chapter 6 of Charles Fayette Taylor's *The Internal-Combustion Engine in Theory and Practice, Volume 1* (MIT Press, Cambridge, Massachusetts, available in paperback), where he discusses intake Mach index.

APPENDIX C **SUGGESTED READING**

The intention of *Sportbike Performance Handbook* is to help you build a better bike. There are a number of useful resources out there, ranging from highly technical manuals to mainstream magazines.

Motorcycle Magazines and Web sites

Magazines and websites are a great source for tuning tips, as well as new bike tests and product reviews. More importantly, they are a good way to keep in touch with your sport. Some of the following magazines can be found at your dealer or at the newsstand. If not, contact the publisher to subscribe.

American Motorcyclist
13515 Yarmouth Dr.
Pickerington, Ohio 43147
614-856-1920
www.ama-cycle.org
Hearken to a mighty chord, played on the official organ of the AMA.

Australian Motorcycle News
P.O. Box 119
73 Atherton Rd.
Oakleigh, Victoria 3166
Australia
+61-3-567-4227
Learn where all that endless, fresh roadracing talent comes from, and how.

Classic Bike
Emap Automotive Ltd
Media House
Lynchwood
Peterborough PE2 6EA

United Kingdom
+44 1733 468099
classic.bike@emap.com
www.classicbike.co.uk
Pretty restorations, often fine historical research.

Classic Racer International
Media Centre
Morton Way
Horncastle
Lincs LN9 6JR

United Kingdom
+44 1507 529529
www.classicracer.com
How can we know where we're going if we don't know where we've been?

Cycle News
P.O. Box 498
2201 Cherry Ave.
Long Beach, CA 90801
310-427-7433
circulation@cyclenews.com
www.cyclenews.com
All the two-wheeled action in newsprint format, 50 times a year for $50.

Cycle World
1499 Monrovia Ave.
Newport Beach, CA 92663
949-720-5300
www.cycleworld.com
This is where I am. *Cycle World* covers the waterfront in journal-of-record style.

Moto Journal
12 Rue Rouget-de-Lisle
92242 Issy-les-Moulineaux cedex
France
+33 1-41-33-37-37
www.moto-journal.fr
France's pillar of bike information. Painless way to improve your language skills.

Moto Tech
United Kingdomwww.racetechmag.com
In effect, Racecar Graphic on two wheels.

SPP
75 Aberdeen Rd.
Emigsville, PA 17318-0437

Motorcycle Consumer News
P.O. Box 6050
Mission Viejo, CA 92690
714-855-8822
editor@mcnews.com
www.mcnews.com
Although pretty sober in tone, this book gets off some good investigative/explanatory articles.

Motorcycle Daily
www.motorcycledaily.com
Daily updates on new motorcycles and other related news.

Motor Cycle News
Media House
Lynch Wood
Peterborough PE2 6EA
United Kingdom
+44 01733 468694

www.motorcyclenews.com
This is the affectionately named "comic" without which the English-speaking racer/enthusiast feels helplessly at sea. Weekly coverage of everything and sometimes more.

Motorcyclist
6420 Wilshire Blvd.
Los Angeles, CA 90048
www.motorcyclistonline.com
Some of my friends say they prefer the youthful outlook of this broad spectrum monthly.

Motorrad
Leuschnerstrasse 1
70174 Stuttgart
Germany
+49 711-182-1374
Europe's Big Gun, which so often, and in ways impenetrable to me, scoops us all.

Performance Bikes
Bushfield House
Orton Centre
Peterborough
Cambridgeshire PE2 5UW United Kingdom
+44 1733 237111
www.performancebikes.co.uk
Looking for that famous British bike magazine irreverence?

Rider
TL Enterprises Inc.
2575 Vista Del Mar Dr.
Ventura, CA 93001
805-667-4100
editor@ridermagazine.com
www.ridermagazine.com
Twelve issues, catering to the odometer-minded.

Riders Club
2-13-3 Tamagawadai, Setagaya-ku
Tokyo 158
Japan
Perfect bound, full of beautiful pictures, jammed with information—all in Japanese.

Roadracing World and Motorcycle Technology
P.O. Box 1428
Lake Elsinore, CA 92531
951-245-6411
www.roadracingworld.com
John Ulrich speaks.

Sportbike
What's left of the former *Cycle* magazine, published annually under the auspices of Cycle World (address same as *Cycle World* above). Good yearly reviews of models, events, personalities with racing/sports slant.

Sport Rider
(same address as *Motorcyclist*)
www.sportrider.com
The view from turn eight, Willow Springs.

Superbike
Leon House
233 High Street Croydon CR9 1HZ
United Kingdom
+44 20 8726 8445
www.superbike.co.uk

Superbike Planet<
www.superbikeplant.com
Regular racing updates

Motorcycle Books

There are a number of books available that will help you further your knowledge of building engines and improving your riding skills. The list below contains some of the better examples. Look for them at your local bookstore, motorcycle dealership, or parts store, or call 1-800-826-6600 for a free catalog from Motorbooks International, which stocks some of these books.

Art and Science of Motorcycle Road Racing
Peter Clifford, Hazleton Publishing, Richmond, Surrey, United Kingdom, 1985.
ISBN 0-905138-35-X
Peter Clifford is currently running the Yamaha 500cc GP team behind Luca Cadalora.

Automotive Fuels Handbook
Keith Owen and TrevorColey. SAE, Warrendale, PA, 1990. ISBN 1-56091-064-X
Somewhat technical, but with a chapter on racing fuels, this one explains fuels in detail.

Automotive Handbook
Bosch, Stuttgart, (avail. from SAE), 1993.
ISBN 1-56091-372-X
This little book contains all sorts of standards, explanations, and descriptions.

Classic Motor Cycle Engines
Vie Willoughby, Motor Racing Publications, Croydon, United Kingdom, 1986.
ISBN 0-947981-10-1
An interesting design review, with commentary on notable designs.

Design of Racing and High Performance Engines
Joseph Harralson (ed.), SAE, Warrendale, PA, 1995. ISBN 1-56091-601-X
This is a collection of important SAE papers related to race engine design, including seminal Honda stuff.

Friction and Lubrication
F. P. Bowden and D. Tabor, Methuen, London, John Wiley, NY, 1956.
A fascinating exposition on the details of friction and lubrication. Try the engineering library—my copy is the only one I've ever seen.

The High-Speed Internal-Combustion Engine
Sir Harry Ricardo, Blackie & Son., London, 1968. ISBN 0-21689-026-8
Sir Harry is one of the founding fathers, and this classic book is still one of the clearest on the subject. Non-mathematical—available from Ricardo—at www.ricardo.com.

Internal Combustion Engine Fundamentals
John B. Heywood, McGraw-Hill, NY, 1988. ISBN 0-07-028637-X
Since the passing of Prof. Taylor (see below), this one has become the BIG BOOK that covers everything.

The Internal Combustion Engine in Theory and Practice (2 Vols.)
Charles Fayette Taylor, MIT Press/John Wiley, Cambridge, MA/NY 1960, 1968 (now avail. in paperback).
Prof. Taylor was head of army aircraft engine development in 1923 and went back to school to see if he could bring order to this field of endeavor. He did, as you will see when you get these books.

Internal Combustion Engines and Air Pollution
Edward F. Obert, Intext, NY, 1973. ISBN 0-7002-2183-2
This excellent text not only presents fundamentals, it also digresses in many useful ways. Written with humor, if you can imagine that.

Internal Combustion Engines: Applied Thermosciences
Colin R. Ferguson, John Wiley, NY, 1986. ISBN 0-471-88129-5
This one is written more from the perspective of heat than mechanics.

Kenny Roberts
Barry Coleman, Arthur Barker Ltd., London, 1982. ISBN 0-213-16825-1
A biography of the famous tough guy, by the man who aided his attempts to take over the world (of GP racing, at least). Inspirational reading for the winter months.

Motocourse
Michael Scott (ed.), Hazleton Publishing, Richmond, Surrey, United Kingdom (avail. Motorbooks in USA annually).
This is the grandest of motorcycle racing coffee-table books, the annual review of Grand Prix road racing. Pictures, technical, rider profiles, race reports. Makes you wish you were rich.

Motorcycle Chassis Design
Tony Foale and Vic Willoughby, Osprey, London, 1984. ISBN 0-85045-560-X
Although this book takes us only to the end of the steel-tube era, it contains the basics and many useful observations.

Motorcycle Dynamics and Rider Control
SAE, Warrendale, PA, 1978.
ISBN 0-89883-200-4
This is another that you'll likely find only at the engineering library, but it does give entry points for handling and stability reading.

Motorcycle Engineering
Phil Irving, Temple Press, London, 1964.
This is the great classic by the late grand old man of the subject—everything British and a few things not, treated in a commonsense way that is still very much worth reading.

Motorcycling Excellence
Motorcycle Safety Foundation, Whitehorse Press, Boston, 1995. ISBN 1884313-01-9
This and other MSF publications are intended to be useful to those who want to become better, more secure riders.

The Racing Motor Cycle
Vic Willoughby, Hamlyn, NY, London, 1980. ISBN 0-600-36342-2
This is a valuable evolutionary, historical volume, to which I refer often.

Superbike Preparation: For Street and Track, Box Stock, and Beyond
Jewel Hendricks, Motorbooks International, Osceola, WI, 1988. ISBN 0-87938-301-1
Mr. Hendricks has raced 50cc machines, been a lifelong fabricator, and even tried a term as AMA tech inspector. This book is full of practical stuff.

Techniques of Motorcycle Road Racing
Kenny Roberts, Hazleton Publishing, Richmond, Surrey, United Kingdom, 1988. ISBN 0-905-138-51-1
If THE MAN writes a book, we'd better read it.

Track Secrets of Champion Road Racers
Alan Cathcart, Osprey, London, 1987. ISBN 0-85045-774-2
Once you're fast, going faster isn't easy. Insights.

Tuning for Speed
Phil Irving, Temple Press, London, 1960.
Now available again, the classic methods explained remain valid today. The author was the designer of Vincent motorcycles. Good reading forever, like Ricardo.

Two-Stroke Tuner's Handbook
Gordon Jennings, HP Books, Tucson, AZ, 1973. ISBN 0-912656-41-7
Are there still any riders who remember two-stroke streetbikes? This is for you, the classic book that first suggested that we cut ports and weld pipes. Jennings is my spiritual uncle.

Winning Motor Cycle Engines
Vie Willoughby, Osprey, London, 1989.
ISBN 0-85045-926-5
Another review and critique of a variety of engine designs. See if you agree with his conclusions.

World Championship Motor Cycle Racing
Mick Woollett, Hamlyn, NY, London, 1980.
ISBN 0-600-36389-9
This is a useful evolutionary history of GP racing from 1949 onward.

INDEX

aerodynamics, engine cooling and, 99
Agostini, Giacomo, 11, 85
air
  box, 56, 58–60
  -cooled heads, 80
  correction, 54
  motion, maintaining in engine, 75
  progressivity, front fork oil level and, 115, 116
airflow
  engine, 29, 30
  slowing down gradually, 32–35
  testing, 31, 32
Akrapovic, 65
Augustine, Kenny, 71, 72
auto shop, selection, 40
Baldwin, Mike, 127, 148, 180
bars, weight reduction, 176
Bazzaz, Ammar, 98
Benelli fours, 18, 25
Bernoulli, Daniel, 34, 51, 65
BMW, 96, 141
Bostrom, Eric, 120
bowl, throat and, 71
brackets, weight reduction, 176
brake
  disc coning, 155, 156
  discs, weight reduction, 176
  fluids, 158, 159
  heat, wheels and, 152
Brake Mean Effective Pressure (BMEP), 27
brakes
  bleeding, 163
  history, 155
  system flexibility, 161, 162
braking stability, 98
braking, late, 134
Branch, Jerry, 49
Brembo, 156, 162
Britten, John, 140, 141
Buell, Erik, 64, 176
bump isolation, spring rate and, 110
Burgess, Jeremy, 49, 97
Cagiva, 137
calipers, 159, 160
  discs and, 155
  multipiston, 156
camdrives, 78–80
carburetion, 22, 50, 51
carburetion, safety, 51
carburetor systems, 51, 52
carburetor, types, 57
carburetors
  slide, 54–56
  tuning slide, 61
  tuning, 61, 62
  vibration and, 58
Carcano, Giulio, 160
Carruthers, Kel, 49
centrifugal compressor, 105, 107
chain, sprockets and, weight reduction, 176
Champion Spark Plug, 90
Chandler, Doug, 134
charge motion, types, 16
chassis
  design, powerband and, 140
  evolution, 101
  material, 137, 138
  racing versus production, 140, 141
  stiffness, 137
  weight distribution, 136, 137
Chickenhawk, 181
clutches, 87–89
Cobas, Antonio, 137
cold starting, 54
combustion, 14, 15
compression ratio, 27, 32
compression, engine, 12, 28
compromise breaking, engine, 31
cooling, engine, 18, 19

Cosworth, 76
Criville, Alex, 38
Crosby, Graeme, 149
Cycle magazine, 40
Cycle News, 175
cylinder, master, fundamentals, 158
damping, 111, 112
Dassault CATIA, 141
Depac, 42
detonation, engine, 27, 28, 173, 174
DiSalvo, Jason, 6, 130
disc
  converting single to twin, 161
  heat, 157
  materials, 156158
discs, calipers and, 155
Dobeck, Mark, 51
Domenicali, Claudio, 98
Doohan, Mick, 108
downdraft, 75, 76
downstream flow loss, 72
Doyle, Peter, 64
Dri-Slide, 170
Ducati, 7, 50, 60, 75–77, 89, 98, 120, 132, 135, 137, 138, 152, 176
Duckworth, Keith, 16, 28, 70
DuHamel, Miguel, 182
DuHamel, Yvon, 8, 176, 182
Dunlop, 142, 146
Dymag Carbon Fiber Reinforced (CFRP) Wheel, 150
dyno testing, 46–49
  alternatives, 47
  carburetor, 49
  correction factor, 47, 48
dyno tuning, overview, 42–44
Dynojet Company, 42, 43, 51
Dynojet Power Commander III, 44, 4750, 57, 68, 90, 93
Earl's Performance Products, 159
  eccentric-vane compressor, 105, 107
Edgar, Graham, 99
Edmonston, 57
Edwards, Colin, 140
electronic motocycle, 95, 96
  future development, 100, 101
  hardware, 98
electronics, protecting, 94
energy efficiency, engine, internal combustion, 13, 14
engine
  braking, 96
  choosing, 36, 38, 39
  compression, 76
  cooling, aerodynamics and, 99
  five-valve, 33
  internal combustion, overview, 12–15
  mixture requirements, 23, 24
  performance, planning for, 6–8
exhaust, 18
  early opening, 13
  engine, 12, 30
exhaust pipe action, overlap and, 30, 31
exhaust pipes, 64–66
  installation, 67, 68
  pipes, slip-on, 67
exhaust port, 72, 73
Factory Pro jet kit, 45
fasteners
  hex-hed, drilling for, 179
  ruined threads, 178, 179
  weight reduction, 177, 178
Femsa, 90
Ferrari, 77
final drive, 86, 87
flame propagation, 16, 17
flame speed, turbulence and, 24–26
footpegs, weight reduction, 176
fork dampers, older, 118, 119

Fox, Geoff, 113, 121
friction coefficient (MU), 160, 161
front fork oil level, air progressivity and, 115, 116
Froude, 42, 43
fuel
  injection, 57, 58
  lead, 171
  management/conservation, 98, 99
  mixing, 13, 14
  wash, 70, 71
fuels, 99
Fuscaldo, Ottavio, 95
G.M.D. Computrack, 121, 128, 131
gasoline
  care, 174
  direct injection, 99, 100
  general information, 172
  private blends, 174
  racing, 171, 172
  reformulated, 171
  storage, 174
  volatility curve, 172, 173
GE, 42, 43
gearboxes, 81–84
Gilera, 137
Gobert, Anthony, 38, 50, 98
Goodyear, 148
Grand Prix of Gibraltar, 8
Grant, Mick, 121
Hailwood, Mike, 137
Hannebrink, Dan, 150
Hansford, Gregg, 121
Harley-Davidson, 41, 48, 69, 144, 159
Hayden, Nicky, 95, 132
Hayden, Roger Lee, 87
header tube size, 66, 67
heat wrap, 67
Heli-Coil, 178, 179
Henning, Todd, 49, 75
Hitachi, 137
Honda, 5, 25, 28, 55, 75, 77, 78, 90, 98, 99, 129, 150, 152, 155, 160
Honda, Soichiro, 5
horsepower, glossary, 184–187
horsepower, reading, 44, 45
Hossack, 137
hot air, ram-air and, 60
Housewarth, Tom, 102
hydraulic
  dampers, 112
  leverage, 159
  lines, 160
  system leverage, 160, 162, 163
idle system, 52, 53
ignition, 14
  advancers, 93, 94
  development, 90, 91
Ilmore, 96
intake
  engine, internal combustion, 12
  flow, post-BDC, 13
  length, 58
  ports, 69
ISR, 156
Johnson, Jocko, 72
Jordan team, 38
Journal of the Japan Society of Mechanical Engineers, 136
Kagayama, Yukio, 101
Kanemoto, Erv, 55, 137, 141
Kawasaki, 17, 48, 61, 77, 78, 82, 87, 98, 120, 138, 150
Kayaba, 113
Kipp, Tom Jr., 33
Kipp, Tom Sr., 169
Krober ignition box, 8
Lauda, Niki, 37
Lawson, Eddie, 8, 9, 40, 48, 108, 121, 130, 155, 163
Lectron, 53, 57
Leonard, Jim, 31
Lockheed, 151
lockwire, drilling for, 179
lubricants, other, 169, 170
lubrication, 19–23, 166–168
main jet, selection, 62, 63
Mamola, Randy, 133
Mansson, 176
Marchesini Cast Magnesium Wheel, 150

Marelli, 100
Mason, Robert, 181
mathematics, performance, 187–189
McCandless, Rex, 5, 135, 137
McConney, Mack, 62
McLaughlin, Steve, 8
Meidensha, 42, 43
Mercedes-Benz, 77
Michelin, 145
Mills, Tony, 148
Mladin, Mat, 50, 64, 130
Models
  AJS 500, 90
  Akashi KR250, 86
  Bimota Tesi, 140
  BMW Kommandogerat, 95
  BMW Telelever, 140
  Britten V-1000, 5
  BSA Gold Star, 77
  Buell 1125R, 176
  Cadillac V-6 CTS, 99
  Cagiva 500, 108
  Cagiva/MV F4, 58
  Ceriani 35mm, 115
  Ducati
    750, 136
    851 twin, 93
    D16RR, 6, 21, 71, 74
    Diana 250, 125
    Superbike, 97, 100
    Testastretta, 73
  Harley-Davidson Sportster, 64
  Harley-Davidson VR Superbike, 152
  Honda
    250, 25, 93
    305 Super Hawk, 74
    450, 49, 72
    500, 38, 136
    900RR, 39
    CB750, 64, 150
    CBR600 F1, 92
    CBR900RR, 45
    Dream 250, 125
    factory 1,025cc, 8
    FWS Daytona V4, 89
    MotoGP, 98
    NR750, 80
    NSR, 56, 138
    RC30, 39
    RC45, 58, 68
    RC166, 18, 80
    RC181, 90, 137
    RC212V, 95
    RS500, 156
    Superbike, 48
    V-4, 132, 149
    V-twin Ascot, 18
  Kawasaki
    1,025cc Superbike, 46, 135, 180
    550, 5
    H2R, 82, 116, 176, 182
    KR250, 21
    KR750, 124, 137
    Z1, 16, 64, 119, 144, 176
    ZX7, 176
    ZX-12R, 65
    Keihin CR, 56
  Lucifer's Hammer, 41
  Manx Norton 500cc, 69
  Modenas KR3 500, 58
  MV 500, 96
  MV-Agusta, 150
  Norton Featherbed, 5, 135, 139
  Norton Manx, 78
  Suzuki
    1,300cc Hayabusa, 8
    1100, 107
    GSX-R, 135
    GSX-R600, 45
    GSX-R750, 45
    GSX-R1100, 118
    Katana 600, 70
  Suzuki-Kawasaki F750, 139
  Triumph 500, 66
  Vincent 1,000cc, 56
  Yamaha
    500cc GP, 138
    750 five-valve, 33
    1000, 107
    F750, 42
    FZ750, 18, 25
    Genesis, 31

GP, 95
Marelli, 100
Monoshock, 114, 117, 138
MotoGP 990, 96
OW31, 149
RADD, 140
TA125, 46
TZ, 119
TZ250, 56, 94
TZ750, 67, 138, 154
YZR, 139
moderation, engine, 39–41
modification, goals, 48, 49
modified, stock versus, reading, 45
Morris, Elliot, 150, 151
Morse, 78
MotoGP, technology needs, 96
motorcycle, fitting, 9–11
Motul, 37
Muzzy, Rob, 40, 46, 48, 49
MV, 6, 78
Nimonic 80, 77
nitrous oxide, 107
Nixon, Gary, 87, 137
O'Brien, Dick, 41, 144
octane, 173
Ohlins, 113, 114, 119, 129, 131
Ohlins TTX, 113, 114, 118
oil pumps, types, 21
oil, 164, 165
  additives, 165, 166
  change frequency, 169
  choices, 170
  synthetic, 168, 169
overlap, engine, internal combustion, 13
overlap, exhaust pipe action and, 30, 31
overrev, 49
Parker, James, 140
peak pressure, 17, 18
Pedrosa, Dani, 132
Penguin Racing School, 182
performance curves, engine, reading, 44–46
performance curves, stock, 46
Pirelli, 101
plug reading, 59
power, engine, internal combustion, 12
powerband, chassis design and, 140
powerjet, 56, 57
Pridmore, Reg, 8
privateer racing, 37
Quarterly, Dale, 118
Rainey, Wayne, 48, 138
ram-air, hot air and, 60
rear springs, 116, 117
rear suspension, 132, 133
Remor, Ing., 137
Renault, 79
reversion, 73, 74
riding positions, 8
riding/racing schools, 180–182
Roberts, Kenny, 34, 58, 114, 120
roots blower, 105–107
Rossi, Valentino, 6, 38, 49, 181
Rowe, Geoffrey, 138
S&S, 57
Schenck, 42
Schlachter, Richard, 180
Schwantz, Kevin, 39
Scott, Gary, 129
sealing, engine, 26, 27
Shenton, Stuart, 111
shifting, clutchless and power, 85, 86
Showa, 113, 119, 129
single-purpose setups, 109
Singleton, Dale, 87
skills, acquiring, 180–183
Snap-On, 29
spark plugs, 91–93
Spencer, Freddie, 8, 133, 146
Spies, Ben, 102, 175
spring rate, bump isolation and, 110
sprockets, chain and, weight reduction, 176
steering dampers, 121
stock, modified versus, reading, 45
Strahlman, Bobby, 41, 90
Stuska, 43
superchargers, types, 105

supercharging, 106, 197
Superflow, 43
  110 Flowbench, 35
  CycleDyn, 44, 47
suspension, 108–110, 113, 114
  chatter, 121, 122
  correct proportion, 112, 113
  instability, 119, 120
  jargon, 122–124
  linkages, 117, 118
  side effects, 110, 111
  sideways, 138–140
  springs, 114, 115
  tuning, adjustments within stock parameters, 124–127
  tuning, pushing the front, 131, 132
  tuning, Supersport, 127–131
Suvorov, Alexander, 182
Suzuki, 5, 48, 50, 77, 78, 93, 100, 150
swingarms, 134, 135
Thede, Paul, 119
thermodynamics, engine, 27
Thompson, Mickey, 110
throat, bowl and, 71
Tilley, Don, 41
tire grip, future development, 101, 102
tire grip, torque curve and, 97
tire, pressure, 149
tire traction, 145, 146
tires, for wet or dry, 148
tires, 142, 143
  radial, 144, 145
  selecting, 148, 149
  sizes, 144
  speed ratings, 143
  stability and, 146
  street choices, 148
titanium, for weight reduction, 178
torque curve, tire grip and, 97
torque, reading, 44, 46
transmission backlash, 84, 85
tread rubber compounds, 147, 148
Triumph, 62, 66
turbocharging, overview, 103–106
turbulence, flame speed and, 24–26
turbulence, need for, 14–17
turning, entering the, 133, 134
Ustinov, Peter, 8
vacuum piston lift speed, 53, 54
valve(s), 77, 78
  desmodromic, 77
  masking, 75
  mass, ratios, 35
  mechanisms, 77
  seat preparation, 71, 72
  seats, 78
  springs, 74, 75
valvetrain elements, 79
vibration, carburetors and, 58
viscosity index, 164, 165
Vukmanovich, George, 133
Wakefield, Bob, 129, 130
water cooling, advantages, 29
weight reduction, overview, 175
wheel
  bearings, 152
  damage, 153
  width, 150
wheels
  air tightness, 153
  brake heat and, 152
  carbon fiber, 152
  cush drives, 152
  magnesium, 151, 152
  wire, 153
Whitelock, Steve, 176
Williams, Jack, 70
Williams, Peter, 150
Willing, Warren, 131
Wilvert, Hurley, 61
Wiseco Piston, 169
Wittner, John, 67, 141
Works Performance, 113
WP Suspension, 129
Wright Brothers, 5
X-Wedge, 57
Yamaha, 6, 34, 77, 93, 97, 100, 129, 130, 137, 138
Yoshimura pipes, 45
Yoshimura, Hideo, 51

192